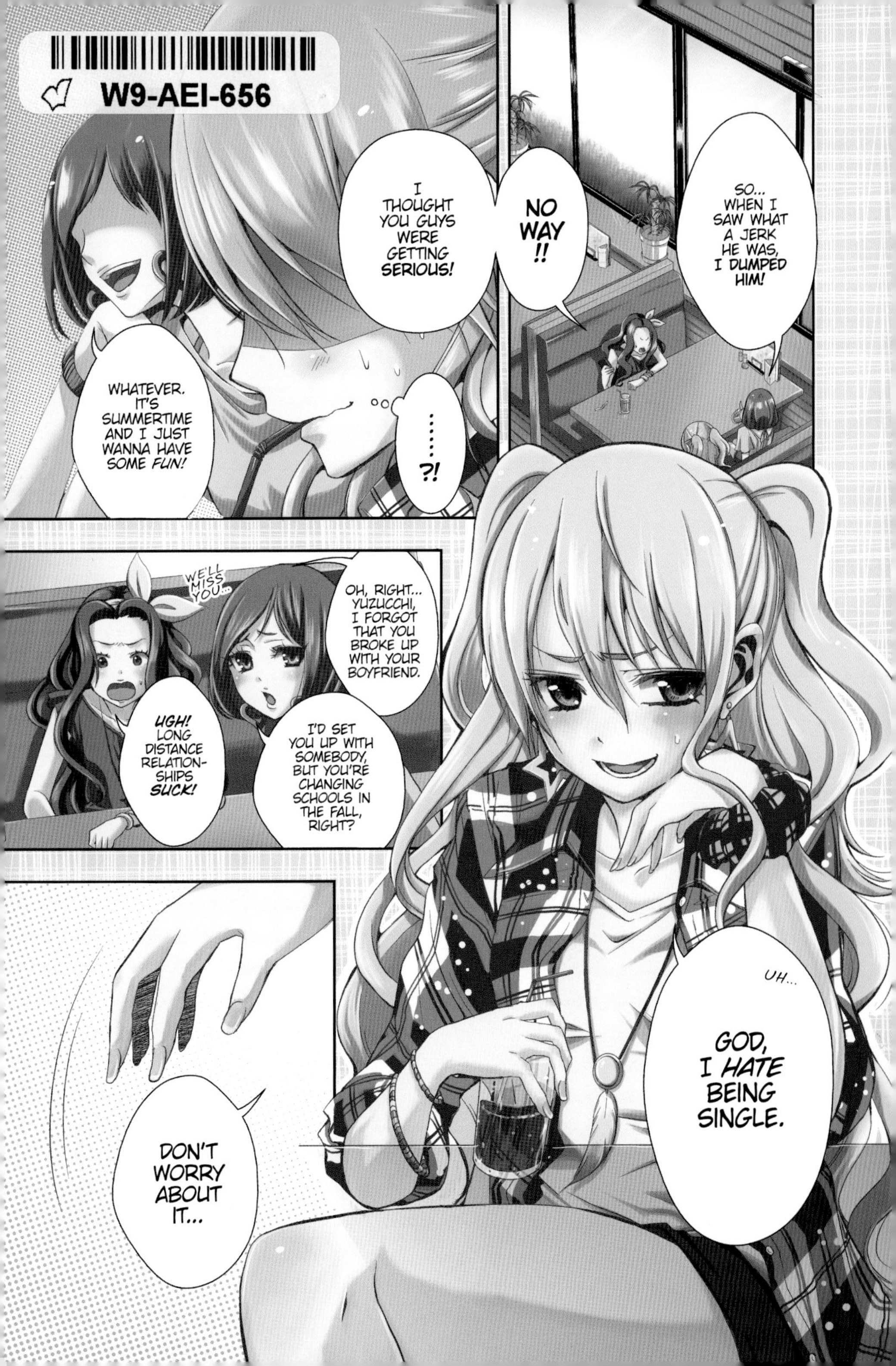
SO... WHEN I SAW WHAT A JERK HE WAS, I DUMPED HIM!
NO WAY!!
I THOUGHT YOU GUYS WERE GETTING SERIOUS!
......?!
WHATEVER. IT'S SUMMERTIME AND I JUST WANNA HAVE SOME *FUN*!
UH...
GOD, I *HATE* BEING SINGLE.
OH, RIGHT... YUZUCCHI, I FORGOT THAT YOU BROKE UP WITH YOUR BOYFRIEND.
WE'LL MISS YOU...
I'D SET YOU UP WITH SOMEBODY, BUT YOU'RE CHANGING SCHOOLS IN THE FALL, RIGHT?
UGH! LONG DISTANCE RELATION-SHIPS *SUCK!*
DON'T WORRY ABOUT IT...

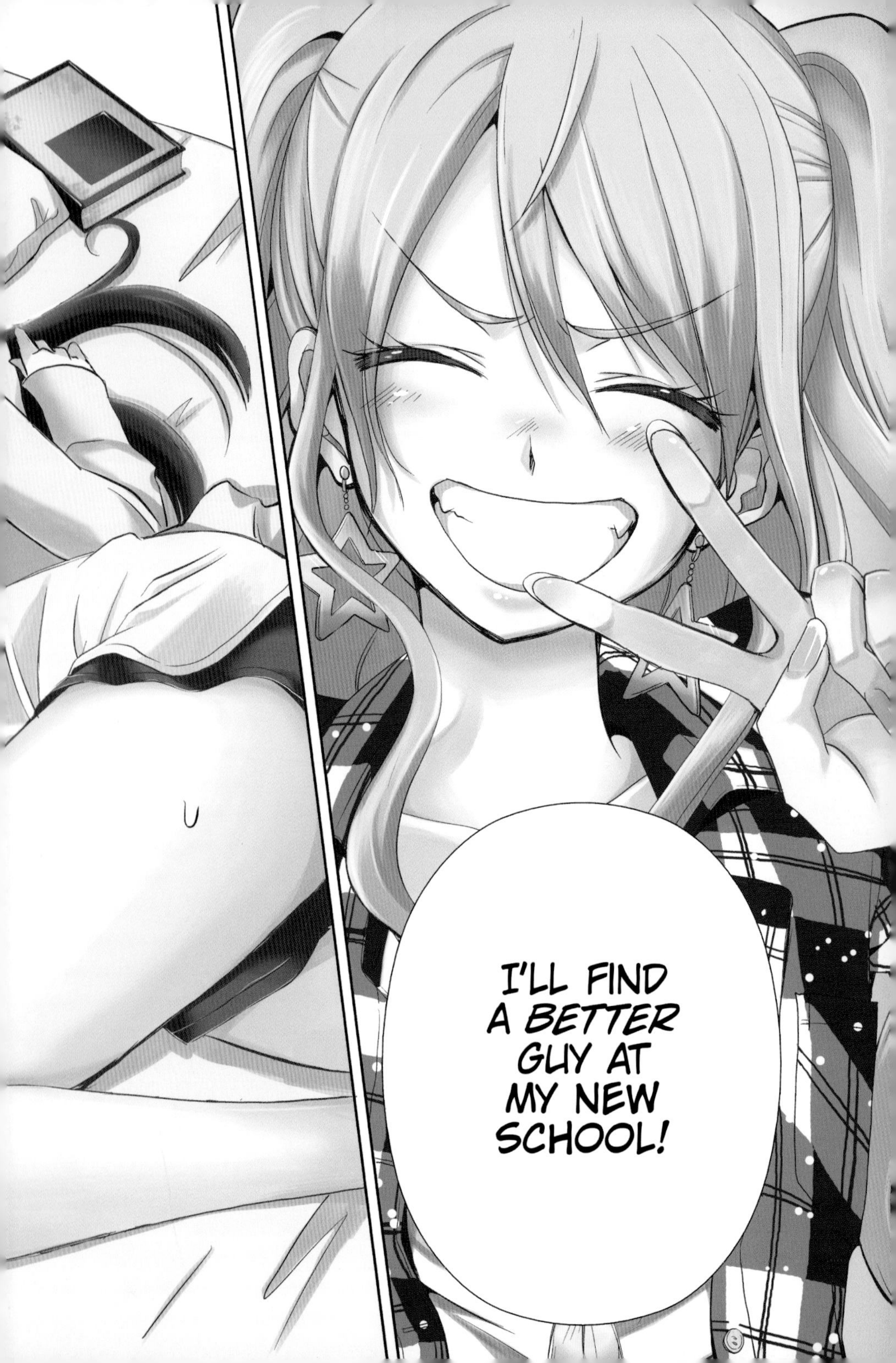
I'LL FIND A *BETTER* GUY AT MY NEW SCHOOL!

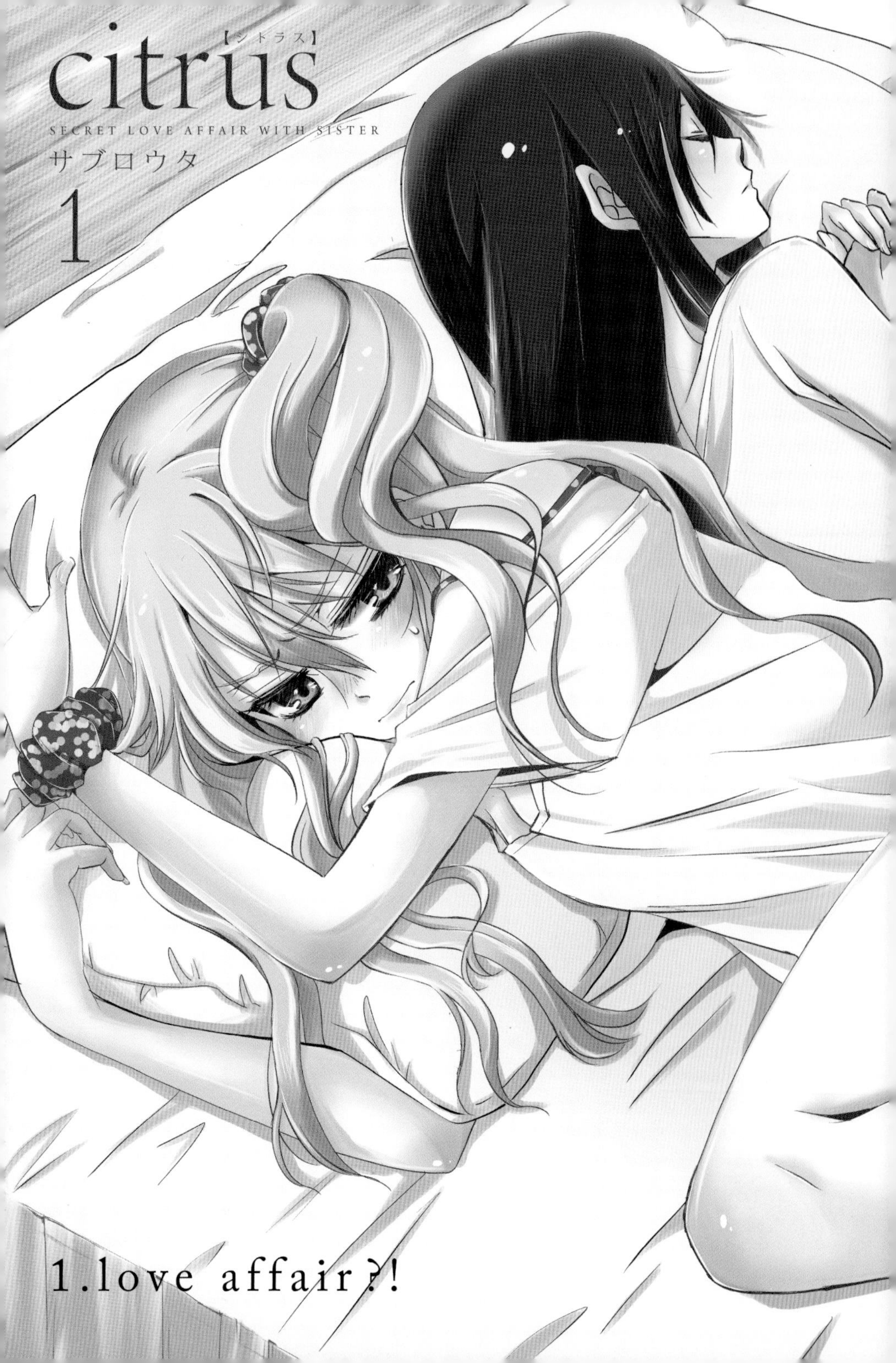
citrus
【シトラス】
SECRET LOVE AFFAIR WITH SISTER
サブロウタ
1
1.love affair?!

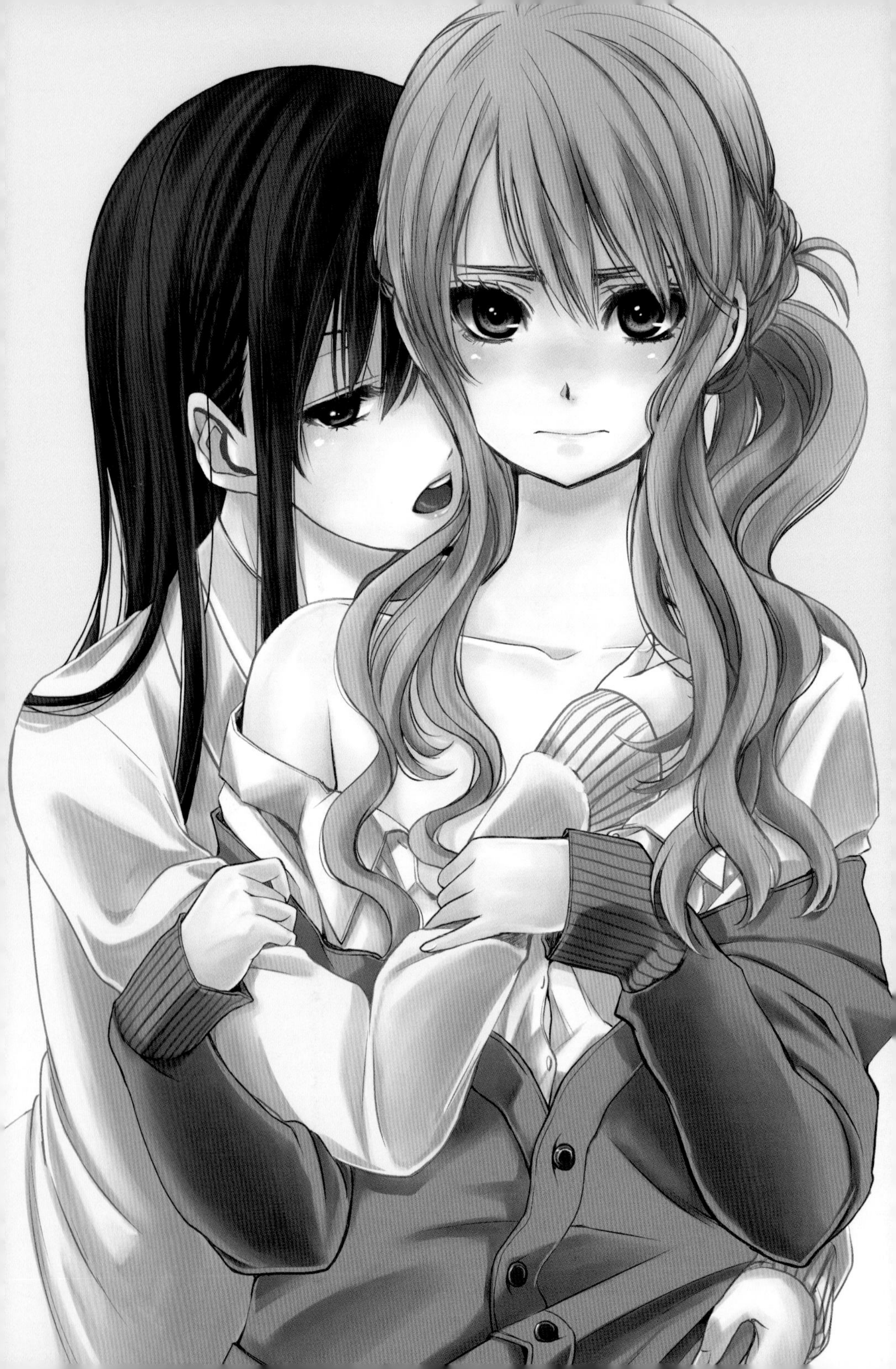

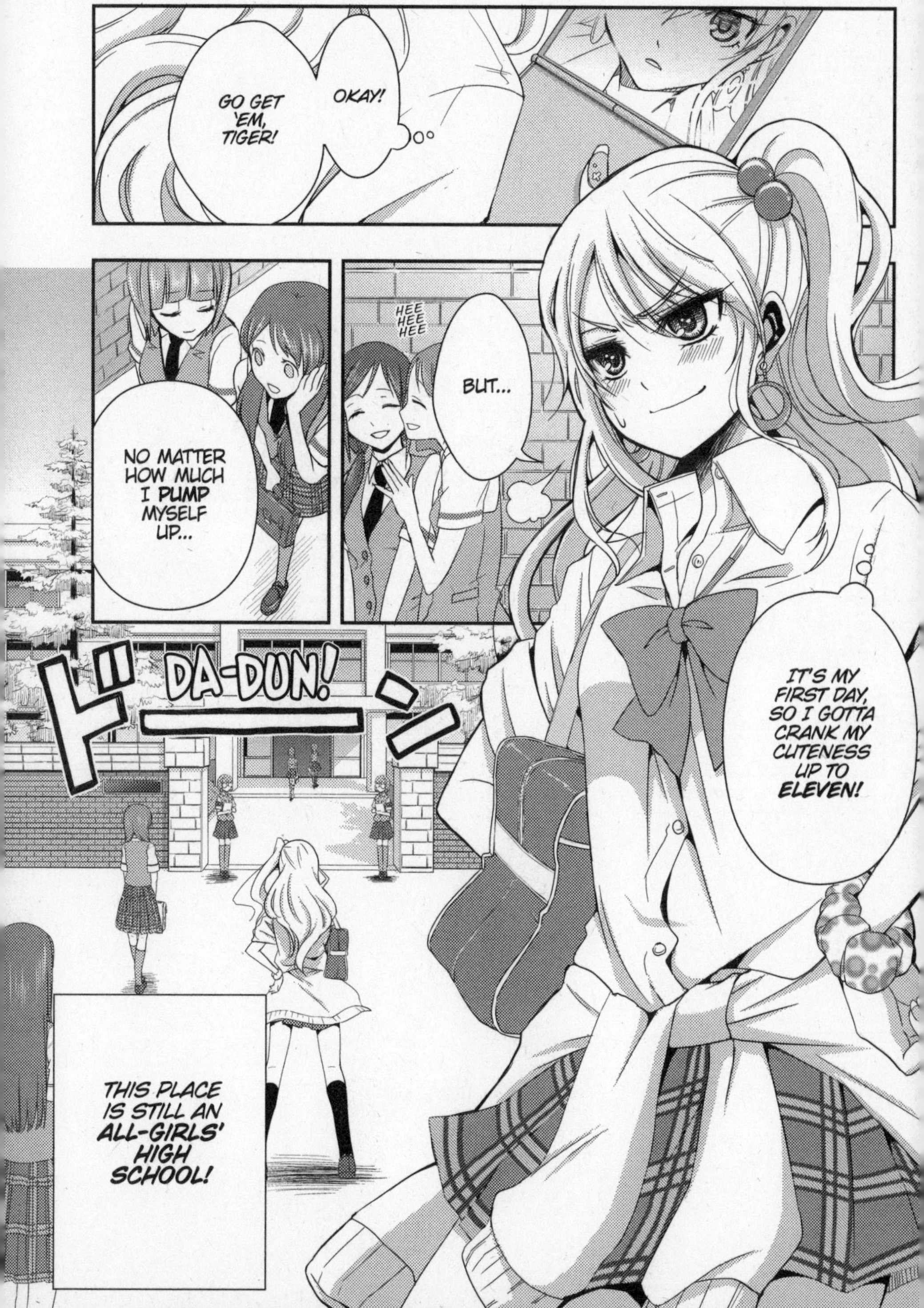
OKAY!
GO GET 'EM, TIGER!
IT'S MY FIRST DAY, SO I GOTTA CRANK MY CUTENESS UP TO **ELEVEN!**
HEE HEE HEE
BUT...
NO MATTER HOW MUCH I **PUMP** MYSELF UP...
DA-DUN!
THIS PLACE IS STILL AN **ALL-GIRLS' HIGH SCHOOL!**

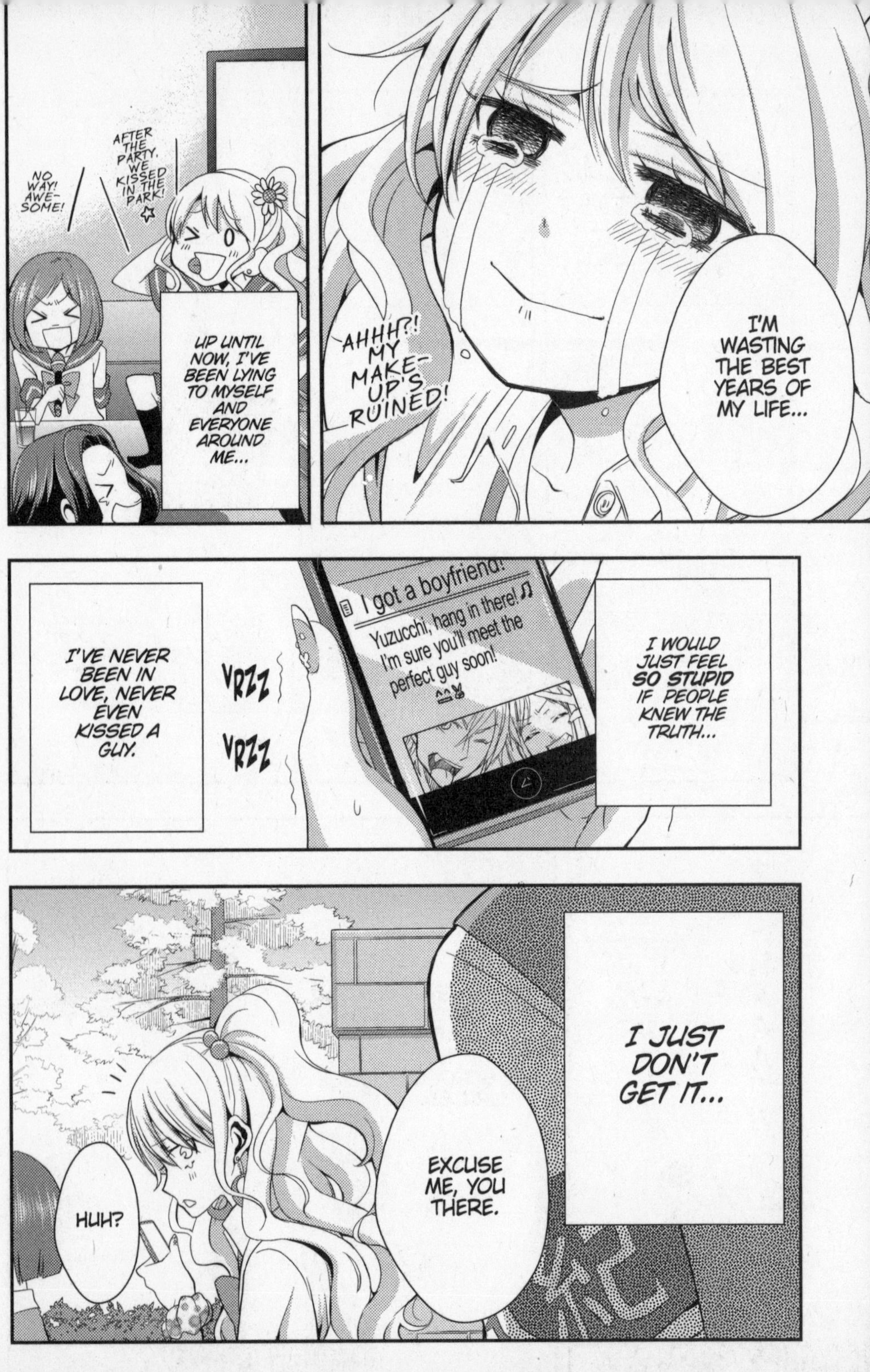
I'M WASTING THE BEST YEARS OF MY LIFE...
AHHH?! MY MAKE-UP'S RUINED!
AFTER THE PARTY, WE KISSED IN THE PARK!
NO WAY! AWESOME!
UP UNTIL NOW, I'VE BEEN LYING TO MYSELF AND EVERYONE AROUND ME...
I WOULD JUST FEEL SO STUPID IF PEOPLE KNEW THE TRUTH...
I got a boyfriend!
Yuzucchi, hang in there! ♫ I'm sure you'll meet the perfect guy soon!
VRZZ
VRZZ
I'VE NEVER BEEN IN LOVE, NEVER EVEN KISSED A GUY.
I JUST DON'T GET IT...
EXCUSE ME, YOU THERE.
HUH?

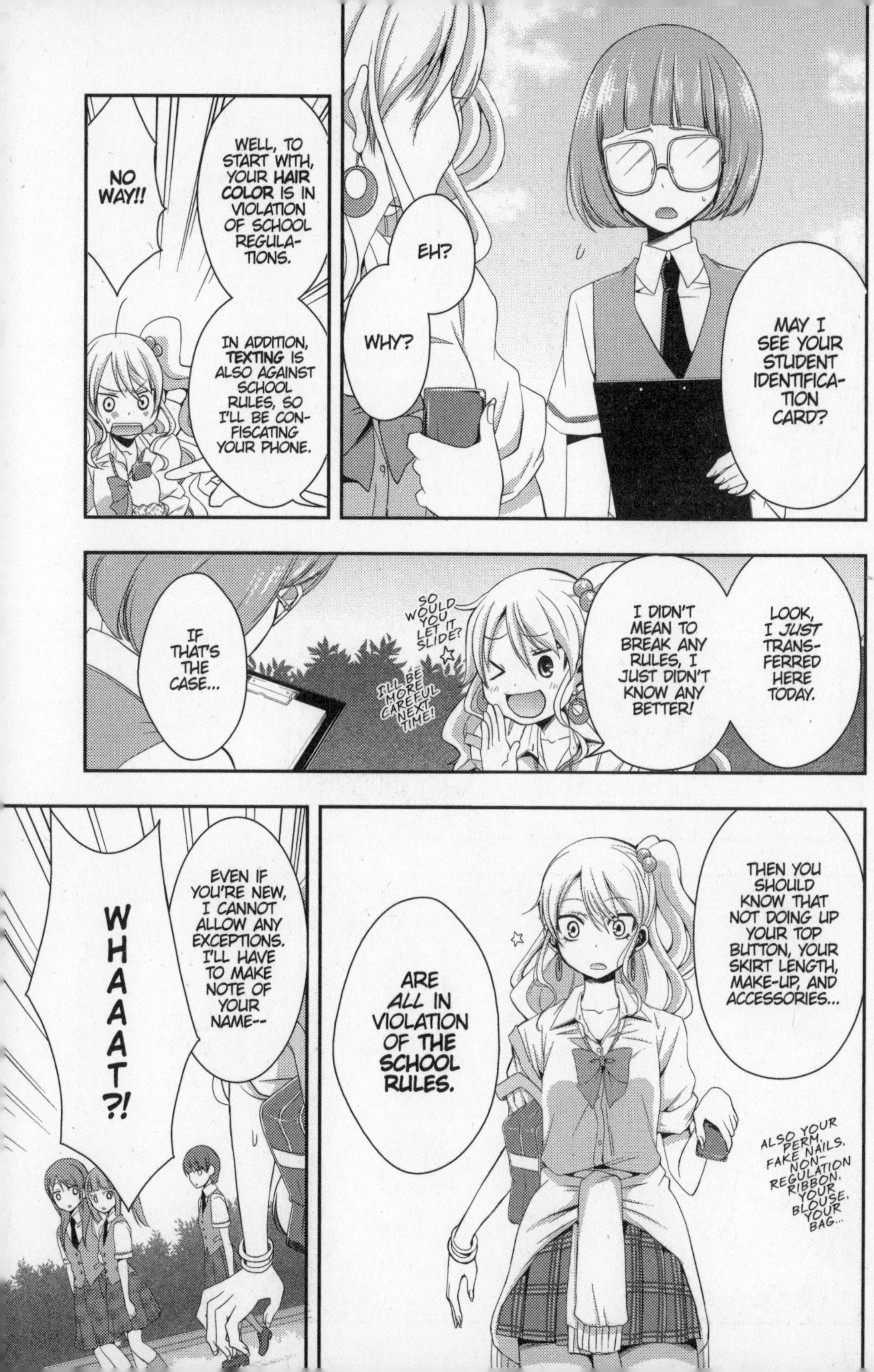
MAY I SEE YOUR STUDENT IDENTIFICATION CARD?
EH?
WHY?
WELL, TO START WITH, YOUR **HAIR COLOR** IS IN VIOLATION OF SCHOOL REGULATIONS.
IN ADDITION, **TEXTING** IS ALSO AGAINST SCHOOL RULES, SO I'LL BE CONFISCATING YOUR PHONE.
NO WAY!!
LOOK, I *JUST* TRANSFERRED HERE TODAY.
I DIDN'T MEAN TO BREAK ANY RULES, I JUST DIDN'T KNOW ANY BETTER!
SO WOULD YOU LET IT SLIDE?
I'LL BE MORE CAREFUL NEXT TIME!
IF THAT'S THE CASE...
THEN YOU SHOULD KNOW THAT NOT DOING UP YOUR TOP BUTTON, YOUR SKIRT LENGTH, MAKE-UP, AND ACCESSORIES...
ARE *ALL* IN VIOLATION OF THE SCHOOL RULES.
ALSO YOUR PERM, FAKE NAILS, NON-REGULATION RIBBON, YOUR BLOUSE, YOUR BAG...
EVEN IF YOU'RE NEW, I CANNOT ALLOW ANY EXCEPTIONS. I'LL HAVE TO MAKE NOTE OF YOUR NAME--
WHAAAAT?!

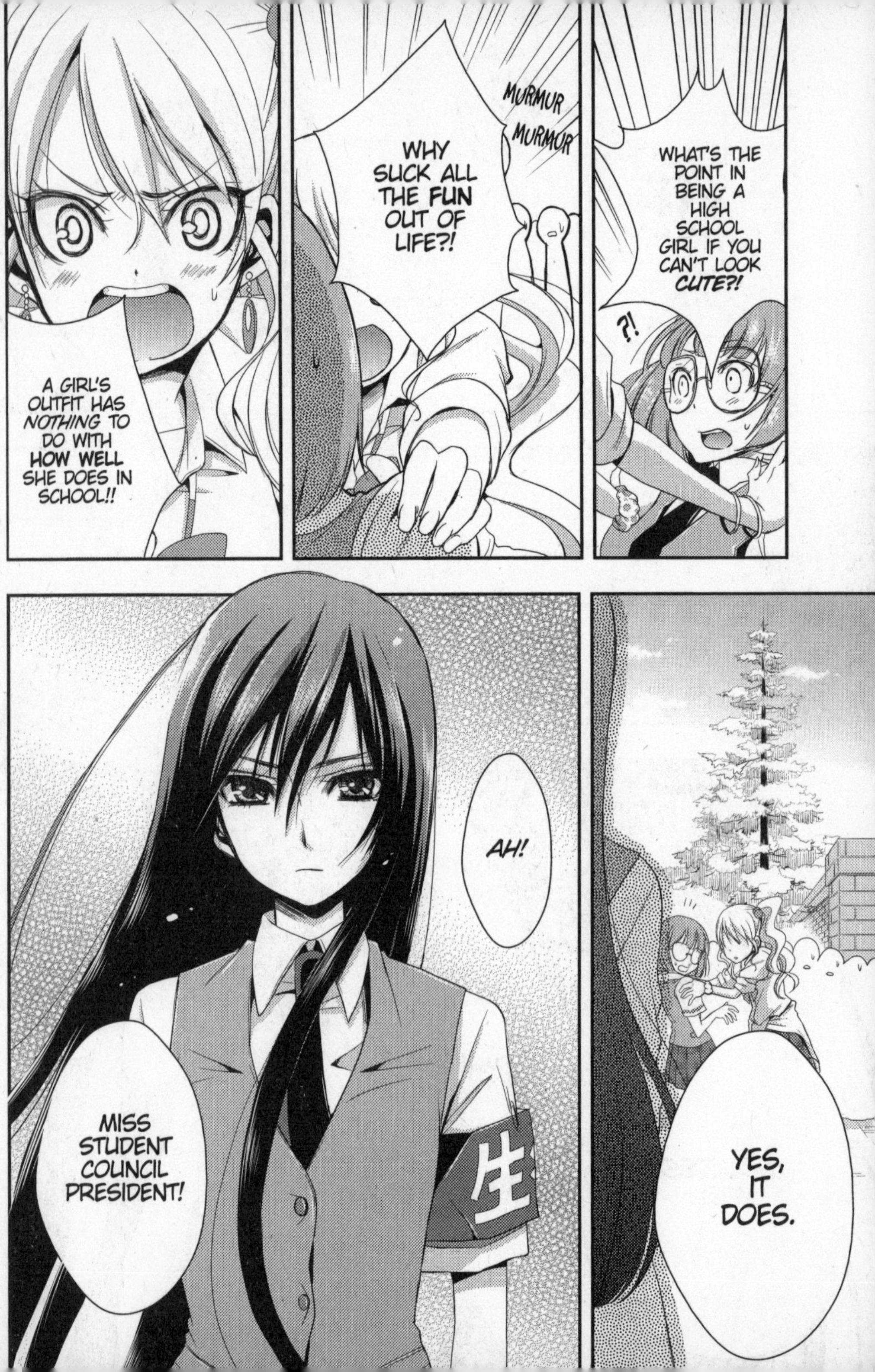
WHAT'S THE POINT IN BEING A HIGH SCHOOL GIRL IF YOU CAN'T LOOK CUTE?!
?!
MURMUR
MURMUR
WHY SUCK ALL THE FUN OUT OF LIFE?!
A GIRL'S OUTFIT HAS NOTHING TO DO WITH HOW WELL SHE DOES IN SCHOOL!!
YES, IT DOES.
AH!
MISS STUDENT COUNCIL PRESIDENT!
生

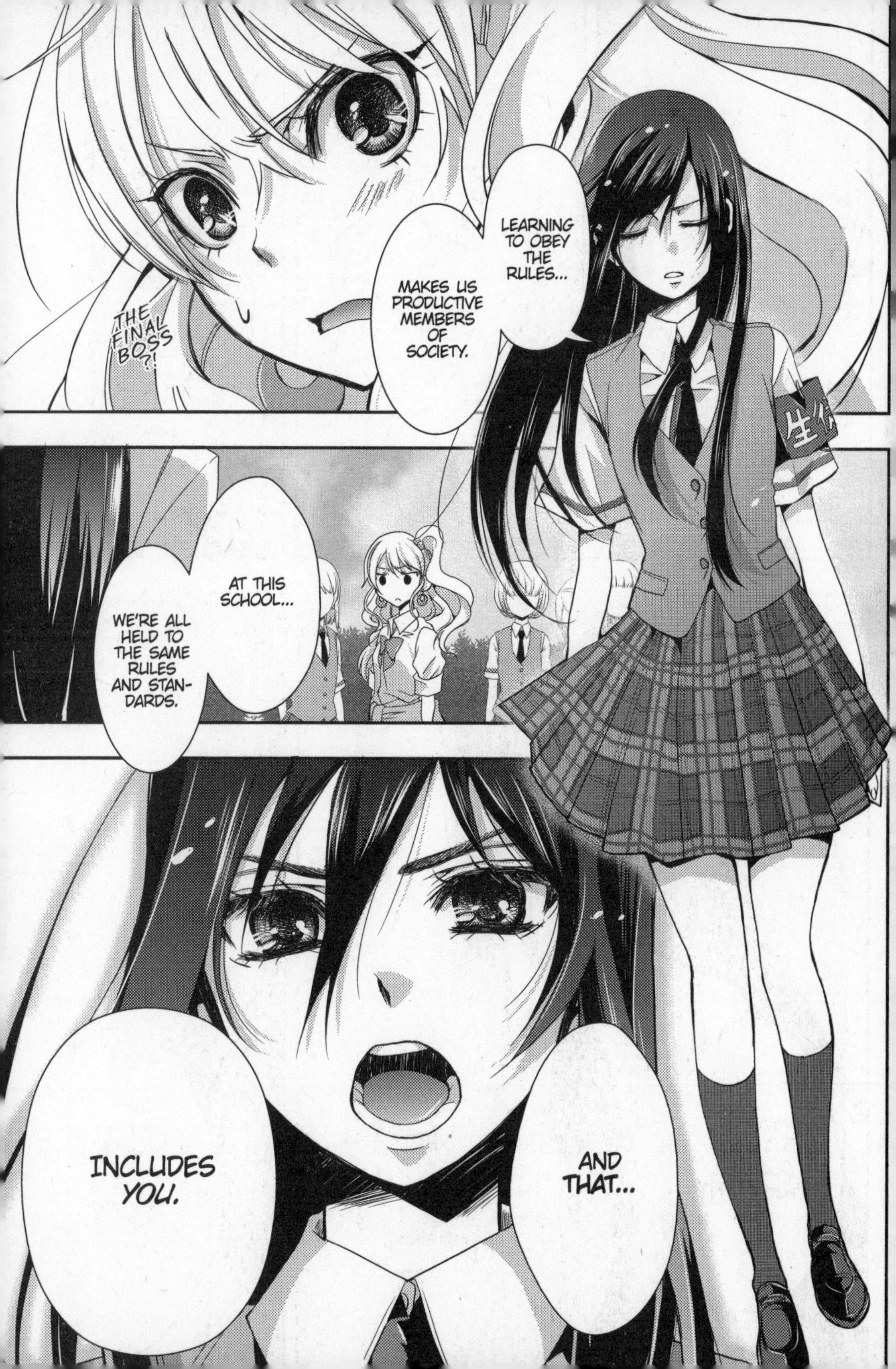
LEARNING TO OBEY THE RULES...
MAKES US PRODUCTIVE MEMBERS OF SOCIETY.
THE FINAL BOSS?!
AT THIS SCHOOL...
WE'RE ALL HELD TO THE SAME RULES AND STAN-DARDS.
AND THAT...
INCLUDES YOU.

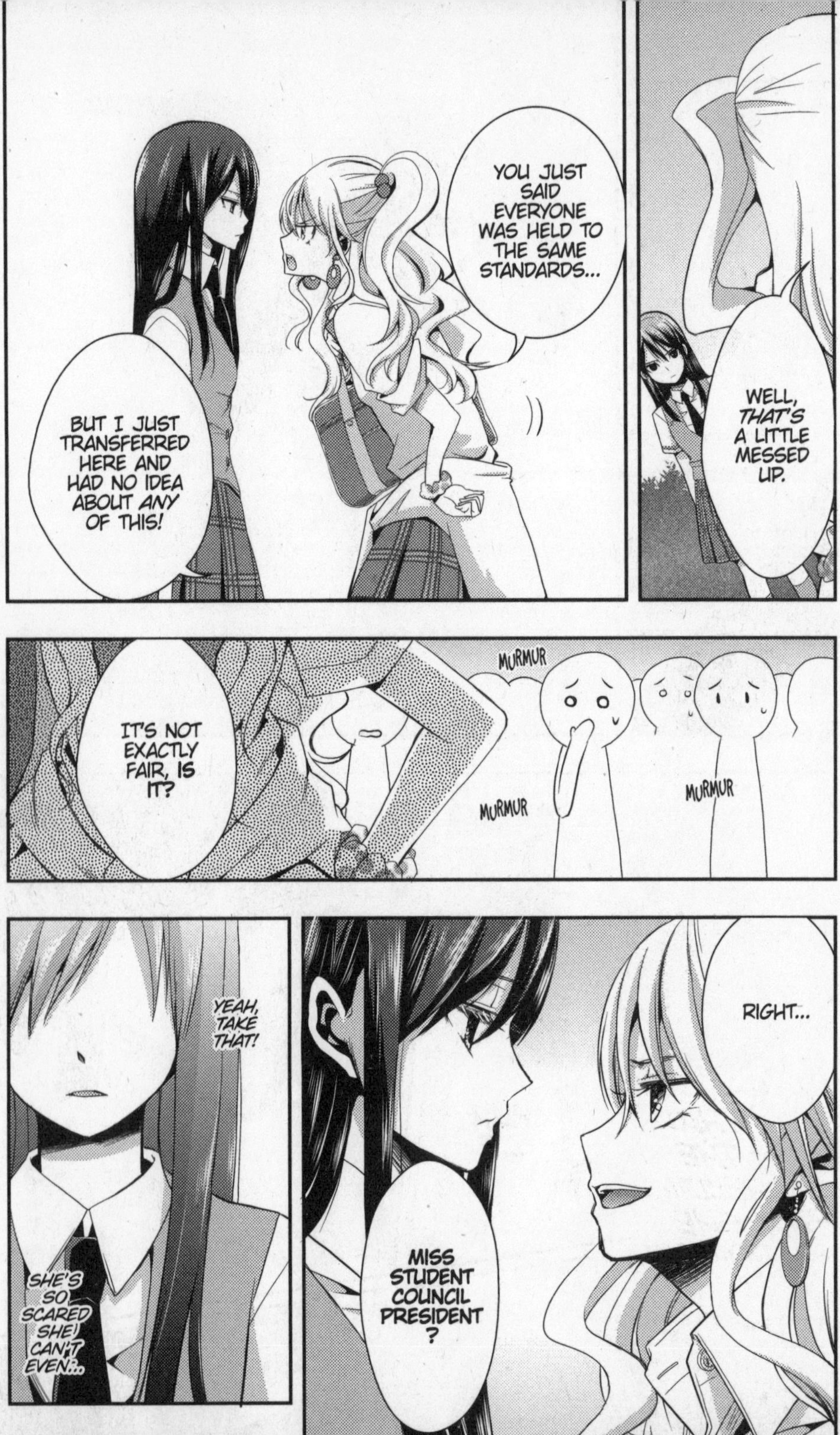
WELL, THAT'S A LITTLE MESSED UP.
YOU JUST SAID EVERYONE WAS HELD TO THE SAME STANDARDS...
BUT I JUST TRANSFERRED HERE AND HAD NO IDEA ABOUT ANY OF THIS!
MURMUR
IT'S NOT EXACTLY FAIR, IS IT?
MURMUR
MURMUR
RIGHT...
MISS STUDENT COUNCIL PRESIDENT?
YEAH, TAKE THAT!
SHE'S SO SCARED SHE CAN'T EVEN...

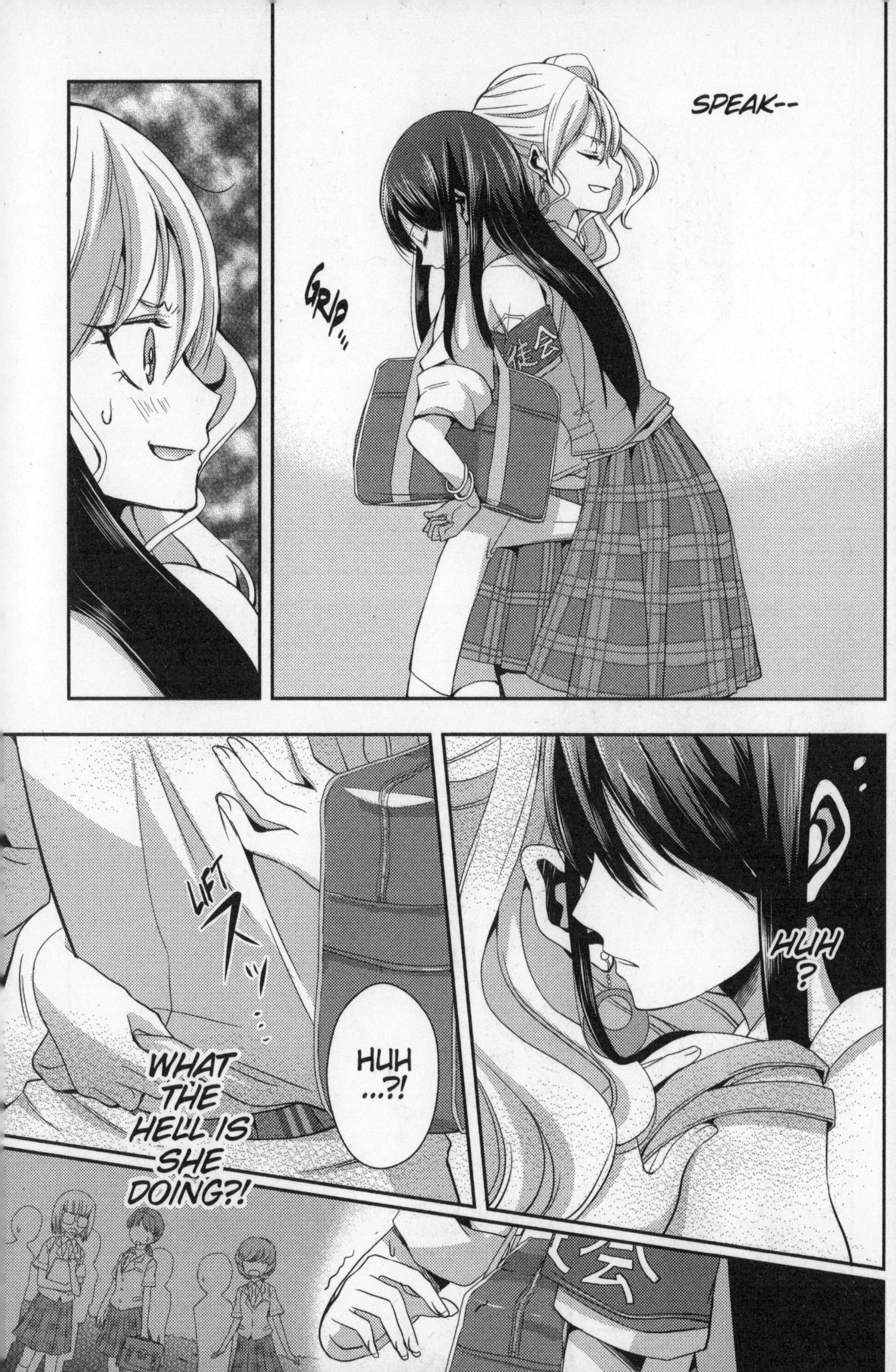
SPEAK--
GRIP...
HUH?
LIFT
スッ...
HUH ...?!
WHAT THE HELL IS SHE DOING?!

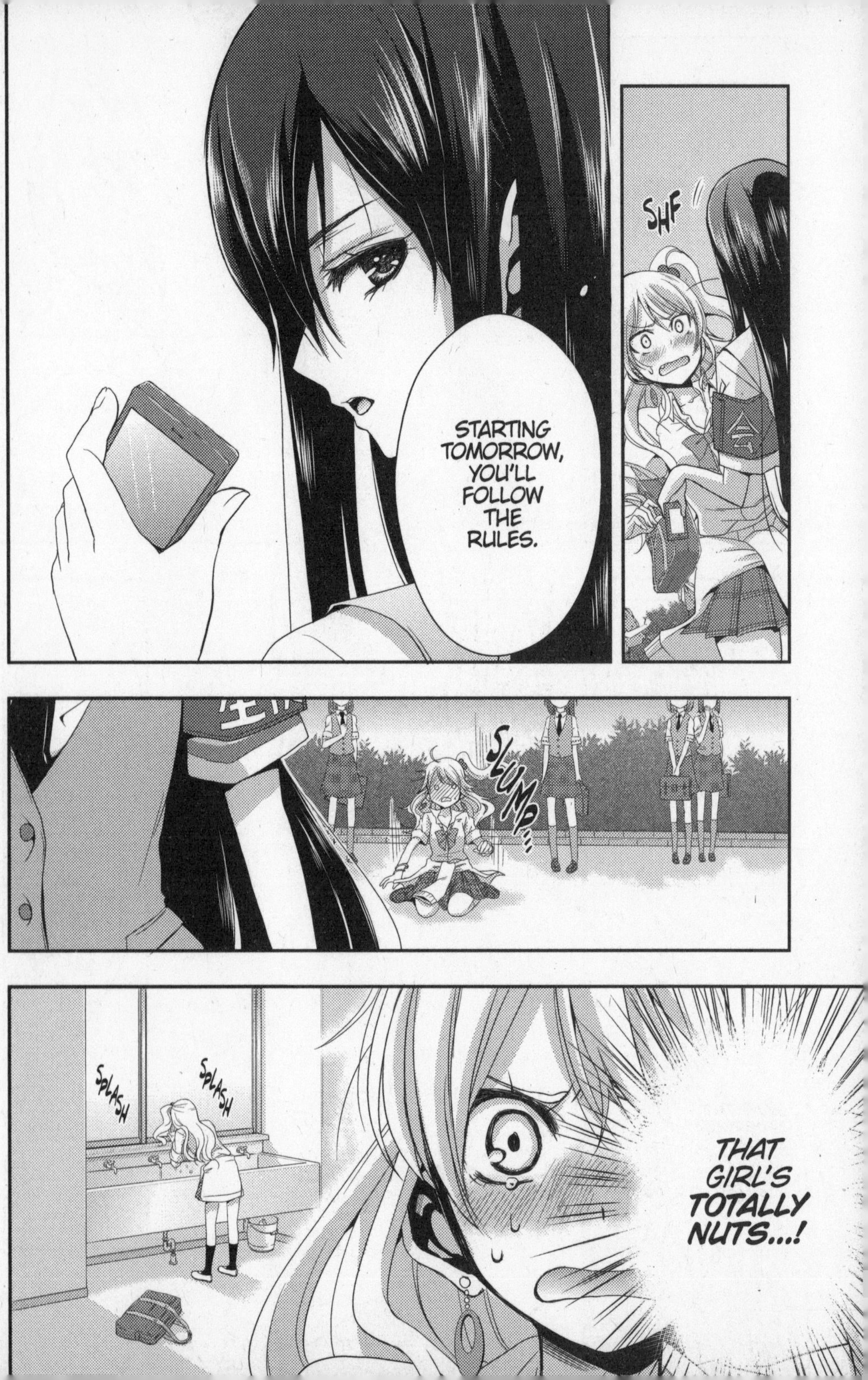
SHF
STARTING TOMORROW, YOU'LL FOLLOW THE RULES.
SLUMP...
THAT GIRL'S TOTALLY NUTS...!
SPLASH
SPLASH

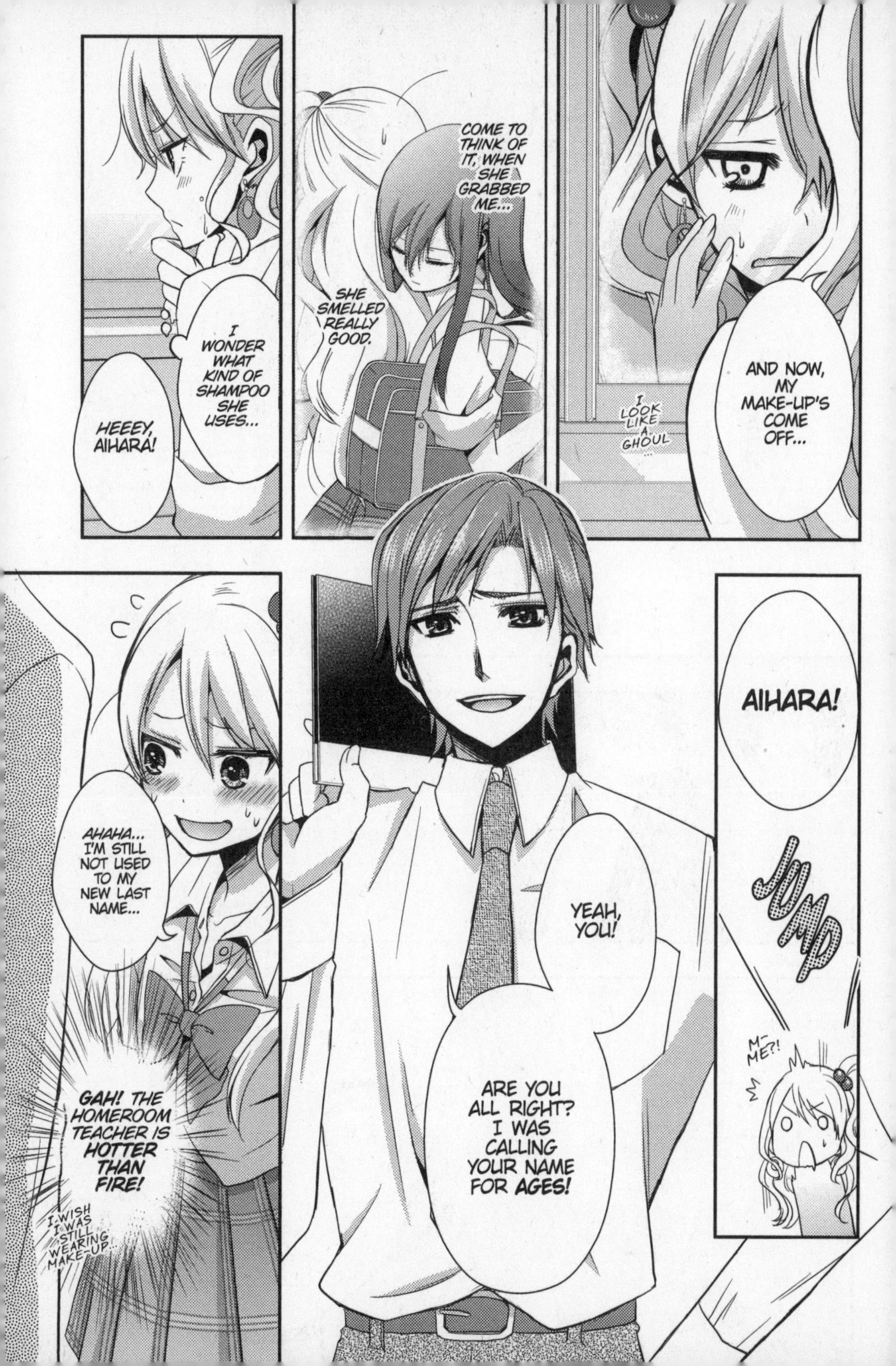
AND NOW, MY MAKE-UP'S COME OFF...
I LOOK LIKE A GHOUL...
COME TO THINK OF IT, WHEN SHE GRABBED ME...
SHE SMELLED REALLY GOOD.
I WONDER WHAT KIND OF SHAMPOO SHE USES...
HEEEY, AIHARA!
AIHARA!
JUMP
M-ME?!
YEAH, YOU!
ARE YOU ALL RIGHT? I WAS CALLING YOUR NAME FOR AGES!
AHAHA... I'M STILL NOT USED TO MY NEW LAST NAME...
GAH! THE HOMEROOM TEACHER IS HOTTER THAN FIRE!
I WISH I WAS STILL WEARING MAKE-UP...

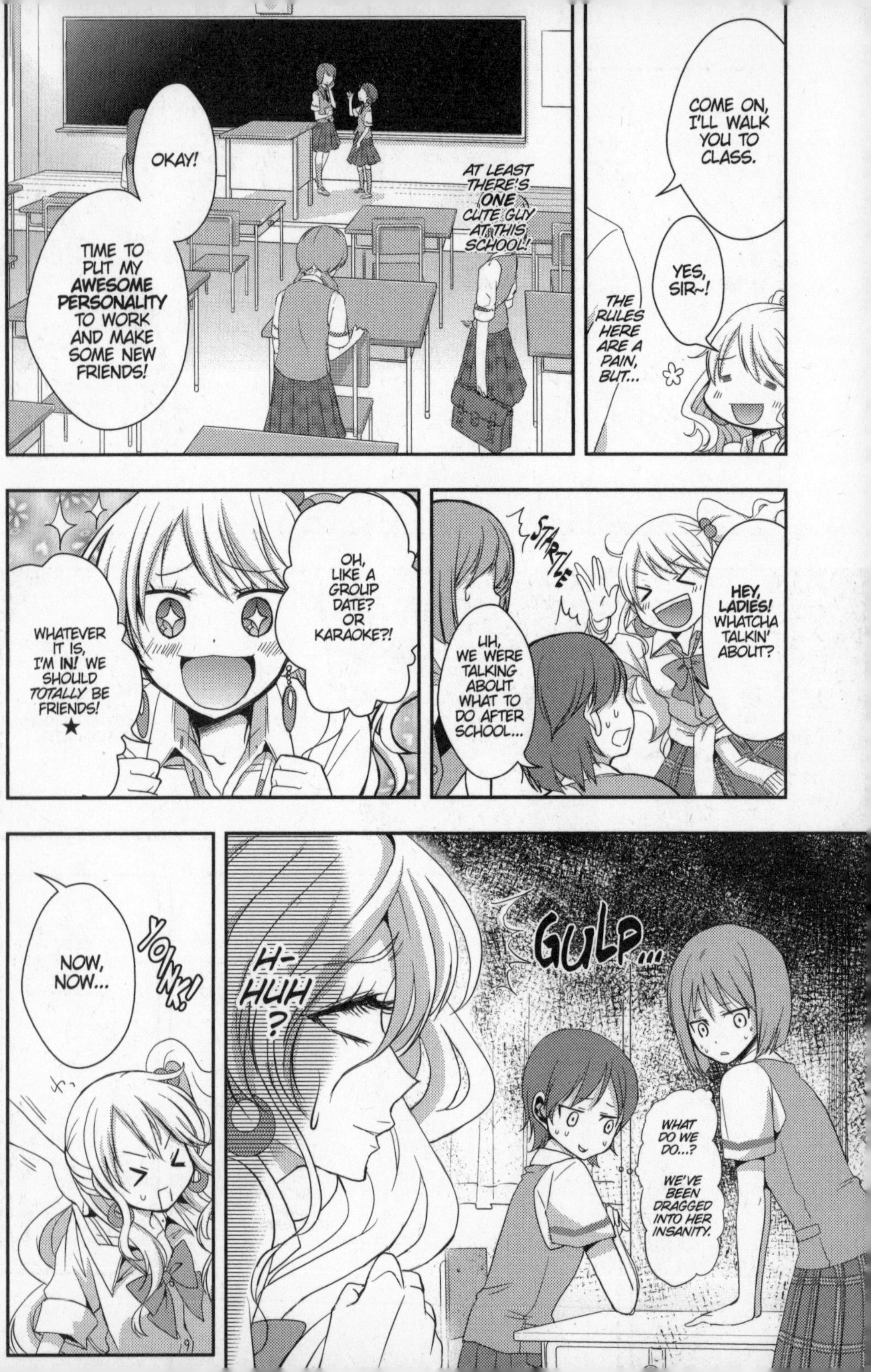
COME ON, I'LL WALK YOU TO CLASS.
YES, SIR~!
THE RULES HERE ARE A PAIN, BUT...
AT LEAST THERE'S ONE CUTE GUY AT THIS SCHOOL!
OKAY!
TIME TO PUT MY AWESOME PERSONALITY TO WORK AND MAKE SOME NEW FRIENDS!
STARTLE
HEY, LADIES! WHATCHA TALKIN' ABOUT?
UH, WE WERE TALKING ABOUT WHAT TO DO AFTER SCHOOL...
OH, LIKE A GROUP DATE? OR KARAOKE?!
WHATEVER IT IS, I'M IN! WE SHOULD TOTALLY BE FRIENDS! ★
GULP...
H-HUH?
WHAT DO WE DO...? WE'VE BEEN DRAGGED INTO HER INSANITY.
YOINK!
NOW, NOW...

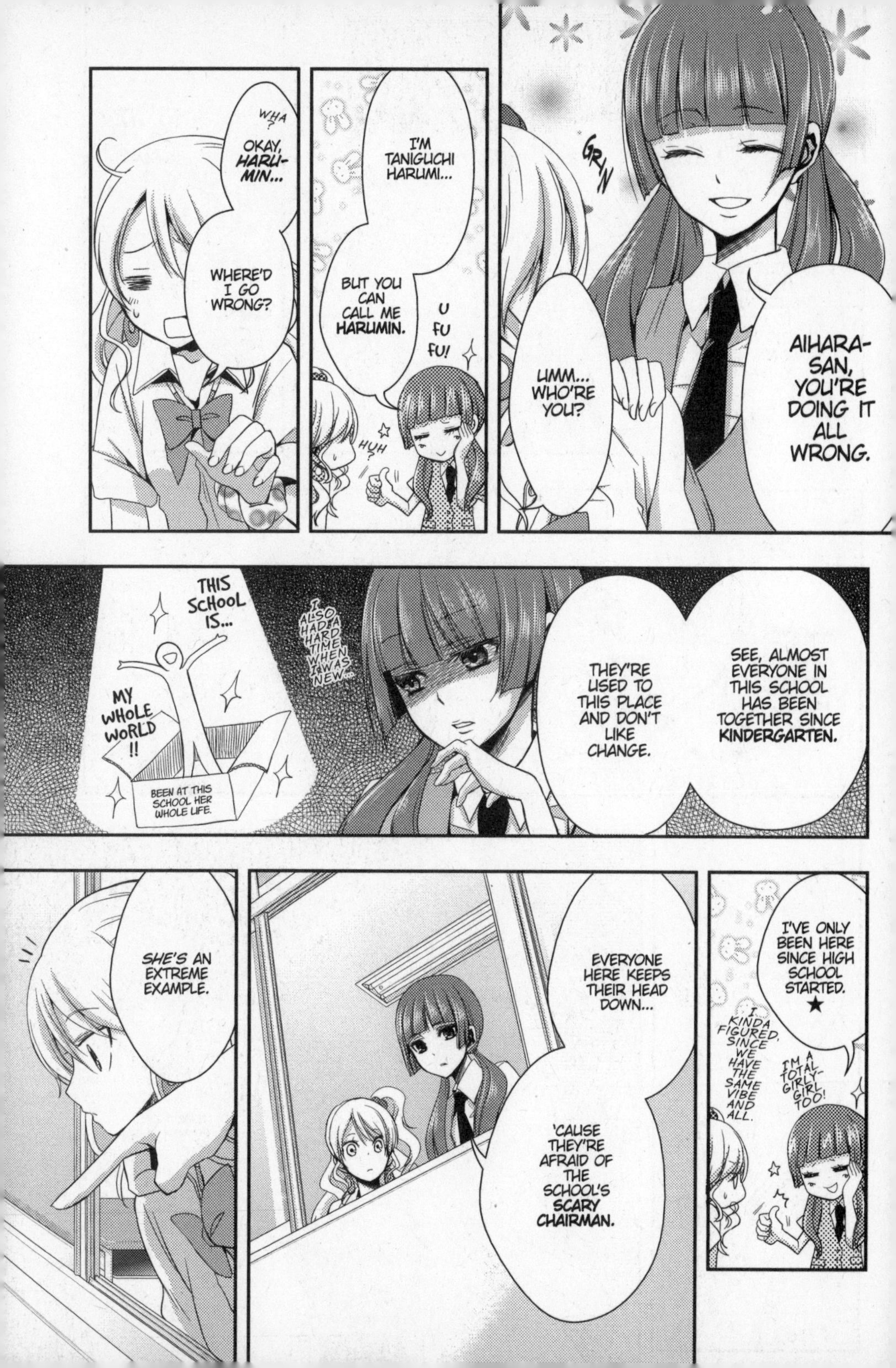

AIHARA-SAN, YOU'RE DOING IT ALL WRONG.
GRIN
UMM... WHO'RE YOU?
I'M TANIGUCHI HARUMI...
BUT YOU CAN CALL ME HARUMIN.
U FU FU!
HUH?
WHA?
OKAY, HARU-MIN...
WHERE'D I GO WRONG?
SEE, ALMOST EVERYONE IN THIS SCHOOL HAS BEEN TOGETHER SINCE KINDERGARTEN.
THEY'RE USED TO THIS PLACE AND DON'T LIKE CHANGE.
I ALSO HAD A HARD TIME WHEN I WAS NEW...
THIS SCHOOL IS...
MY WHOLE WORLD !!
BEEN AT THIS SCHOOL HER WHOLE LIFE.
I'VE ONLY BEEN HERE SINCE HIGH SCHOOL STARTED. ★
I'M A TOTAL GIRLY-GIRL TOO!
I KINDA FIGURED, SINCE WE HAVE THE SAME VIBE AND ALL.
EVERYONE HERE KEEPS THEIR HEAD DOWN...
'CAUSE THEY'RE AFRAID OF THE SCHOOL'S SCARY CHAIRMAN.
SHE'S AN EXTREME EXAMPLE.

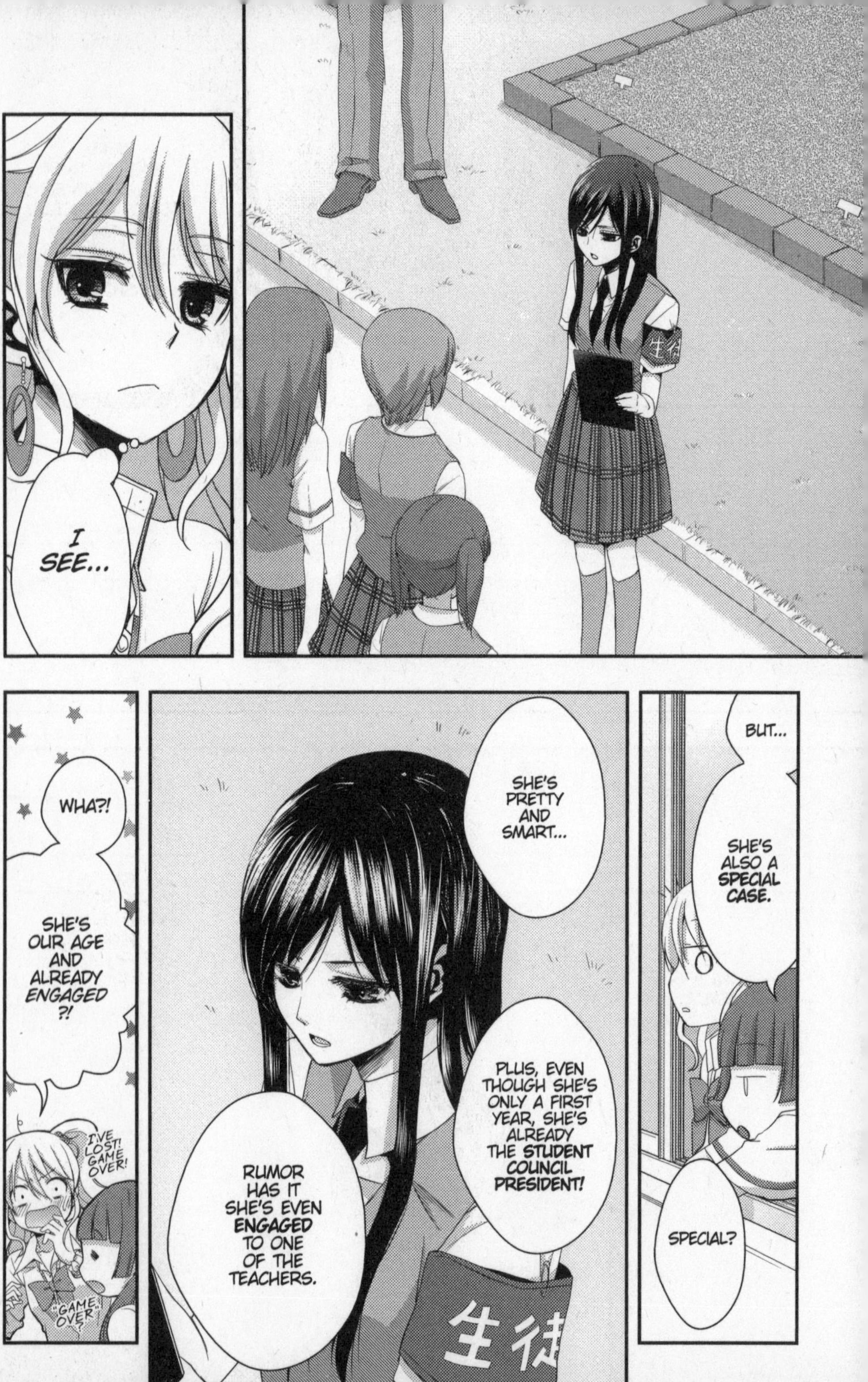
I SEE...
BUT...
SHE'S ALSO A **SPECIAL CASE.**
SPECIAL?
SHE'S PRETTY AND SMART...
PLUS, EVEN THOUGH SHE'S ONLY A FIRST YEAR, SHE'S ALREADY THE **STUDENT COUNCIL PRESIDENT!**
RUMOR HAS IT SHE'S EVEN **ENGAGED** TO ONE OF THE TEACHERS.
生徒
WHA?!
SHE'S OUR AGE AND ALREADY ENGAGED ?!
I'VE LOST! GAME OVER!
"GAME OVER"?

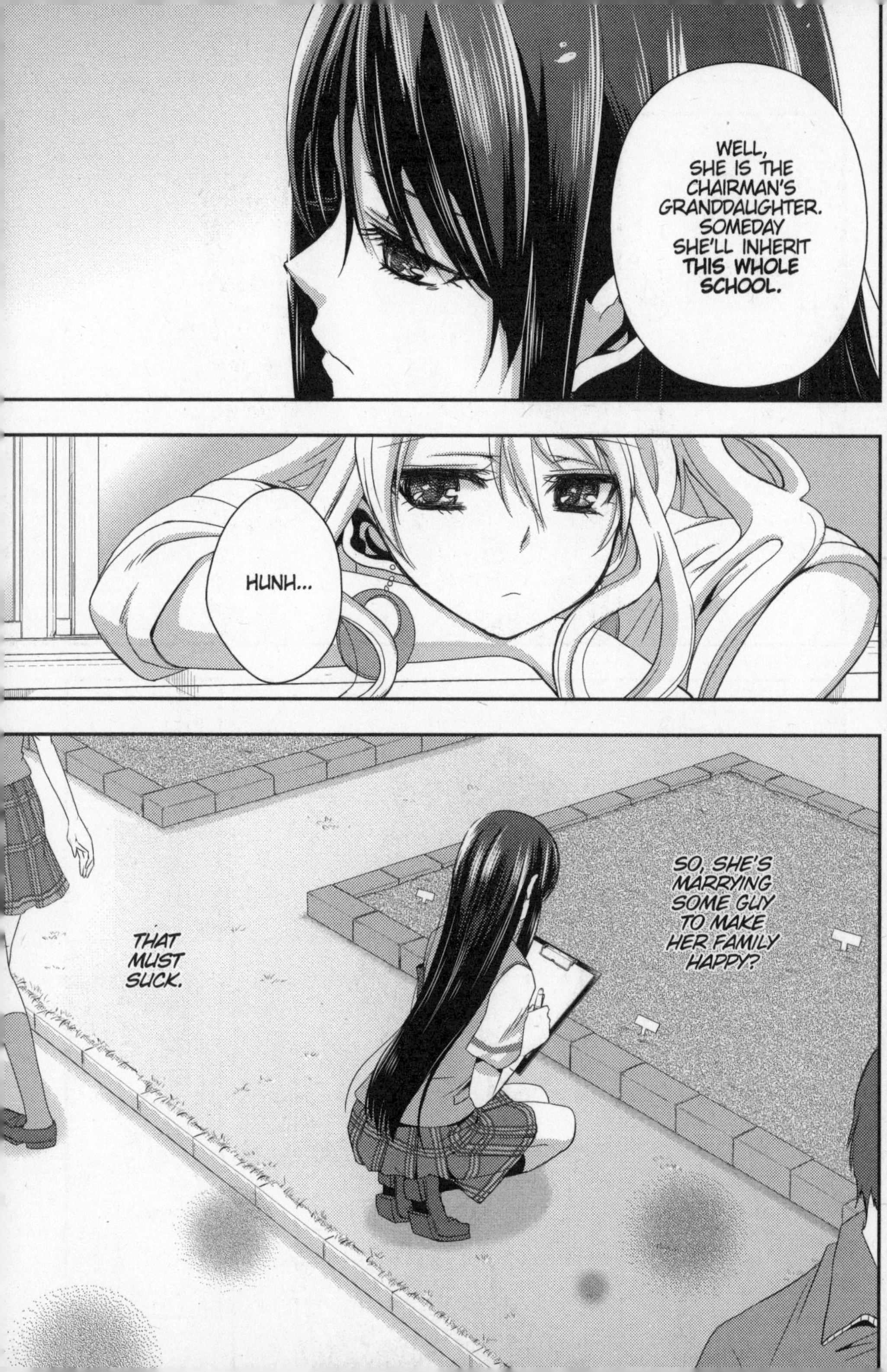
WELL, SHE IS THE CHAIRMAN'S GRANDDAUGHTER. SOMEDAY SHE'LL INHERIT THIS WHOLE SCHOOL.
HUNH...
SO, SHE'S MARRYING SOME GUY TO MAKE HER FAMILY HAPPY?
THAT MUST SUCK.

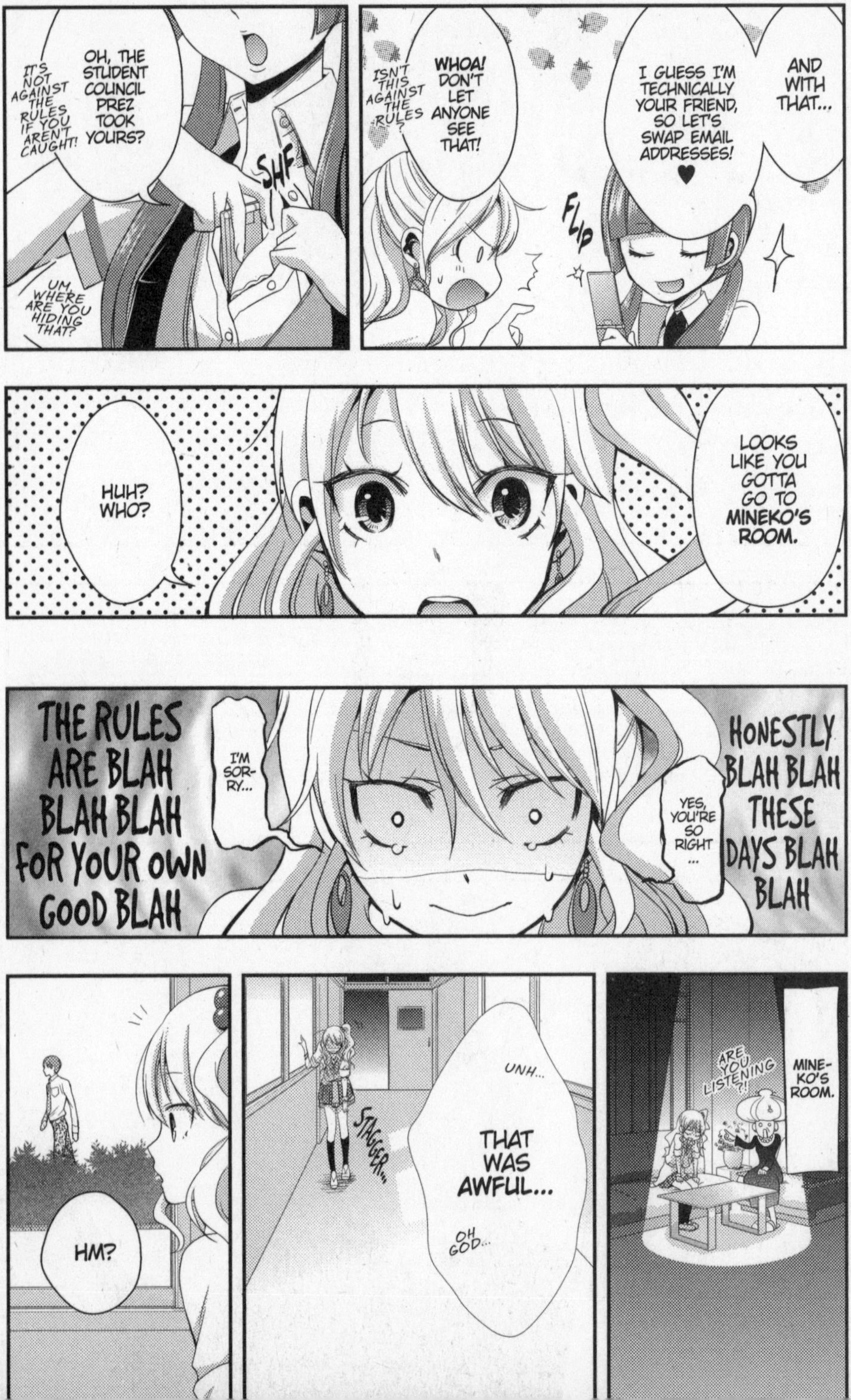
AND WITH THAT...
I GUESS I'M TECHNICALLY YOUR FRIEND, SO LET'S SWAP EMAIL ADDRESSES! ♥
FLIP
WHOA! DON'T LET ANYONE SEE THAT!
ISN'T THIS AGAINST THE RULES?
OH, THE STUDENT COUNCIL PREZ TOOK YOURS?
IT'S NOT AGAINST THE RULES IF YOU AREN'T CAUGHT!
SHF
UM, WHERE ARE YOU HIDING THAT?
LOOKS LIKE YOU GOTTA GO TO MINEKO'S ROOM.
HUH? WHO?
HONESTLY BLAH BLAH THESE DAYS BLAH BLAH
YES, YOU'RE SO RIGHT...
I'M SORRY...
THE RULES ARE BLAH BLAH BLAH FOR YOUR OWN GOOD BLAH
MINEKO'S ROOM.
ARE YOU LISTENING?!
UNH...
THAT WAS AWFUL...
OH GOD...
STAGGER...
HM?

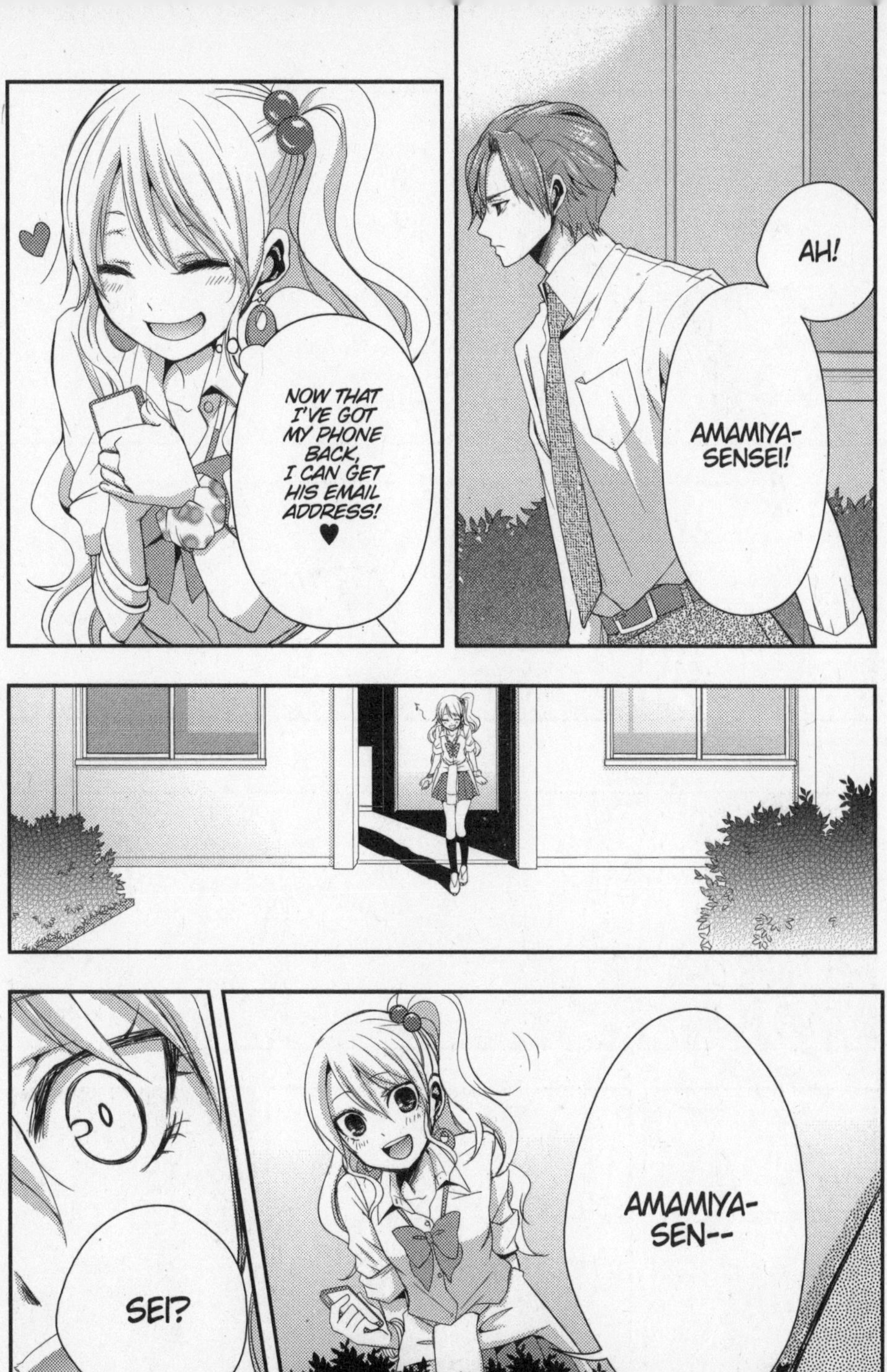
AH!
AMAMIYA-SENSEI!
NOW THAT I'VE GOT MY PHONE BACK, I CAN GET HIS EMAIL ADDRESS! ♥
AMAMIYA-SEN--
SEI?

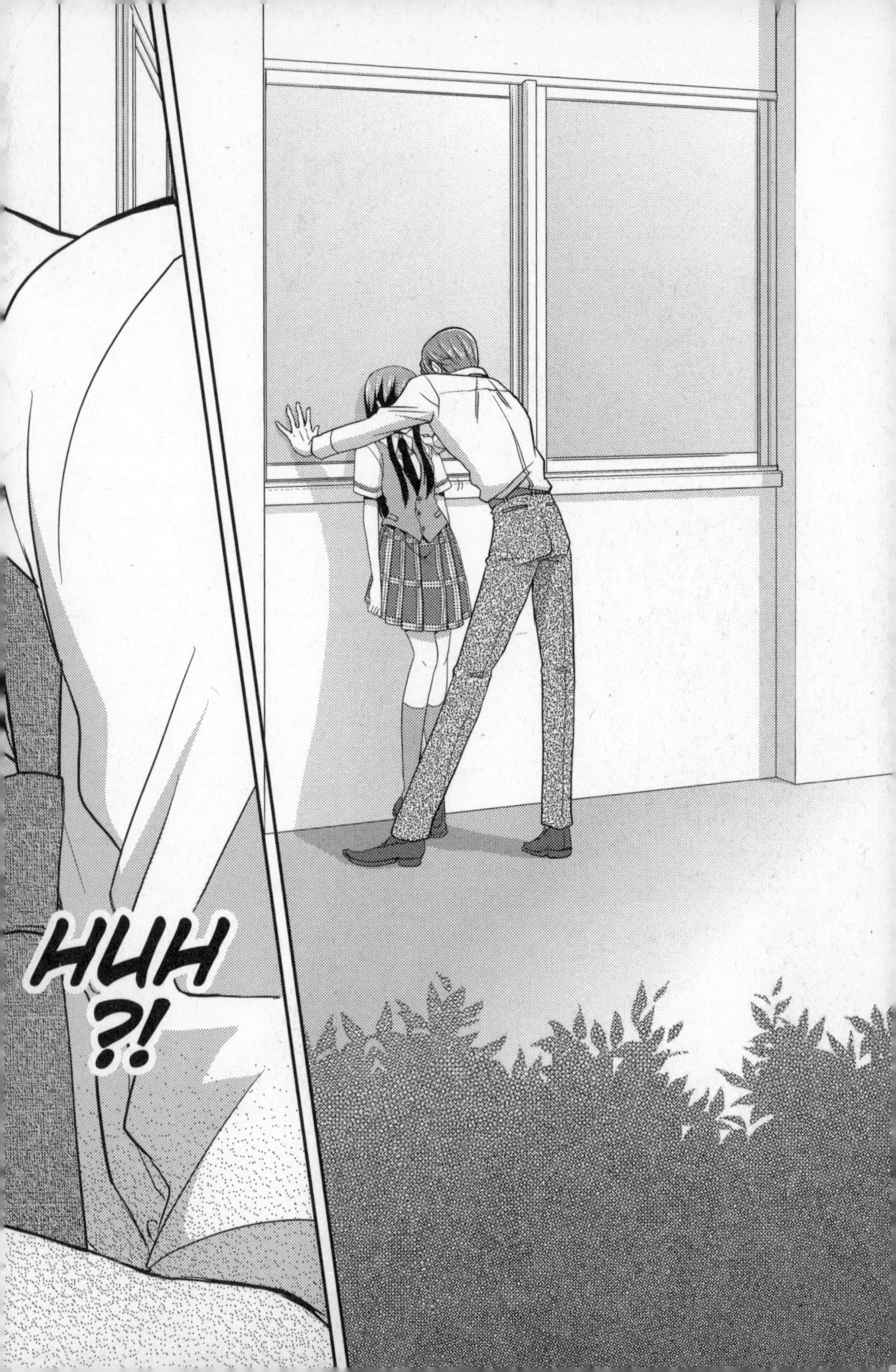
HUH
?!

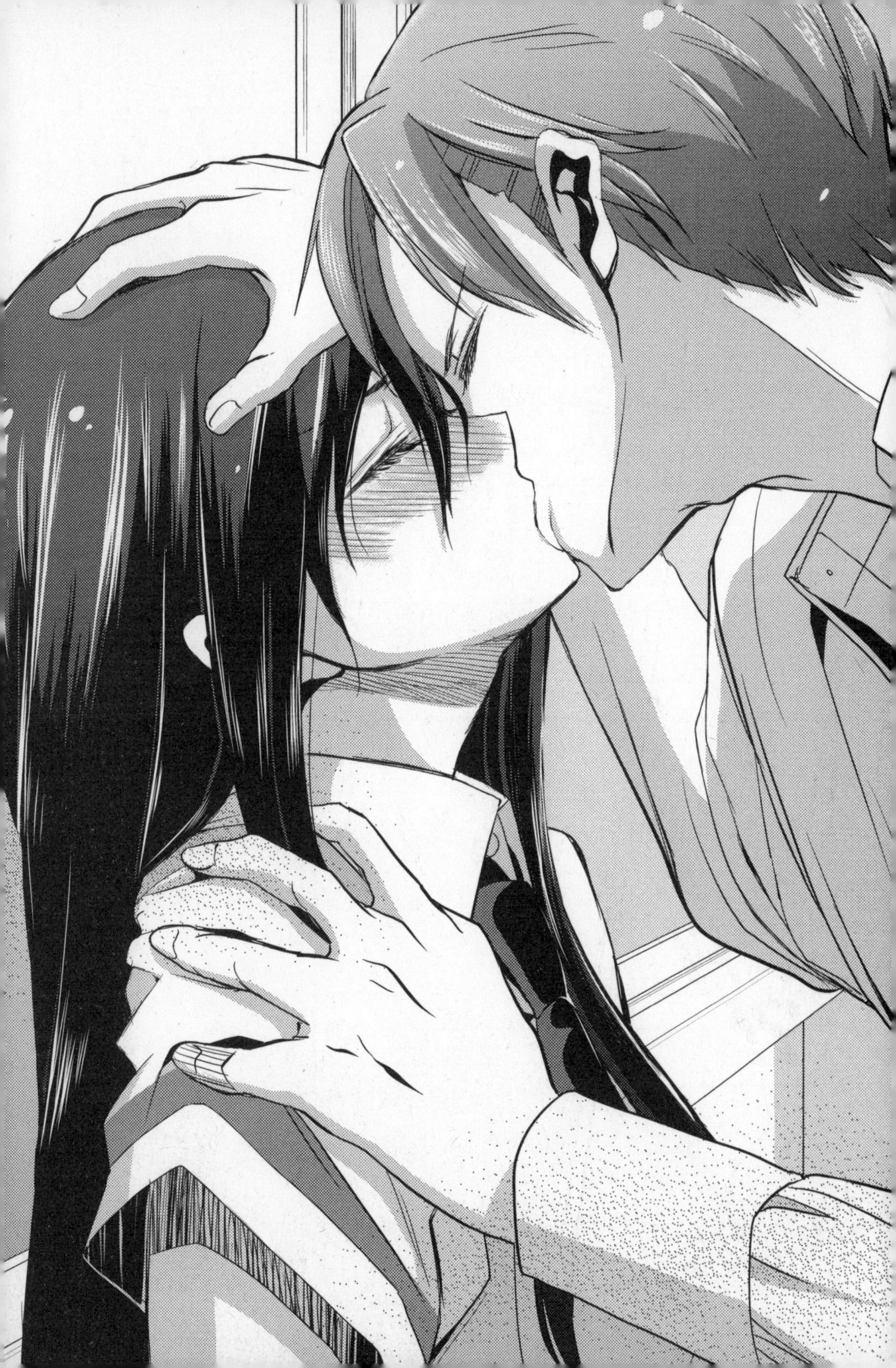

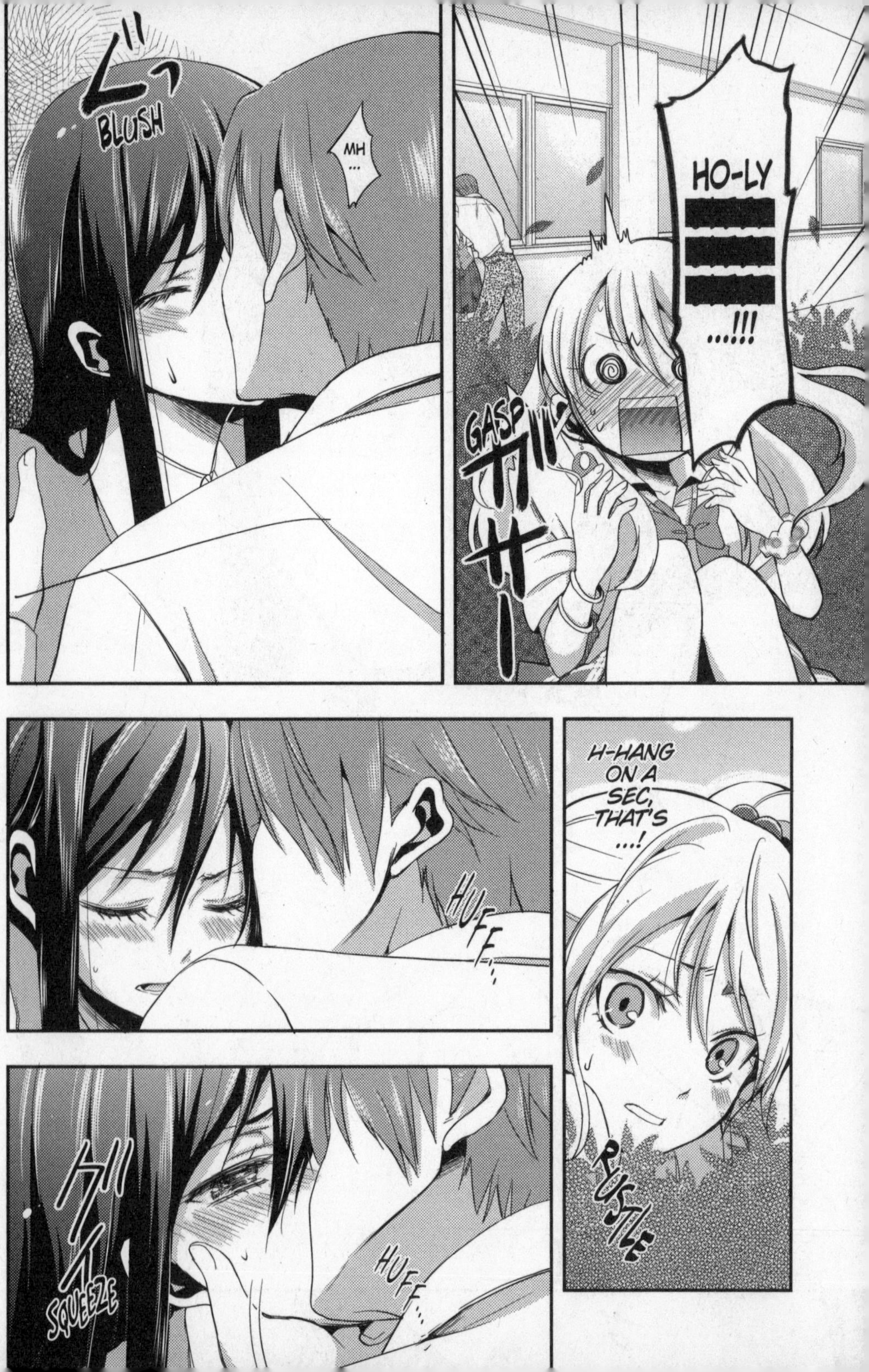
HO-LY
[redacted]
...!!!
GASP
BLUSH
MH
...
H-HANG ON A SEC, THAT'S ...!
RUSTLE
HUFF...
SQUEEZE
HUFF...

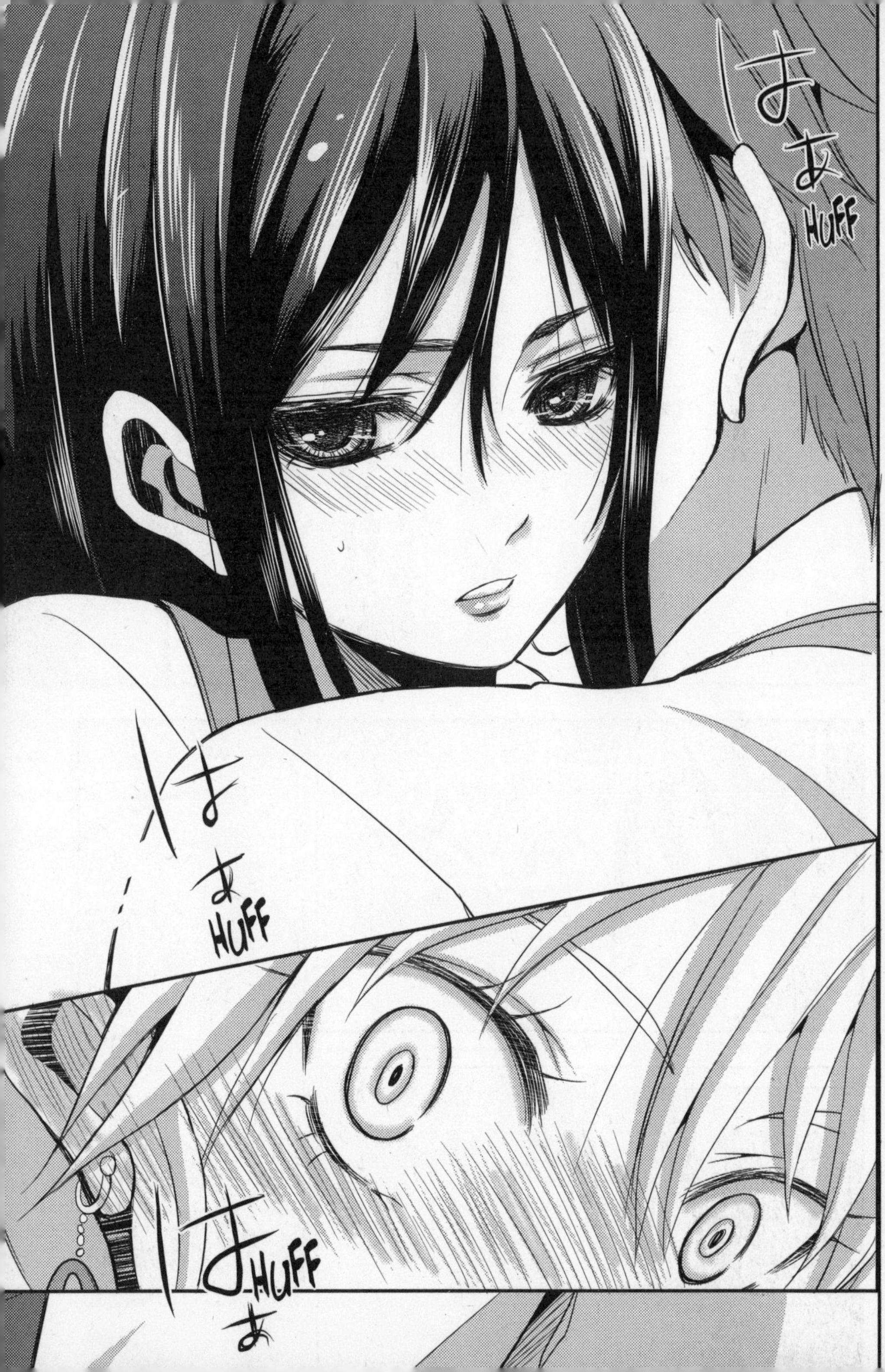
はぁ
HUFF
はぁ…
HUFF
はぁ
HUFF

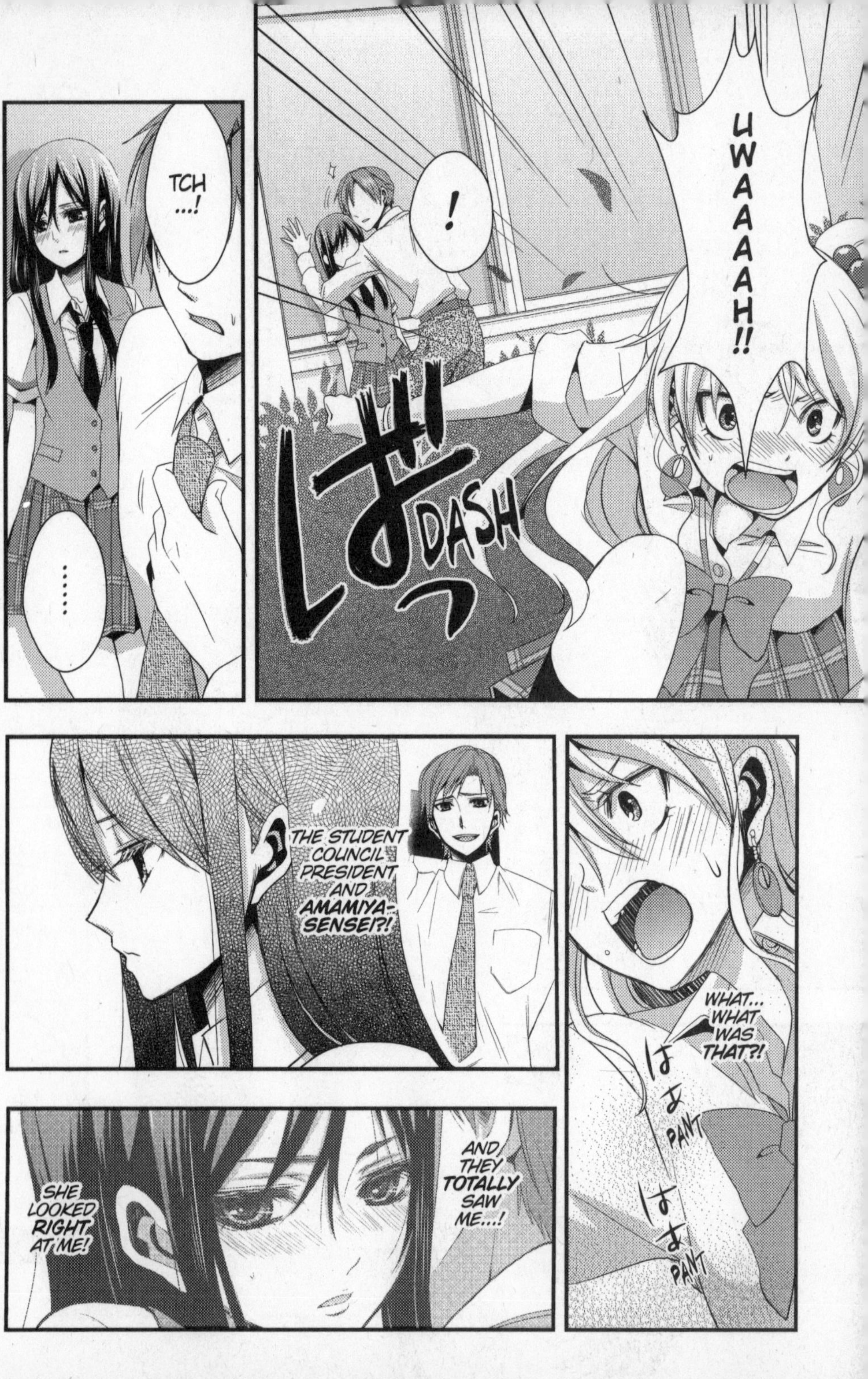
UWAAAAAH!!
!
しゅっ DASH
TCH ...!
......
WHAT... WHAT WAS THAT?!
はぁ PANT
はぁ PANT
THE STUDENT COUNCIL PRESIDENT AND AMAMIYA-SENSEI?!
AND THEY TOTALLY SAW ME...!
SHE LOOKED RIGHT AT ME!

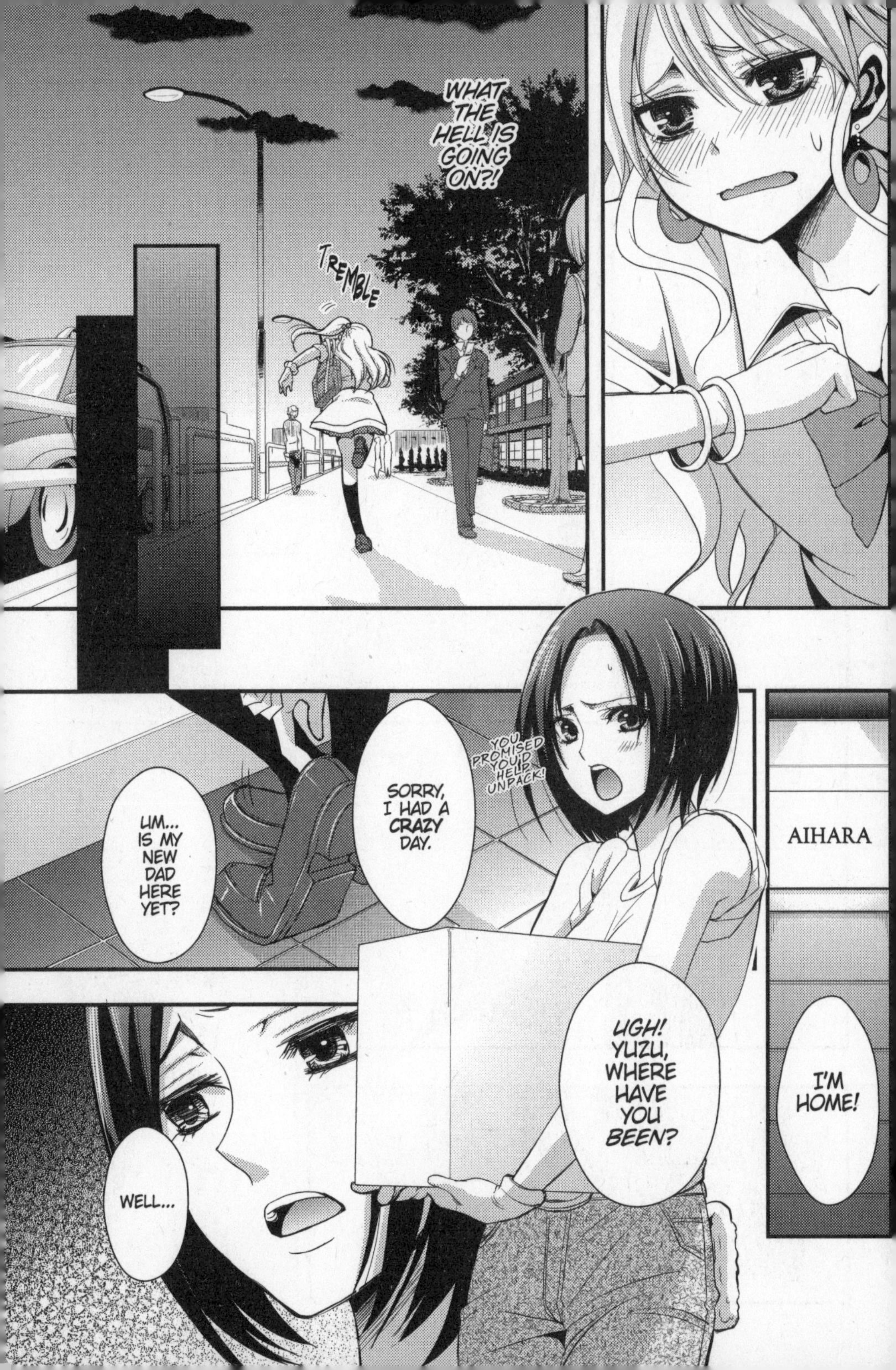
WHAT THE HELL IS GOING ON?!
TREMBLE
AIHARA
I'M HOME!
UGH! YUZU, WHERE HAVE YOU BEEN?
YOU PROMISED YOU'D HELP UNPACK!
SORRY, I HAD A CRAZY DAY.
UM... IS MY NEW DAD HERE YET?
WELL...

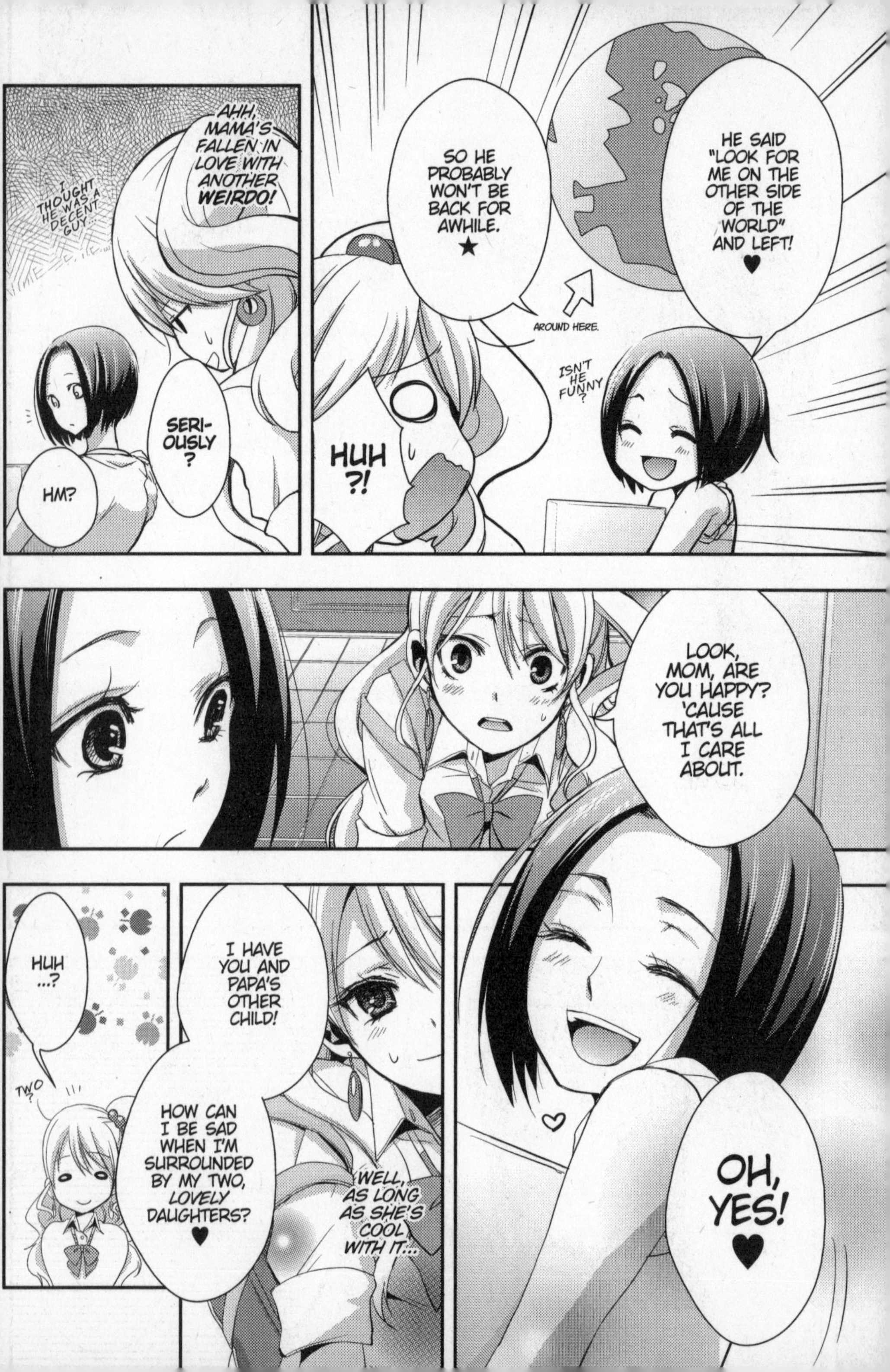
HE SAID "LOOK FOR ME ON THE OTHER SIDE OF THE "WORLD" AND LEFT! ♥
AROUND HERE.
ISN'T HE FUNNY?
SO HE PROBABLY WON'T BE BACK FOR AWHILE. ★
HUH ?!
AHH, MAMA'S FALLEN IN LOVE WITH ANOTHER WEIRDO!
I THOUGHT HE WAS A DECENT GUY...
SERIOUSLY?
HM?
LOOK, MOM, ARE YOU HAPPY? 'CAUSE THAT'S ALL I CARE ABOUT.
OH, YES! ♥
I HAVE YOU AND PAPA'S OTHER CHILD!
HOW CAN I BE SAD WHEN I'M SURROUNDED BY MY TWO, LOVELY DAUGHTERS? ♥
WELL, AS LONG AS SHE'S COOL WITH IT...
HUH ...?
TWO ?

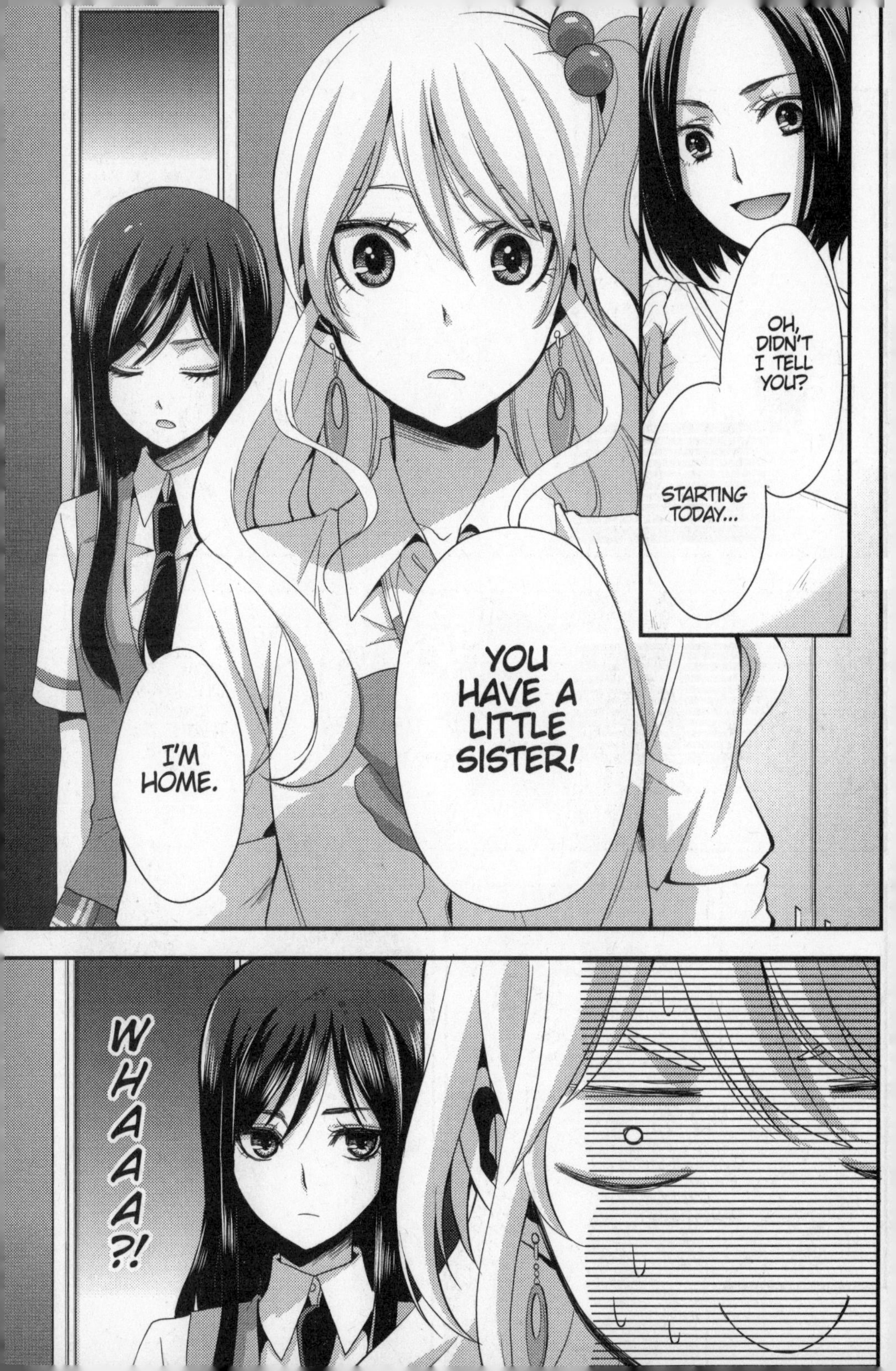
OH, DIDN'T I TELL YOU?
STARTING TODAY...
YOU HAVE A LITTLE SISTER!
I'M HOME.
WHAAAA?!

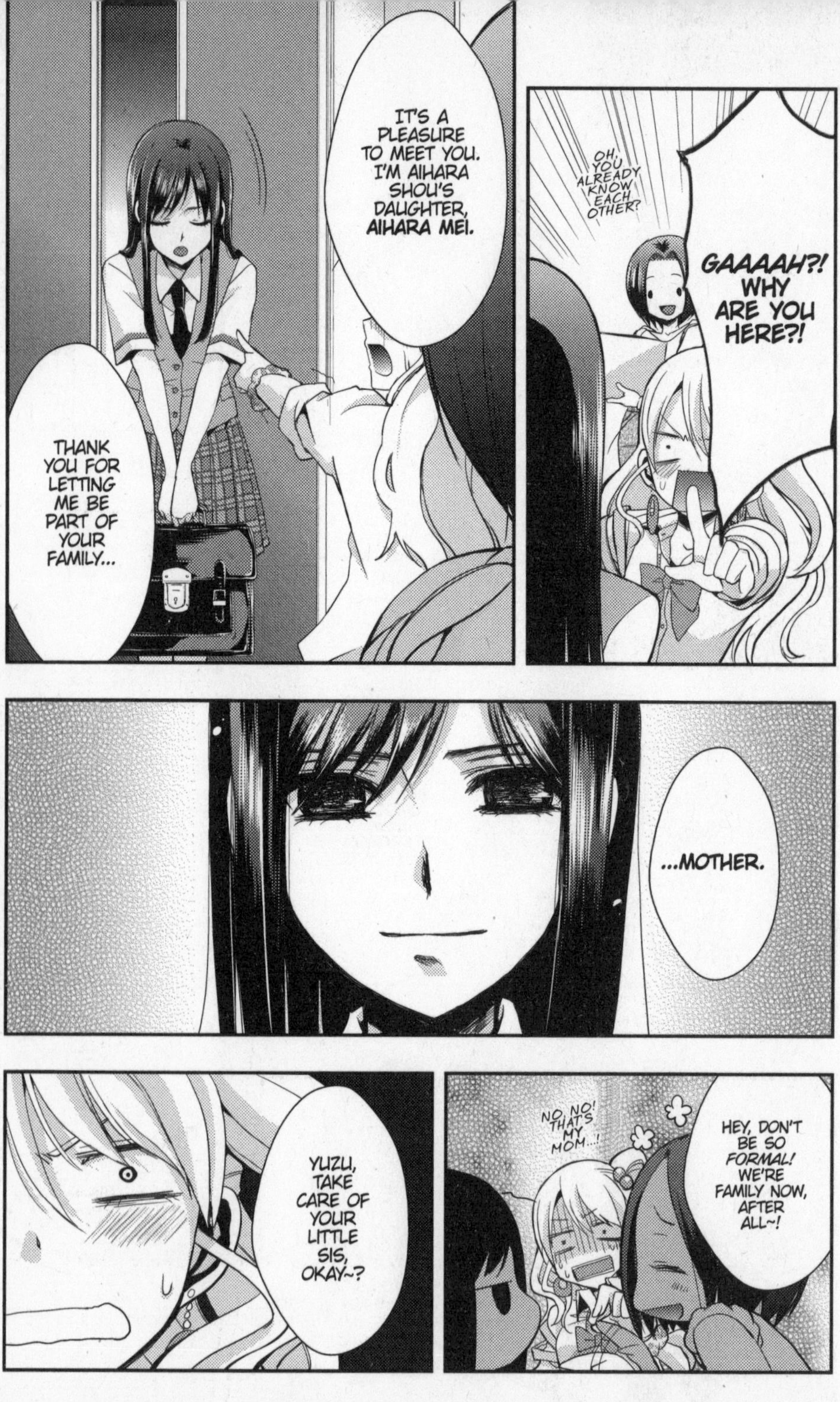
GAAAAH?! WHY ARE YOU HERE?!
OH, YOU ALREADY KNOW EACH OTHER?
IT'S A PLEASURE TO MEET YOU. I'M AIHARA SHOU'S DAUGHTER, AIHARA MEI.
THANK YOU FOR LETTING ME BE PART OF YOUR FAMILY...
...MOTHER.
HEY, DON'T BE SO *FORMAL!* WE'RE FAMILY NOW, AFTER ALL~!
NO NO! THAT'S MY MOM...!
YUZU, TAKE CARE OF YOUR LITTLE SIS, OKAY~?

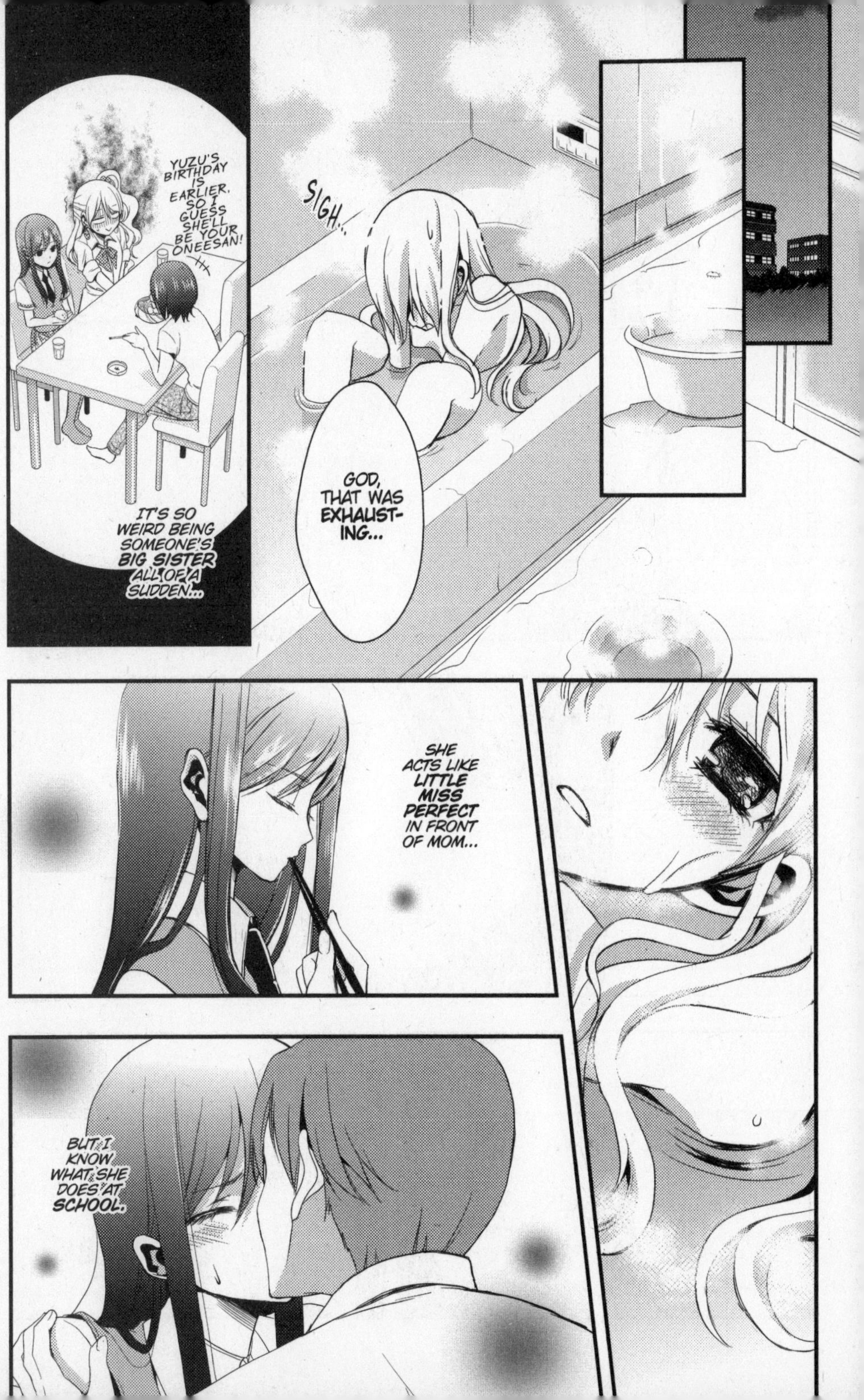
SIGH...
GOD, THAT WAS EXHAUSTING...
YUZU'S BIRTHDAY IS EARLIER, SO I GUESS SHE'LL BE YOUR ONEESAN!
IT'S SO WEIRD BEING SOMEONE'S BIG SISTER ALL OF A SUDDEN...
SHE ACTS LIKE LITTLE MISS PERFECT IN FRONT OF MOM...
BUT I KNOW WHAT SHE DOES AT SCHOOL.

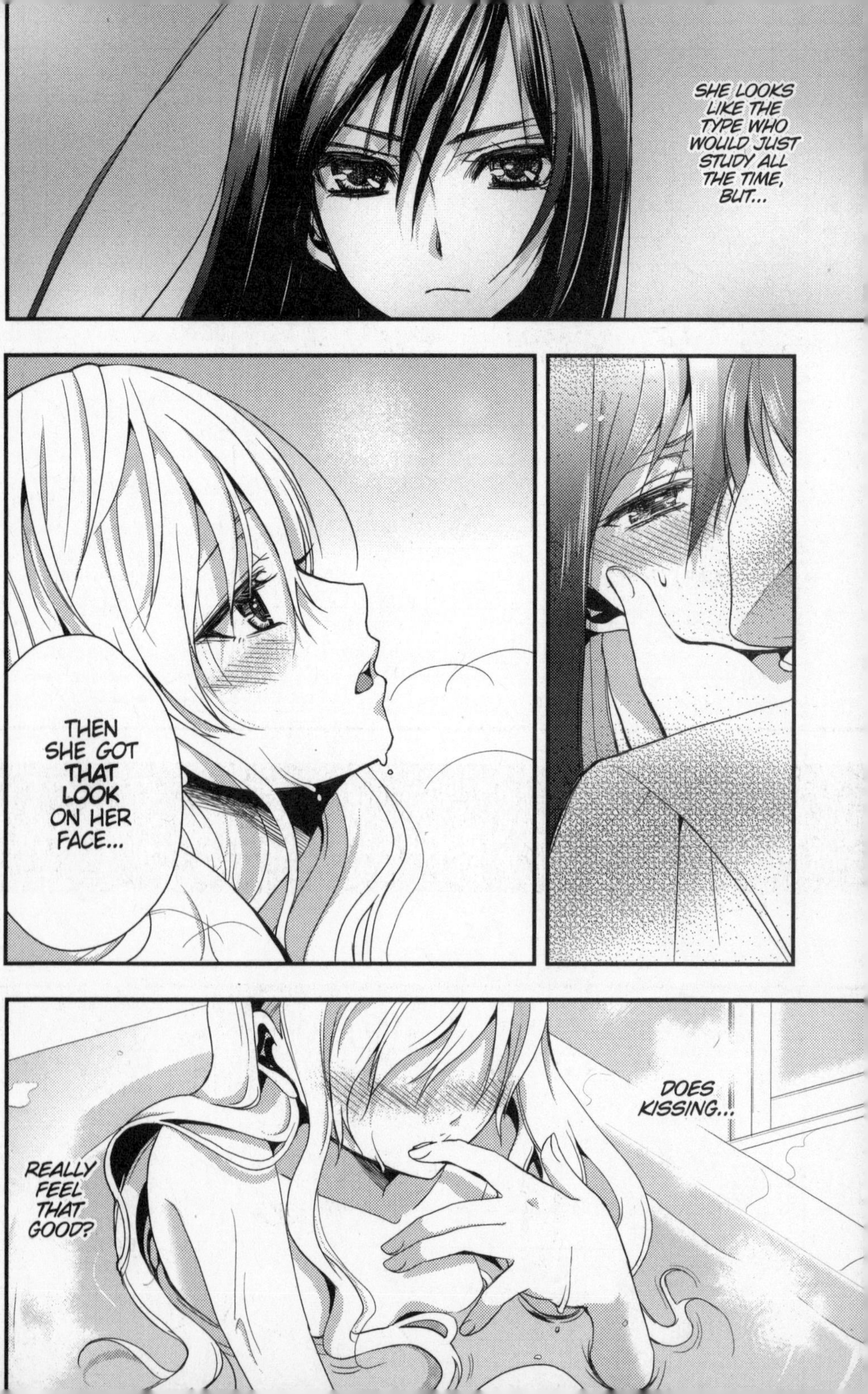
SHE LOOKS LIKE THE TYPE WHO WOULD JUST STUDY ALL THE TIME, BUT...
THEN SHE GOT THAT LOOK ON HER FACE...
DOES KISSING...
REALLY FEEL THAT GOOD?

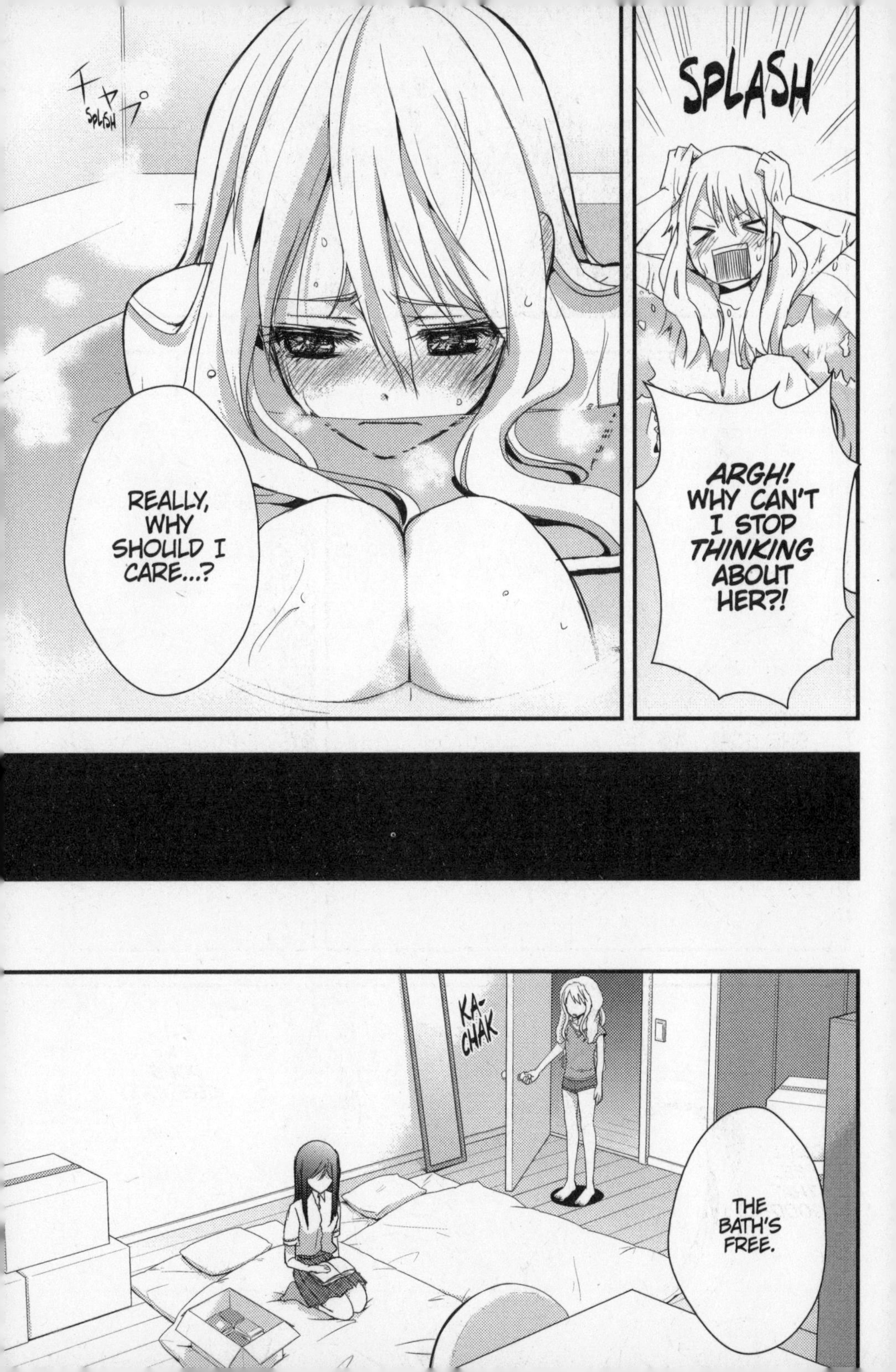
SPLASH
ARGH! WHY CAN'T I STOP THINKING ABOUT HER?!
チャプ
SPLASH
REALLY, WHY SHOULD I CARE...?
KA-CHAK
THE BATH'S FREE.

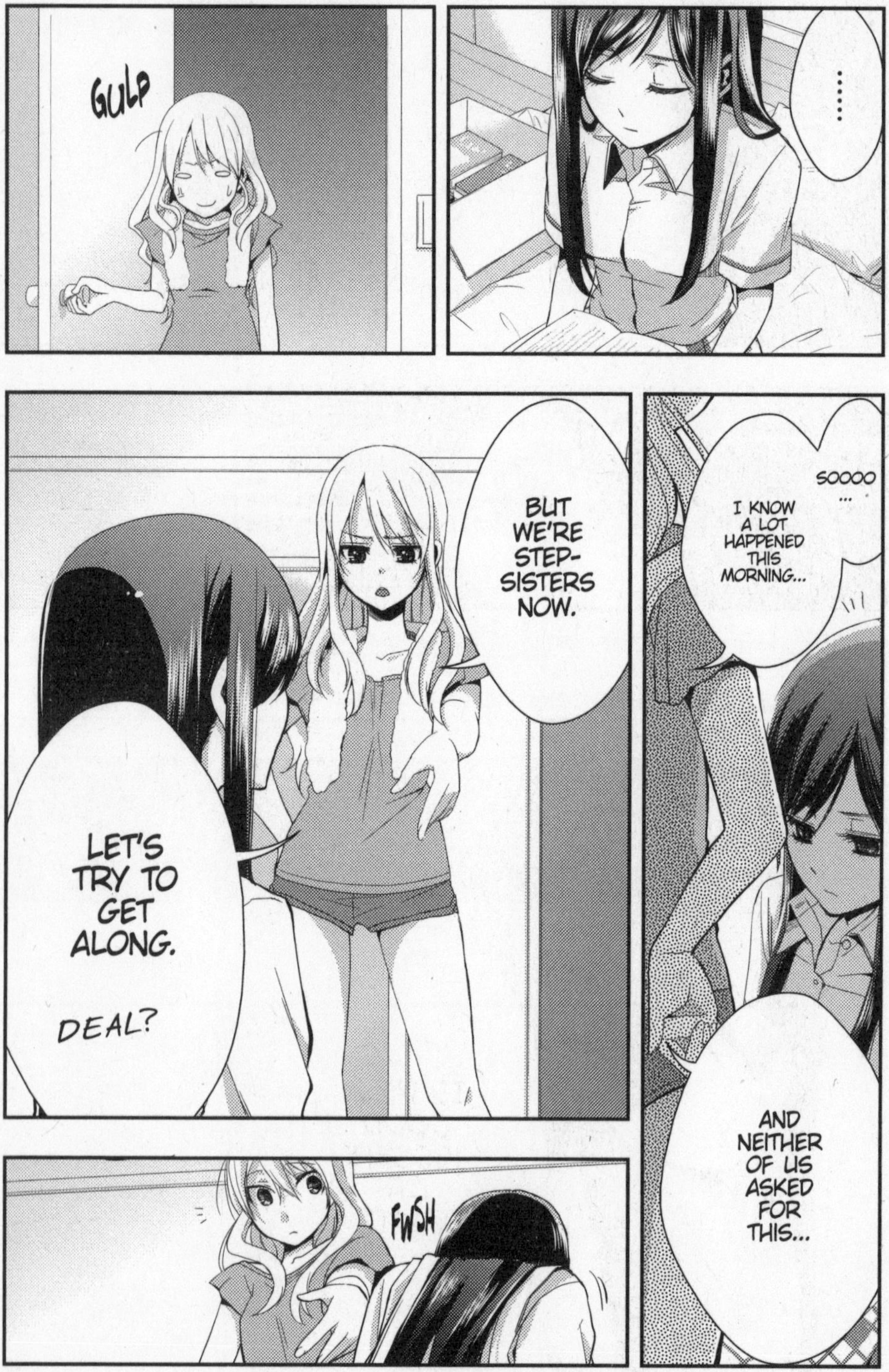
......
GULP
SOOOO ...
I KNOW A LOT HAPPENED THIS MORNING...
AND NEITHER OF US ASKED FOR THIS...
BUT WE'RE STEP-SISTERS NOW.
LET'S TRY TO GET ALONG.
DEAL?
FWSH

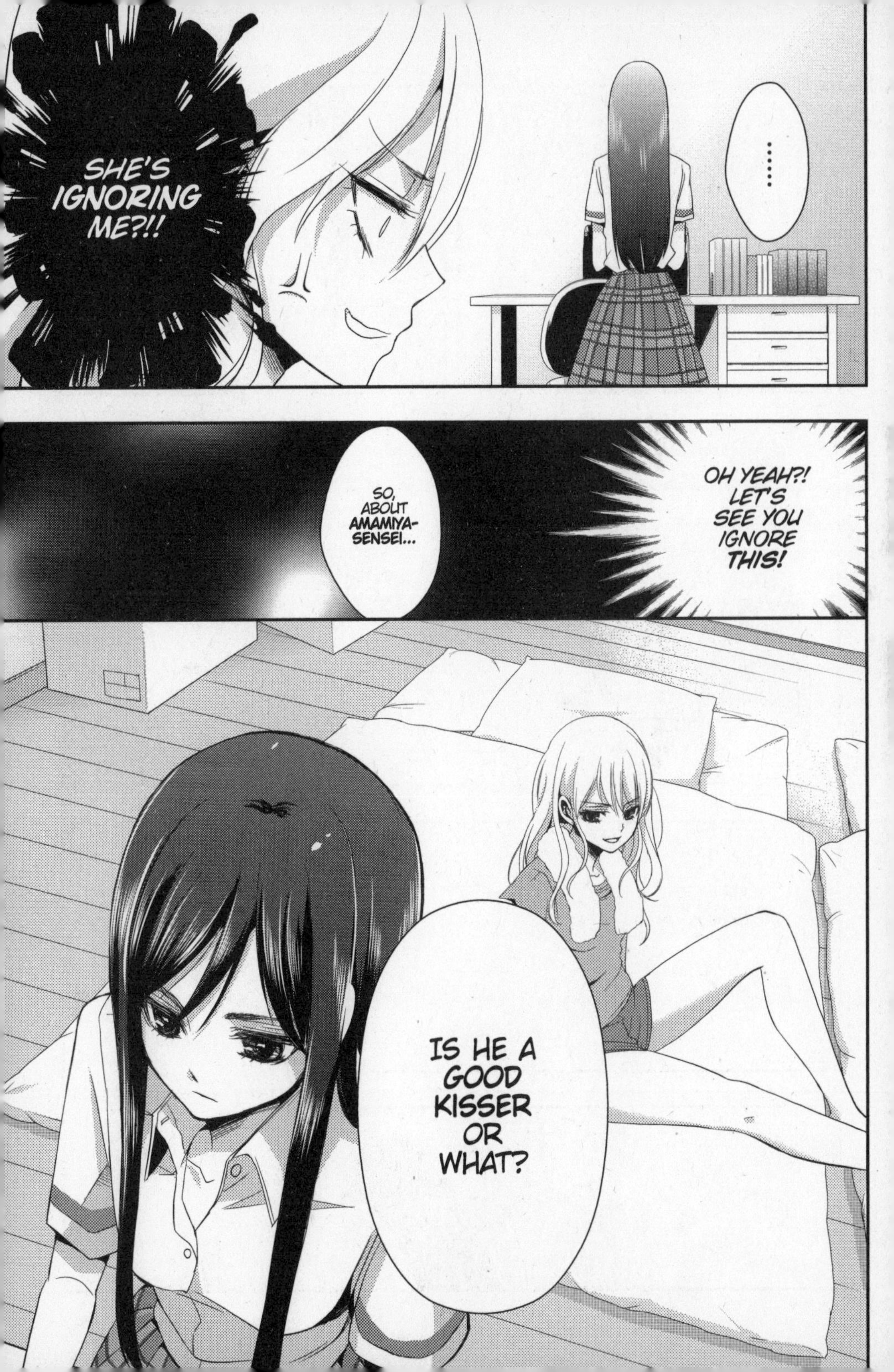
......
SHE'S IGNORING ME?!!
OH YEAH?! LET'S SEE YOU IGNORE THIS!
SO, ABOUT AMAMIYA-SENSEI...
IS HE A GOOD KISSER OR WHAT?

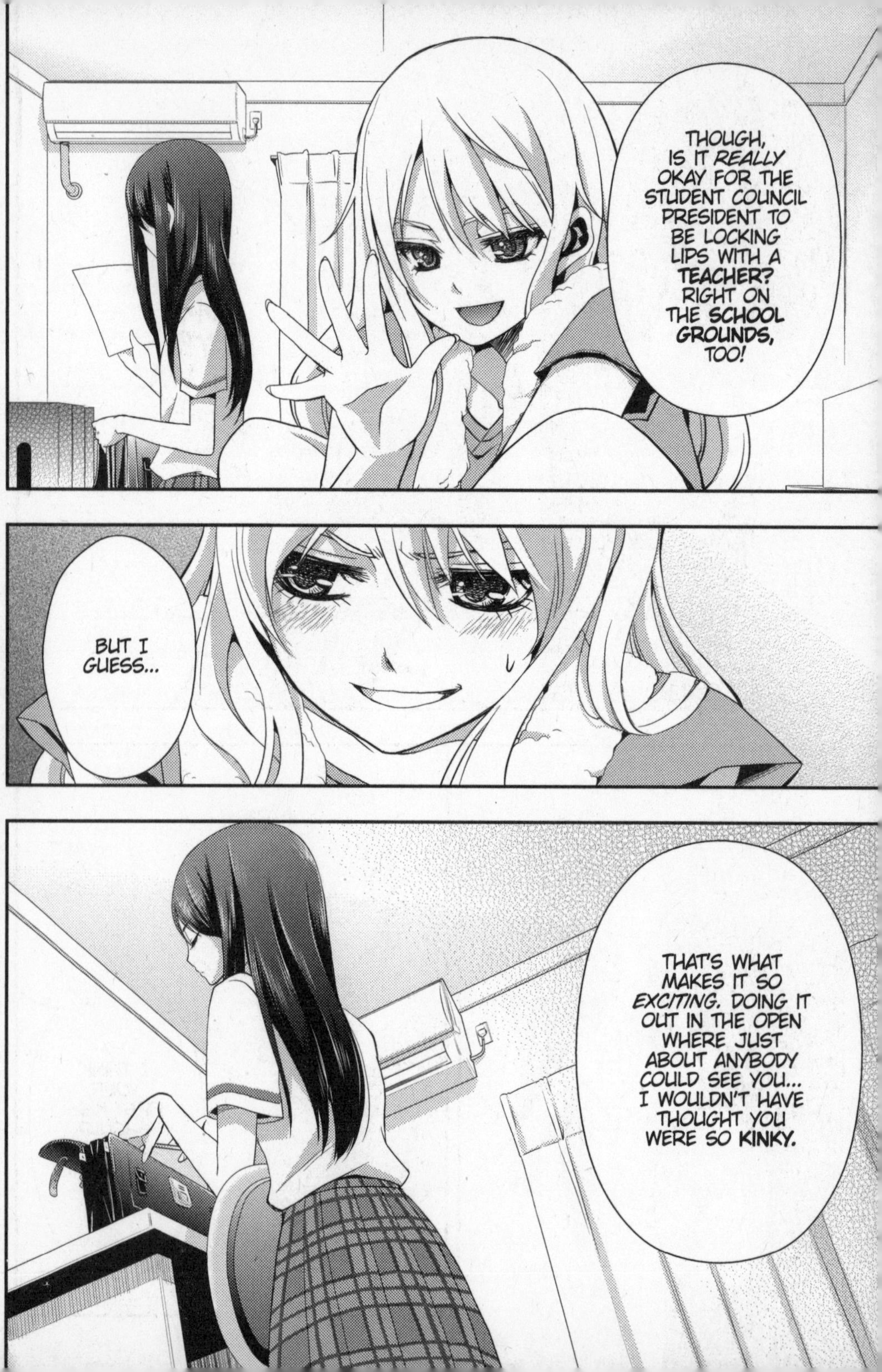
THOUGH, IS IT *REALLY* OKAY FOR THE STUDENT COUNCIL PRESIDENT TO BE LOCKING LIPS WITH A **TEACHER?** RIGHT ON THE **SCHOOL GROUNDS,** TOO!
BUT I GUESS...
THAT'S WHAT MAKES IT SO *EXCITING.* DOING IT OUT IN THE OPEN WHERE JUST ABOUT ANYBODY COULD SEE YOU... I WOULDN'T HAVE THOUGHT YOU WERE SO **KINKY.**

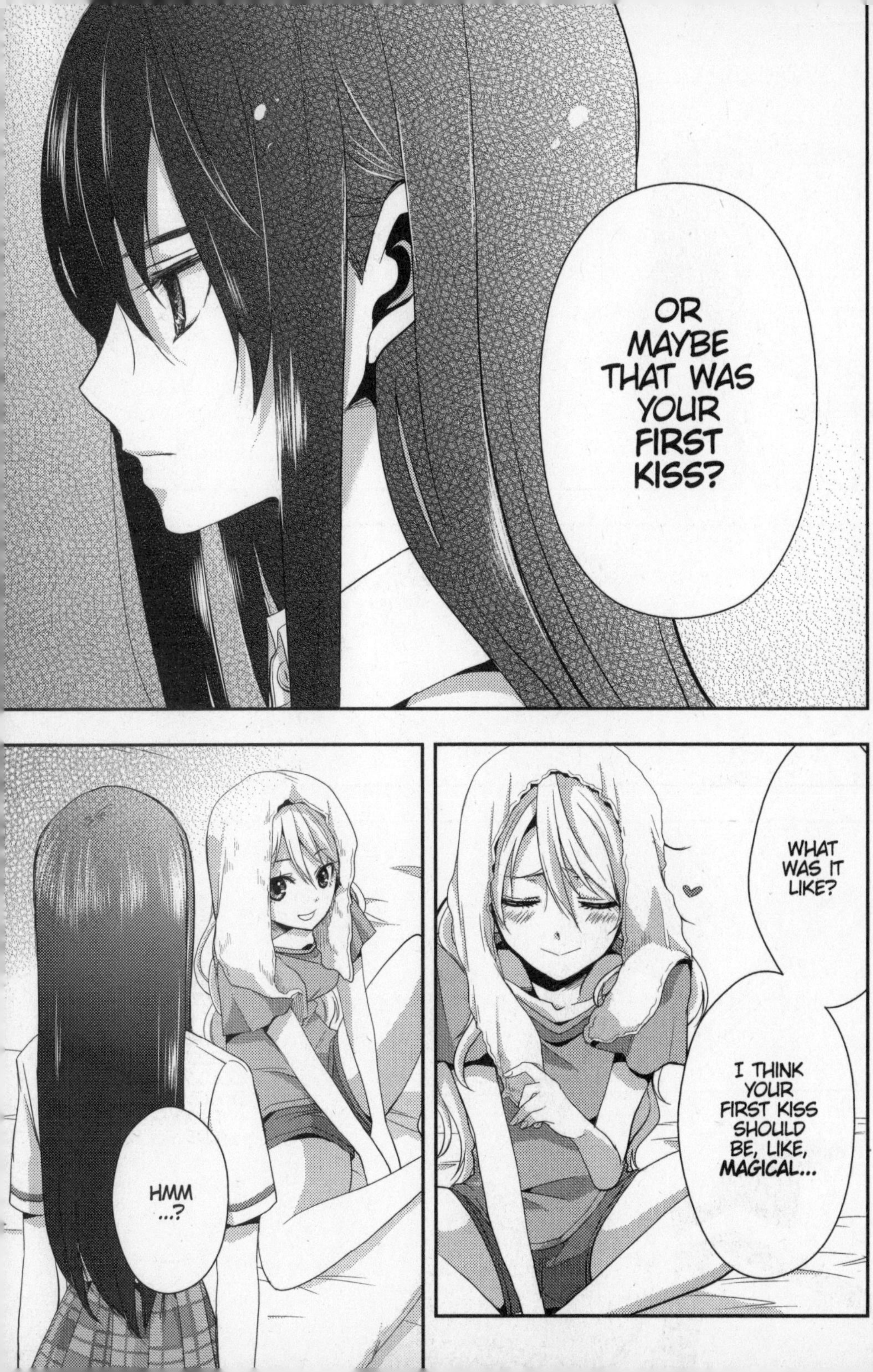
OR MAYBE THAT WAS YOUR FIRST KISS?
WHAT WAS IT LIKE?
I THINK YOUR FIRST KISS SHOULD BE, LIKE, MAGICAL...
HMM ...?

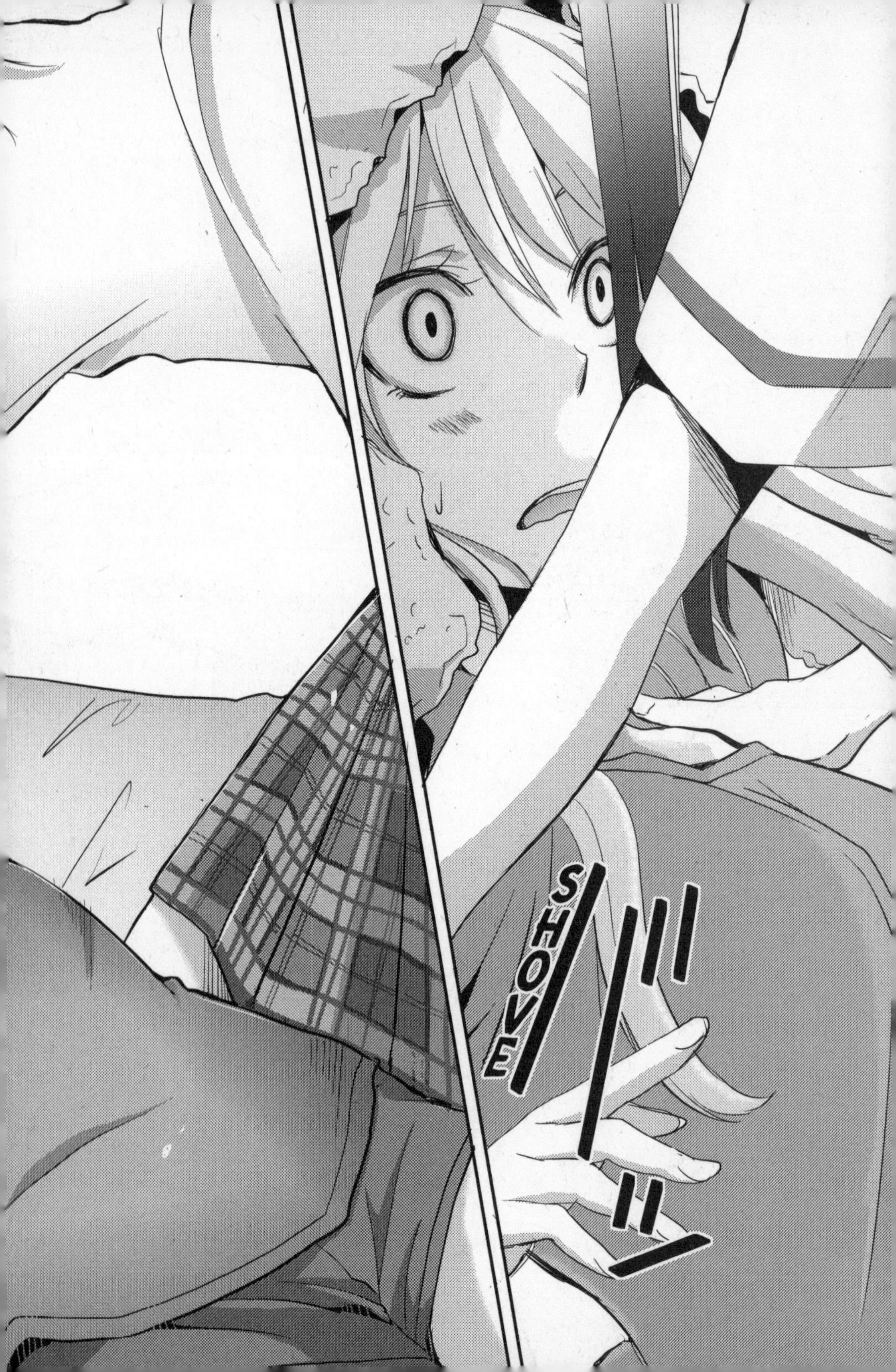
SHOVE

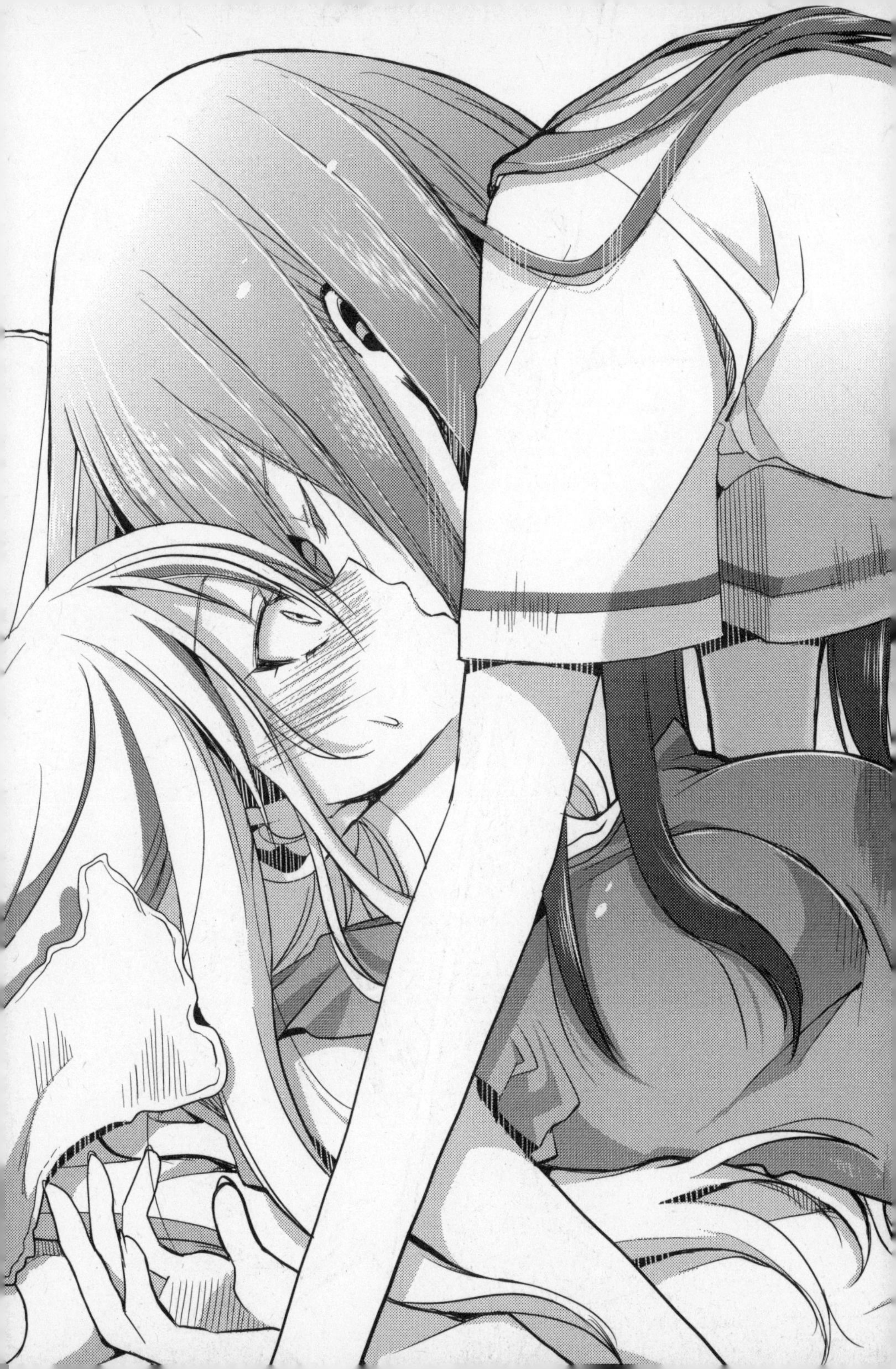

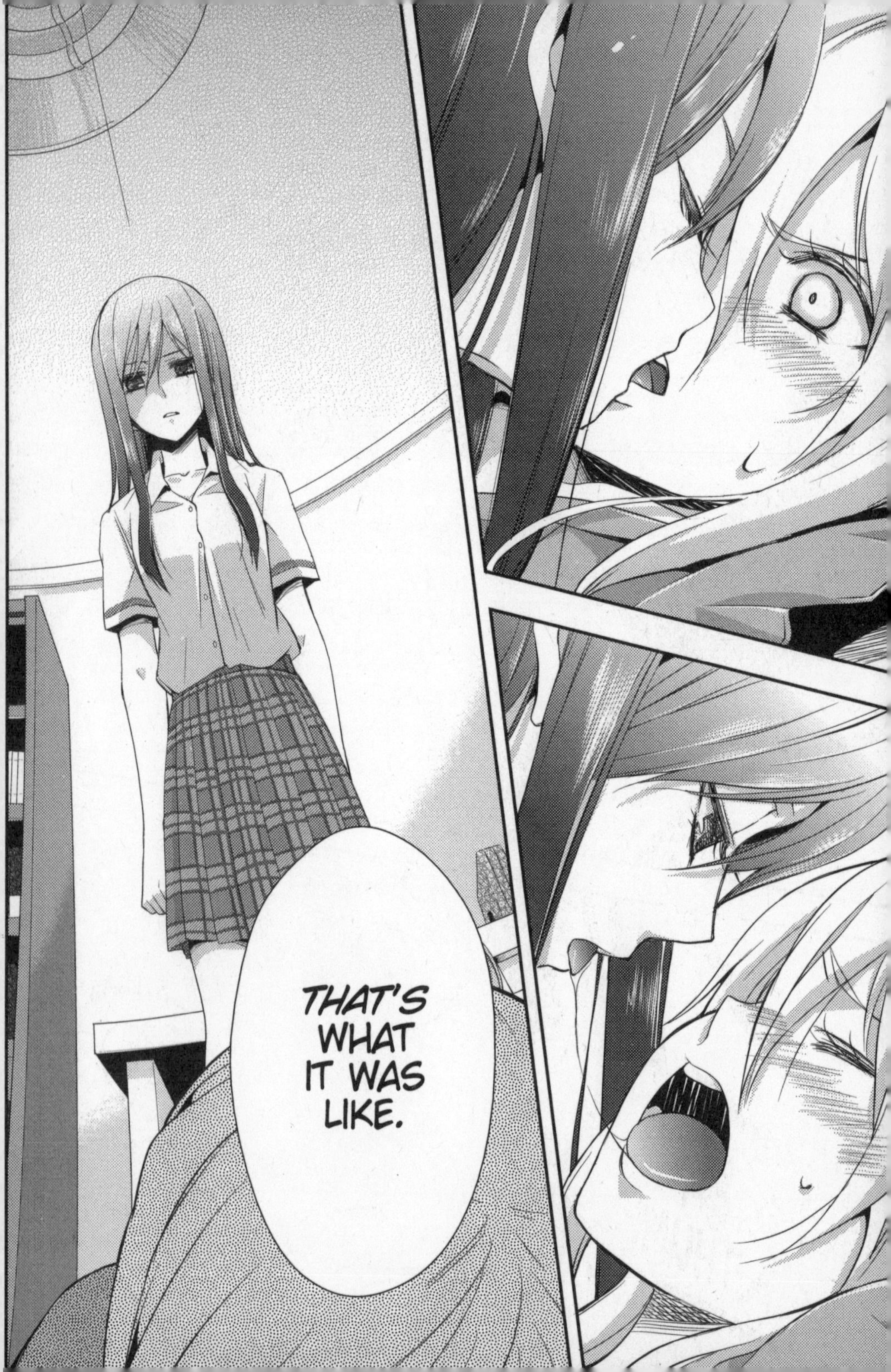
THAT'S WHAT IT WAS LIKE.

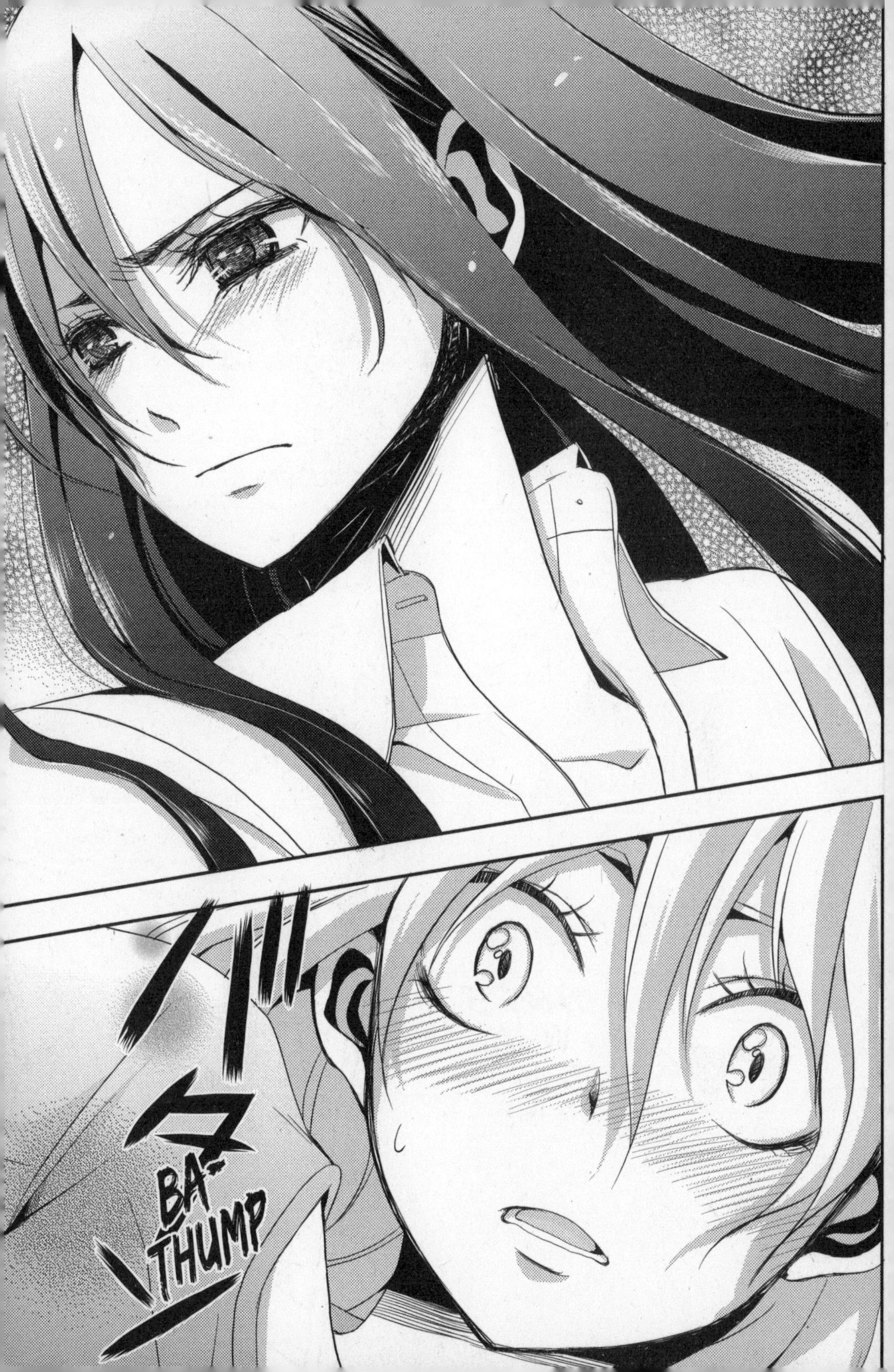
BA-THUMP

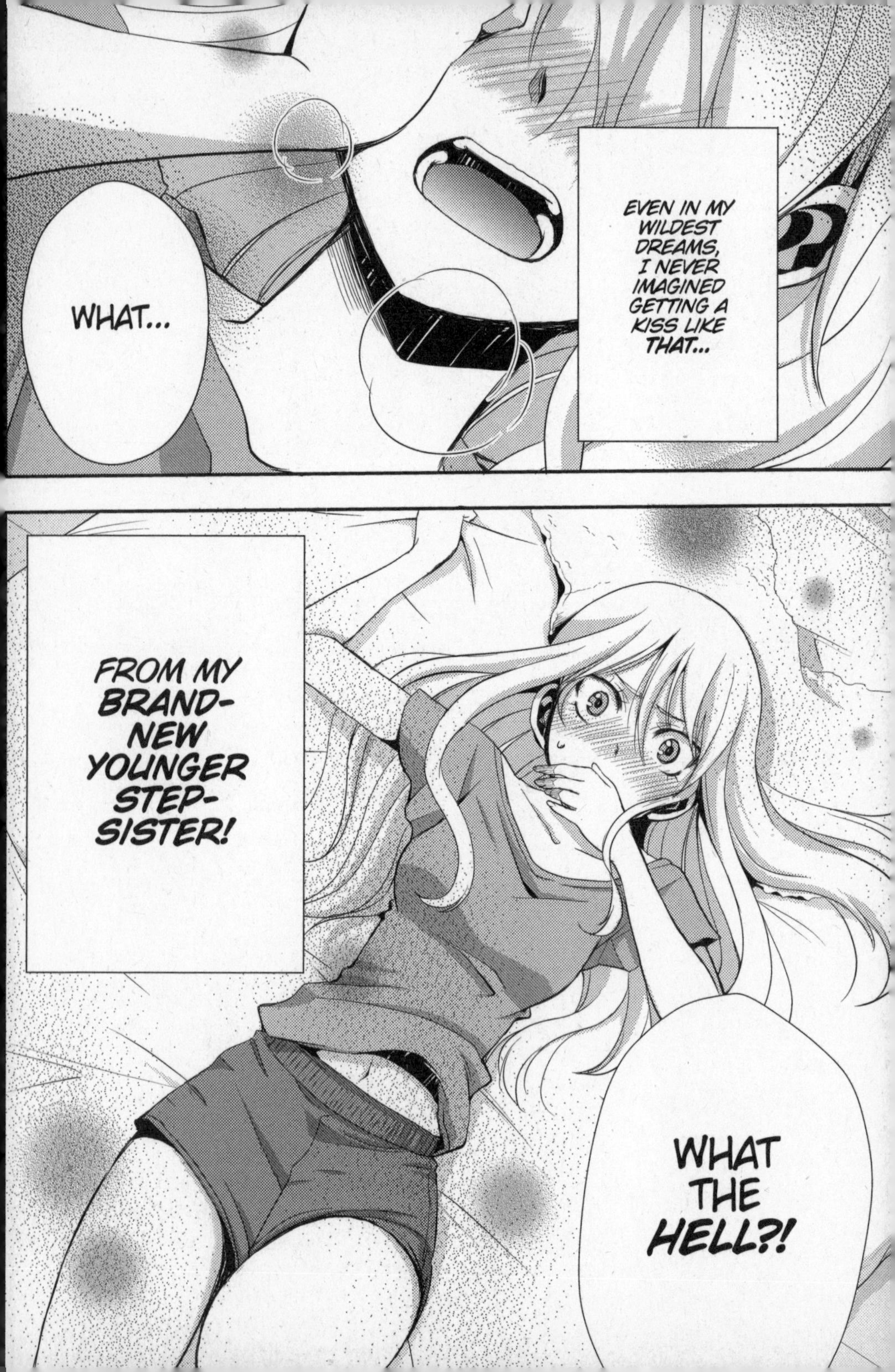
EVEN IN MY WILDEST DREAMS, I NEVER IMAGINED GETTING A KISS LIKE THAT...
WHAT...
FROM MY BRAND-NEW YOUNGER STEP-SISTER!
WHAT THE HELL?!

citrus
【シトラス】
SECRET LOVE AFFAIR WITH SISTER

citrus

SABUROUTA PRESENTS SECRET LOVE AFFAIR WITH SISTER

1

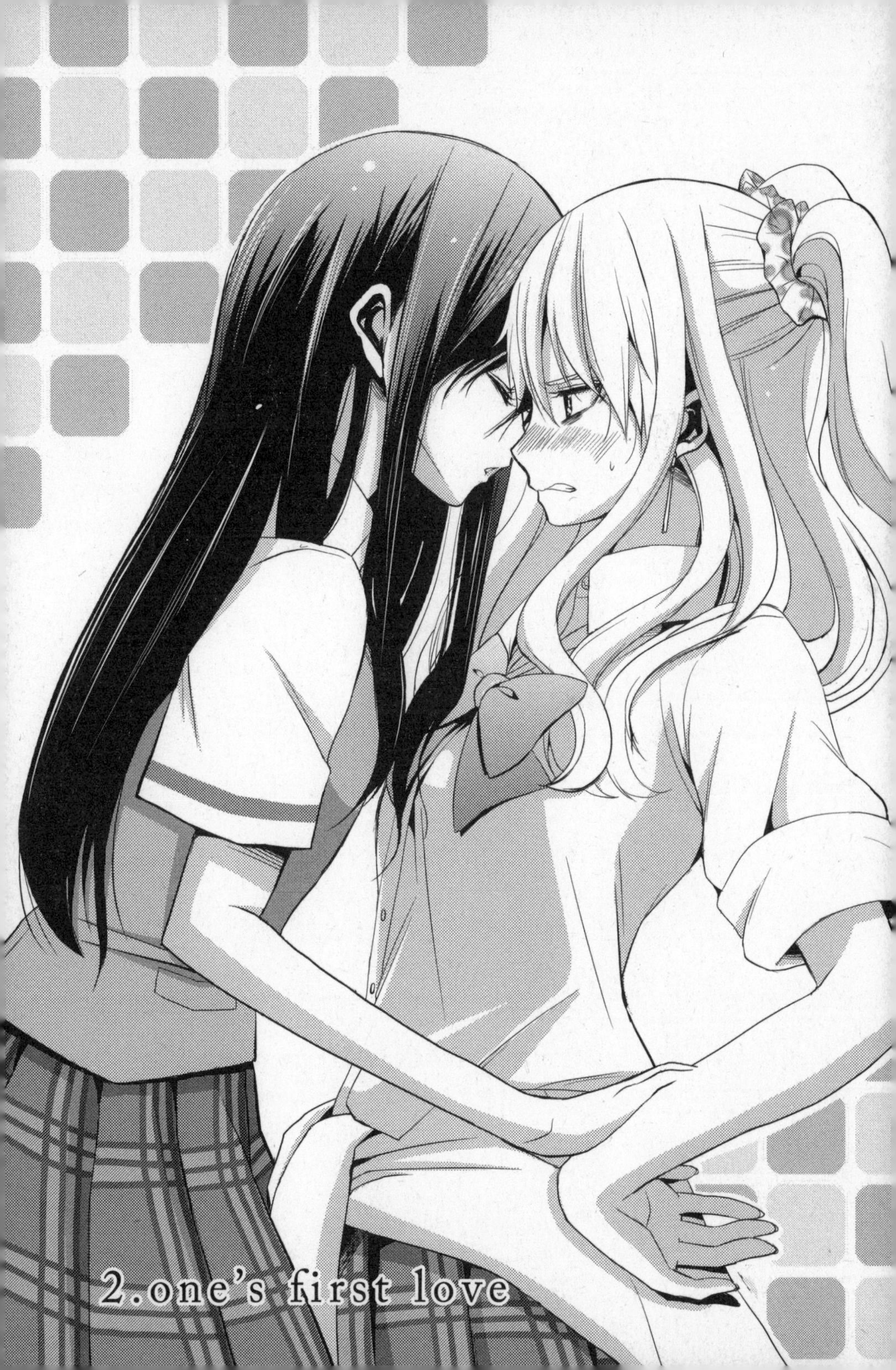
2.one's first love

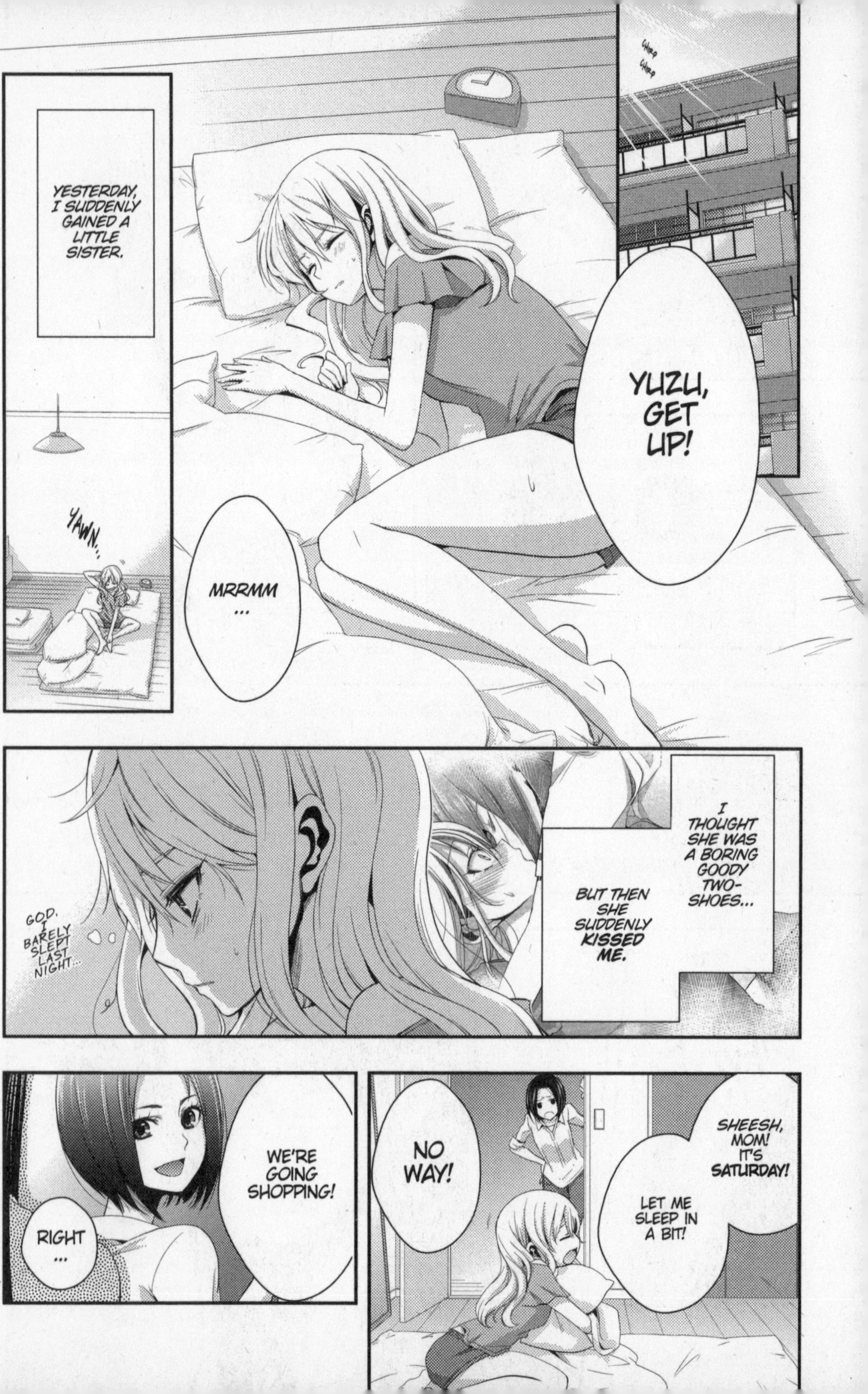
CHIRP
CHIRP
YUZU, GET UP!
MRRMM...
YESTERDAY, I SUDDENLY GAINED A LITTLE SISTER.
YAWN...
I THOUGHT SHE WAS A BORING GOODY TWO-SHOES...
BUT THEN SHE SUDDENLY KISSED ME.
GOD, I BARELY SLEPT LAST NIGHT...
SHEESH, MOM! IT'S SATURDAY!
LET ME SLEEP IN A BIT!
NO WAY!
WE'RE GOING SHOPPING!
RIGHT...

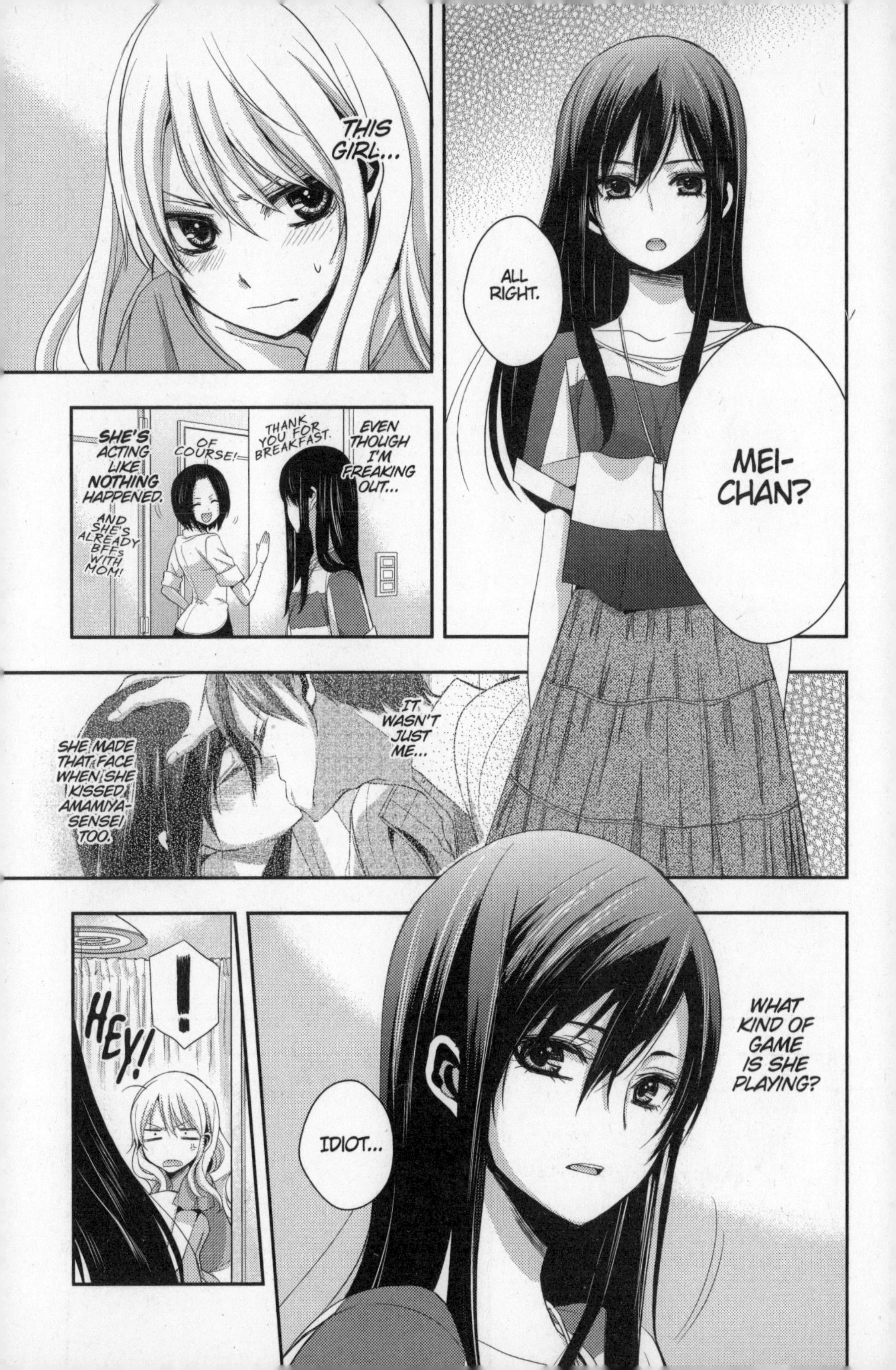
MEI-CHAN?
ALL RIGHT.
THIS GIRL...
EVEN THOUGH I'M FREAKING OUT...
THANK YOU FOR BREAKFAST.
OF COURSE!
SHE'S ACTING LIKE NOTHING HAPPENED.
AND SHE'S ALREADY BFFs WITH MOM!
IT WASN'T JUST ME...
SHE MADE THAT FACE WHEN SHE KISSED AMAMIYA-SENSEI TOO.
WHAT KIND OF GAME IS SHE PLAYING?
IDIOT...
!
HEY!

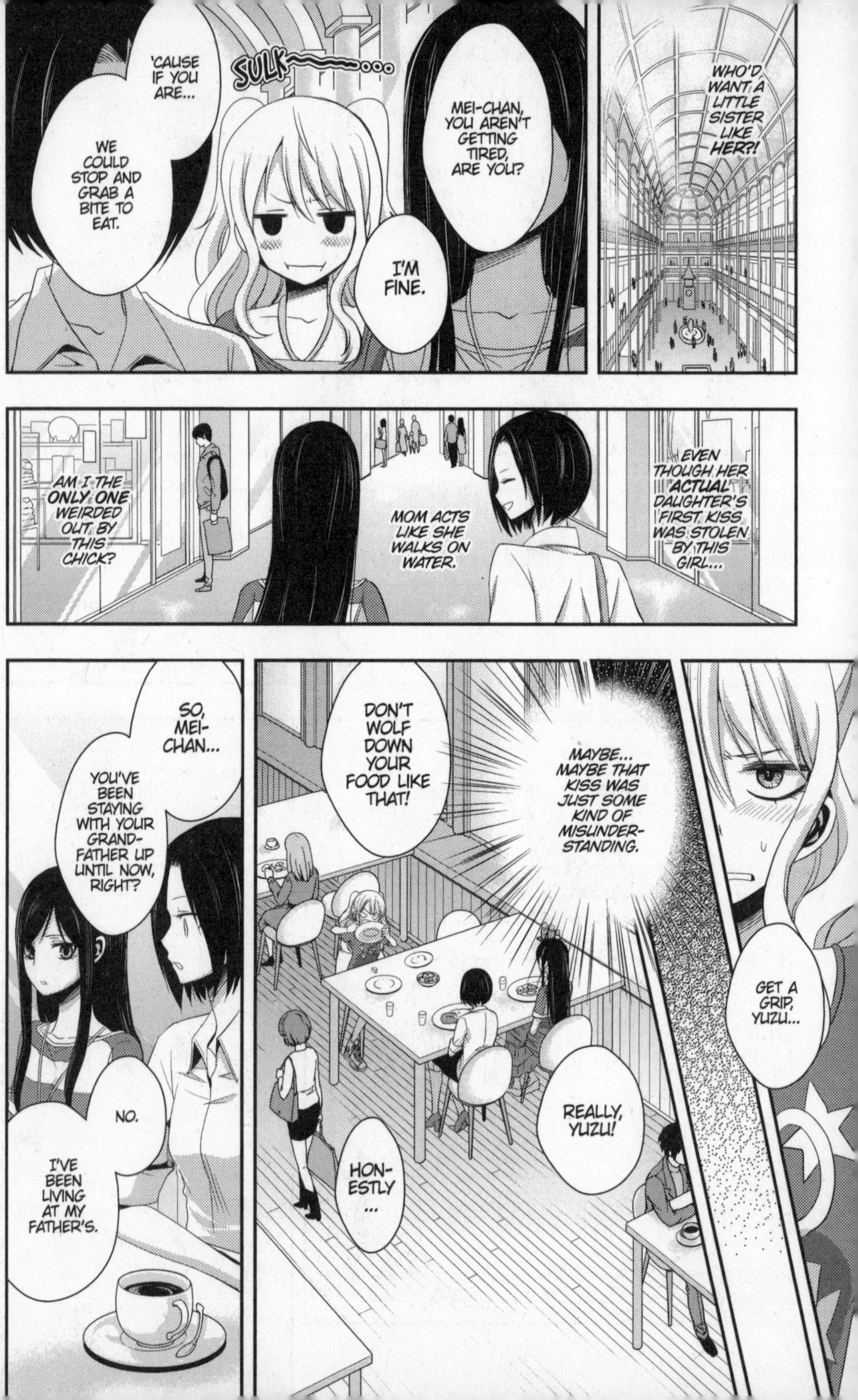
WHO'D WANT A LITTLE SISTER LIKE HER?!
MEI-CHAN, YOU AREN'T GETTING TIRED, ARE YOU?
SULK~~~...
'CAUSE IF YOU ARE...
WE COULD STOP AND GRAB A BITE TO EAT.
I'M FINE.
EVEN THOUGH HER ACTUAL DAUGHTER'S FIRST KISS WAS STOLEN BY THIS GIRL...
MOM ACTS LIKE SHE WALKS ON WATER.
AM I THE ONLY ONE WEIRDED OUT BY THIS CHICK?
MAYBE... MAYBE THAT KISS WAS JUST SOME KIND OF MISUNDER-STANDING.
GET A GRIP, YUZU...
DON'T WOLF DOWN YOUR FOOD LIKE THAT!
REALLY, YUZU!
HON-ESTLY...
SO, MEI-CHAN...
YOU'VE BEEN STAYING WITH YOUR GRAND-FATHER UP UNTIL NOW, RIGHT?
NO.
I'VE BEEN LIVING AT MY FATHER'S.

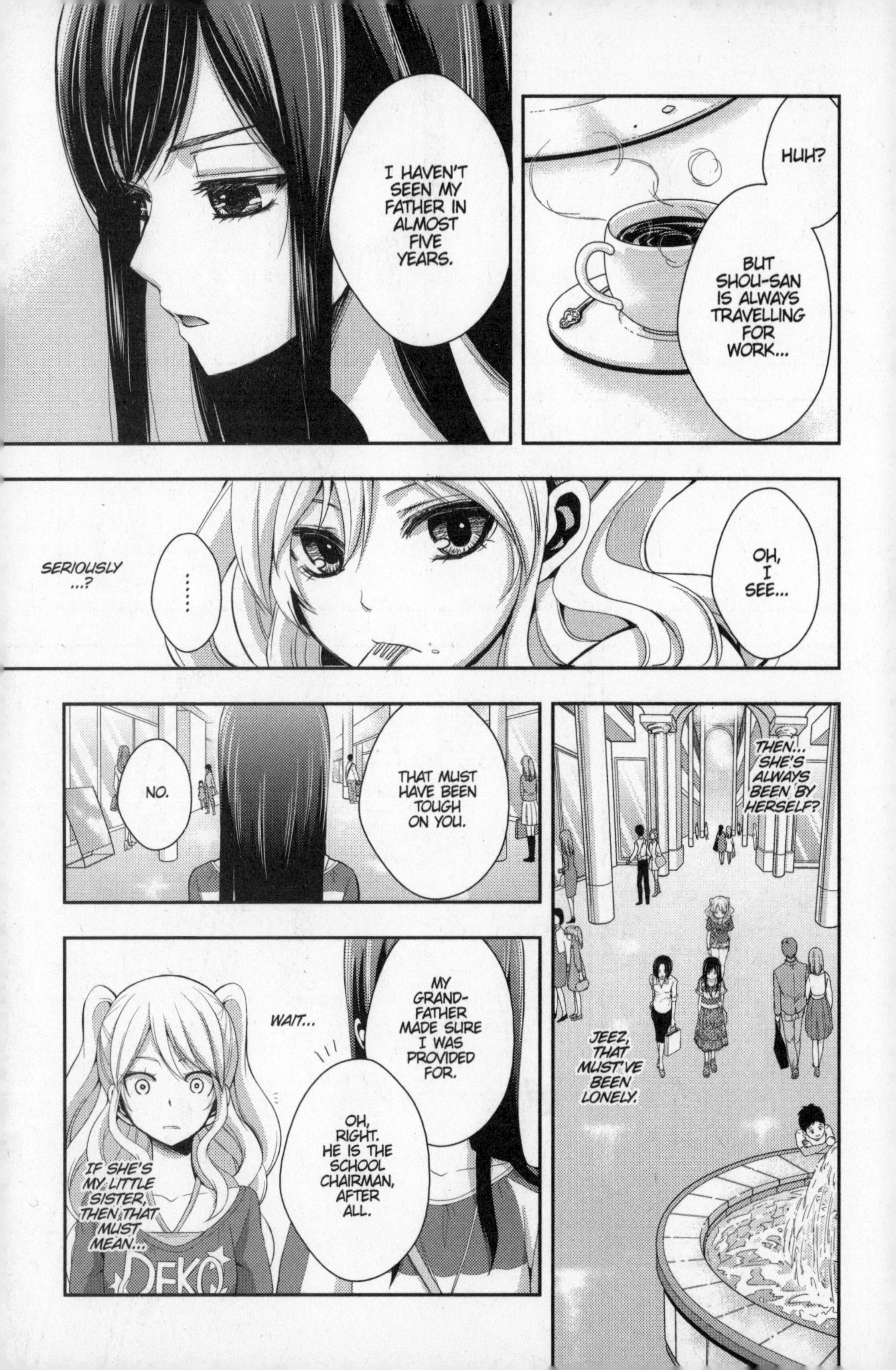
HUH?
BUT SHOU-SAN IS ALWAYS TRAVELLING FOR WORK...
I HAVEN'T SEEN MY FATHER IN ALMOST FIVE YEARS.
OH, I SEE...
......
SERIOUSLY ...?
THEN... SHE'S ALWAYS BEEN BY HERSELF?
JEEZ, THAT MUST'VE BEEN LONELY.
THAT MUST HAVE BEEN TOUGH ON YOU.
NO.
MY GRAND-FATHER MADE SURE I WAS PROVIDED FOR.
WAIT...
OH, RIGHT. HE IS THE SCHOOL CHAIRMAN, AFTER ALL.
IF SHE'S MY LITTLE SISTER, THEN THAT MUST MEAN...
DEKO

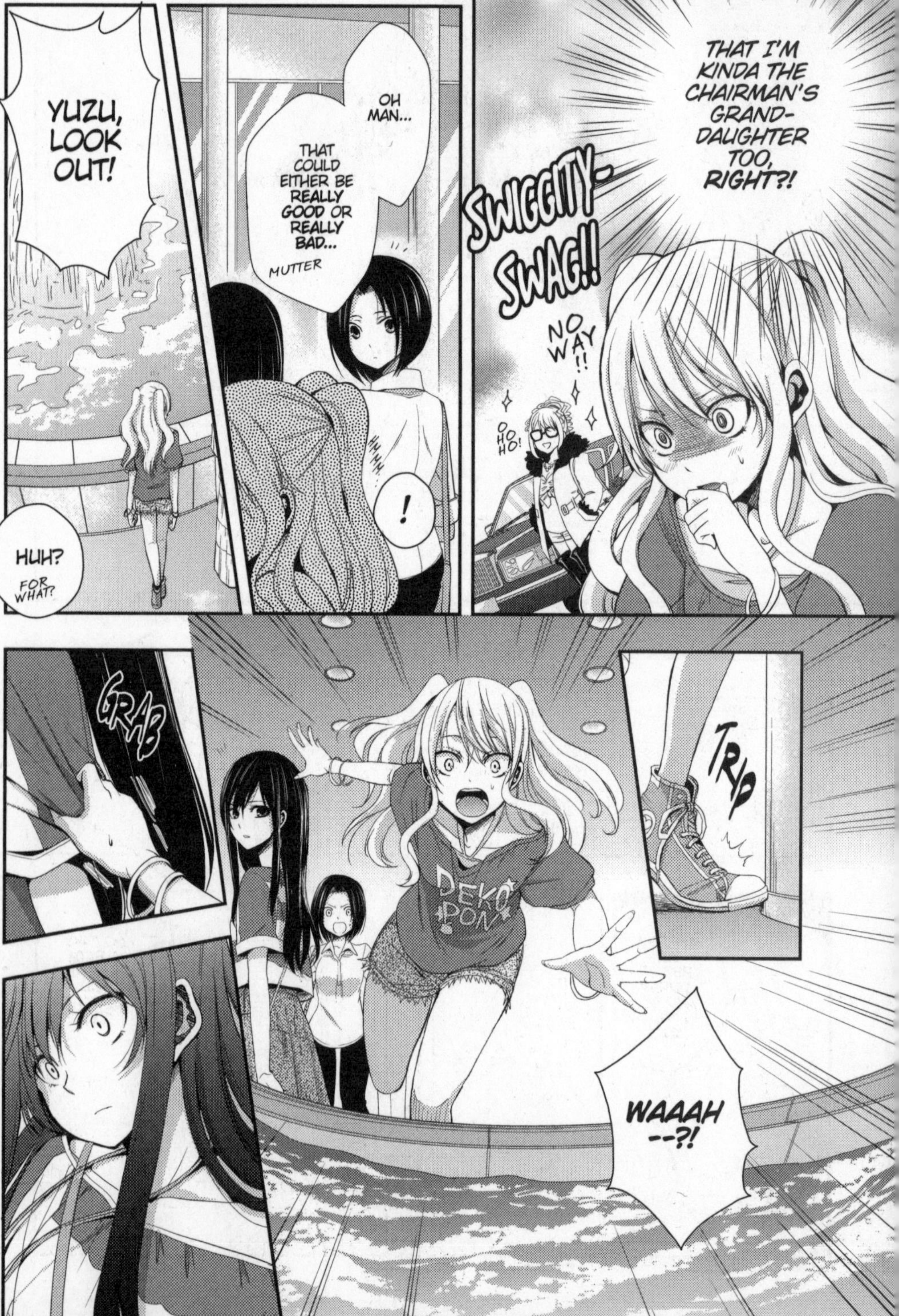
THAT I'M KINDA THE CHAIRMAN'S GRAND-DAUGHTER TOO, RIGHT?!
SWIGGITY-SWAG!!
NO WAY!!
OHOHO!
OH MAN...
THAT COULD EITHER BE REALLY GOOD OR REALLY BAD...
MUTTER
!
YUZU, LOOK OUT!
HUH?
FOR WHAT?
TRIP
WAAAH--?!
GRAB

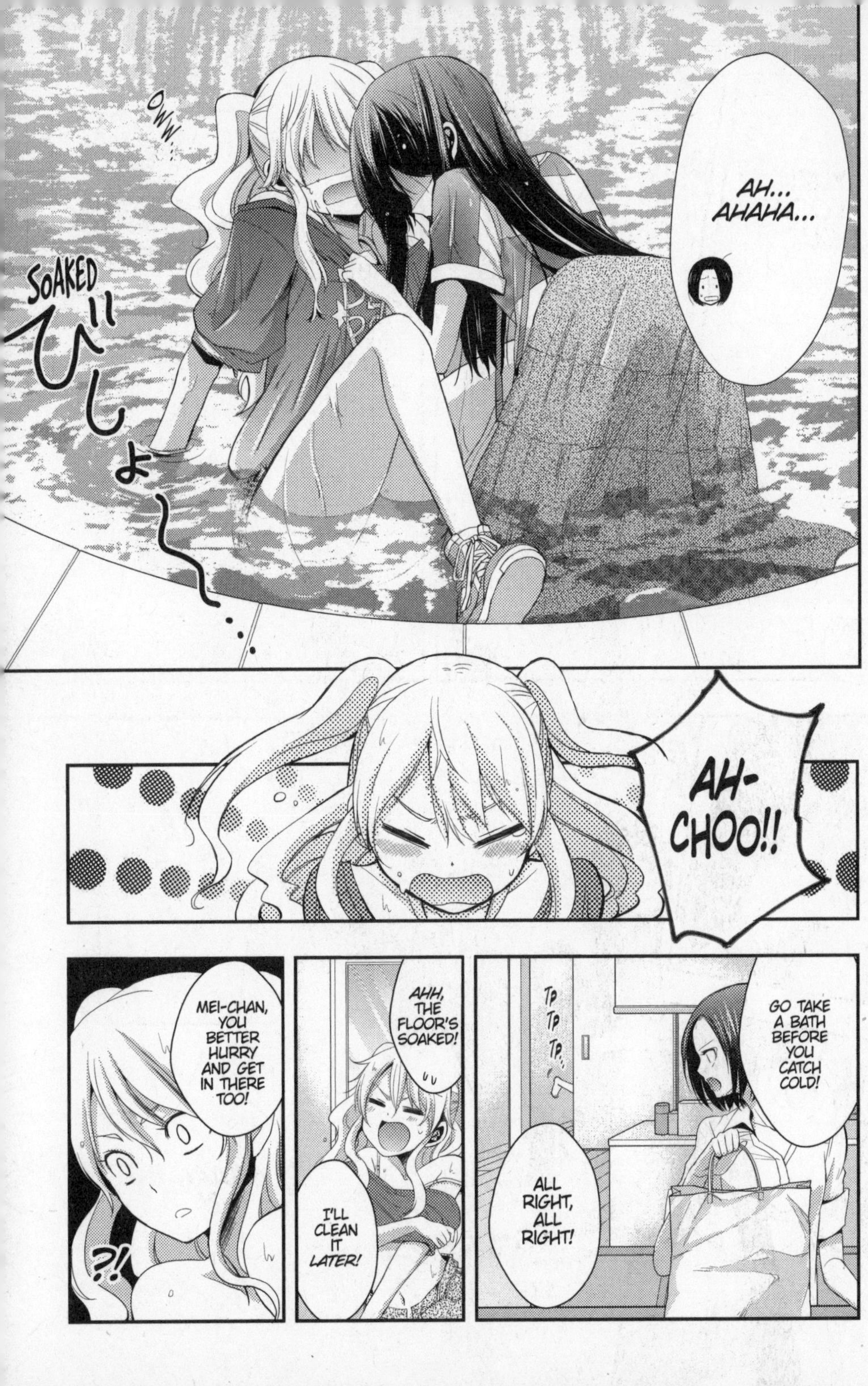
AH... AHAHA...
OWW...
SOAKED
びしょ～～...
AH-CHOO!!
GO TAKE A BATH BEFORE YOU CATCH COLD!
Tp Tp Tp...
ALL RIGHT, ALL RIGHT!
AHH, THE FLOOR'S SOAKED!
I'LL CLEAN IT LATER!
MEI-CHAN, YOU BETTER HURRY AND GET IN THERE TOO!
?!

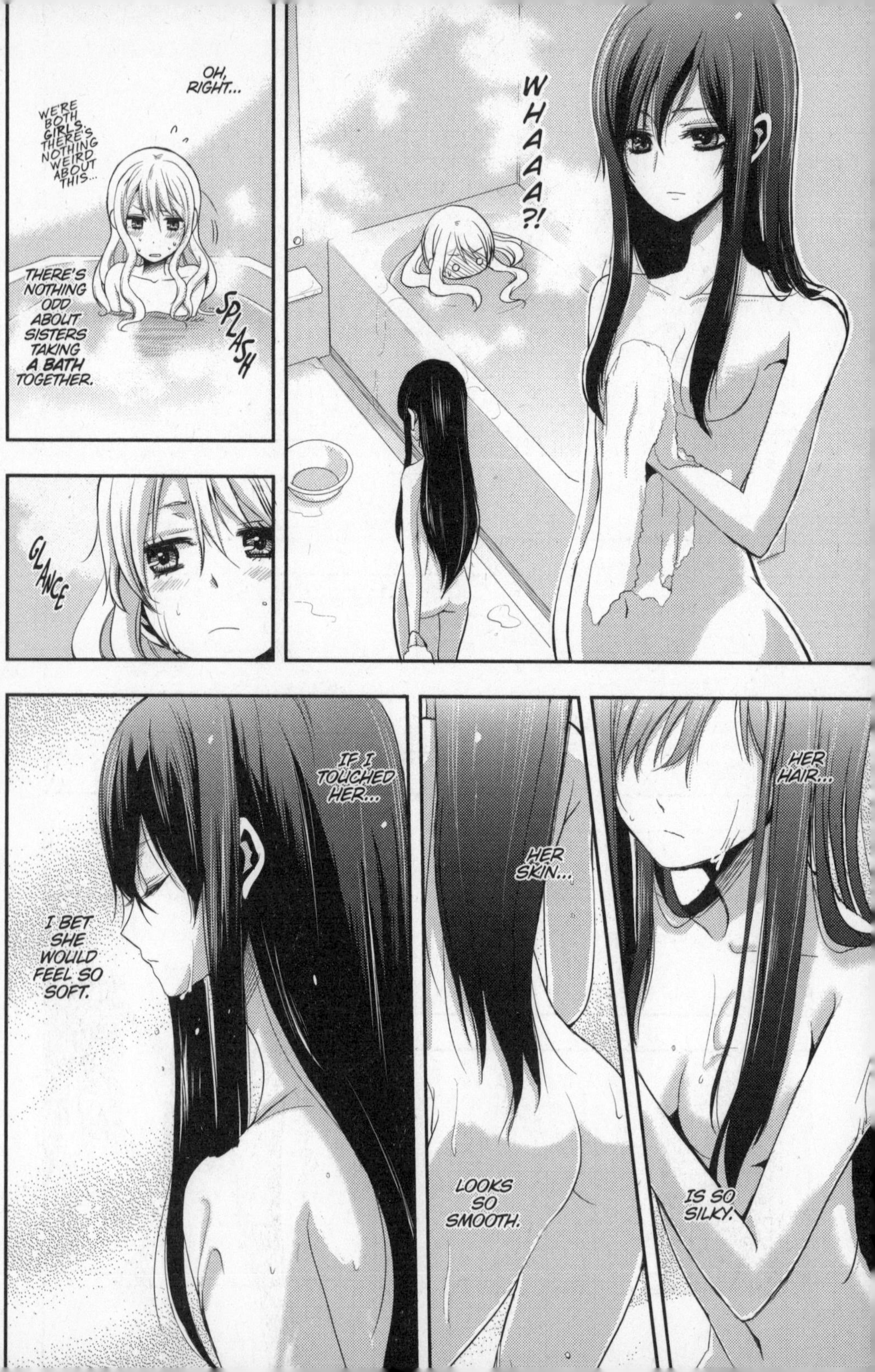
WHAAAA?!
OH, RIGHT...
WE'RE BOTH GIRLS. THERE'S NOTHING WEIRD ABOUT THIS...
THERE'S NOTHING ODD ABOUT SISTERS TAKING A BATH TOGETHER.
SPLASH
GLANCE
HER HAIR...
IS SO SILKY.
HER SKIN...
LOOKS SO SMOOTH.
IF I TOUCHED HER...
I BET SHE WOULD FEEL SO SOFT.

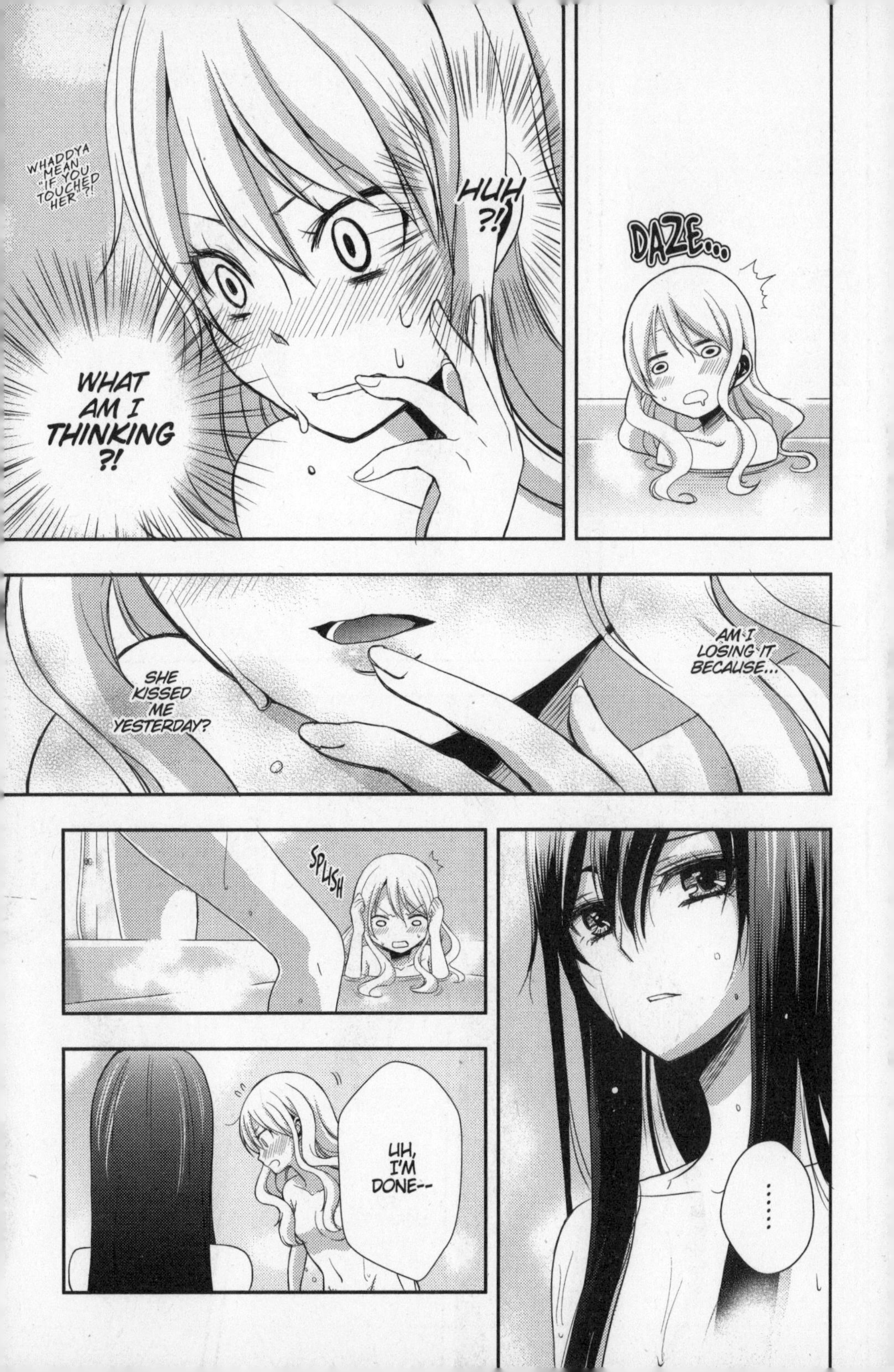
DAZE...
HUH ?!
WHADDYA MEAN "IF YOU TOUCHED HER"?!
WHAT AM I THINKING ?!
AM I LOSING IT BECAUSE...
SHE KISSED ME YESTERDAY?
......
SPLUSH
UH, I'M DONE--

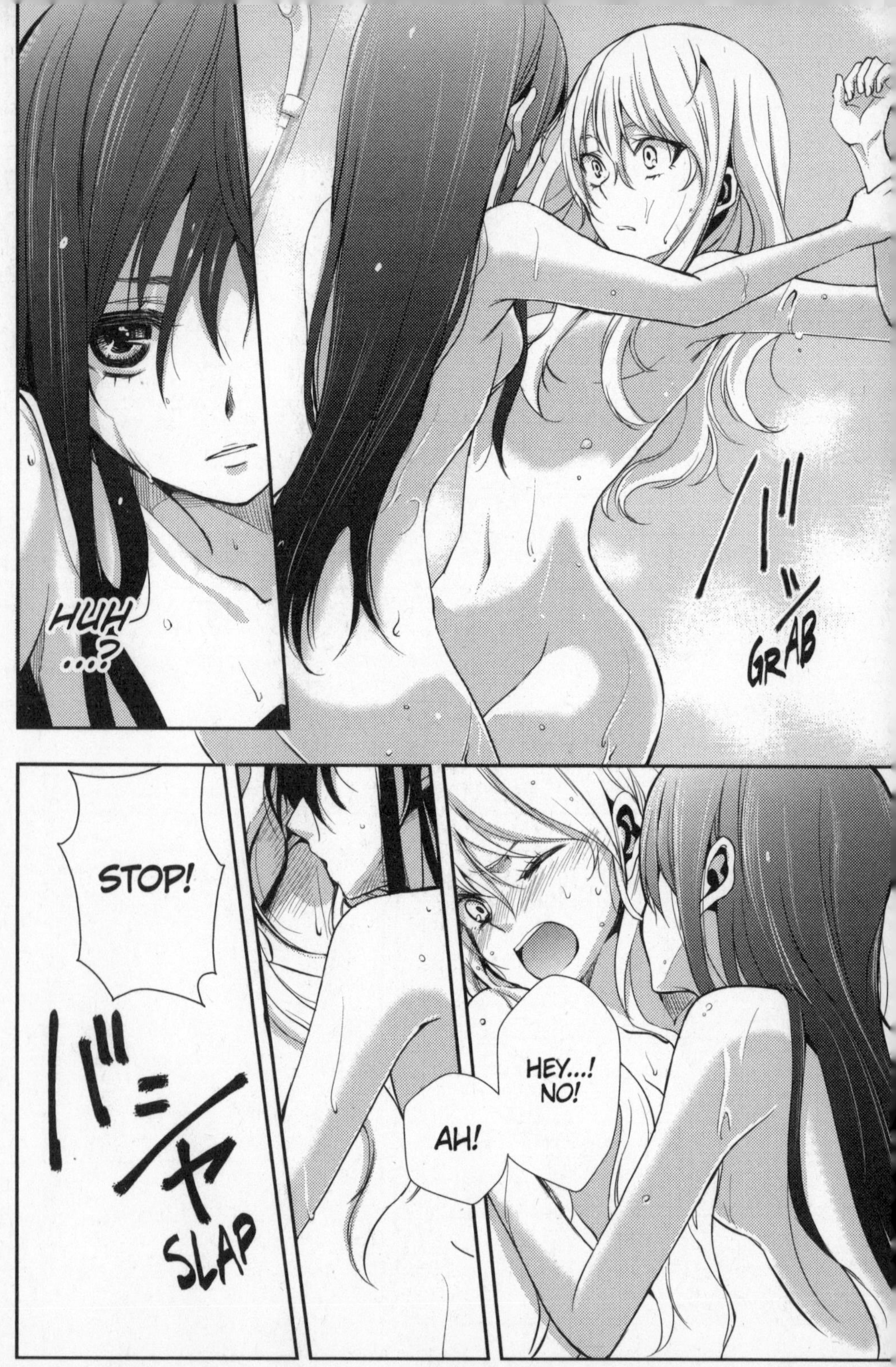
GRAB
HUH...?
HEY...! NO!
AH!
STOP!
SLAP

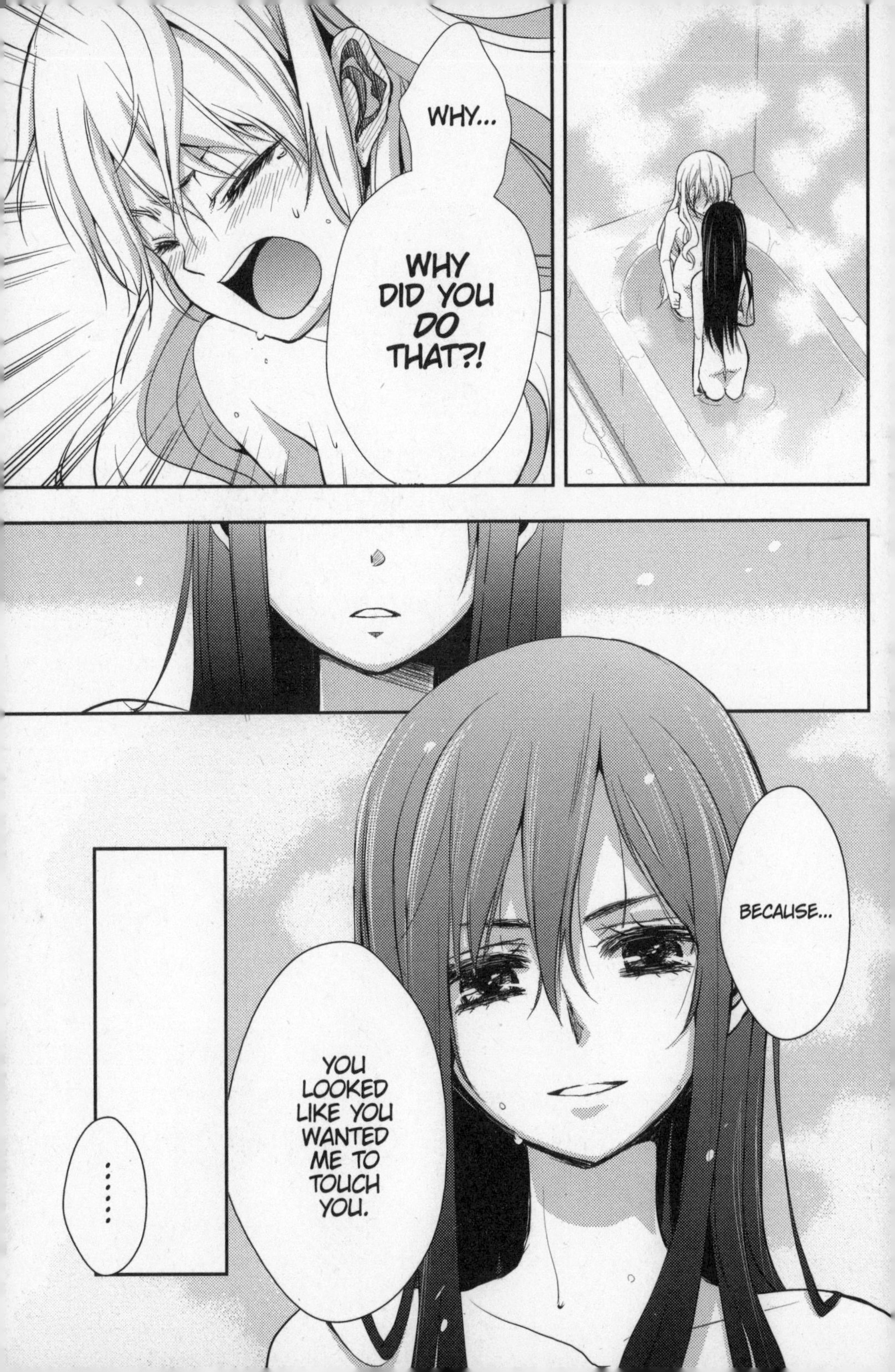
WHY...
WHY DID YOU DO THAT?!
BECAUSE...
YOU LOOKED LIKE YOU WANTED ME TO TOUCH YOU.
......

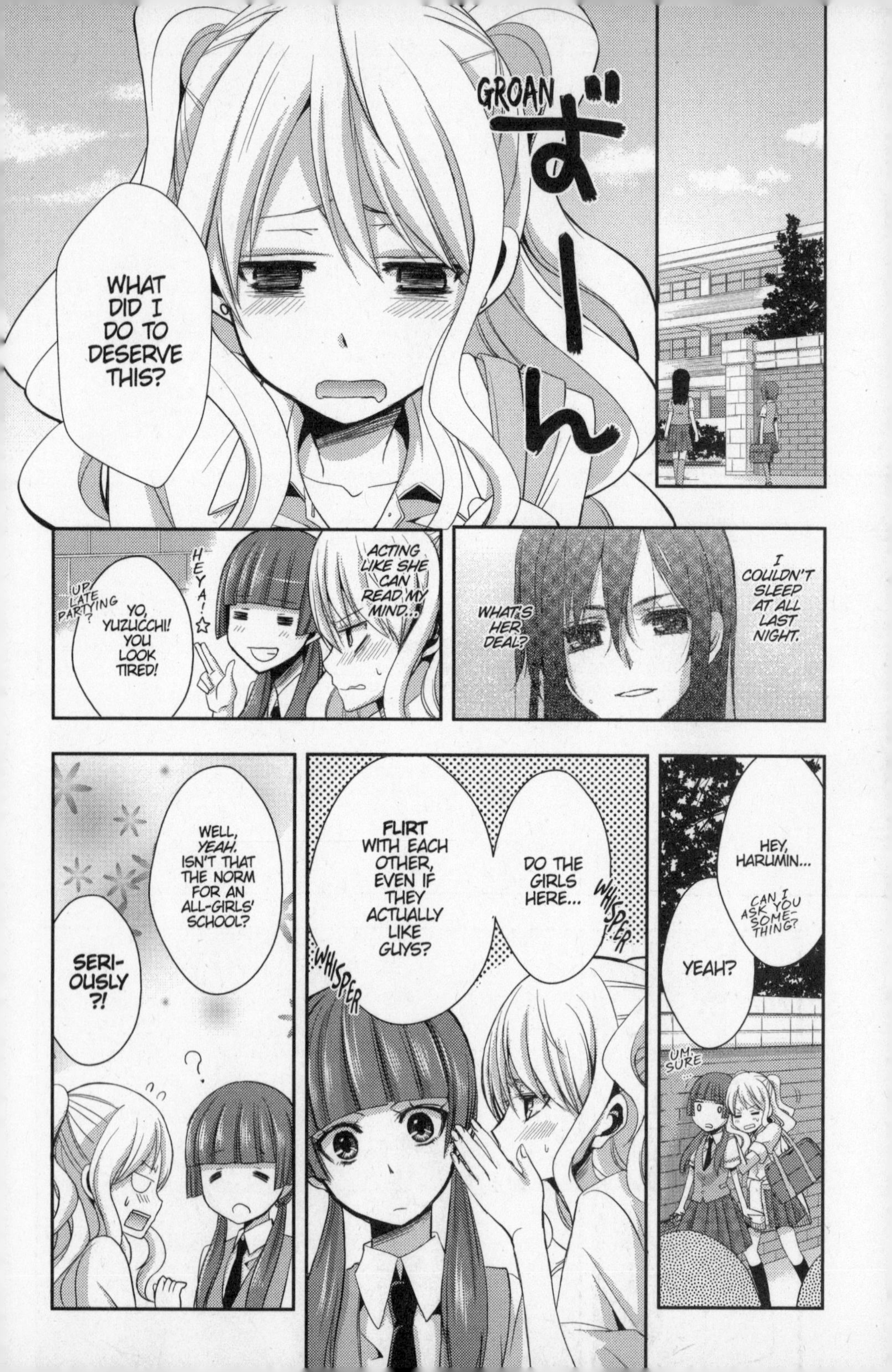
GROAN
ずーん
WHAT DID I DO TO DESERVE THIS?
I COULDN'T SLEEP AT ALL LAST NIGHT.
WHAT'S HER DEAL?
HEYA!☆
YO, YUZUCCHI! YOU LOOK TIRED!
UP LATE PARTYING?
ACTING LIKE SHE CAN READ MY MIND...
HEY, HARUMIN...
CAN I ASK YOU SOME-THING?
YEAH?
UM, SURE...
DO THE GIRLS HERE...
WHISPER
FLIRT WITH EACH OTHER, EVEN IF THEY ACTUALLY LIKE GUYS?
WHISPER
WELL, YEAH. ISN'T THAT THE NORM FOR AN ALL-GIRLS' SCHOOL?
SERI-OUSLY?!
?

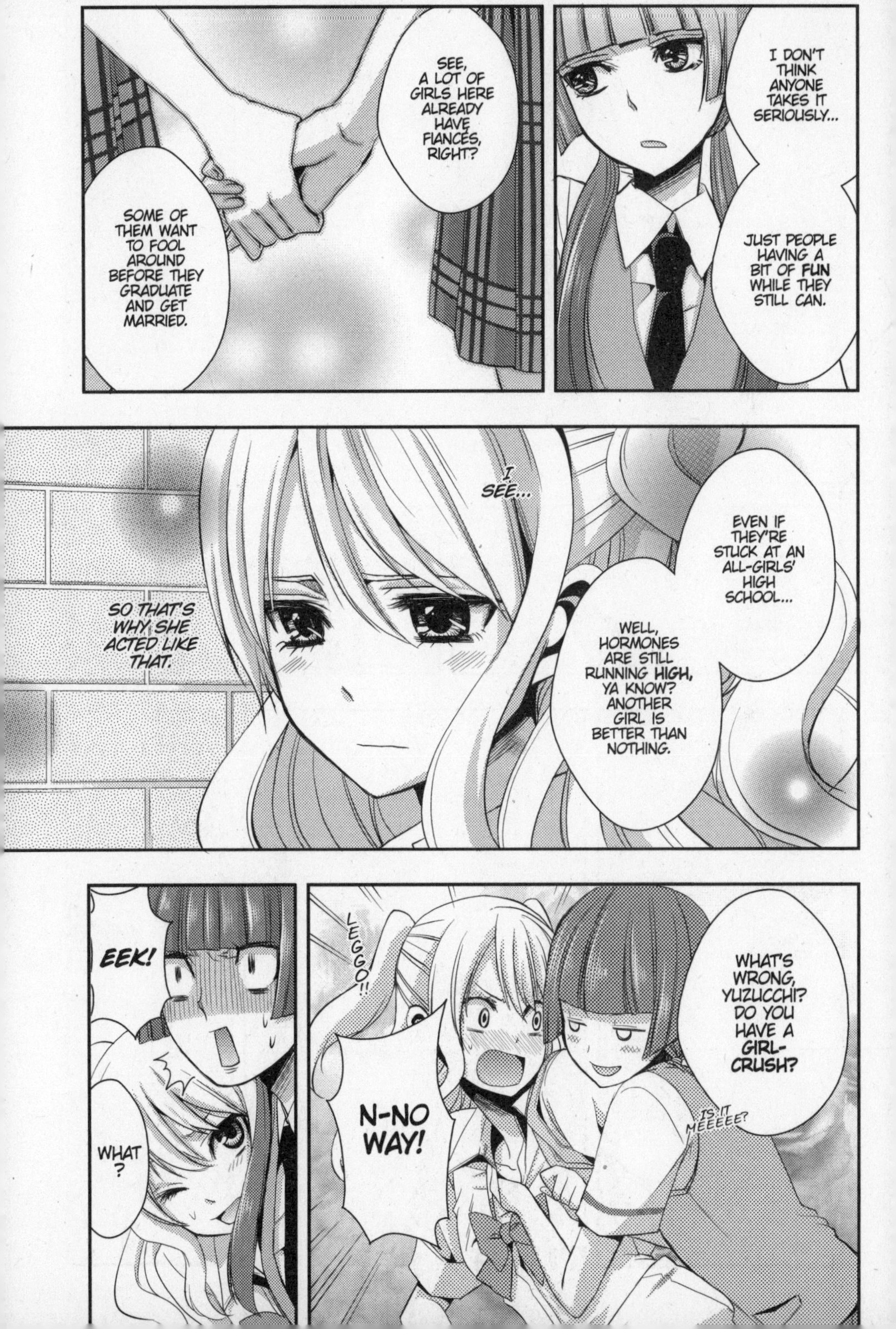
I DON'T THINK ANYONE TAKES IT SERIOUSLY...
JUST PEOPLE HAVING A BIT OF FUN WHILE THEY STILL CAN.
SEE, A LOT OF GIRLS HERE ALREADY HAVE FIANCÉS, RIGHT?
SOME OF THEM WANT TO FOOL AROUND BEFORE THEY GRADUATE AND GET MARRIED.
EVEN IF THEY'RE STUCK AT AN ALL-GIRLS' HIGH SCHOOL...
I SEE...
WELL, HORMONES ARE STILL RUNNING HIGH, YA KNOW? ANOTHER GIRL IS BETTER THAN NOTHING.
SO THAT'S WHY SHE ACTED LIKE THAT.
WHAT'S WRONG, YUZUCCHI? DO YOU HAVE A GIRL-CRUSH?
IS IT MEEEEEE?
LEGGO!!
N-NO WAY!
EEK!
WHAT?

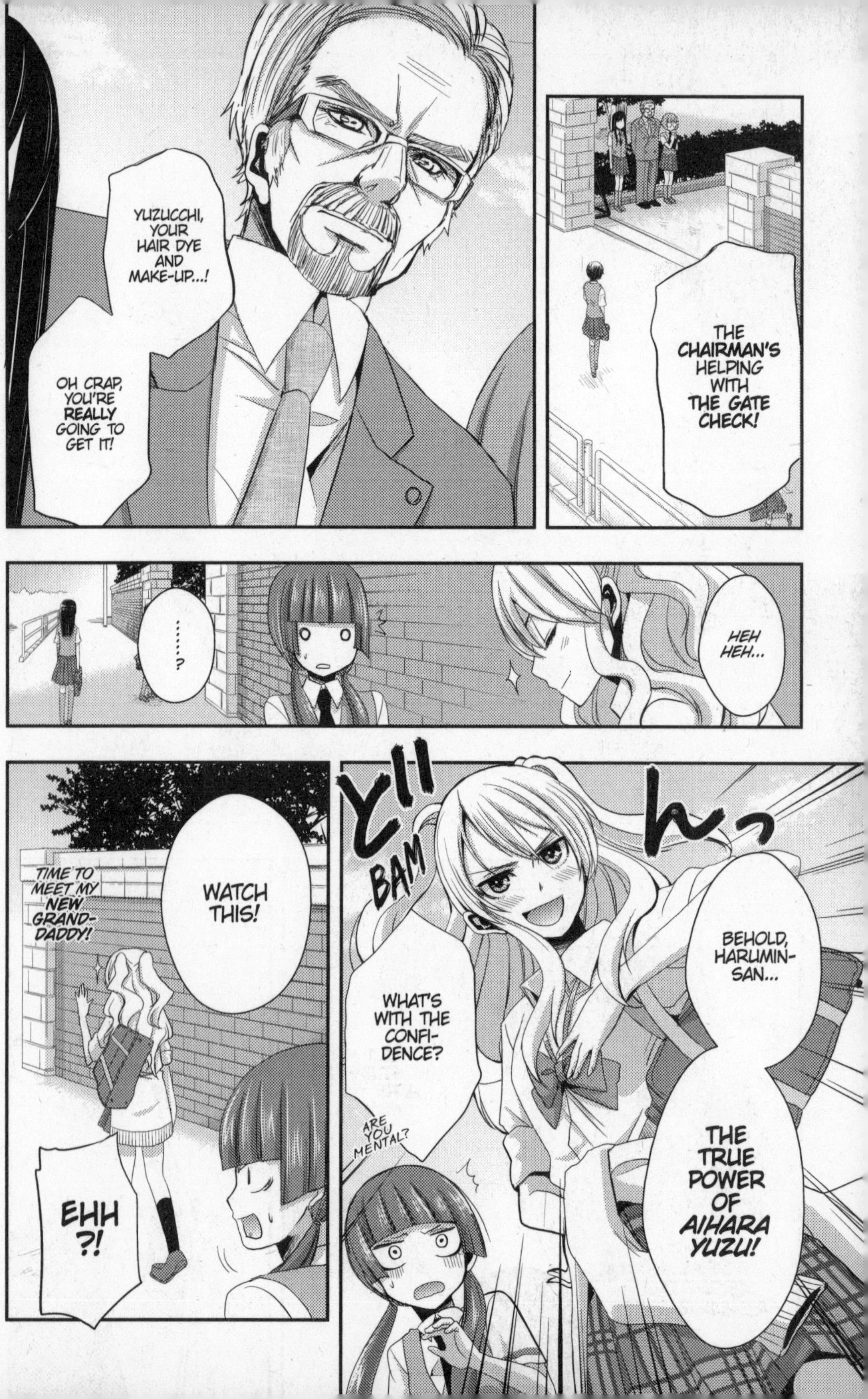

THE CHAIRMAN'S HELPING WITH THE GATE CHECK!
YUZUCCHI, YOUR HAIR DYE AND MAKE-UP...!
OH CRAP, YOU'RE REALLY GOING TO GET IT!
HEH HEH...
......?
どんっ
BAM
BEHOLD, HARUMIN-SAN...
THE TRUE POWER OF AIHARA YUZU!
WHAT'S WITH THE CONFIDENCE?
ARE YOU MENTAL?
WATCH THIS!
TIME TO MEET MY NEW GRAND-DADDY!
EHH ?!

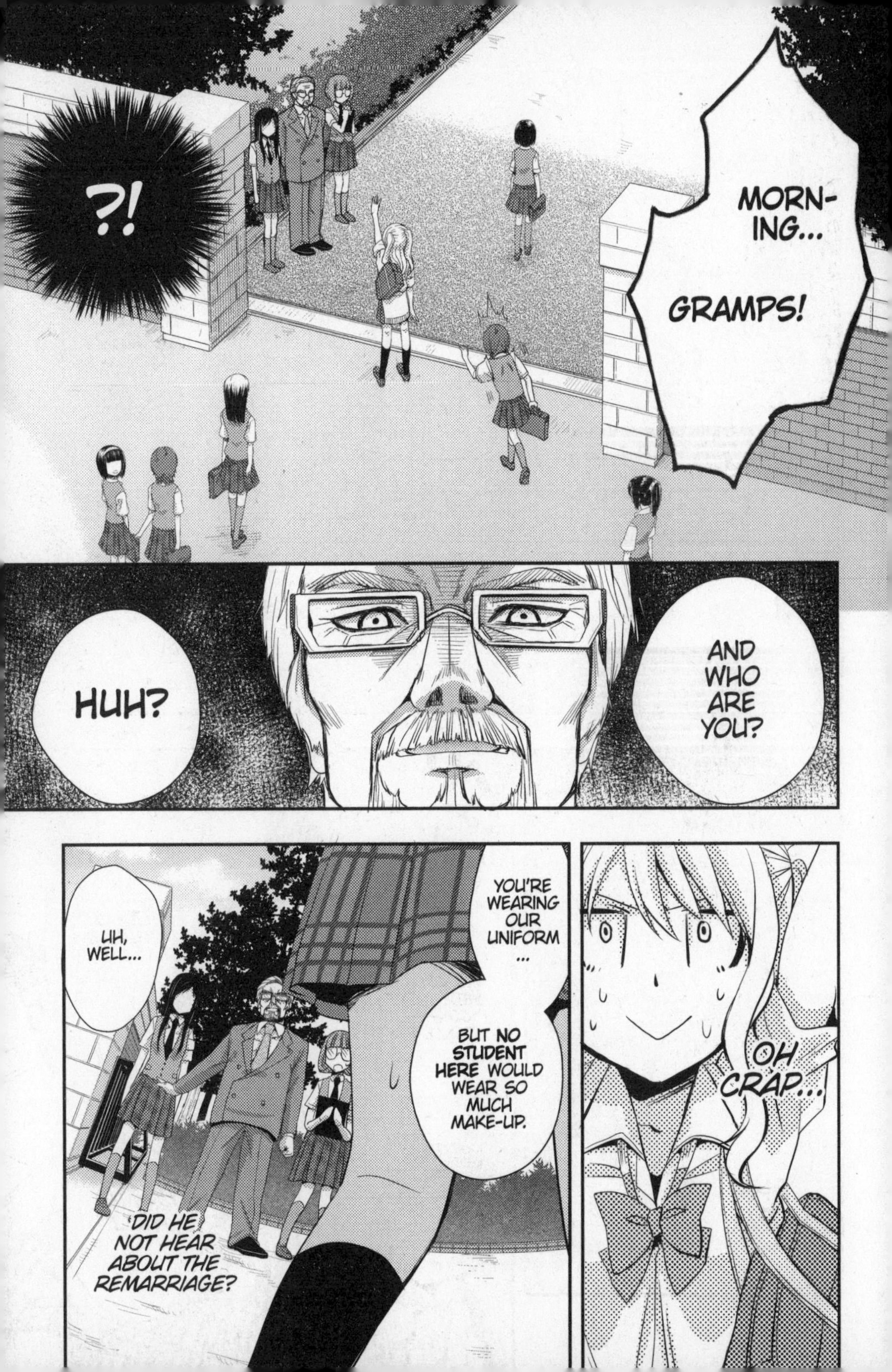
MORN-ING...
GRAMPS!
?!
AND WHO ARE YOU?
HUH?
OH CRAP...
YOU'RE WEARING OUR UNIFORM ...
BUT NO STUDENT HERE WOULD WEAR SO MUCH MAKE-UP.
UH, WELL...
DID HE NOT HEAR ABOUT THE REMARRIAGE?

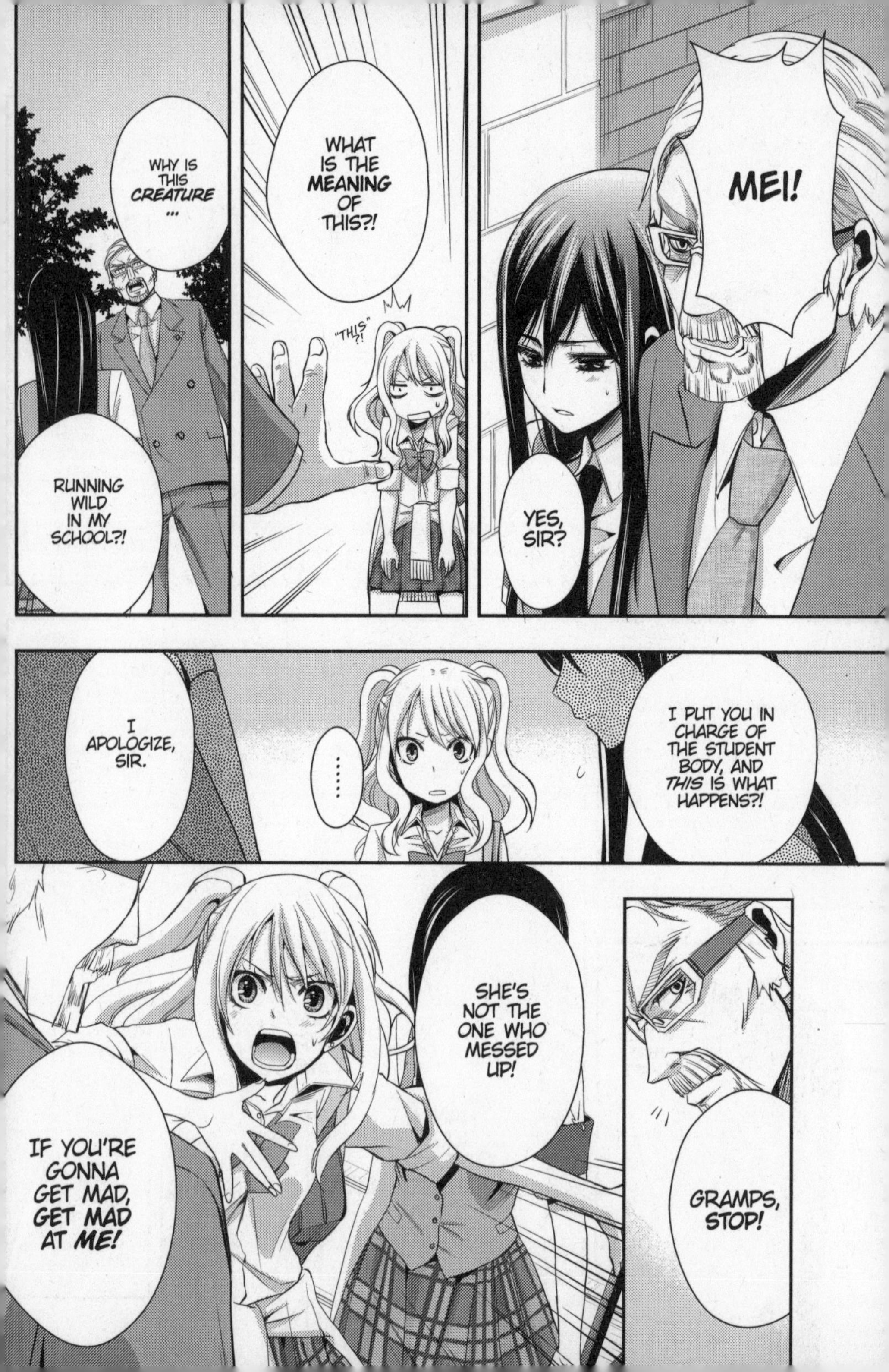
MEI!
YES, SIR?
WHAT IS THE MEANING OF THIS?!
"THIS"?!
WHY IS THIS CREATURE ...
RUNNING WILD IN MY SCHOOL?!
I PUT YOU IN CHARGE OF THE STUDENT BODY, AND THIS IS WHAT HAPPENS?!
......
I APOLOGIZE, SIR.
GRAMPS, STOP!
SHE'S NOT THE ONE WHO MESSED UP!
IF YOU'RE GONNA GET MAD, GET MAD AT ME!

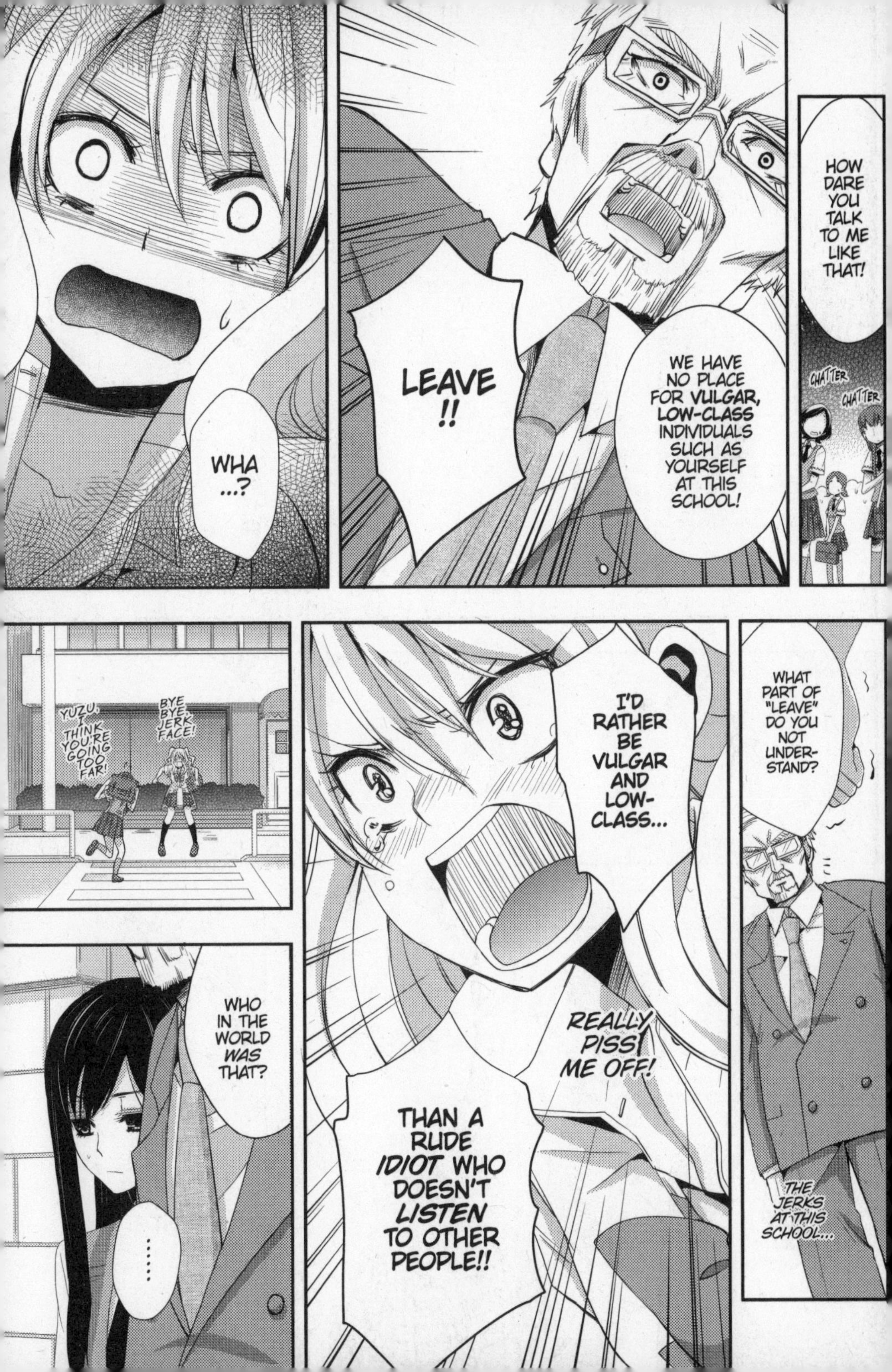

HOW DARE YOU TALK TO ME LIKE THAT!
CHATTER
CHATTER
WE HAVE NO PLACE FOR VULGAR, LOW-CLASS INDIVIDUALS SUCH AS YOURSELF AT THIS SCHOOL!
LEAVE !!
WHA ...?
WHAT PART OF "LEAVE" DO YOU NOT UNDER-STAND?
THE JERKS AT THIS SCHOOL...
I'D RATHER BE VULGAR AND LOW-CLASS...
REALLY PISS ME OFF!
THAN A RUDE IDIOT WHO DOESN'T LISTEN TO OTHER PEOPLE!!
BYE BYE, JERK FACE!
YUZU, I THINK YOU'RE GOING TOO FAR!
WHO IN THE WORLD WAS THAT?
......

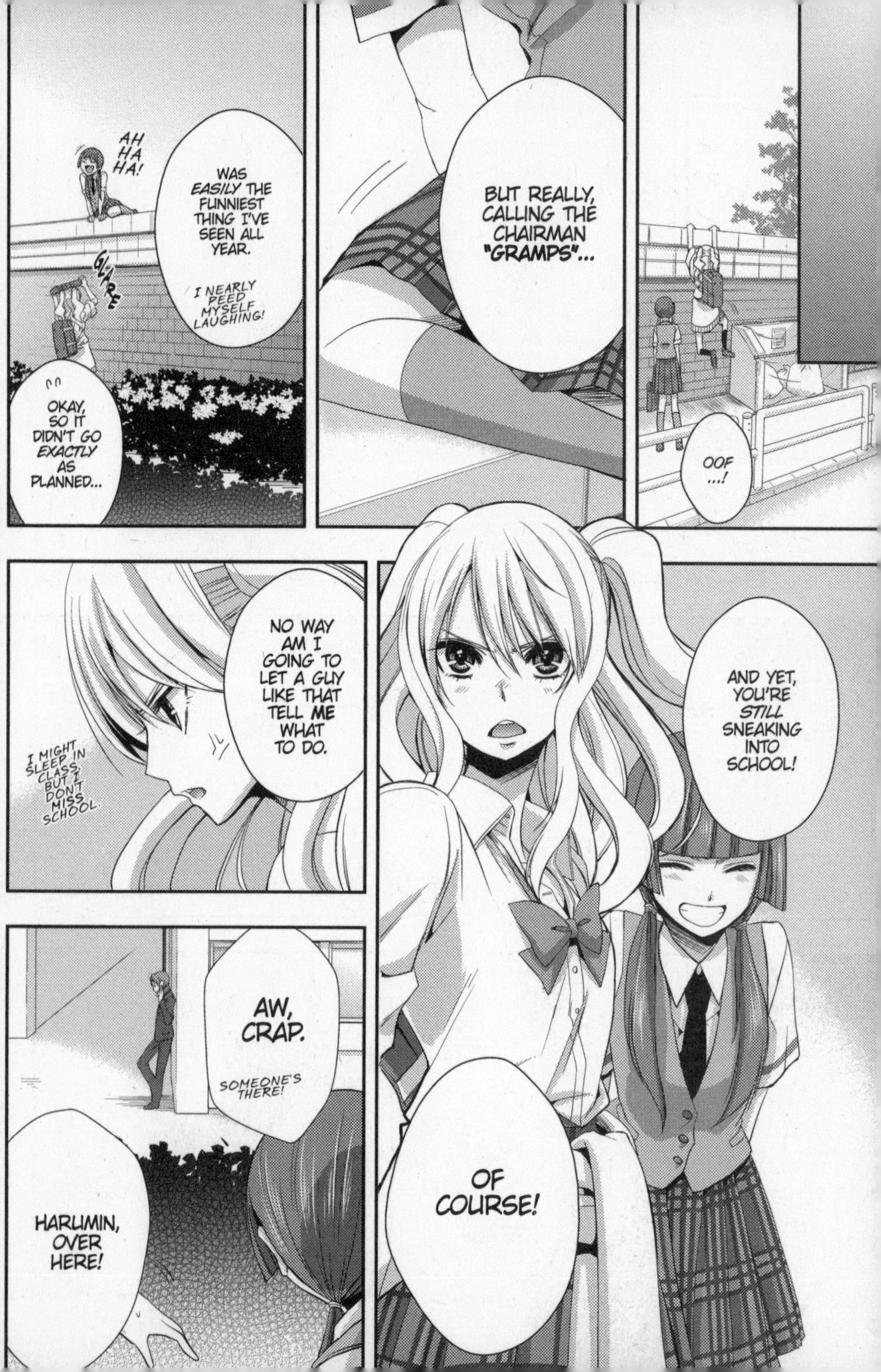
OOF ...!
BUT REALLY, CALLING THE CHAIRMAN "GRAMPS"...
AH HA HA!
WAS EASILY THE FUNNIEST THING I'VE SEEN ALL YEAR.
I NEARLY PEED MYSELF LAUGHING!
GLARE
OKAY, SO IT DIDN'T GO EXACTLY AS PLANNED...
AND YET, YOU'RE STILL SNEAKING INTO SCHOOL!
OF COURSE!
NO WAY AM I GOING TO LET A GUY LIKE THAT TELL ME WHAT TO DO.
I MIGHT SLEEP IN CLASS, BUT I DON'T MISS SCHOOL.
AW, CRAP.
SOMEONE'S THERE!
HARUMIN, OVER HERE!

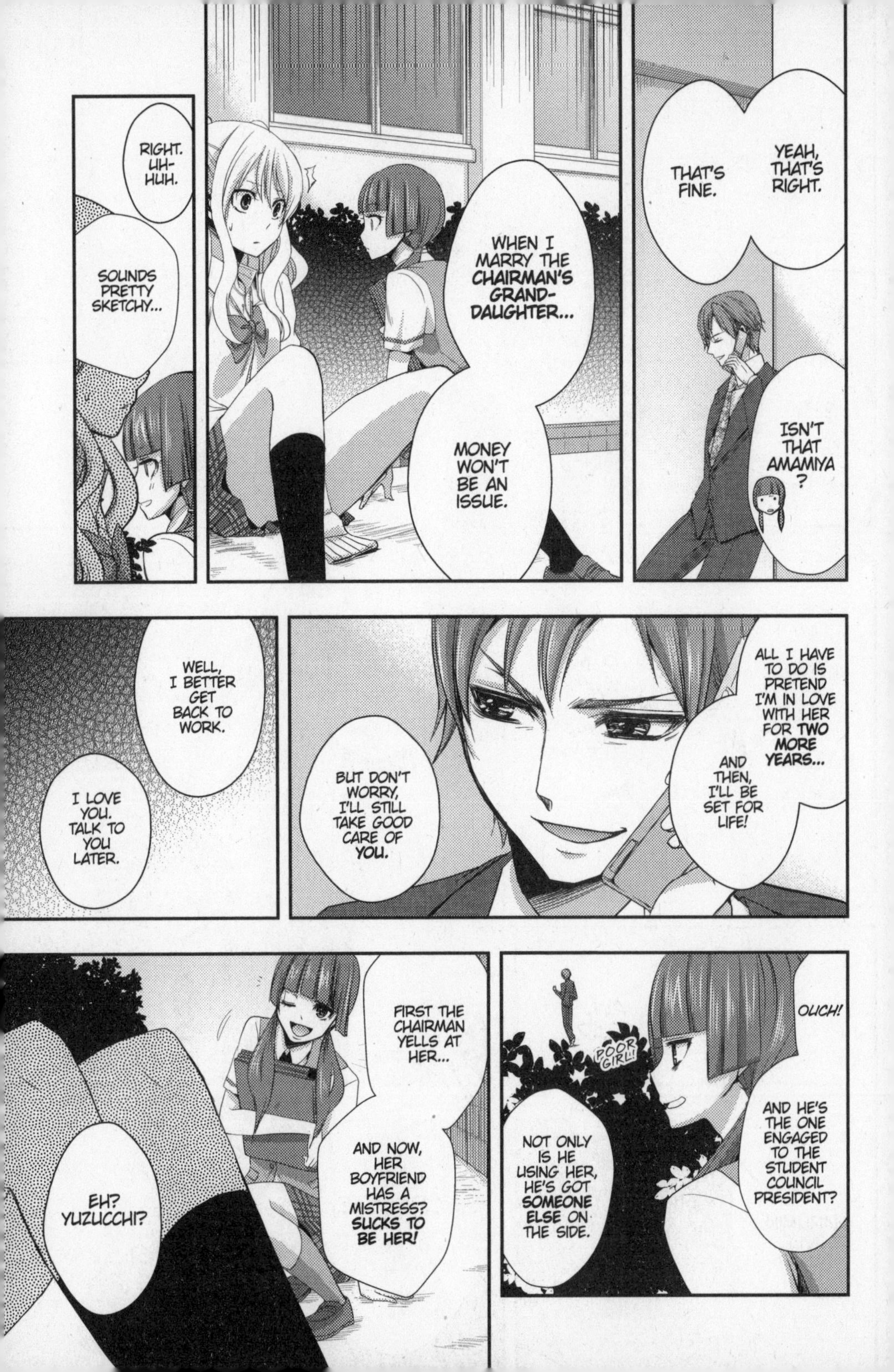
YEAH, THAT'S RIGHT.
THAT'S FINE.
ISN'T THAT AMAMIYA?
WHEN I MARRY THE CHAIRMAN'S GRAND-DAUGHTER...
MONEY WON'T BE AN ISSUE.
RIGHT. UH-HUH.
SOUNDS PRETTY SKETCHY...
ALL I HAVE TO DO IS PRETEND I'M IN LOVE WITH HER FOR TWO MORE YEARS...
AND THEN, I'LL BE SET FOR LIFE!
BUT DON'T WORRY, I'LL STILL TAKE GOOD CARE OF YOU.
WELL, I BETTER GET BACK TO WORK.
I LOVE YOU. TALK TO YOU LATER.
OUCH!
POOR GIRL!
AND HE'S THE ONE ENGAGED TO THE STUDENT COUNCIL PRESIDENT?
NOT ONLY IS HE USING HER, HE'S GOT SOMEONE ELSE ON THE SIDE.
FIRST THE CHAIRMAN YELLS AT HER...
AND NOW, HER BOYFRIEND HAS A MISTRESS? SUCKS TO BE HER!
EH? YUZUCCHI?

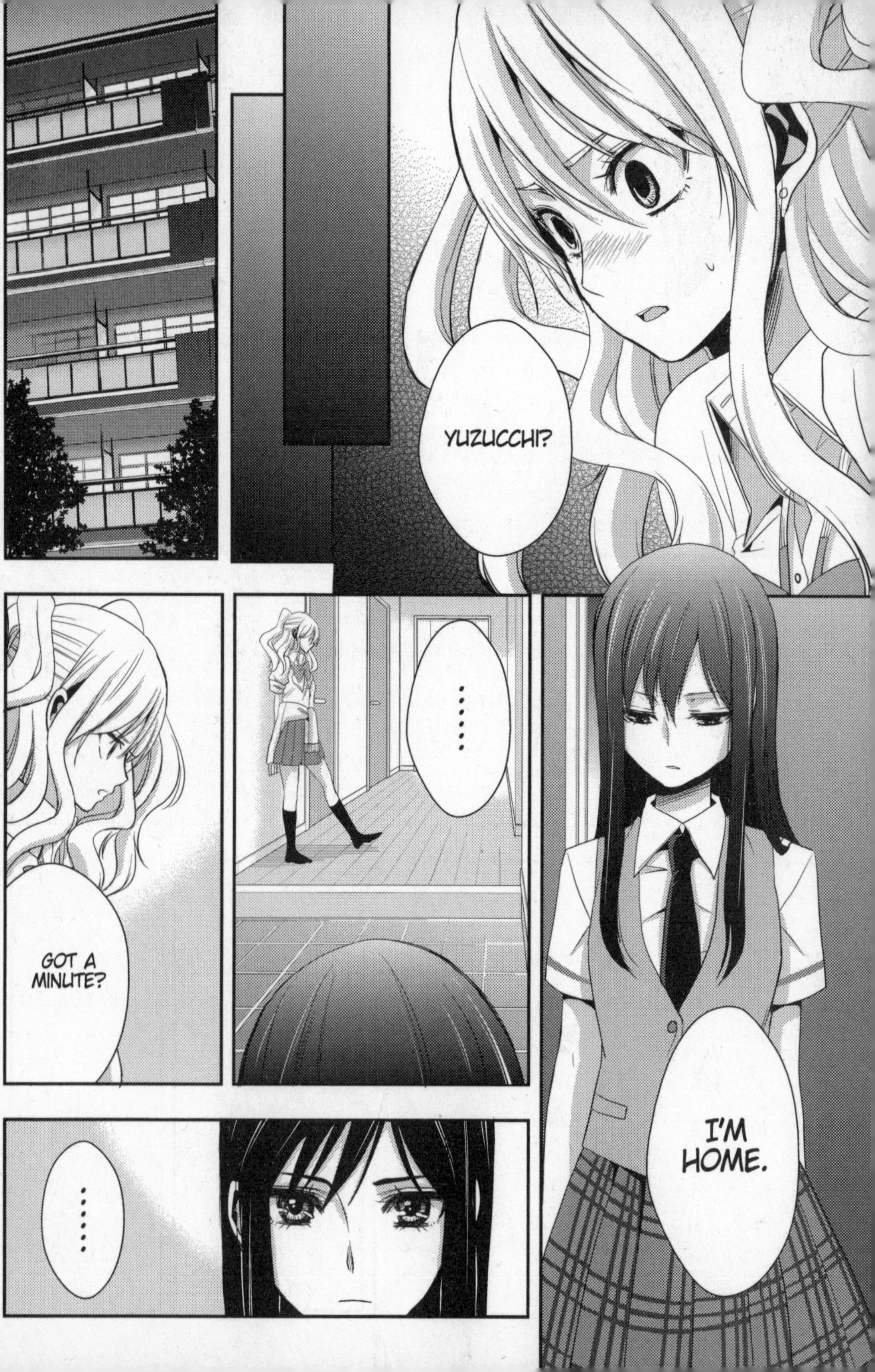
YUZUCCHI?
I'M HOME.
......
GOT A MINUTE?
......

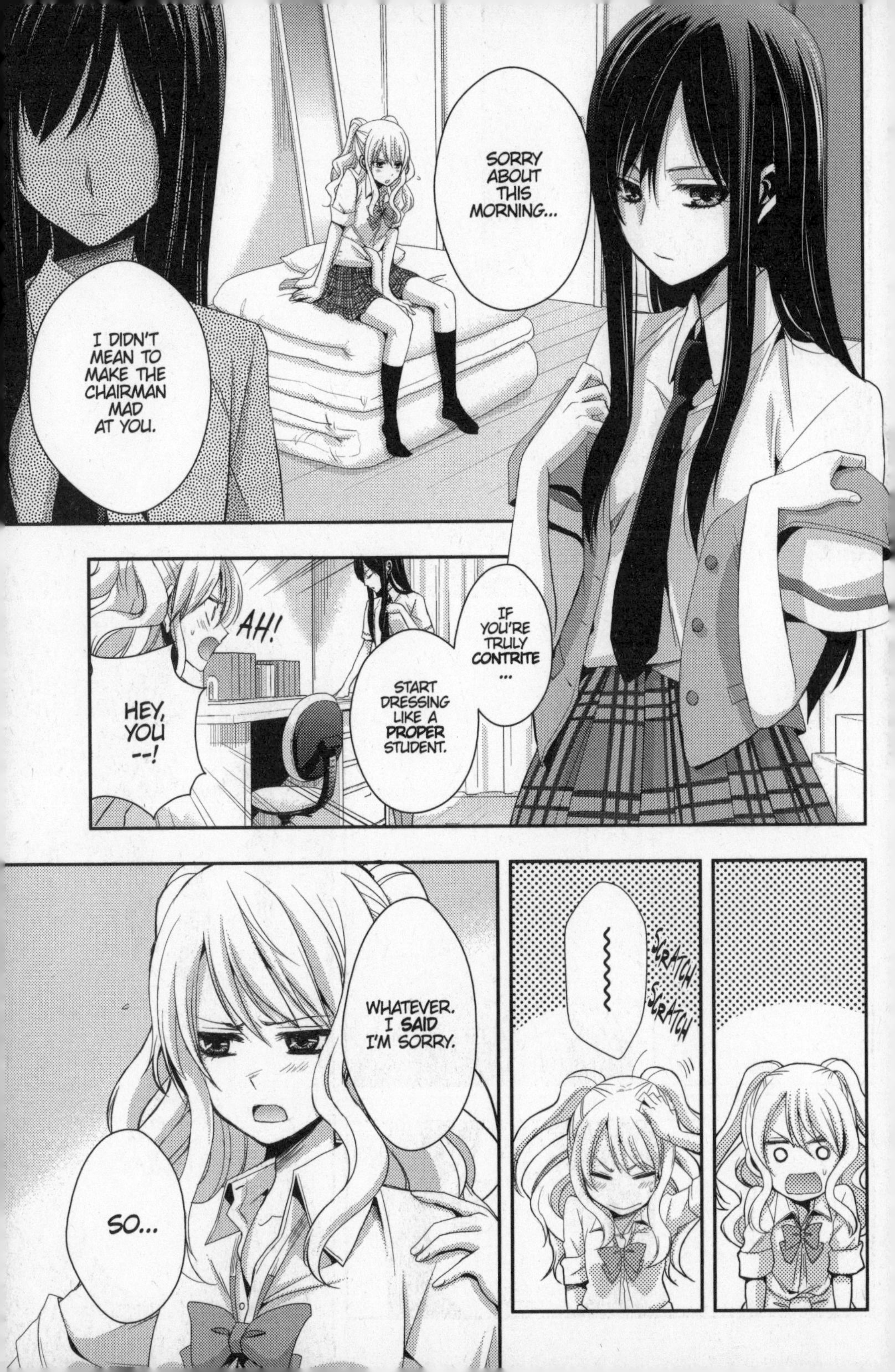
SORRY ABOUT THIS MORNING...
I DIDN'T MEAN TO MAKE THE CHAIRMAN MAD AT YOU.
IF YOU'RE TRULY CONTRITE ...
START DRESSING LIKE A PROPER STUDENT.
AH!
HEY, YOU --!
SCRATCH SCRATCH
WHATEVER. I SAID I'M SORRY.
SO...

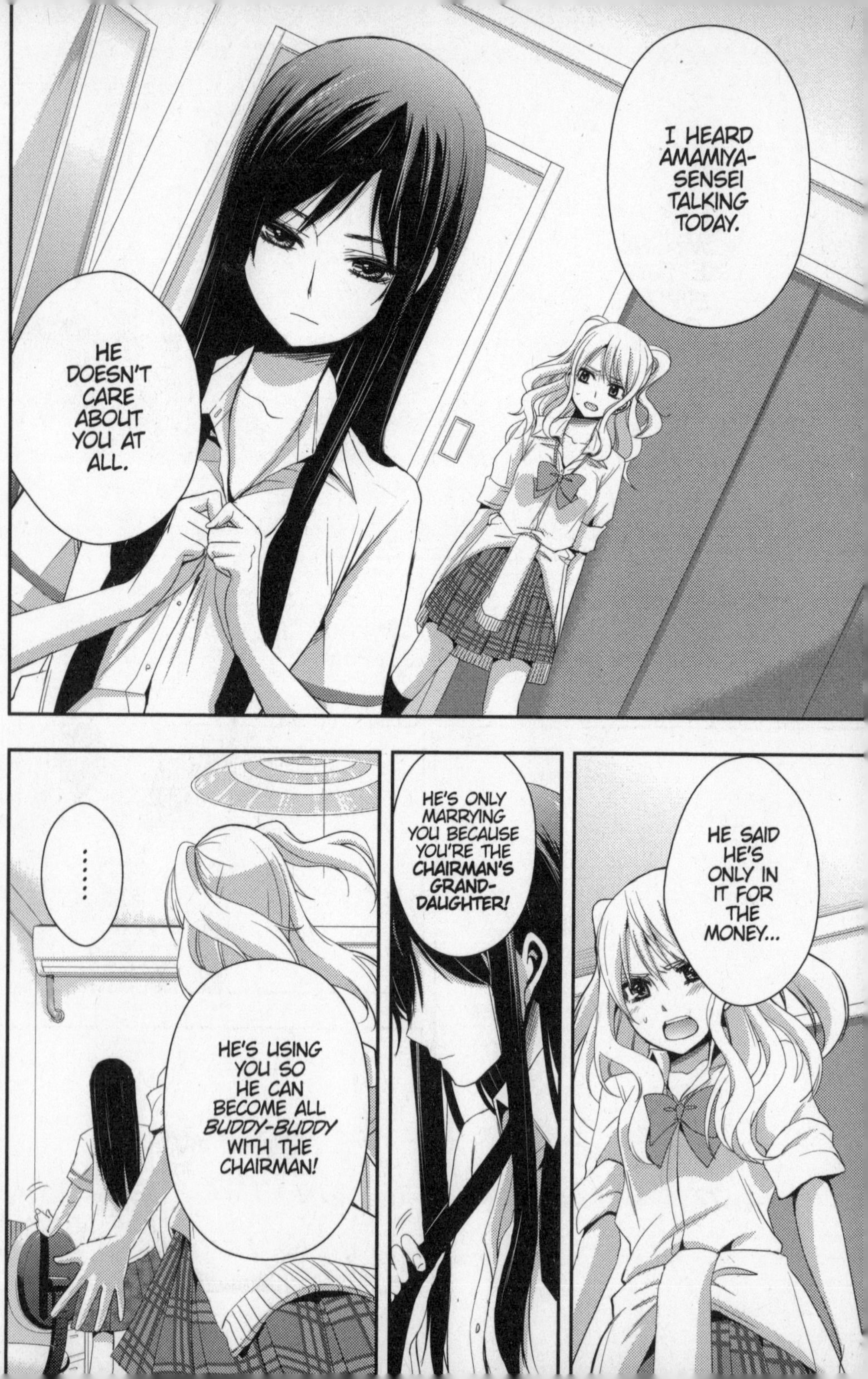
I HEARD AMAMIYA-SENSEI TALKING TODAY.
HE DOESN'T CARE ABOUT YOU AT ALL.
HE SAID HE'S ONLY IN IT FOR THE MONEY...
HE'S ONLY MARRYING YOU BECAUSE YOU'RE THE CHAIRMAN'S GRAND-DAUGHTER!
......
HE'S USING YOU SO HE CAN BECOME ALL *BUDDY-BUDDY* WITH THE CHAIRMAN!

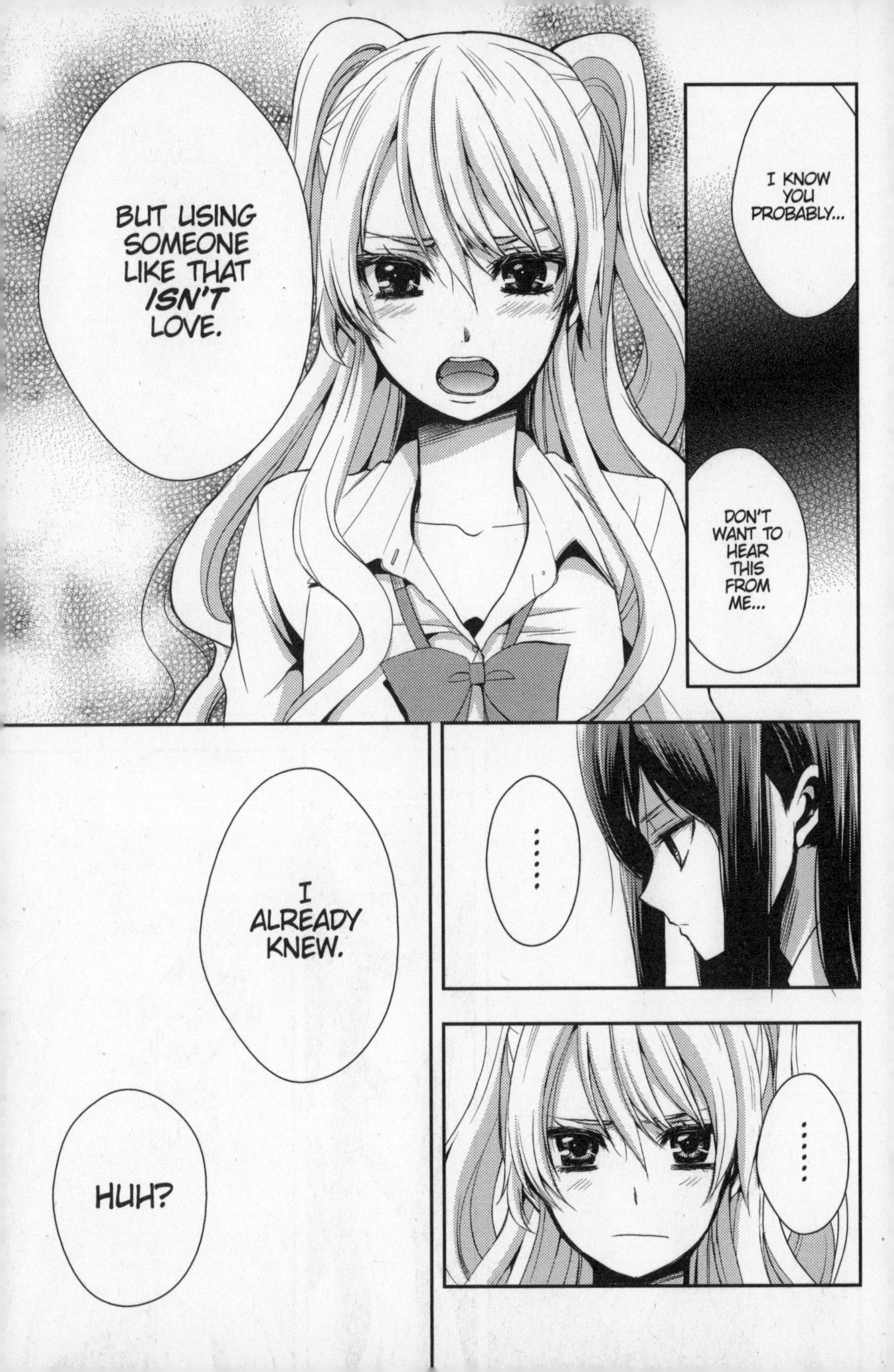
I KNOW YOU PROBABLY...
DON'T WANT TO HEAR THIS FROM ME...
BUT USING SOMEONE LIKE THAT *ISN'T* LOVE.
......
......
I ALREADY KNEW.
HUH?

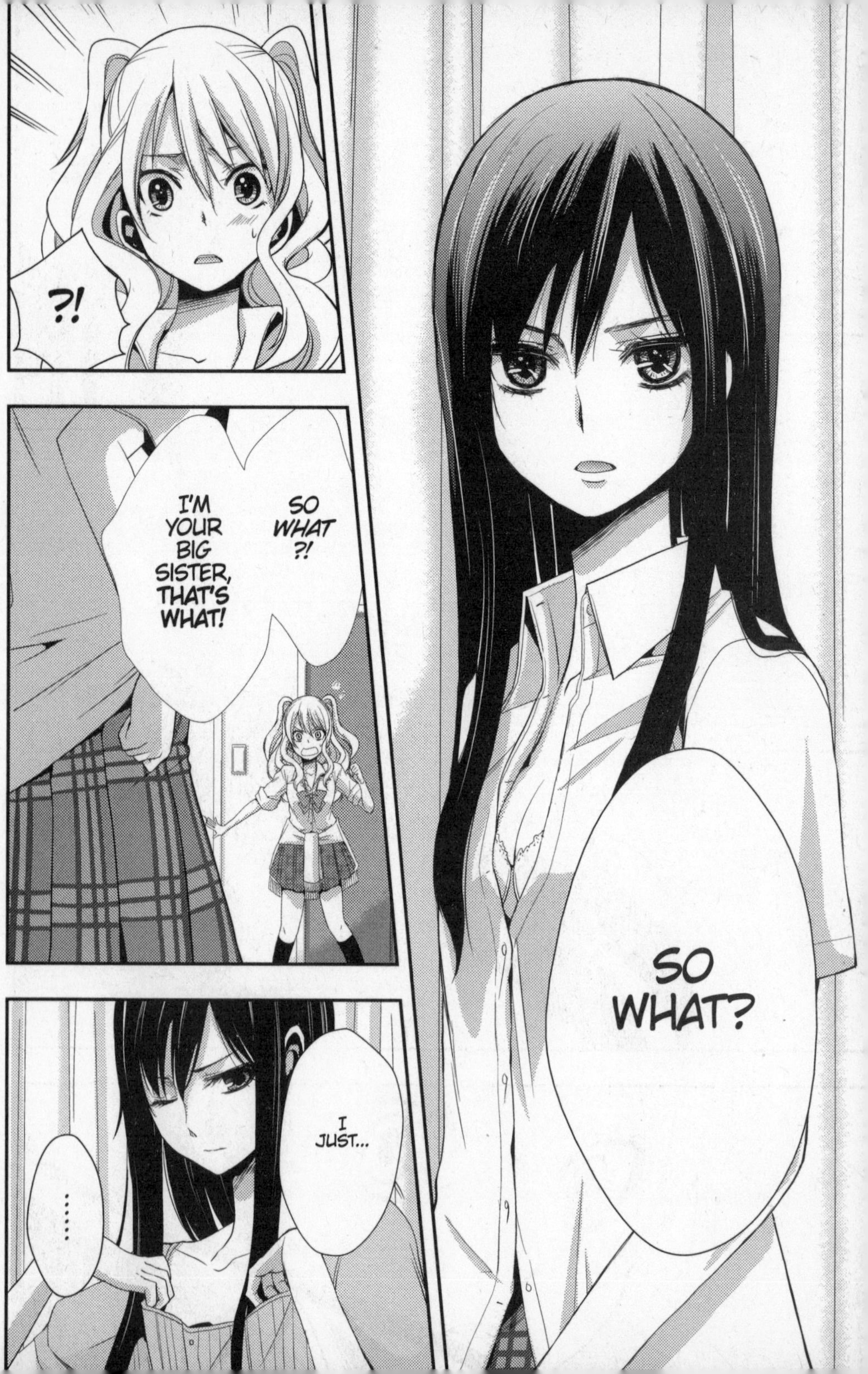
SO WHAT?
?!
SO WHAT ?!
I'M YOUR BIG SISTER, THAT'S WHAT!
I JUST...
......

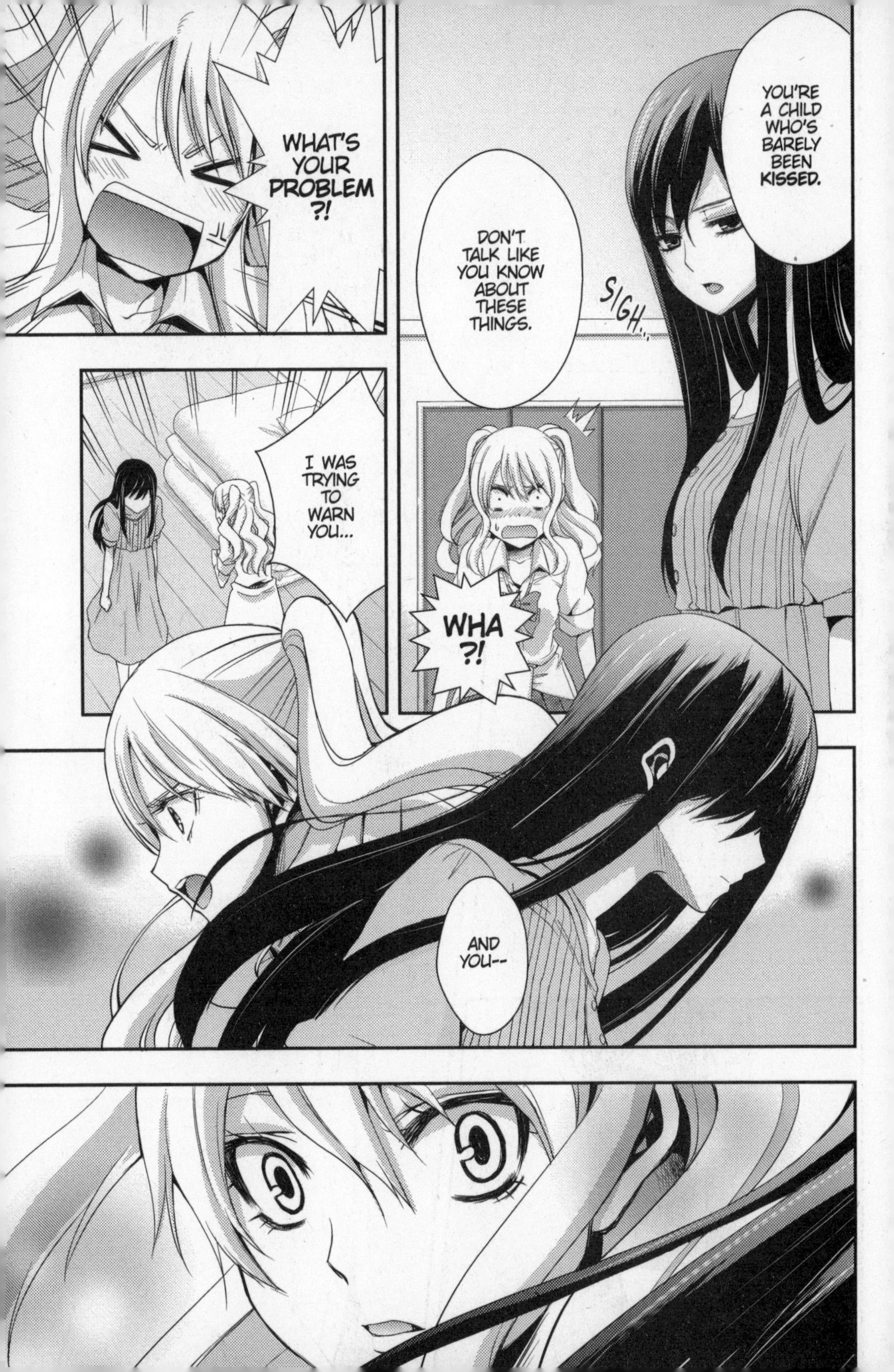
YOU'RE A CHILD WHO'S BARELY BEEN KISSED.
WHA ?!
WHAT'S YOUR PROBLEM ?!
DON'T TALK LIKE YOU KNOW ABOUT THESE THINGS.
SIGH...
I WAS TRYING TO WARN YOU...
AND YOU--

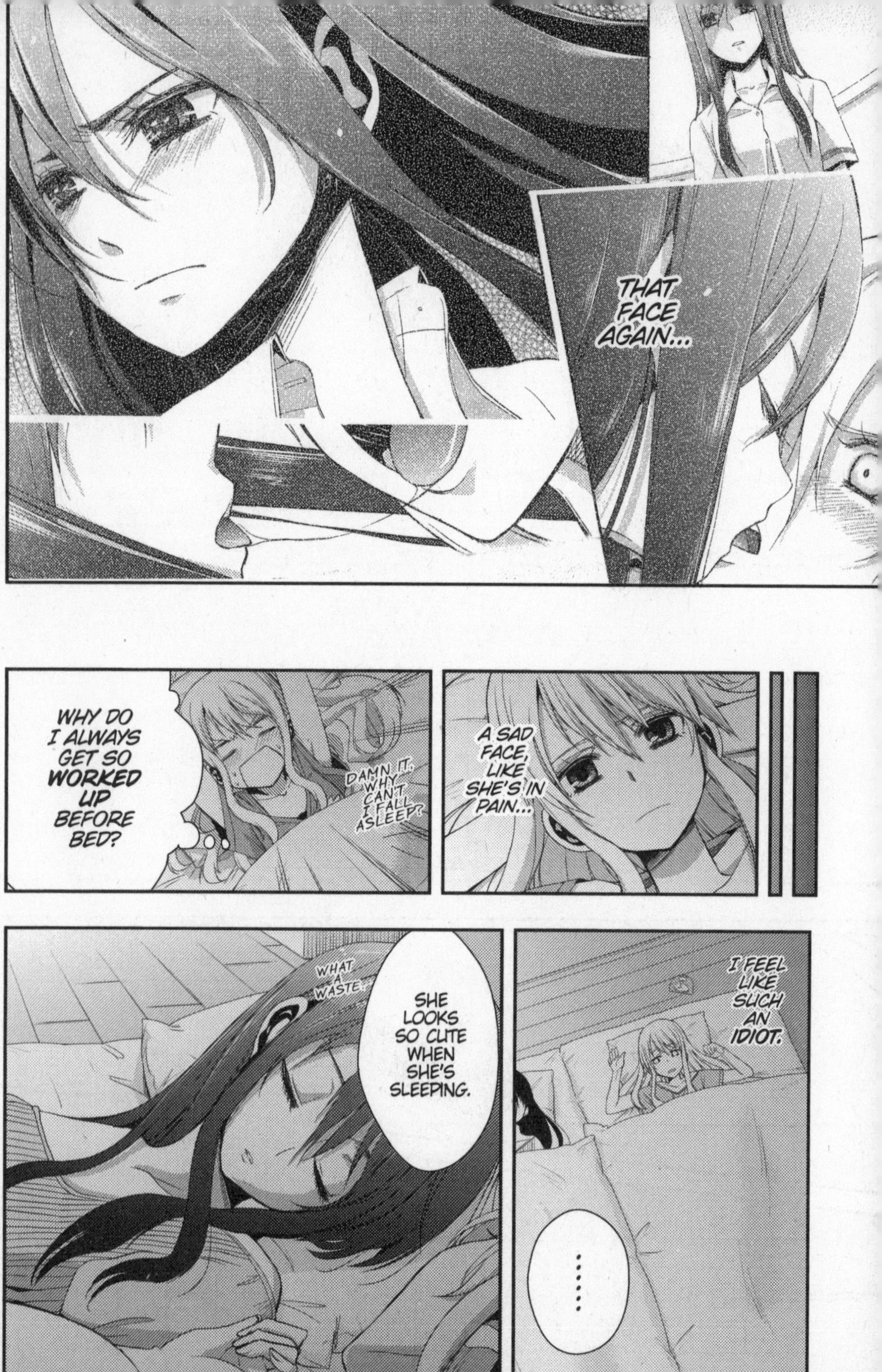
THAT FACE AGAIN...
A SAD FACE, LIKE SHE'S IN PAIN...
DAMN IT. WHY CAN'T I FALL ASLEEP?
WHY DO I ALWAYS GET SO WORKED UP BEFORE BED?
I FEEL LIKE SUCH AN IDIOT.
......
SHE LOOKS SO CUTE WHEN SHE'S SLEEPING.
WHAT A WASTE...

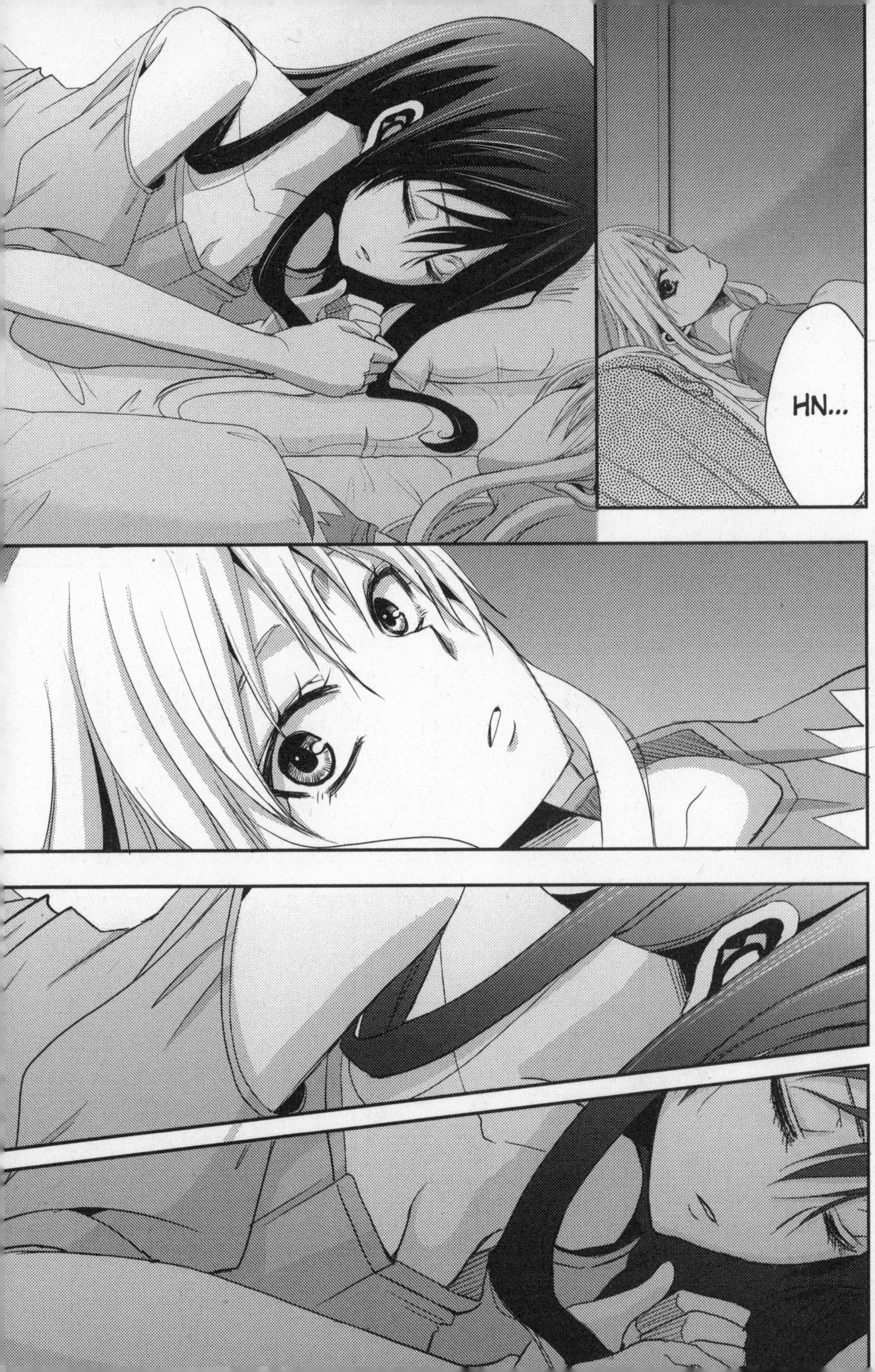
HN...

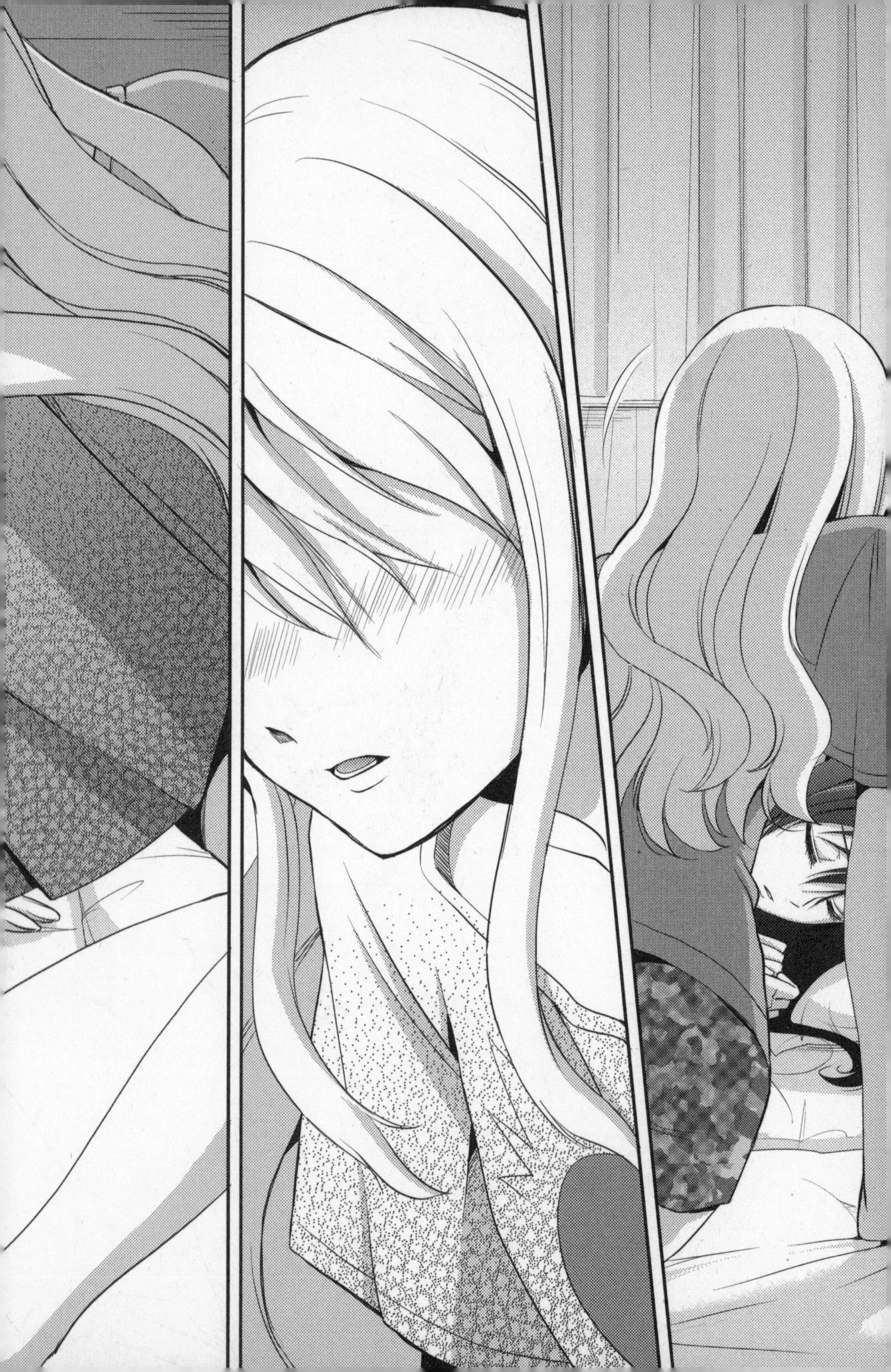

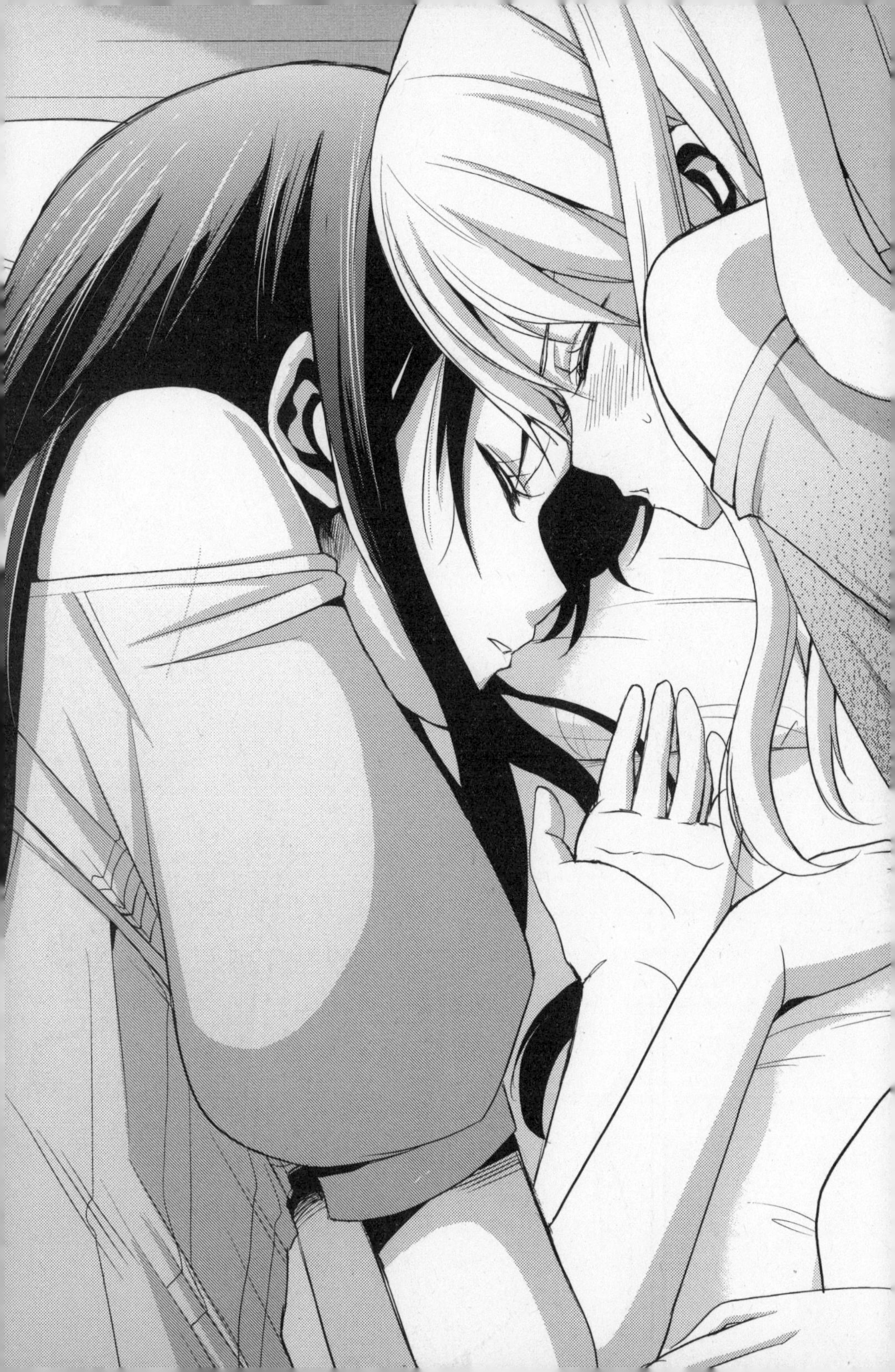

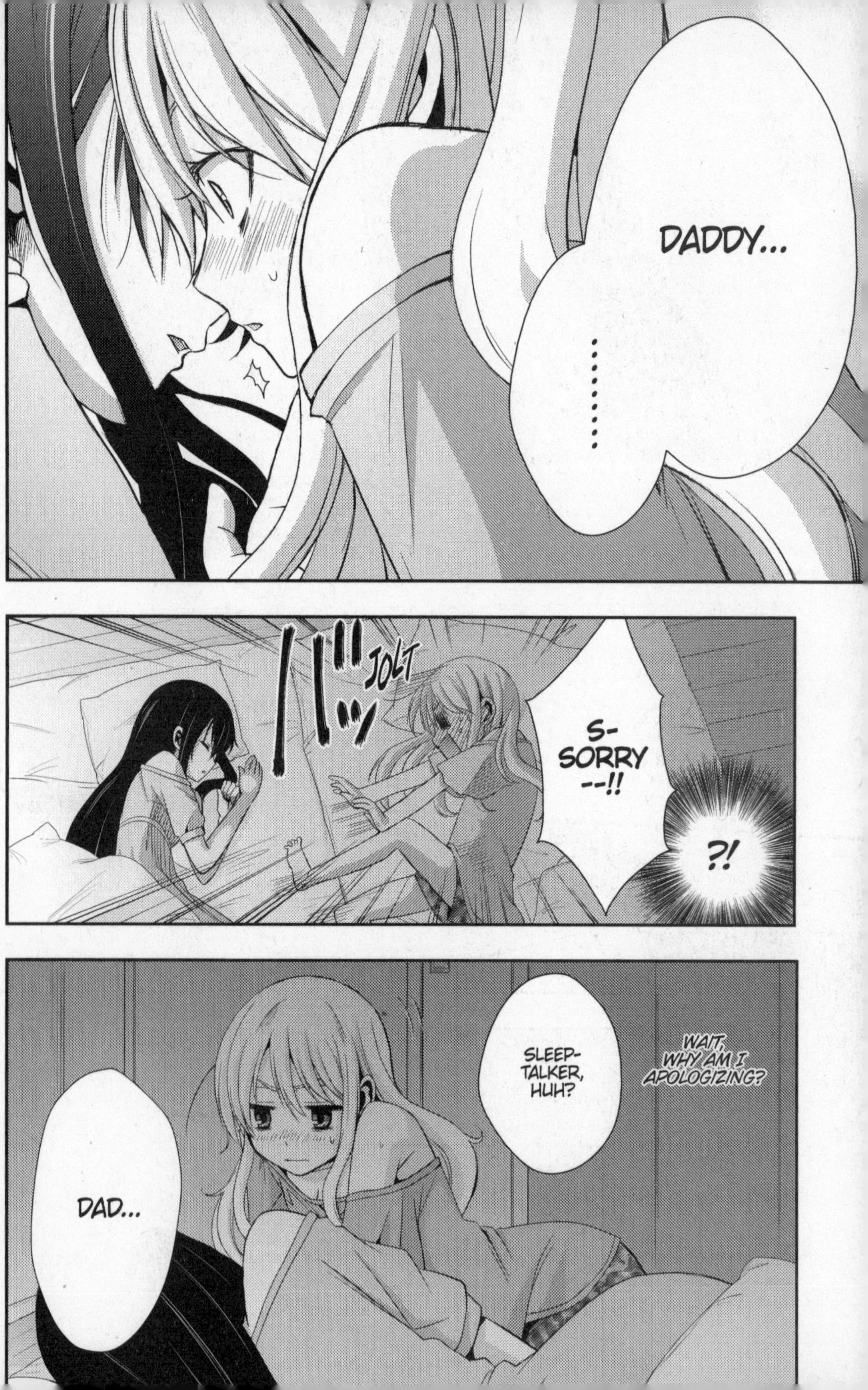
DADDY...
......
?!
S-SORRY--!!
JOLT
WAIT, WHY AM I APOLOGIZING?
SLEEP-TALKER, HUH?
DAD...

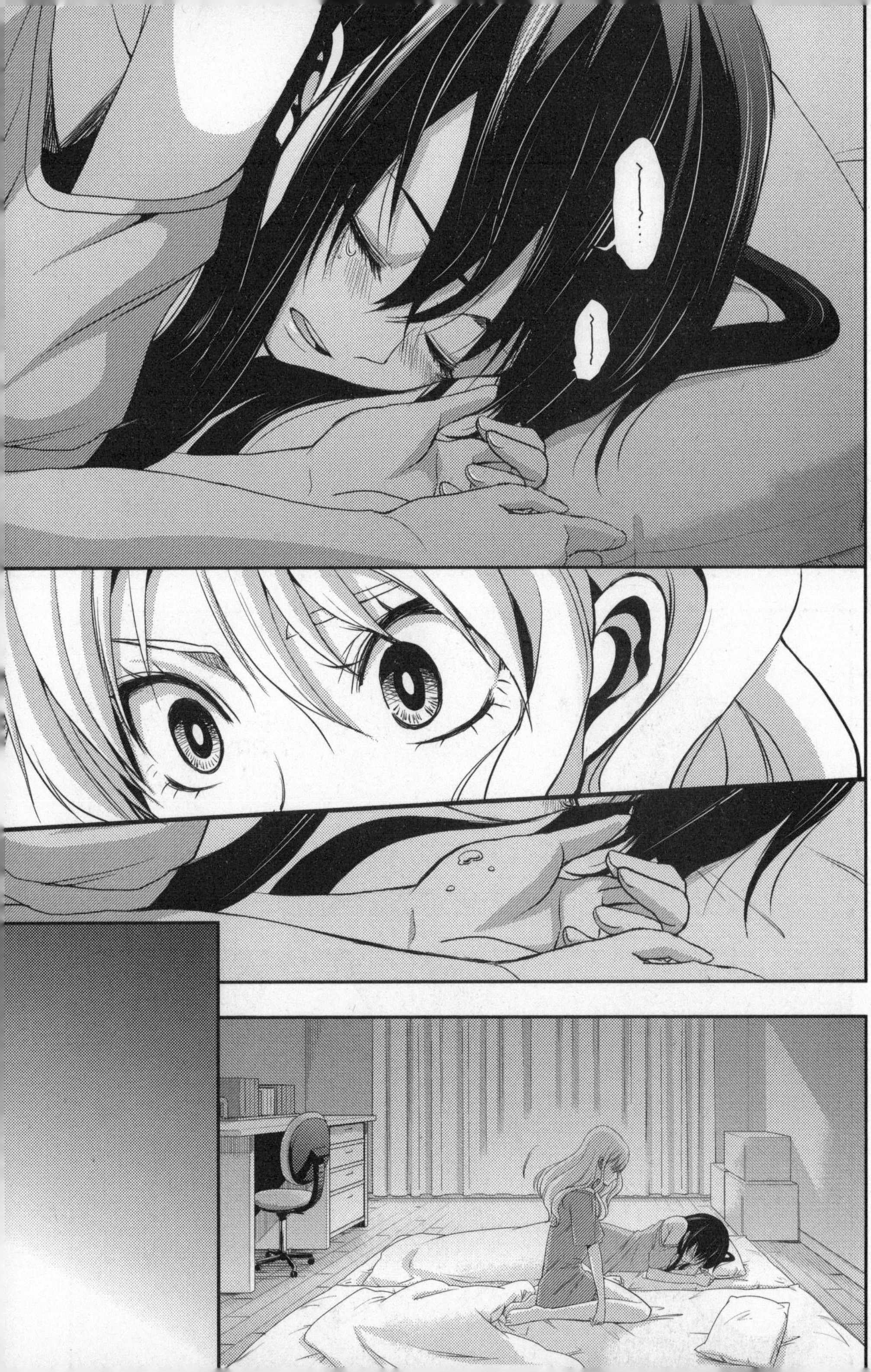

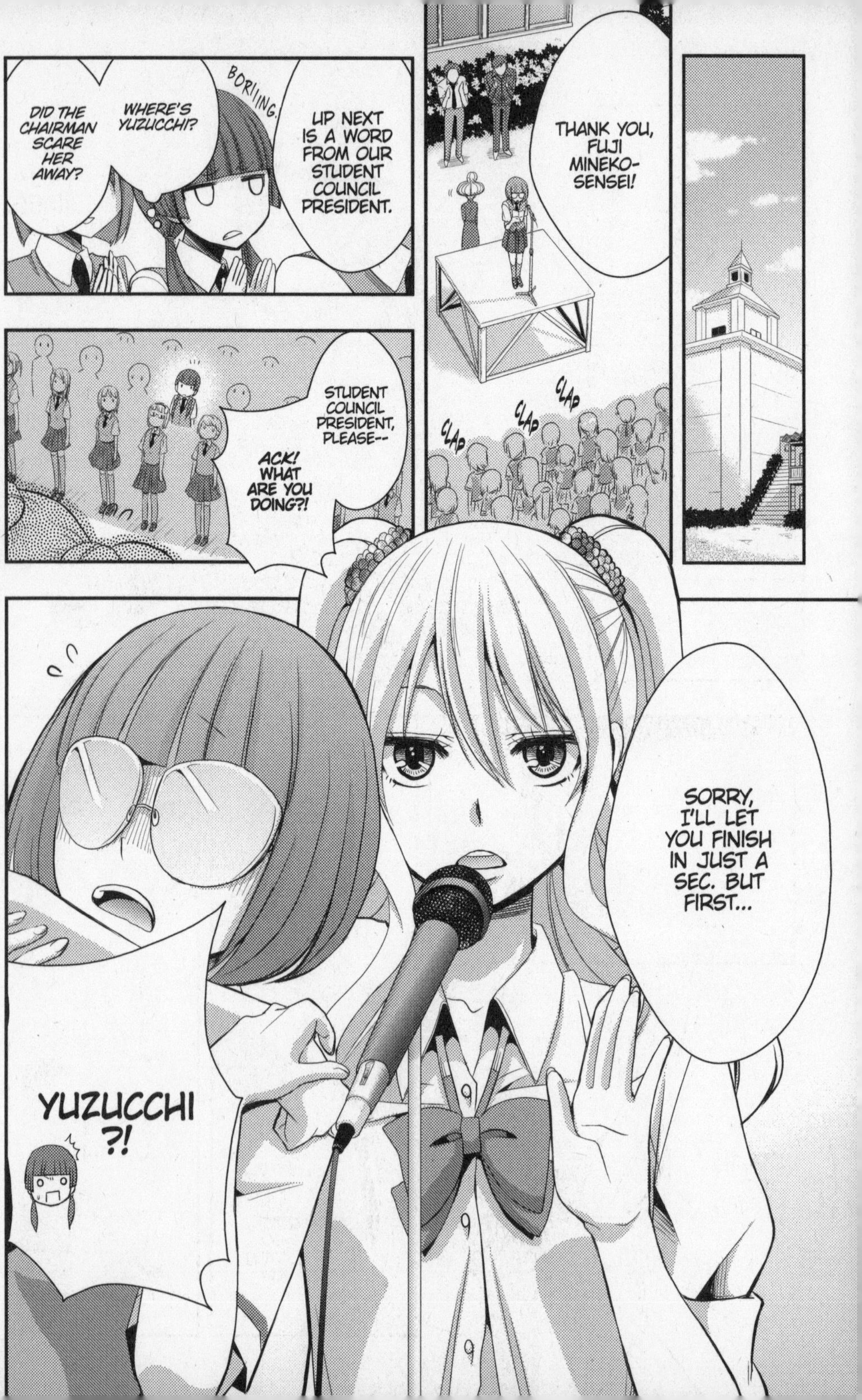
THANK YOU, FUJI MINEKO-SENSEI!
CLAP
CLAP
CLAP
UP NEXT IS A WORD FROM OUR STUDENT COUNCIL PRESIDENT.
BORIIING.
WHERE'S YUZUCCHI?
DID THE CHAIRMAN SCARE HER AWAY?
STUDENT COUNCIL PRESIDENT, PLEASE--
ACK! WHAT ARE YOU DOING?!
SORRY, I'LL LET YOU FINISH IN JUST A SEC. BUT FIRST...
YUZUCCHI ?!

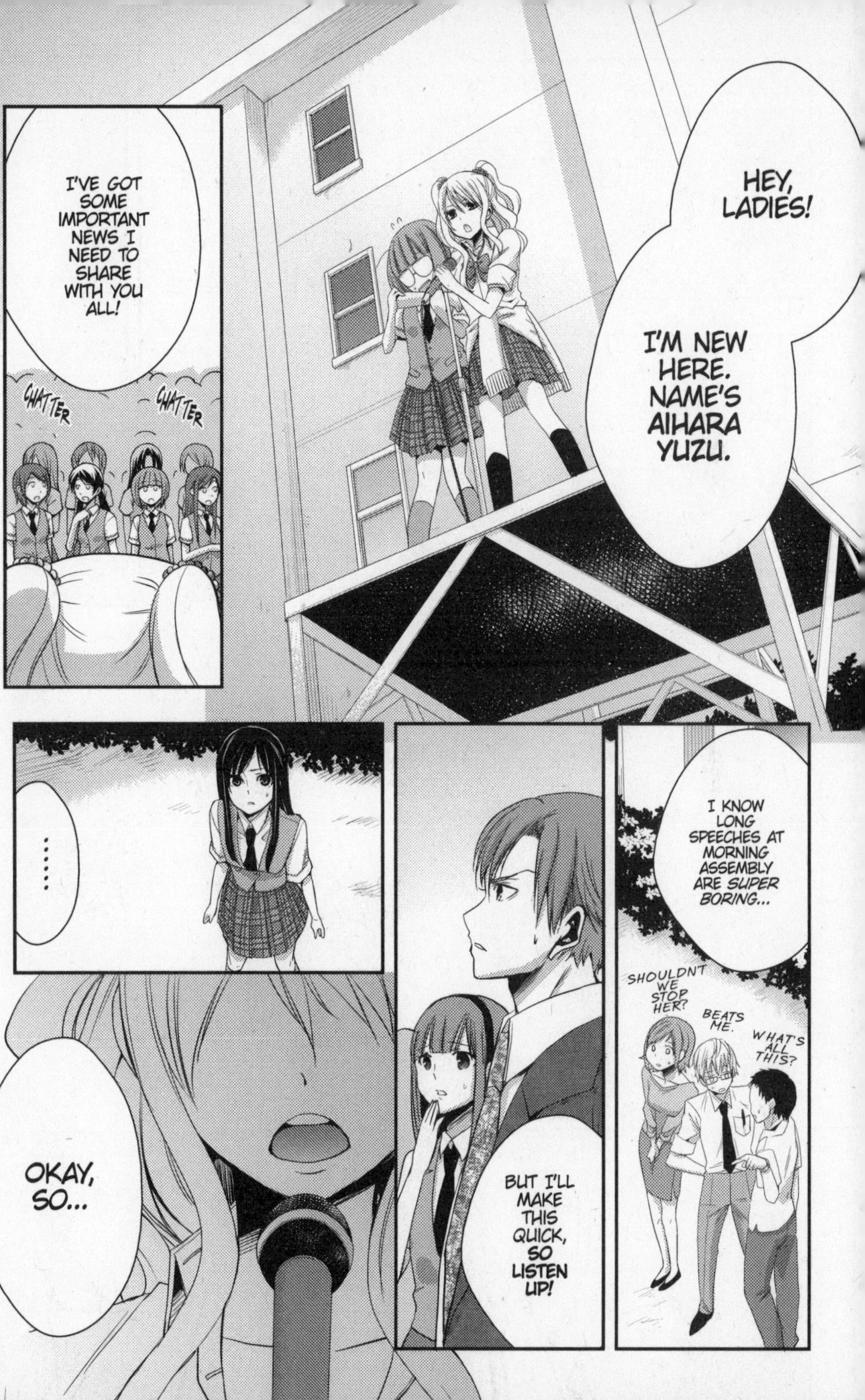
HEY, LADIES!
I'M NEW HERE. NAME'S AIHARA YUZU.
I'VE GOT SOME IMPORTANT NEWS I NEED TO SHARE WITH YOU ALL!
CHATTER
CHATTER
I KNOW LONG SPEECHES AT MORNING ASSEMBLY ARE SUPER BORING...
SHOULDN'T WE STOP HER?
BEATS ME.
WHAT'S ALL THIS?
BUT I'LL MAKE THIS QUICK, SO LISTEN UP!
......
OKAY, SO...

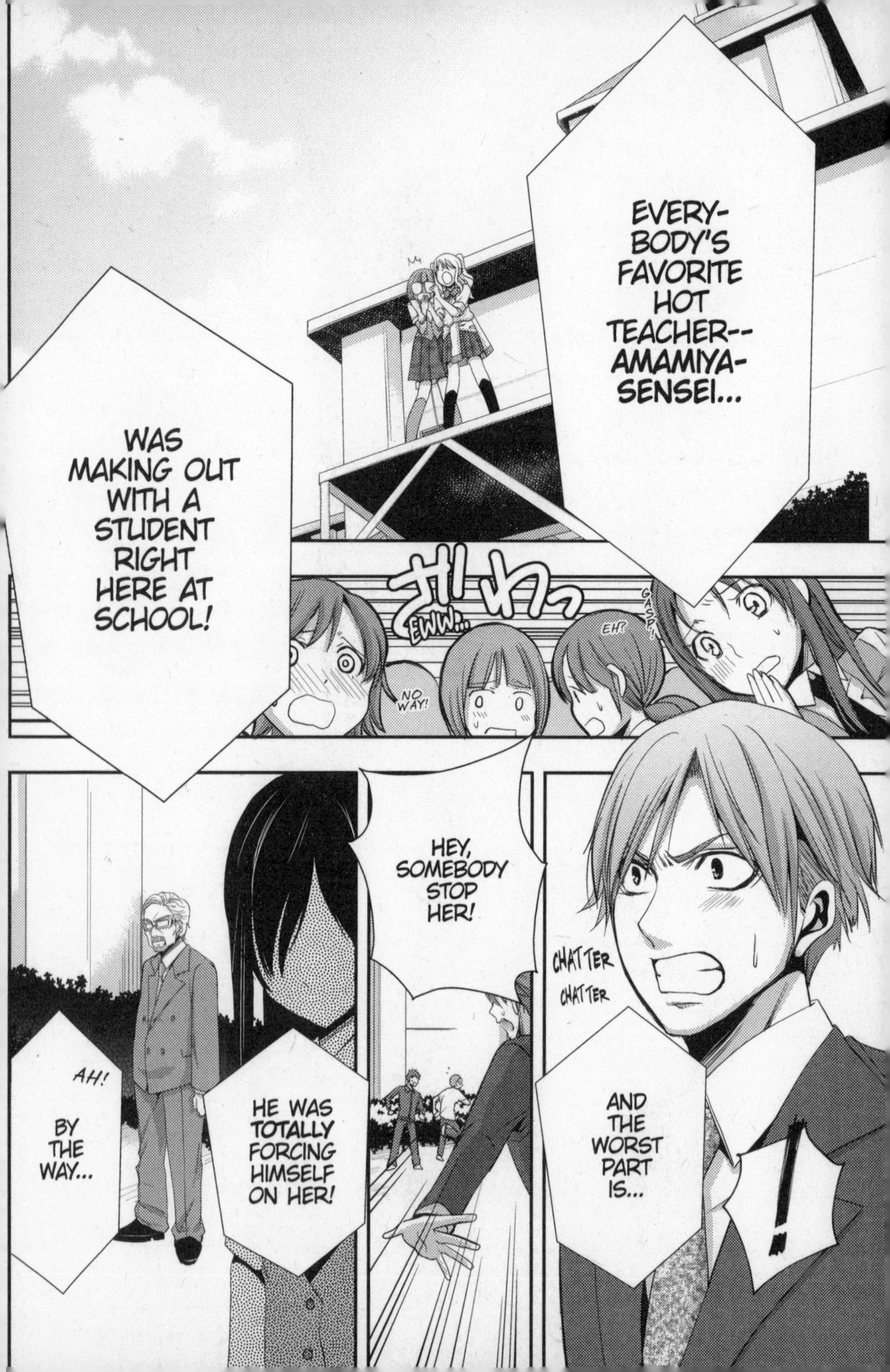
EVERY-BODY'S FAVORITE HOT TEACHER--AMAMIYA-SENSEI...
WAS MAKING OUT WITH A STUDENT RIGHT HERE AT SCHOOL!
ざわっ
GASP!
EH?
NO WAY!
EWW...
CHATTER
CHATTER
AND THE WORST PART IS...
!
HEY, SOMEBODY STOP HER!
HE WAS TOTALLY FORCING HIMSELF ON HER!
AH!
BY THE WAY...

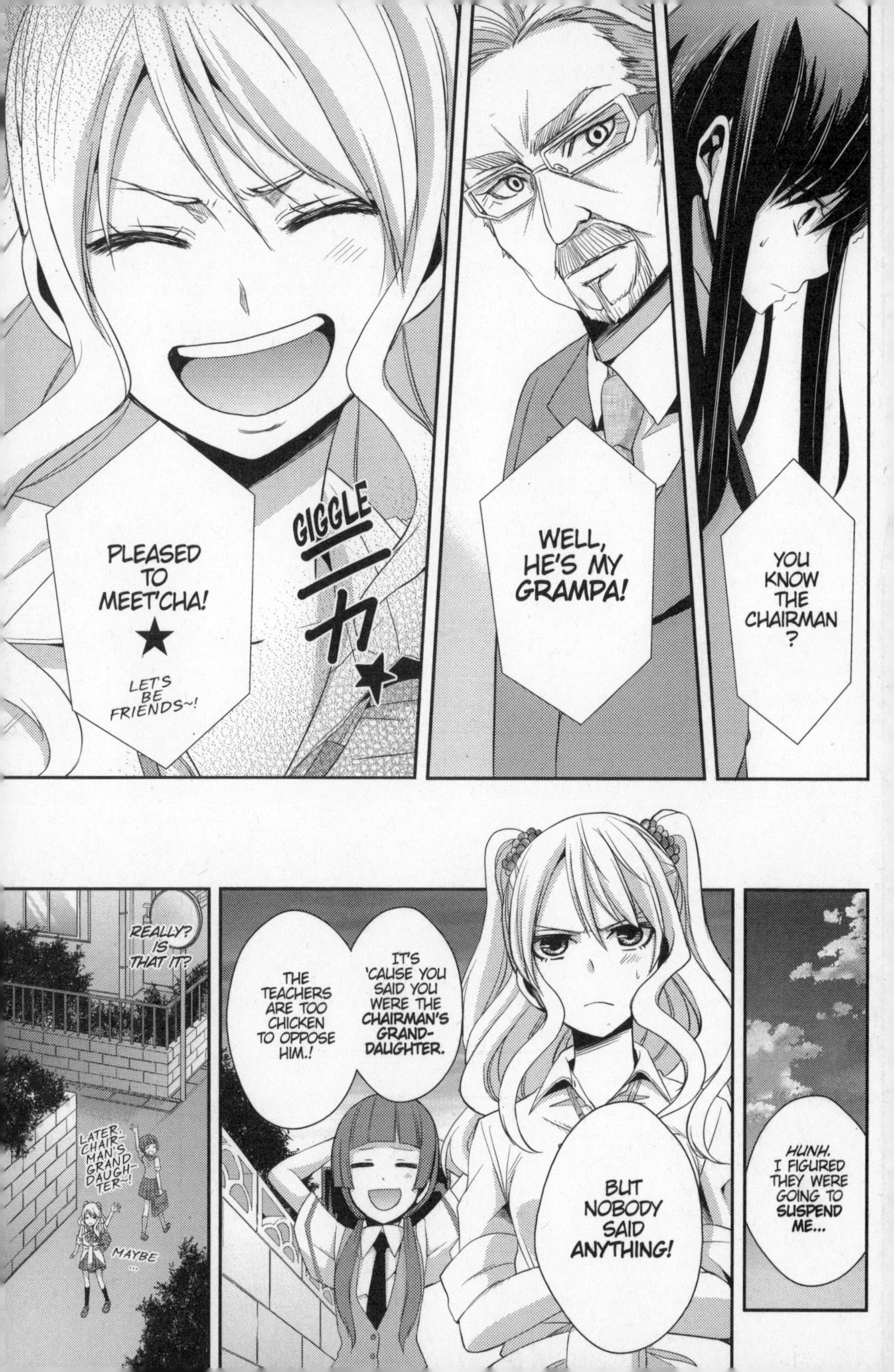
YOU KNOW THE CHAIRMAN?
WELL, HE'S MY GRAMPA!
PLEASED TO MEET'CHA! ★
LET'S BE FRIENDS~!
GIGGLE
HUNH. I FIGURED THEY WERE GOING TO SUSPEND ME...
BUT NOBODY SAID ANYTHING!
IT'S 'CAUSE YOU SAID YOU WERE THE CHAIRMAN'S GRAND-DAUGHTER.
THE TEACHERS ARE TOO CHICKEN TO OPPOSE HIM.!
REALLY? IS THAT IT?
LATER- CHAIR-MAN'S GRAND-DAUGH-TER~!
MAYBE...

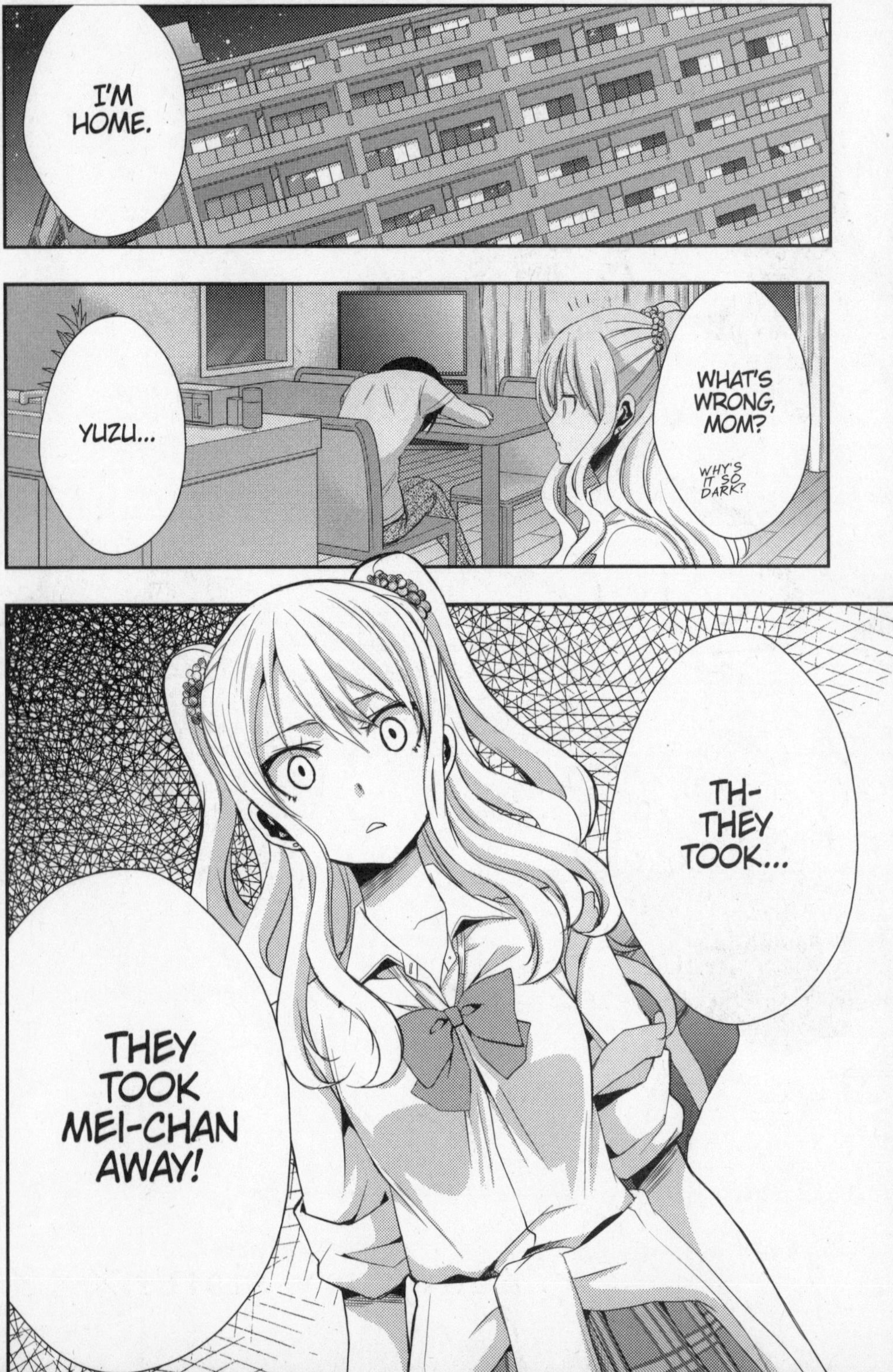
I'M HOME.
WHAT'S WRONG, MOM?
WHY'S IT SO DARK?
YUZU...
TH- THEY TOOK...
THEY TOOK MEI-CHAN AWAY!

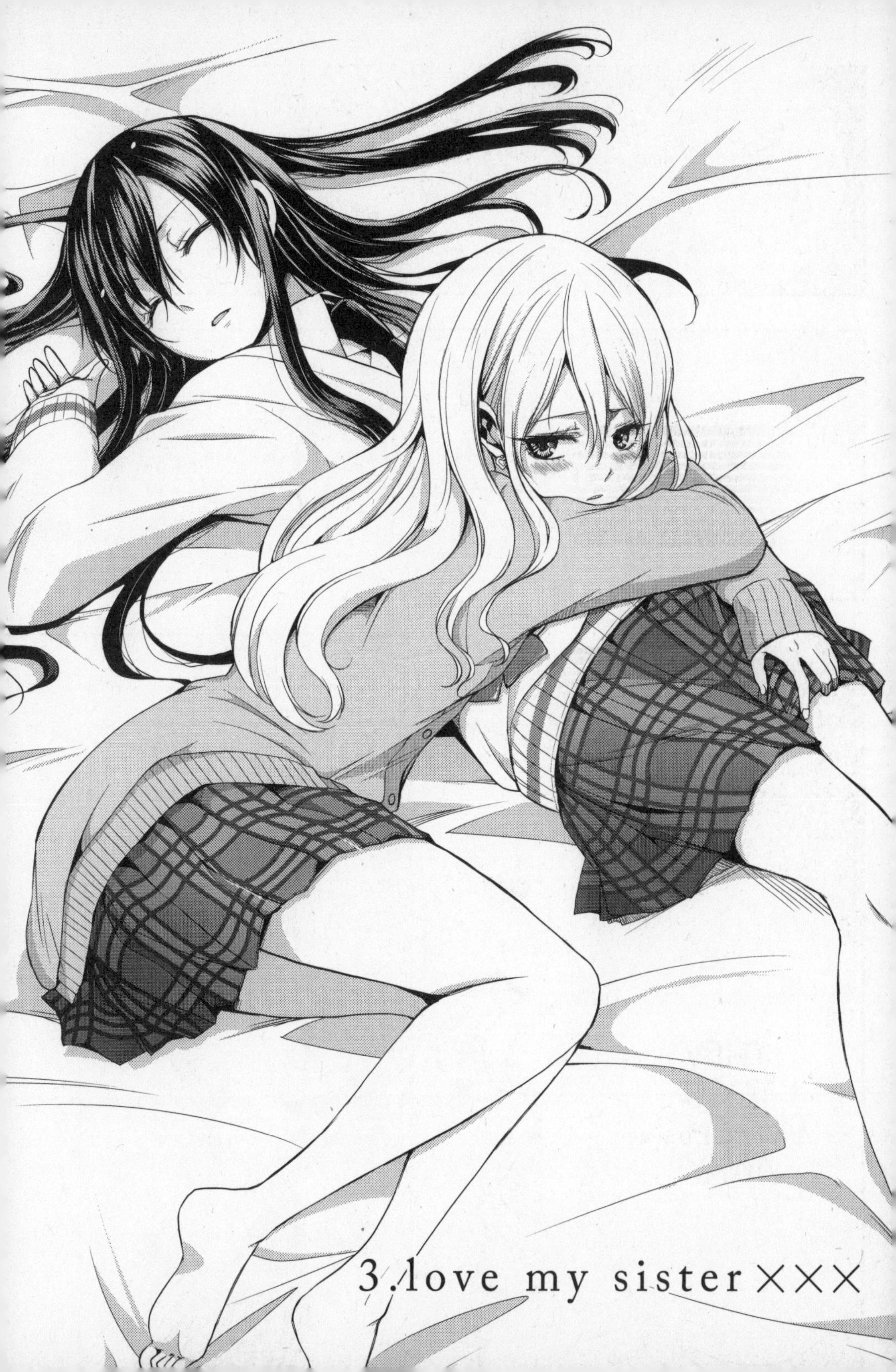
3.love my sister×××

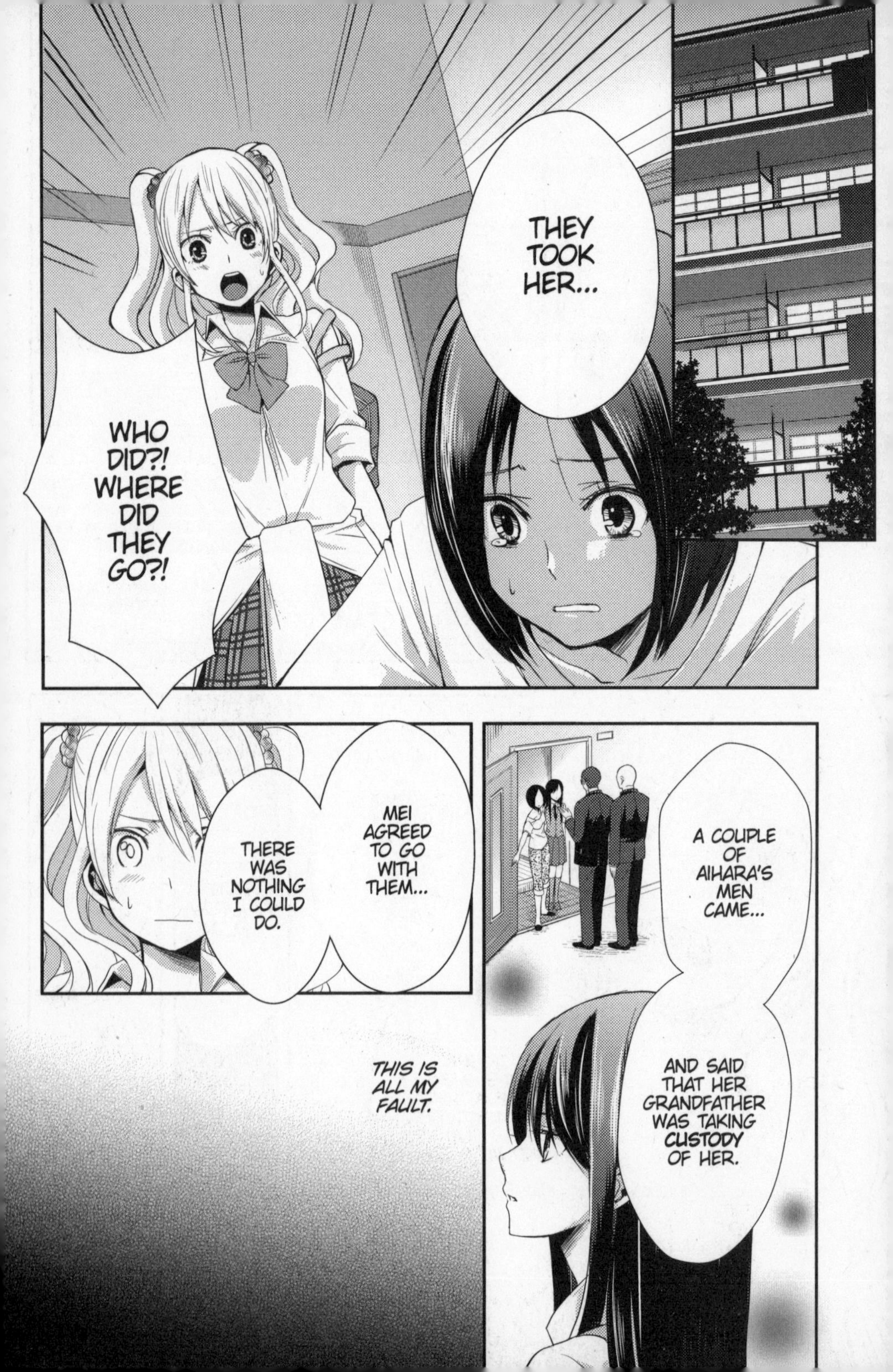
THEY TOOK HER...
WHO DID?! WHERE DID THEY GO?!
A COUPLE OF AIHARA'S MEN CAME...
AND SAID THAT HER GRANDFATHER WAS TAKING CUSTODY OF HER.
MEI AGREED TO GO WITH THEM...
THERE WAS NOTHING I COULD DO.
THIS IS ALL MY FAULT.

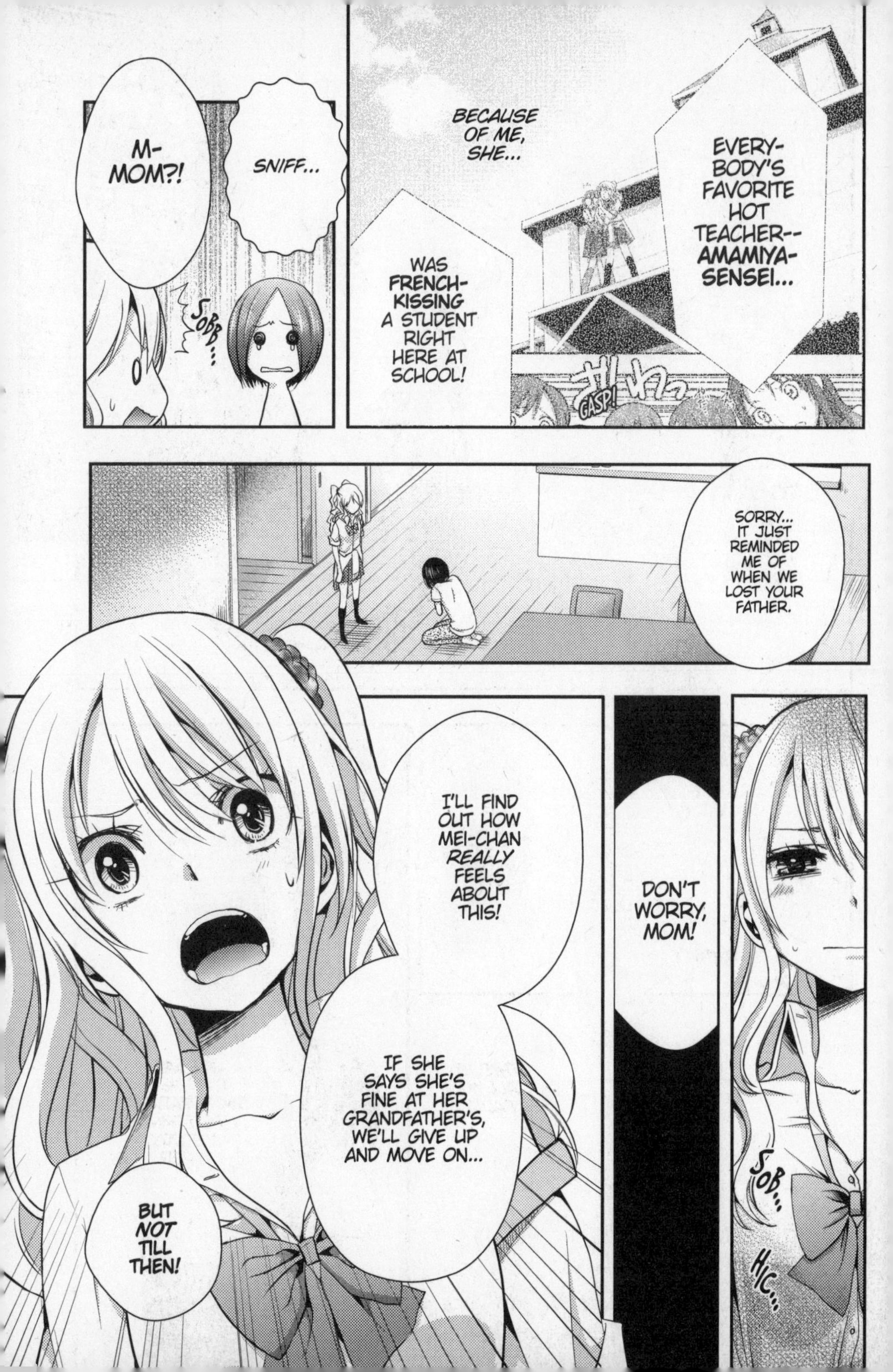
EVERY-BODY'S FAVORITE HOT TEACHER--AMAMIYA-SENSEI...
BECAUSE OF ME, SHE...
WAS FRENCH-KISSING A STUDENT RIGHT HERE AT SCHOOL!
ざわっ
GASP!
SNIFF...
M-MOM?!
SOBB...
SORRY... IT JUST REMINDED ME OF WHEN WE LOST YOUR FATHER.
SOB...
HIC...
DON'T WORRY, MOM!
I'LL FIND OUT HOW MEI-CHAN *REALLY* FEELS ABOUT THIS!
IF SHE SAYS SHE'S FINE AT HER GRANDFATHER'S, WE'LL GIVE UP AND MOVE ON...
BUT *NOT* TILL THEN!

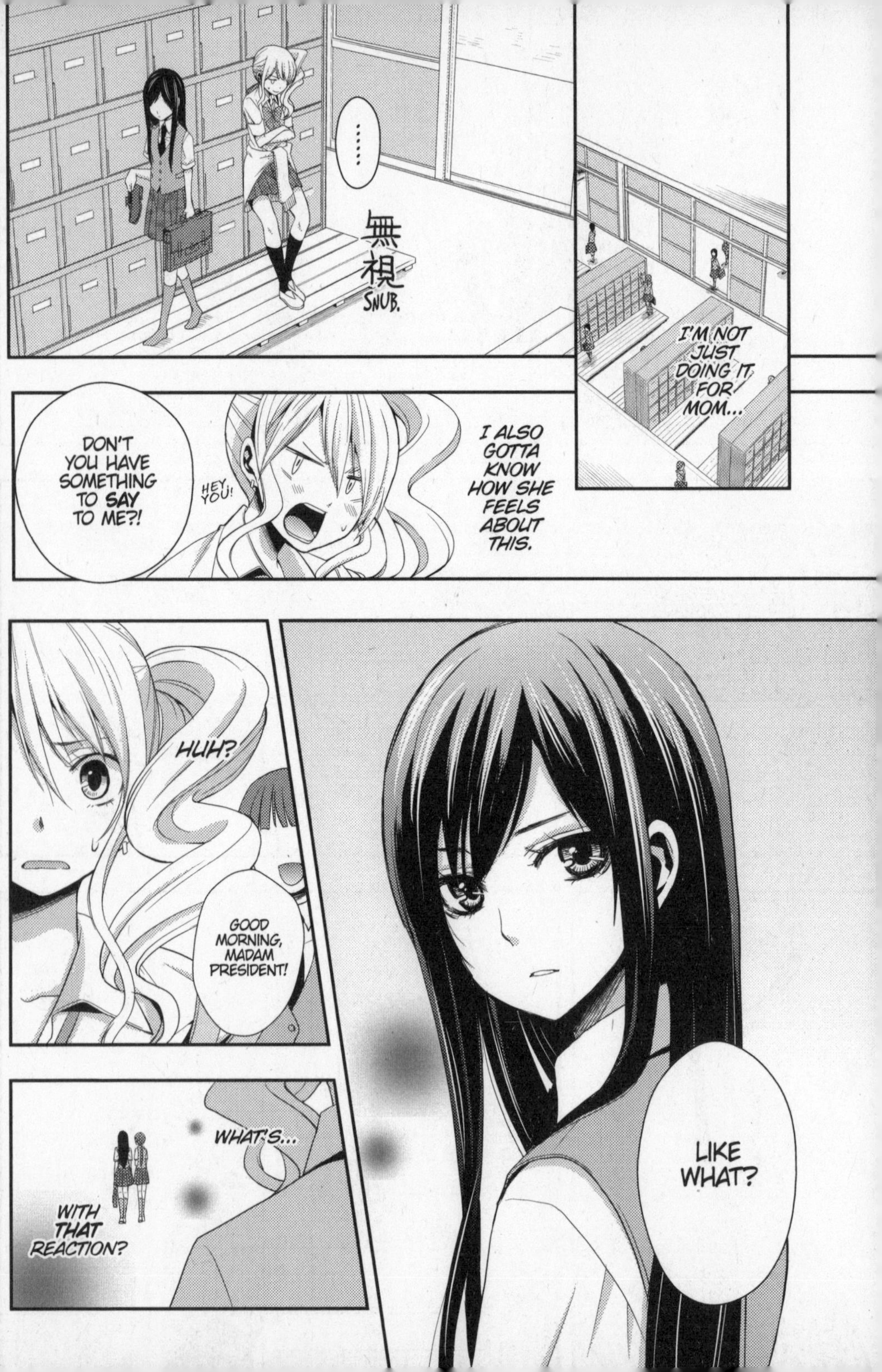
I'M NOT JUST DOING IT FOR MOM...
......
無視
SNUB.
I ALSO GOTTA KNOW HOW SHE FEELS ABOUT THIS.
HEY, YOU!
DON'T YOU HAVE SOMETHING TO SAY TO ME?!
LIKE WHAT?
HUH?
GOOD MORNING, MADAM PRESIDENT!
WHAT'S...
WITH THAT REACTION?

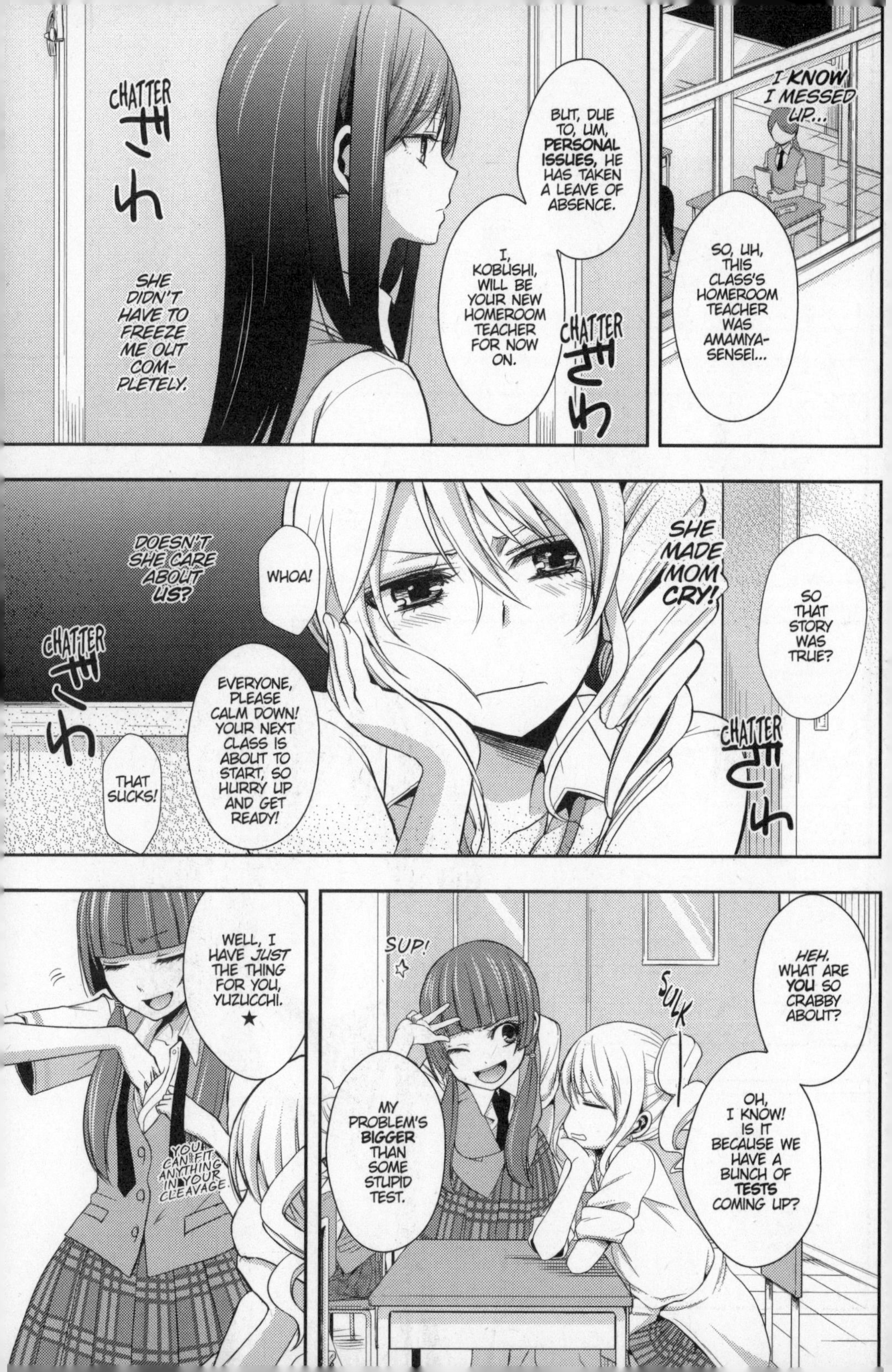
I KNOW I MESSED UP...
SO, UH, THIS CLASS'S HOMEROOM TEACHER WAS AMAMIYA-SENSEI...
BUT, DUE TO, UM, PERSONAL ISSUES, HE HAS TAKEN A LEAVE OF ABSENCE.
CHATTER ざわ
I, KOBUSHI, WILL BE YOUR NEW HOMEROOM TEACHER FOR NOW ON.
CHATTER ざわ
SHE DIDN'T HAVE TO FREEZE ME OUT COMPLETELY.
SHE MADE MOM CRY!
SO THAT STORY WAS TRUE?
CHATTER ざわ
WHOA!
DOESN'T SHE CARE ABOUT US?
CHATTER ざわ
EVERYONE, PLEASE CALM DOWN! YOUR NEXT CLASS IS ABOUT TO START, SO HURRY UP AND GET READY!
THAT SUCKS!
HEH. WHAT ARE YOU SO CRABBY ABOUT?
SULK
SUP!
OH, I KNOW! IS IT BECAUSE WE HAVE A BUNCH OF TESTS COMING UP?
MY PROBLEM'S BIGGER THAN SOME STUPID TEST.
WELL, I HAVE JUST THE THING FOR YOU, YUZUCCHI. ★
YOU CAN FIT ANYTHING IN YOUR CLEAVAGE.

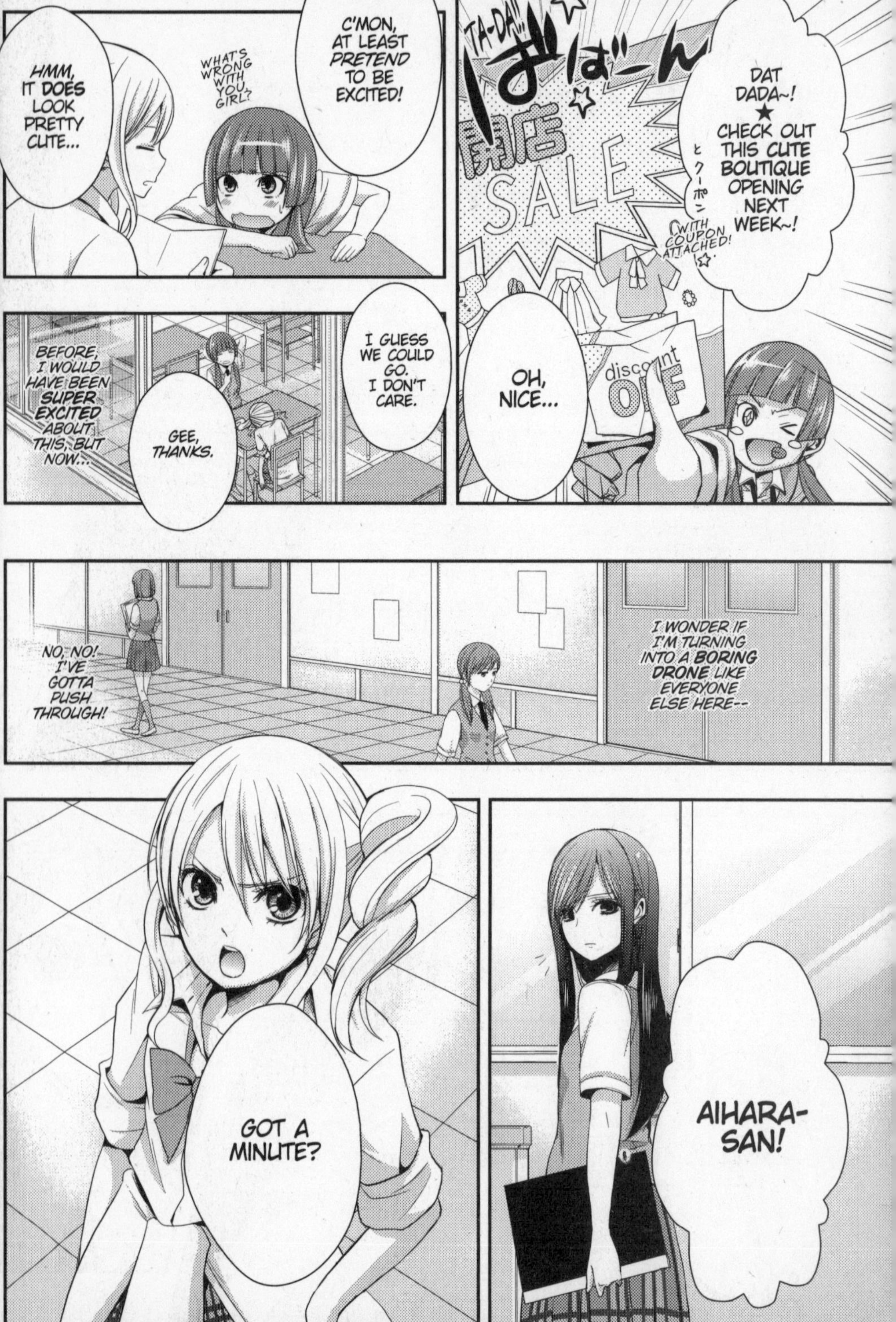
TA-DA!!
開店
SALE
とクーポン
WITH COUPON ATTACHED!
discount
OFF
DAT DADA~! ★ CHECK OUT THIS CUTE BOUTIQUE OPENING NEXT WEEK~!
OH, NICE...
C'MON, AT LEAST PRETEND TO BE EXCITED!
WHAT'S WRONG WITH YOU, GIRL?
HMM, IT DOES LOOK PRETTY CUTE...
I GUESS WE COULD GO. I DON'T CARE.
GEE, THANKS.
BEFORE, I WOULD HAVE BEEN SUPER EXCITED ABOUT THIS, BUT NOW...
I WONDER IF I'M TURNING INTO A BORING DRONE LIKE EVERYONE ELSE HERE--
NO, NO! I'VE GOTTA PUSH THROUGH!
AIHARA-SAN!
GOT A MINUTE?

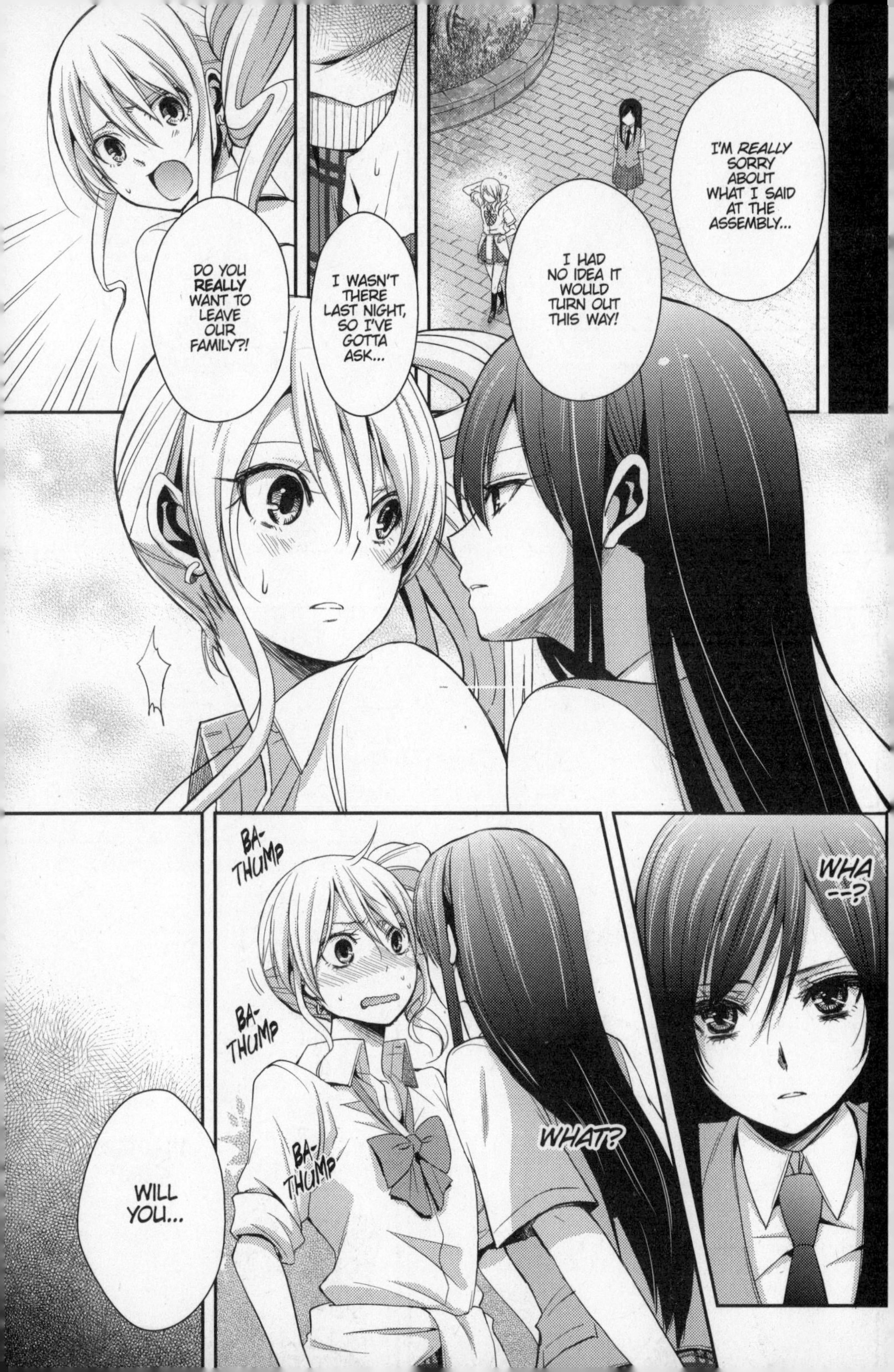

I'M *REALLY* SORRY ABOUT WHAT I SAID AT THE ASSEMBLY...
I HAD NO IDEA IT WOULD TURN OUT THIS WAY!
I WASN'T THERE LAST NIGHT, SO I'VE GOTTA ASK...
DO YOU **REALLY** WANT TO LEAVE OUR FAMILY?!
WHA--?
BA-THUMP
BA-THUMP
WHAT?
BA-THUMP
WILL YOU...

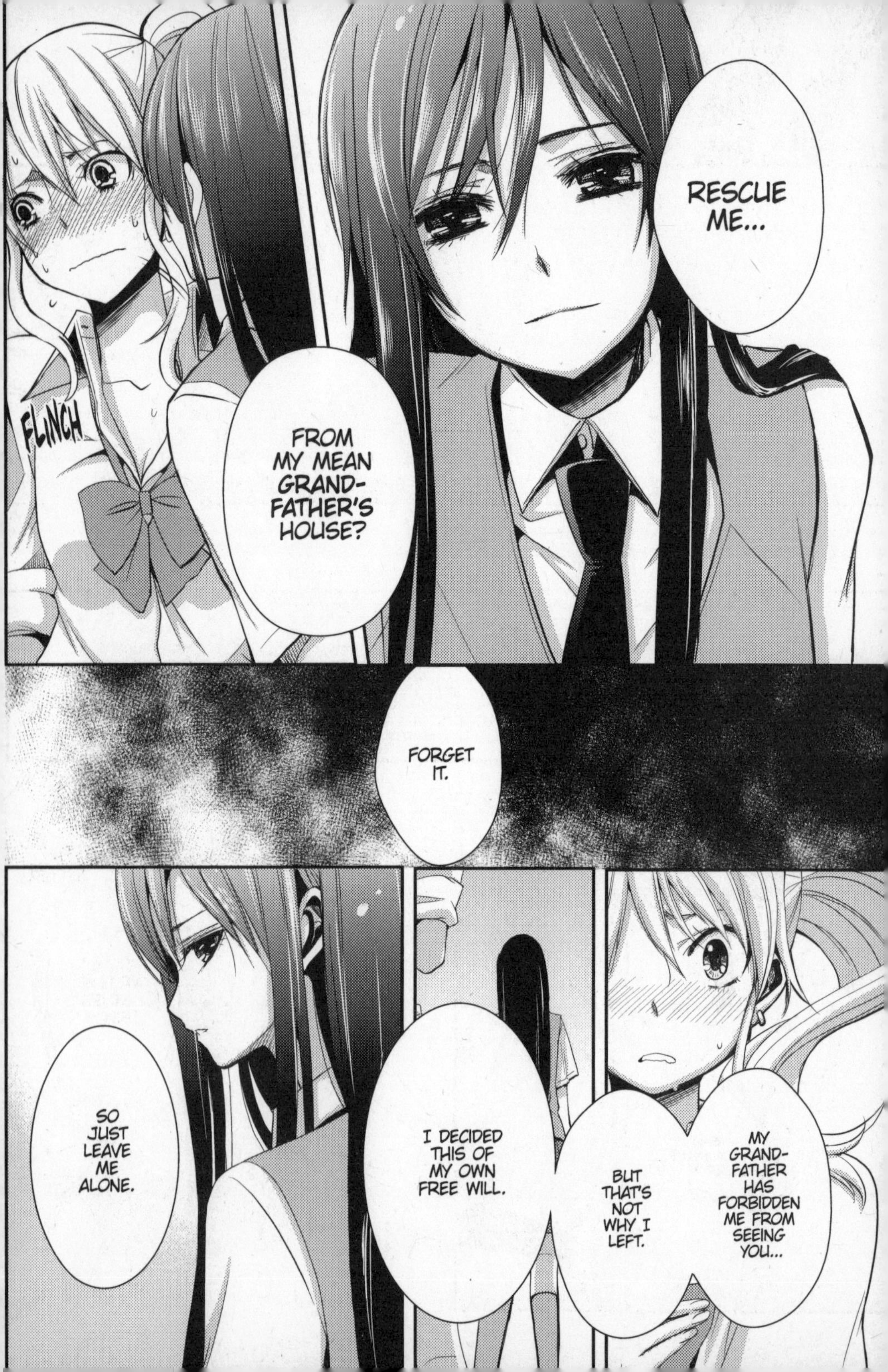
RESCUE ME...
FROM MY MEAN GRAND-FATHER'S HOUSE?
FLINCH
FORGET IT.
MY GRAND-FATHER HAS FORBIDDEN ME FROM SEEING YOU...
BUT THAT'S NOT WHY I LEFT.
I DECIDED THIS OF MY OWN FREE WILL.
SO JUST LEAVE ME ALONE.

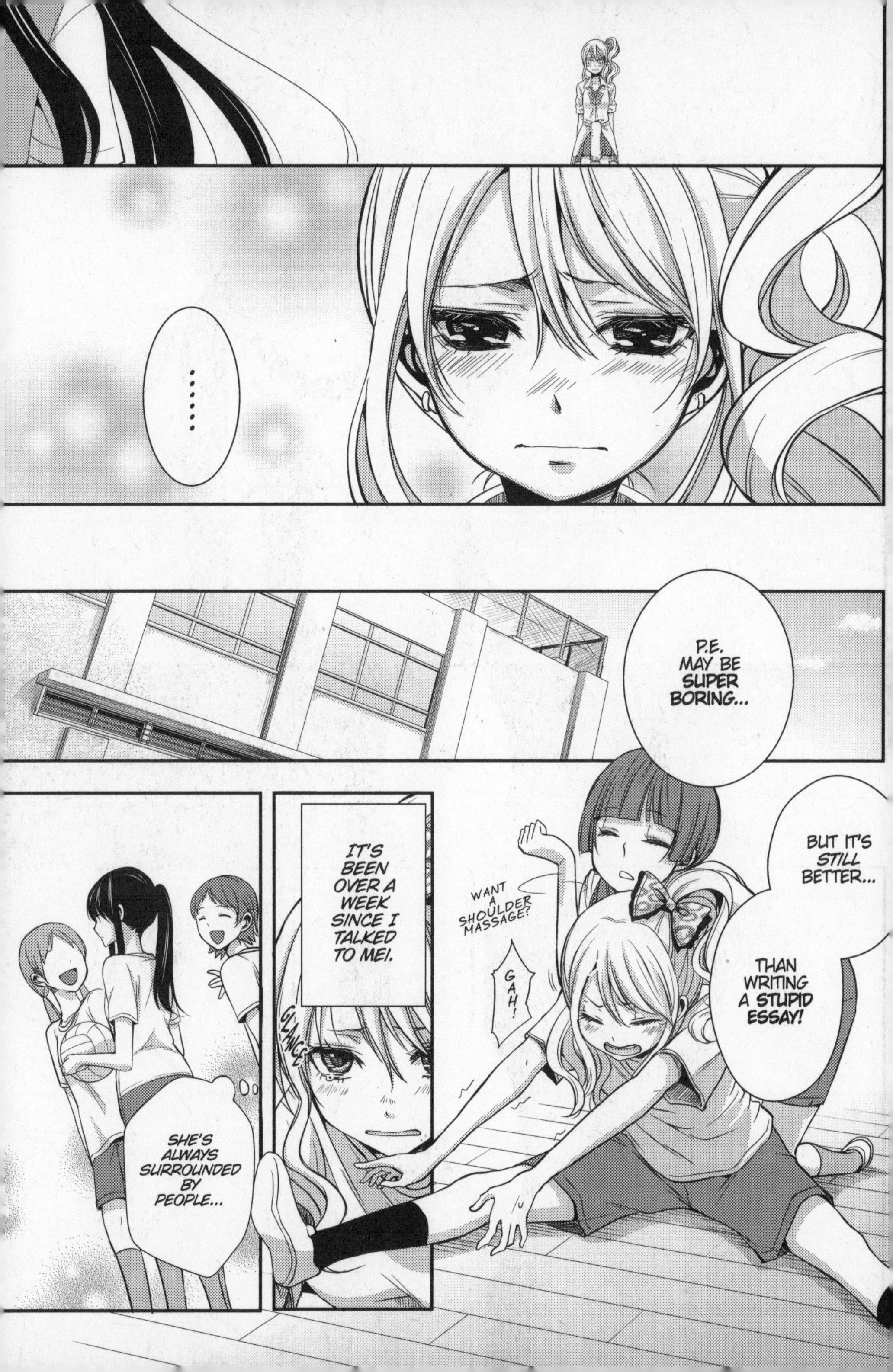
......
P.E. MAY BE SUPER BORING...
BUT IT'S STILL BETTER...
THAN WRITING A STUPID ESSAY!
WANT A SHOULDER MASSAGE?
GAH!
IT'S BEEN OVER A WEEK SINCE I TALKED TO MEI.
GLANCE
SHE'S ALWAYS SURROUNDED BY PEOPLE...

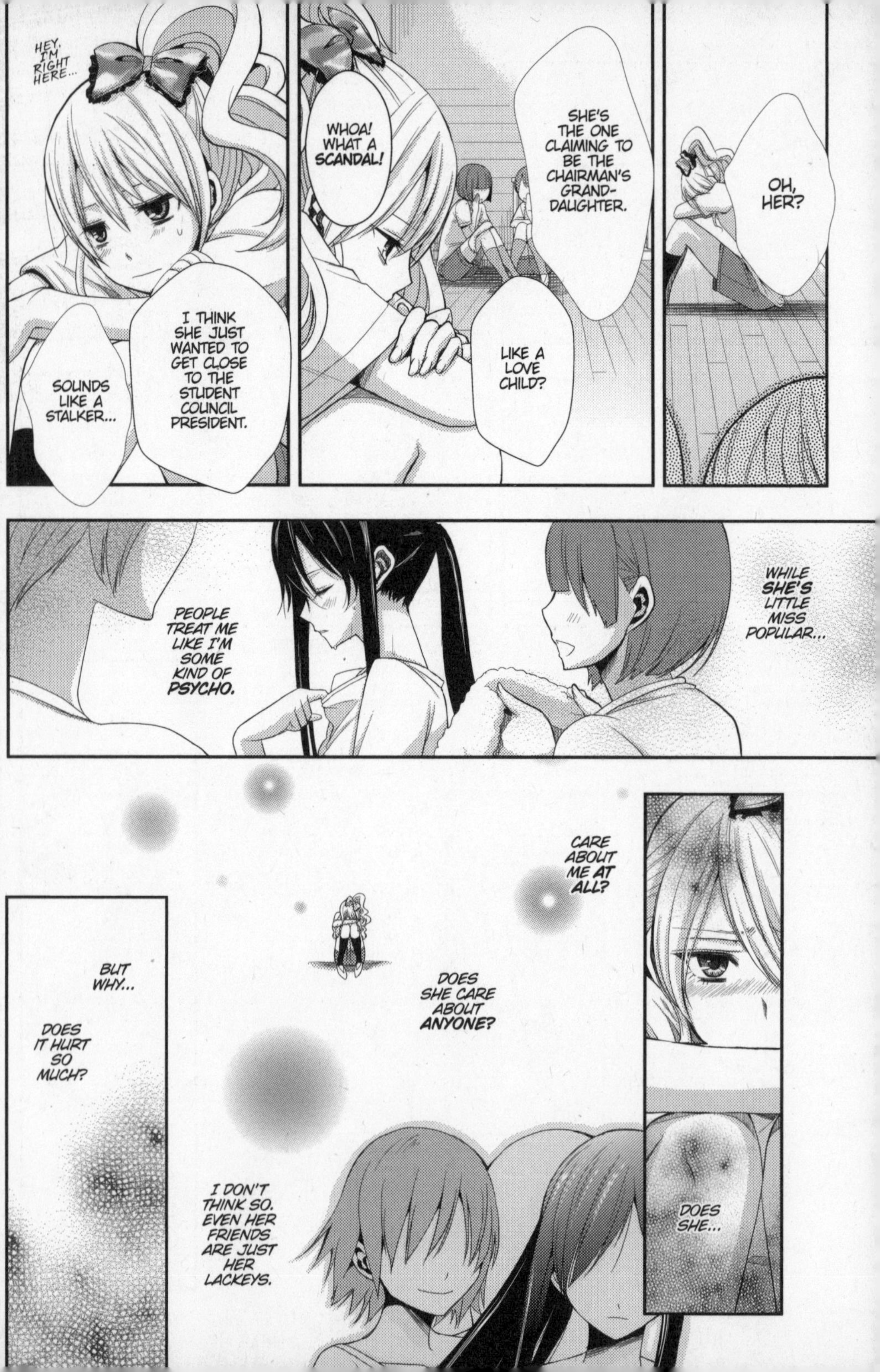
OH, HER?
SHE'S THE ONE CLAIMING TO BE THE CHAIRMAN'S GRAND-DAUGHTER.
WHOA! WHAT A SCANDAL!
LIKE A LOVE CHILD?
HEY, I'M RIGHT HERE...
I THINK SHE JUST WANTED TO GET CLOSE TO THE STUDENT COUNCIL PRESIDENT.
SOUNDS LIKE A STALKER...
WHILE SHE'S LITTLE MISS POPULAR...
PEOPLE TREAT ME LIKE I'M SOME KIND OF PSYCHO.
DOES SHE...
CARE ABOUT ME AT ALL?
DOES SHE CARE ABOUT ANYONE?
I DON'T THINK SO. EVEN HER FRIENDS ARE JUST HER LACKEYS.
BUT WHY...
DOES IT HURT SO MUCH?

CLENCH...

WHY DO I EVEN CARE?

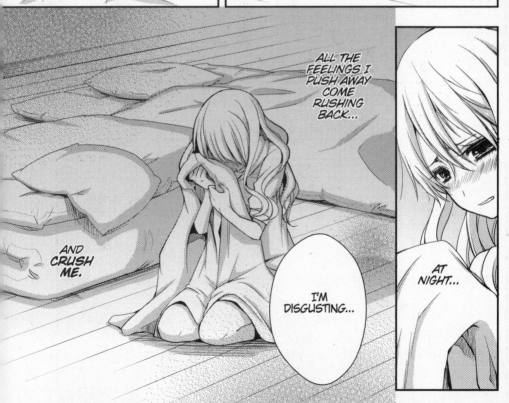

ALL THE FEELINGS I PUSH AWAY COME RUSHING BACK...

AND CRUSH ME.

I'M DISGUSTING...

AT NIGHT...

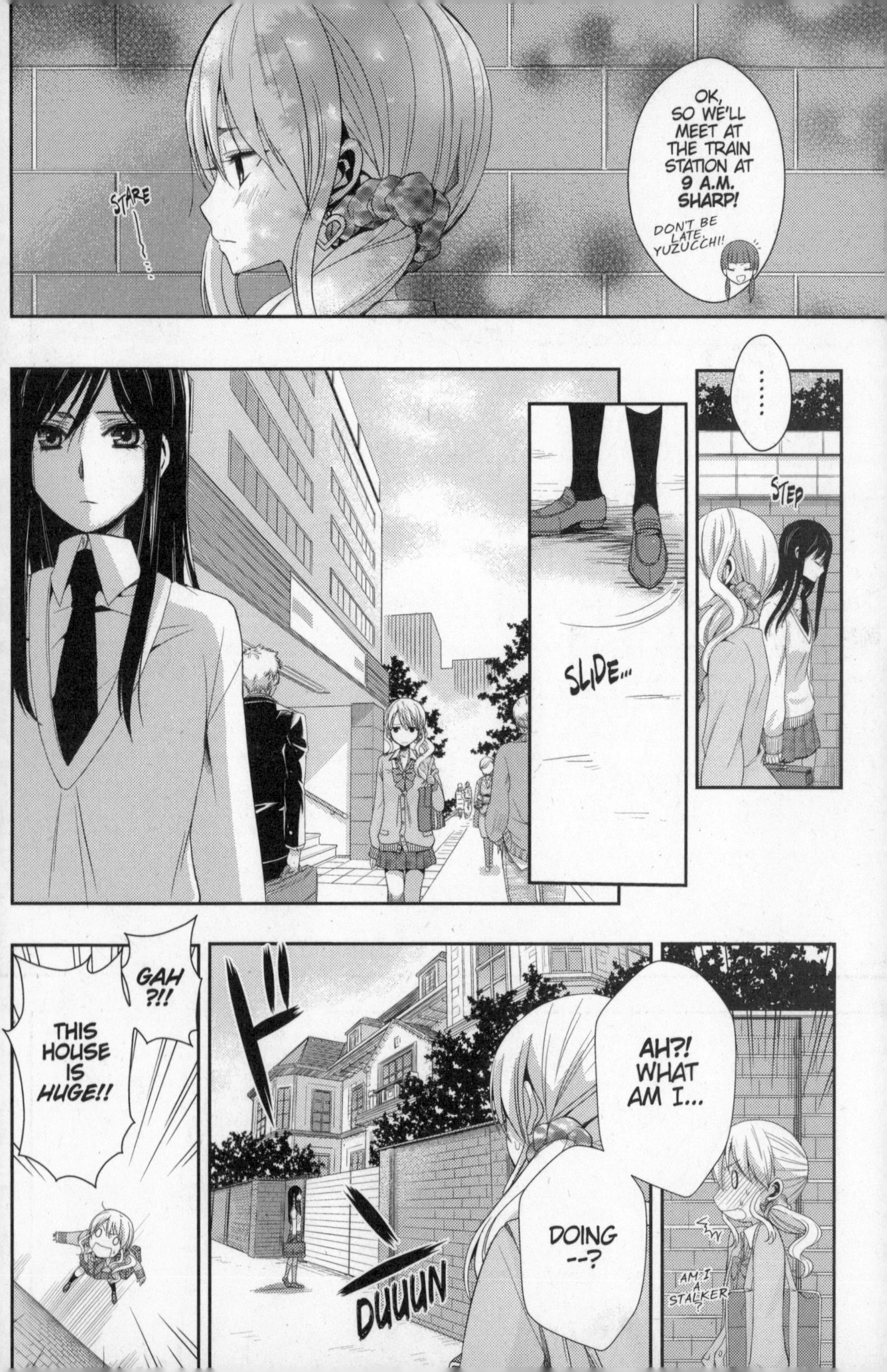
OK, SO WE'LL MEET AT THE TRAIN STATION AT 9 A.M. SHARP!
DON'T BE LATE, YUZUCCHI!!
STARE
......
STEP
SLIDE...
AH?! WHAT AM I...
DOING --?
AM I A STALKER?
DUUUN
GAH ?!!
THIS HOUSE IS HUGE!!

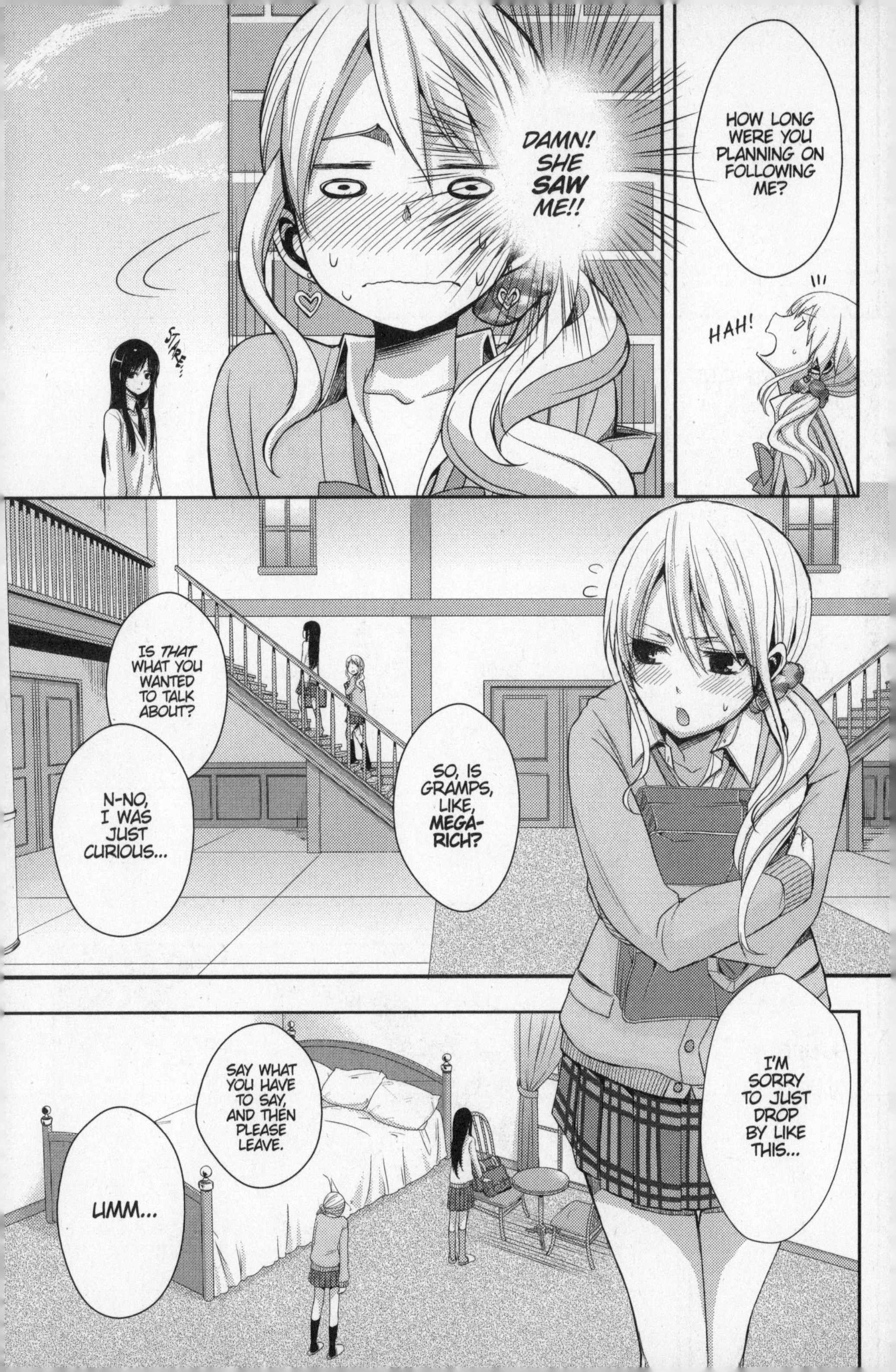
HOW LONG WERE YOU PLANNING ON FOLLOWING ME?
HAH!
DAMN! SHE SAW ME!!
STARE...
SO, IS GRAMPS, LIKE, MEGA-RICH?
IS *THAT* WHAT YOU WANTED TO TALK ABOUT?
N-NO, I WAS JUST CURIOUS...
I'M SORRY TO JUST DROP BY LIKE THIS...
SAY WHAT YOU HAVE TO SAY, AND THEN PLEASE LEAVE.
UMM...

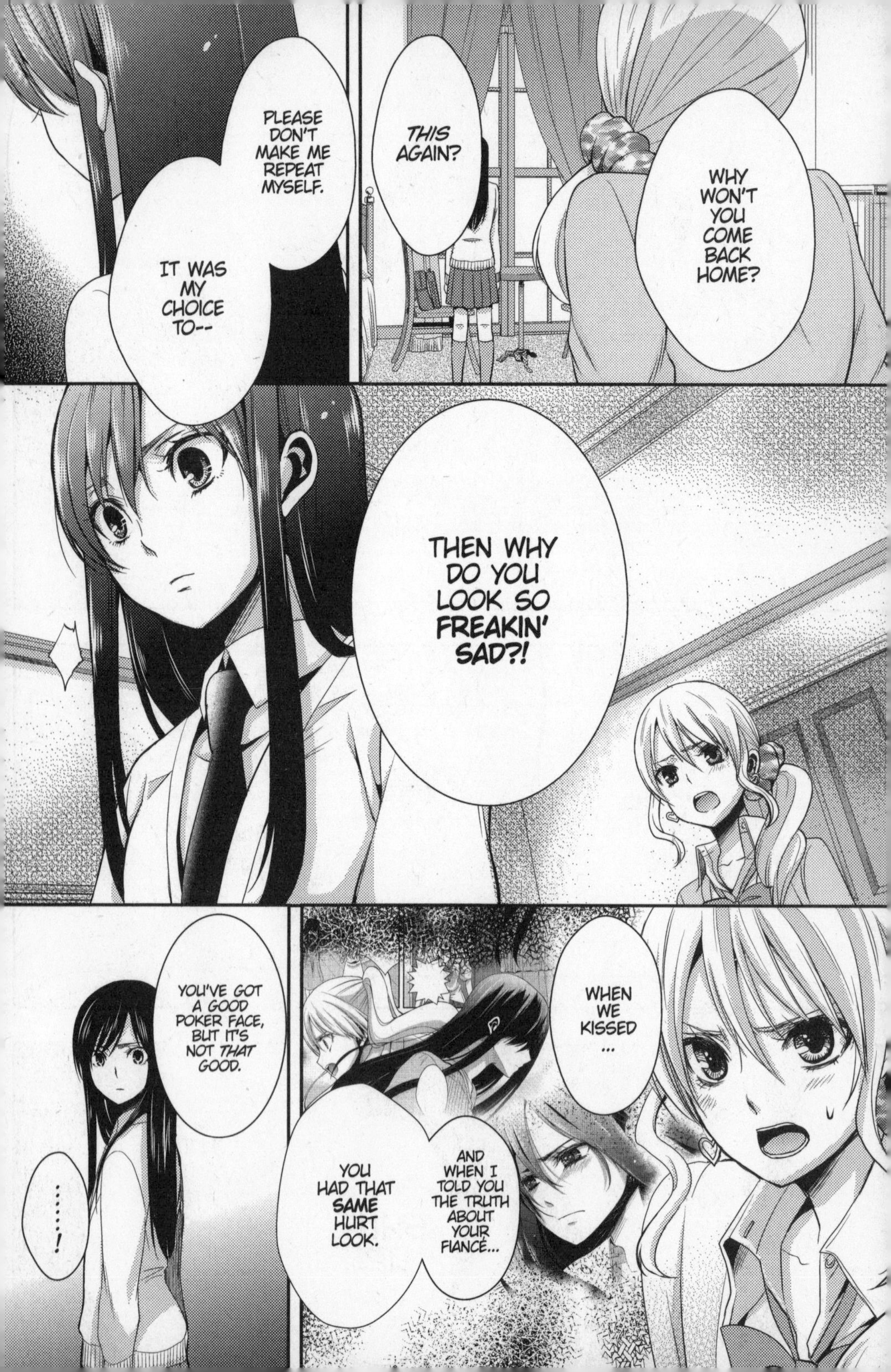
WHY WON'T YOU COME BACK HOME?
THIS AGAIN?
PLEASE DON'T MAKE ME REPEAT MYSELF.
IT WAS MY CHOICE TO--
THEN WHY DO YOU LOOK SO FREAKIN' SAD?!
WHEN WE KISSED...
AND WHEN I TOLD YOU THE TRUTH ABOUT YOUR FIANCÉ...
YOU HAD THAT **SAME** HURT LOOK.
YOU'VE GOT A GOOD POKER FACE, BUT IT'S NOT *THAT* GOOD.
......!

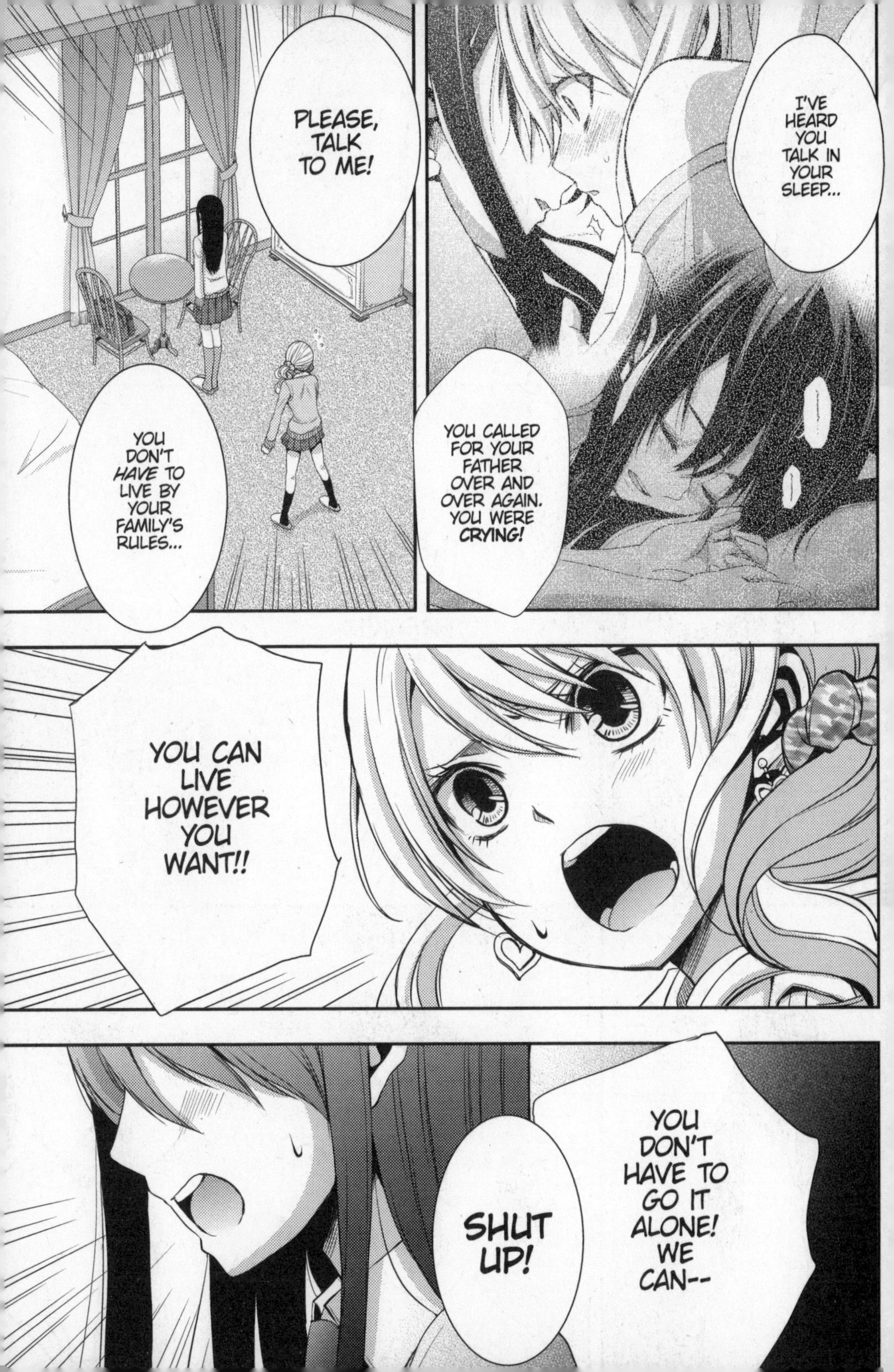
I'VE HEARD YOU TALK IN YOUR SLEEP...
YOU CALLED FOR YOUR FATHER OVER AND OVER AGAIN. YOU WERE CRYING!
PLEASE, TALK TO ME!
YOU DON'T *HAVE* TO LIVE BY YOUR FAMILY'S RULES...
YOU CAN LIVE HOWEVER YOU WANT!!
YOU DON'T HAVE TO GO IT ALONE! WE CAN--
SHUT UP!

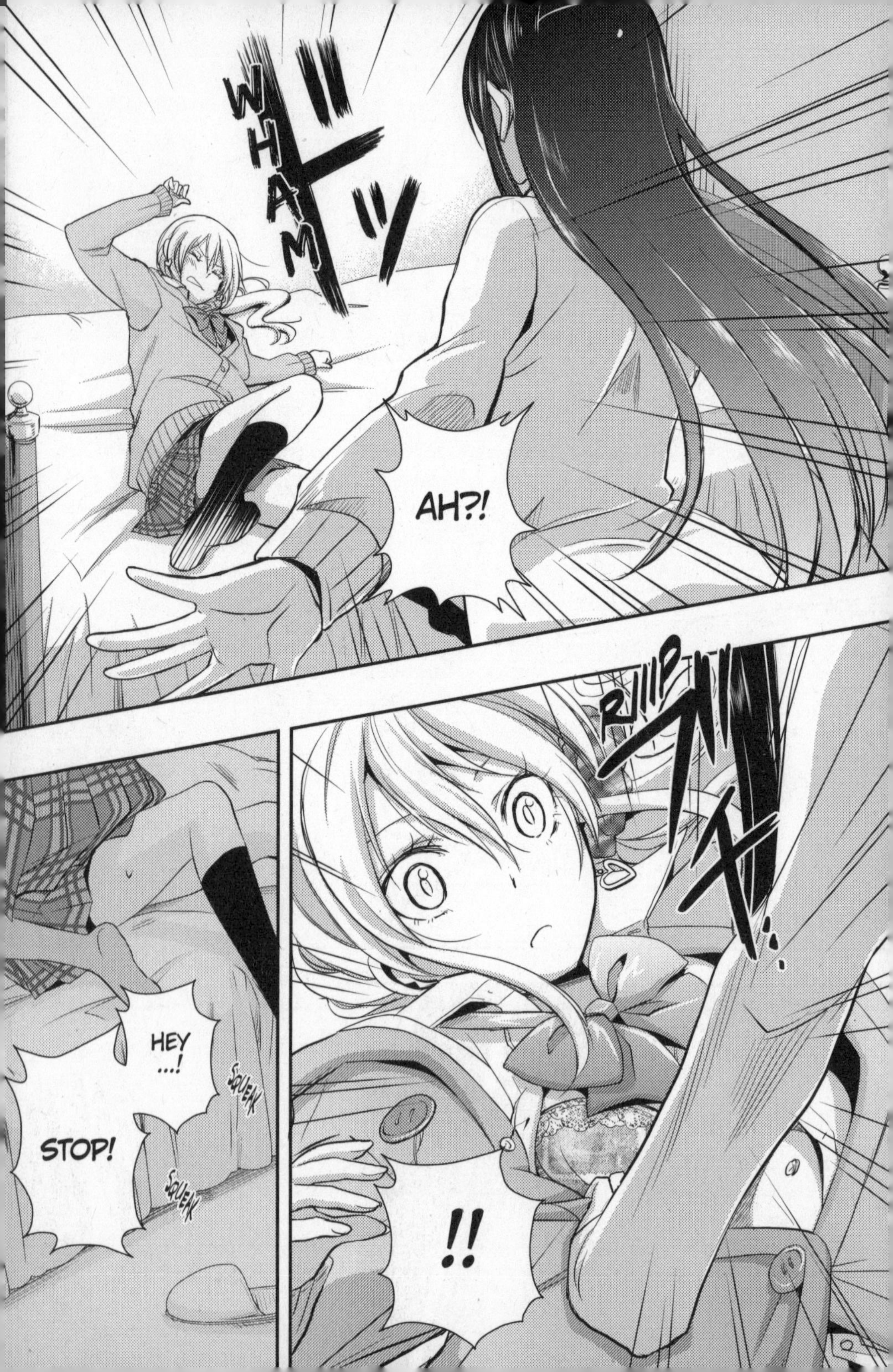
WHAM
AH?!
RIIIP
!!
HEY ...!
SQUEAK
STOP!
SQUEAK

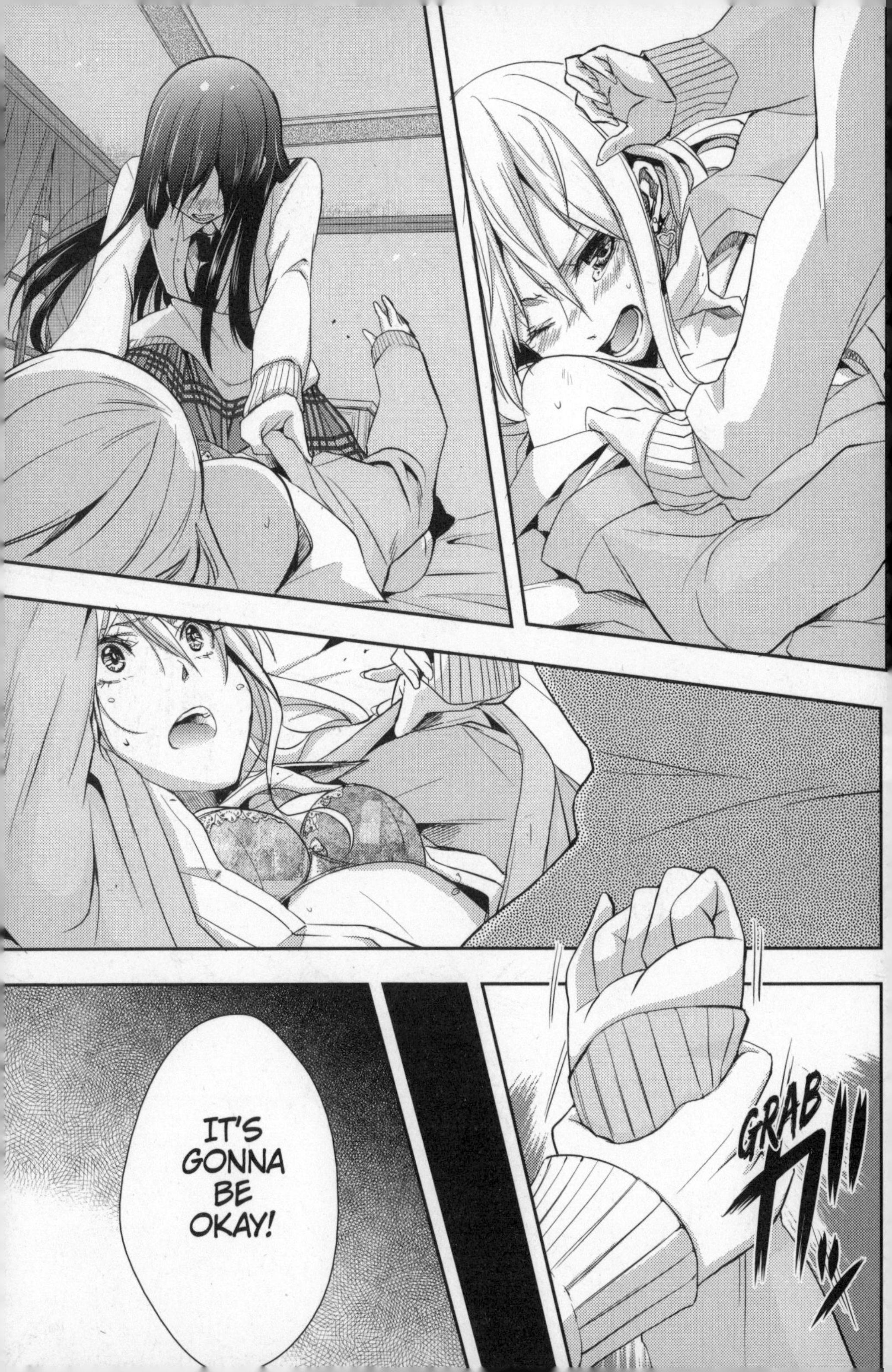
GRAB
IT'S GONNA BE OKAY!

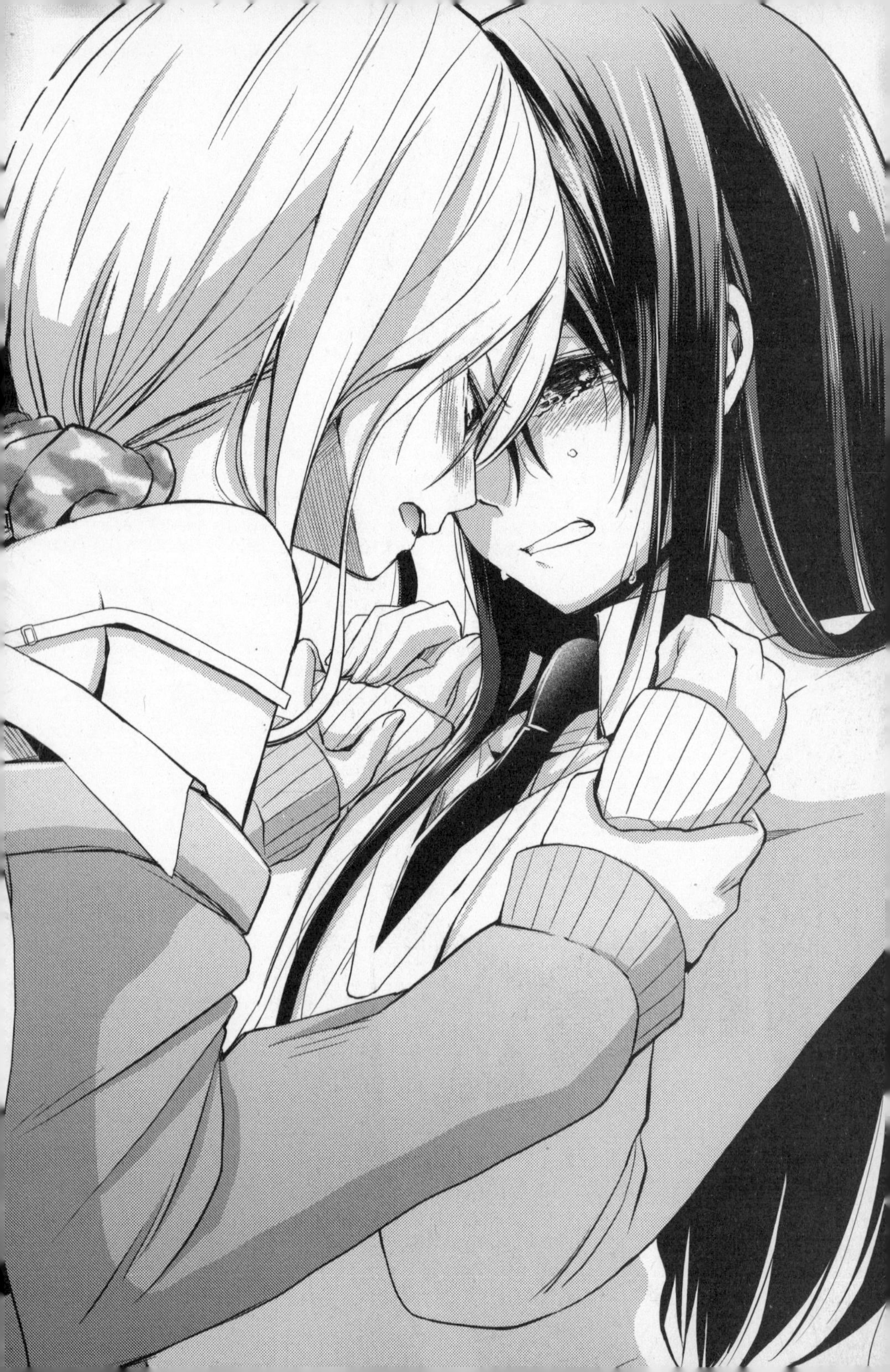

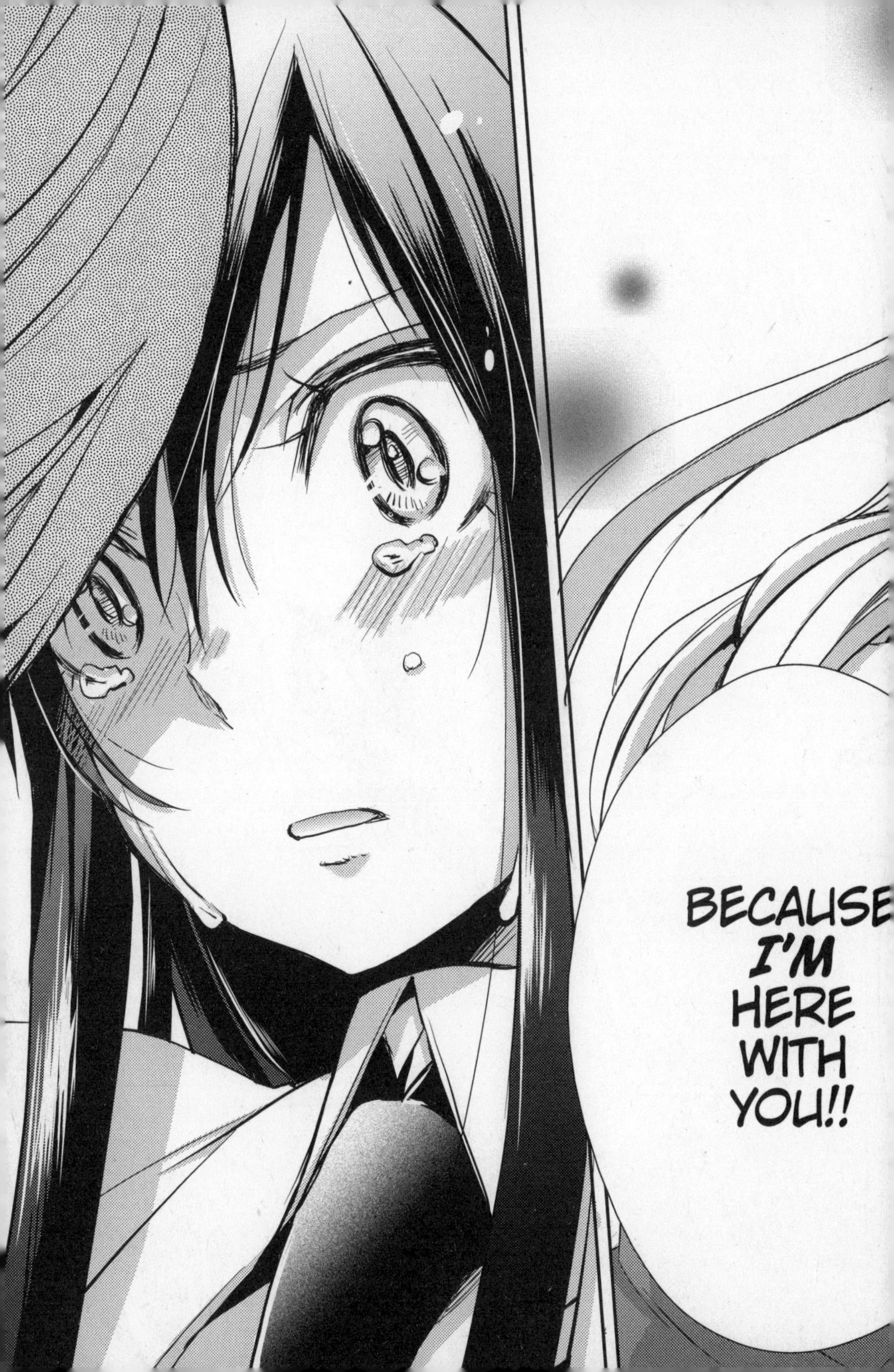
BECAUSE *I'M* HERE WITH YOU!!

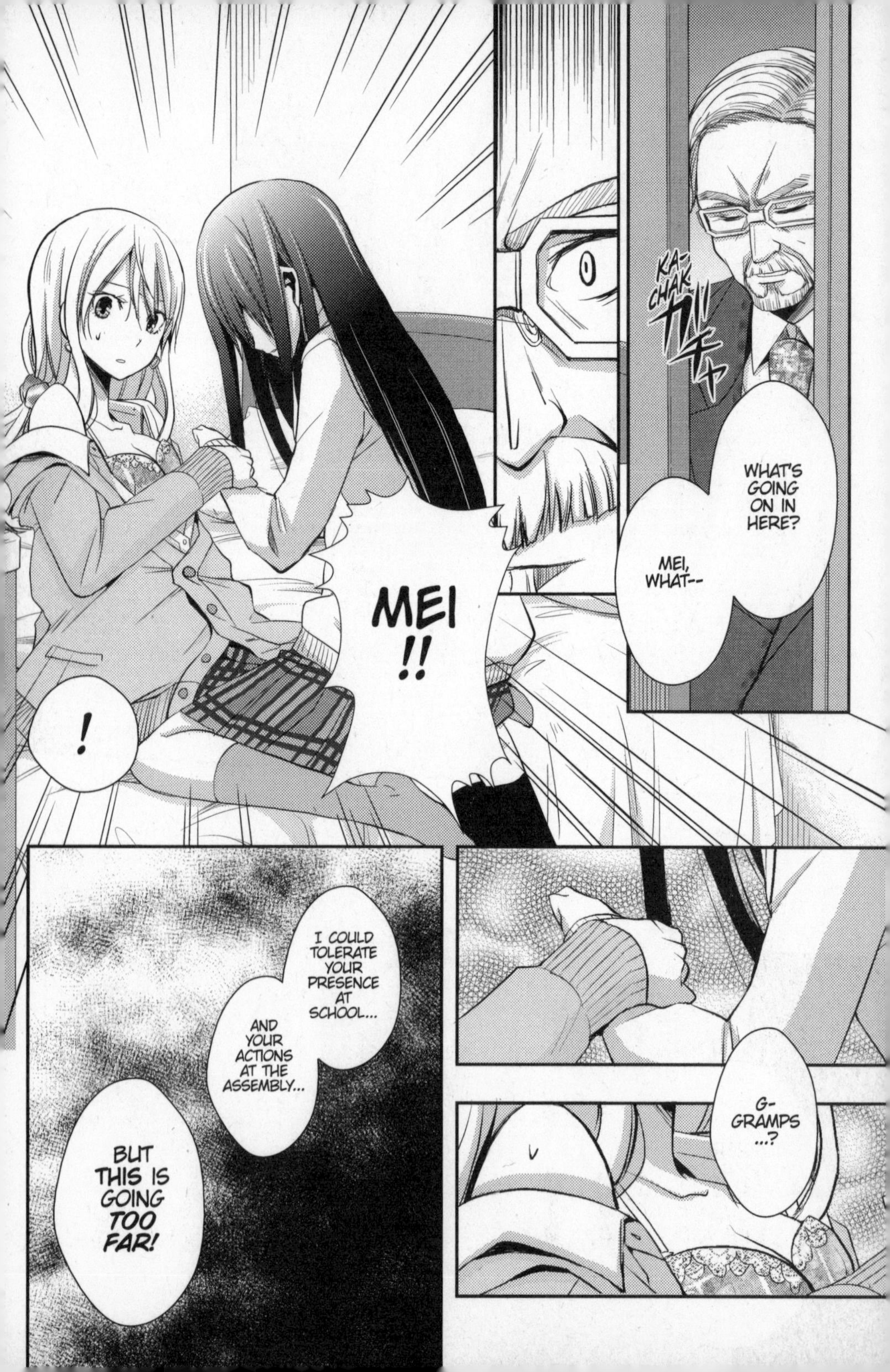
KA-CHAK
WHAT'S GOING ON IN HERE?
MEI, WHAT--
MEI !!
!
G-GRAMPS ...?
I COULD TOLERATE YOUR PRESENCE AT SCHOOL...
AND YOUR ACTIONS AT THE ASSEMBLY...
BUT THIS IS GOING TOO FAR!

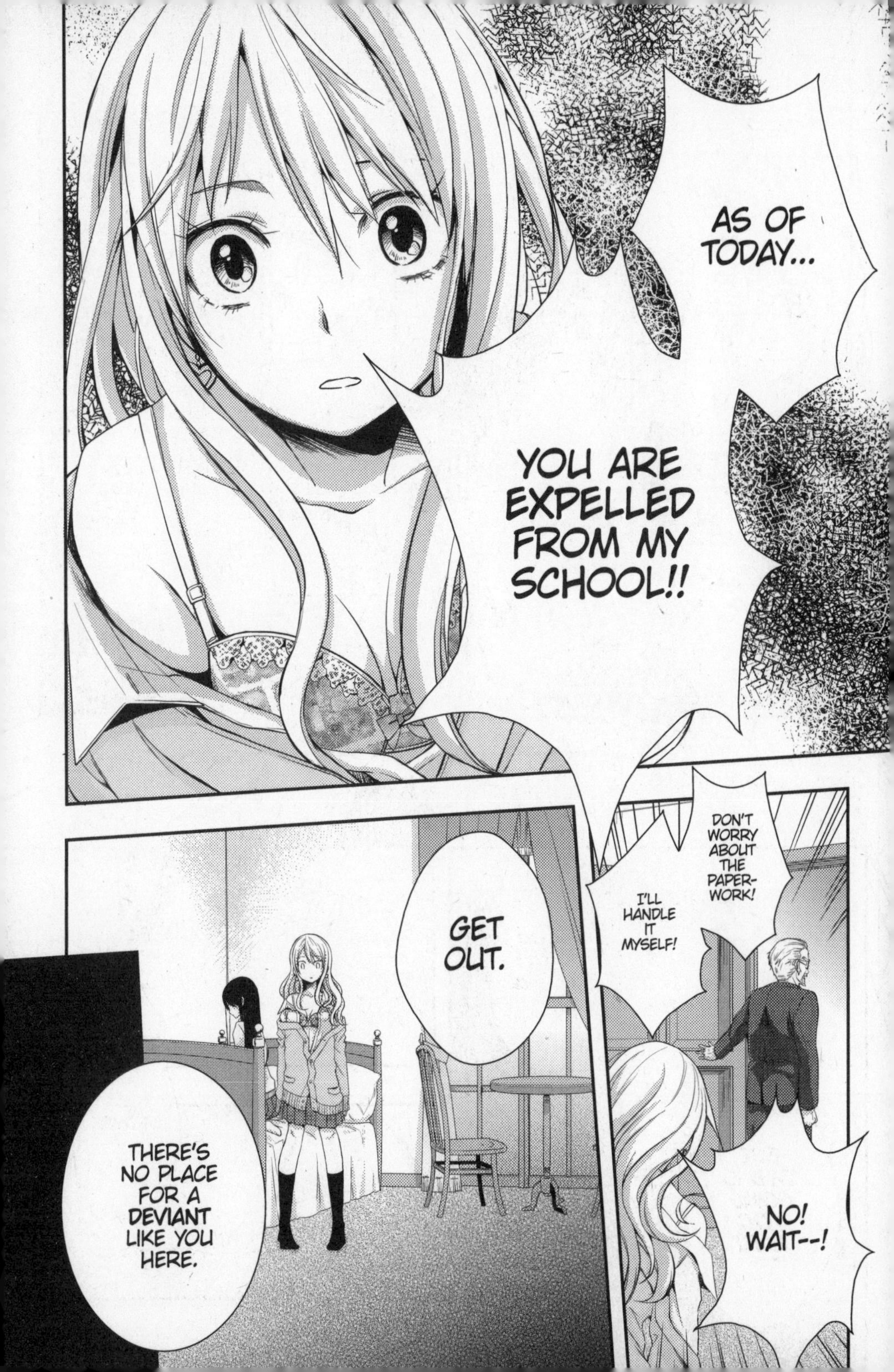
AS OF TODAY...
YOU ARE EXPELLED FROM MY SCHOOL!!
DON'T WORRY ABOUT THE PAPER-WORK!
I'LL HANDLE IT MYSELF!
NO! WAIT--!
GET OUT.
THERE'S NO PLACE FOR A DEVIANT LIKE YOU HERE.

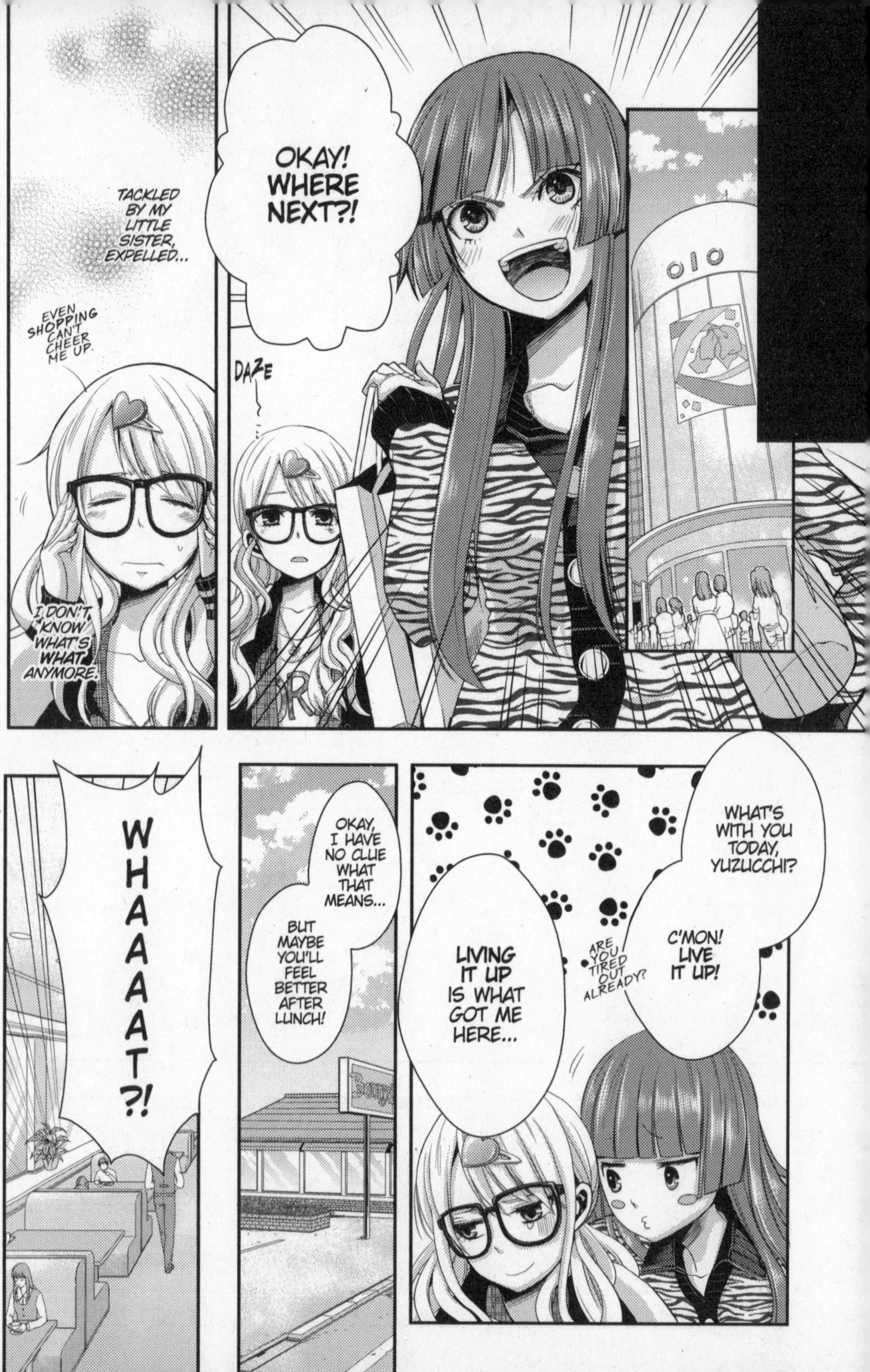
OKAY! WHERE NEXT?!
DAZE
TACKLED BY MY LITTLE SISTER, EXPELLED...
EVEN SHOPPING CAN'T CHEER ME UP.
I DON'T KNOW WHAT'S WHAT ANYMORE.
WHAT'S WITH YOU TODAY, YUZUCCHI?
C'MON! LIVE IT UP!
ARE YOU TIRED OUT ALREADY?
LIVING IT UP IS WHAT GOT ME HERE...
OKAY, I HAVE NO CLUE WHAT THAT MEANS...
BUT MAYBE YOU'LL FEEL BETTER AFTER LUNCH!
WHAAAAAT?!

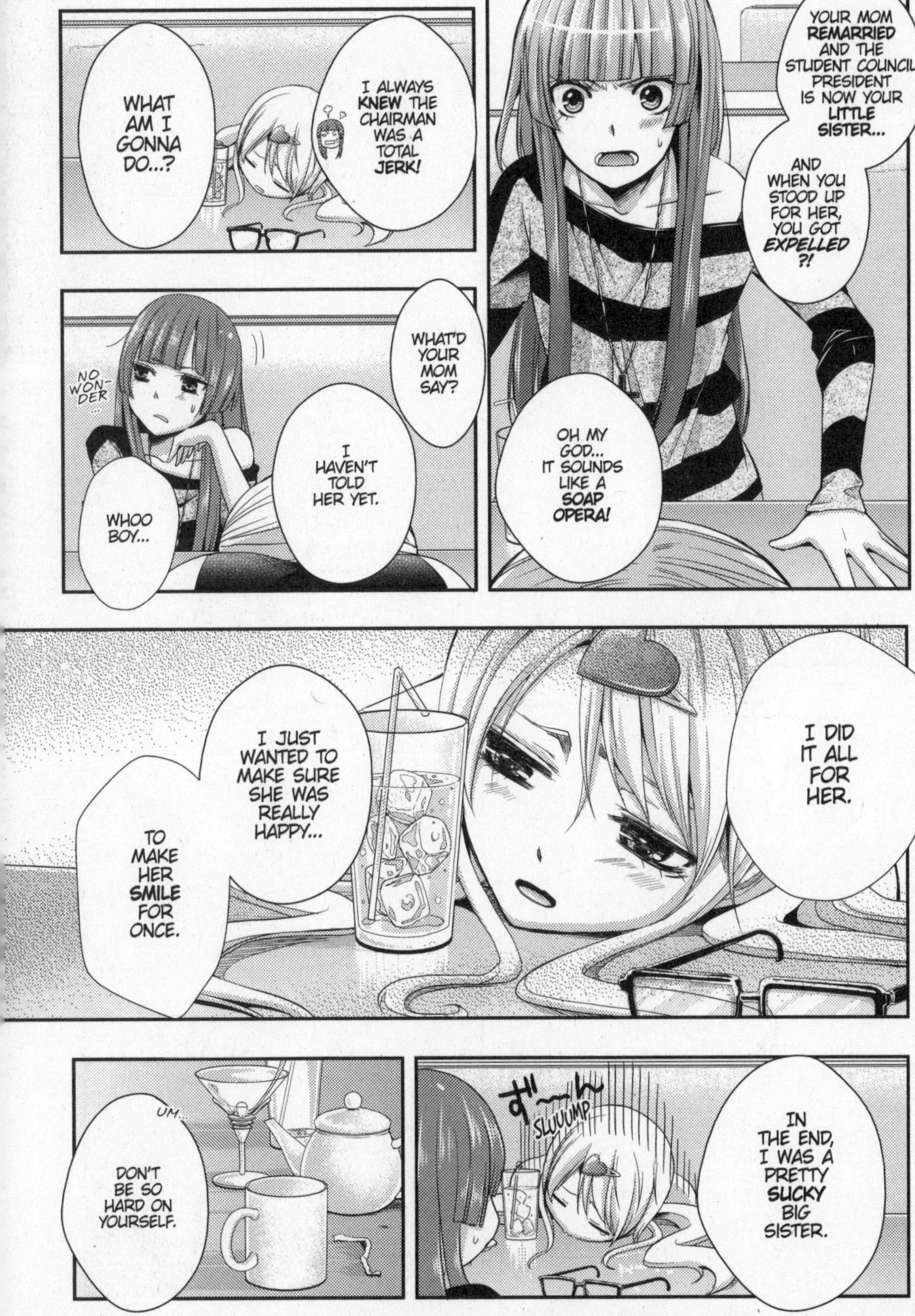
YOUR MOM REMARRIED AND THE STUDENT COUNCIL PRESIDENT IS NOW YOUR LITTLE SISTER...
AND WHEN YOU STOOD UP FOR HER, YOU GOT EXPELLED?!
OH MY GOD... IT SOUNDS LIKE A SOAP OPERA!
I ALWAYS KNEW THE CHAIRMAN WAS A TOTAL JERK!
WHAT AM I GONNA DO...?
WHAT'D YOUR MOM SAY?
I HAVEN'T TOLD HER YET.
NO WONDER...
WHOO BOY...
I DID IT ALL FOR HER.
I JUST WANTED TO MAKE SURE SHE WAS REALLY HAPPY...
TO MAKE HER SMILE FOR ONCE.
ず〜〜ん
SLUUUMP
IN THE END, I WAS A PRETTY SUCKY BIG SISTER.
UM...
DON'T BE SO HARD ON YOURSELF.

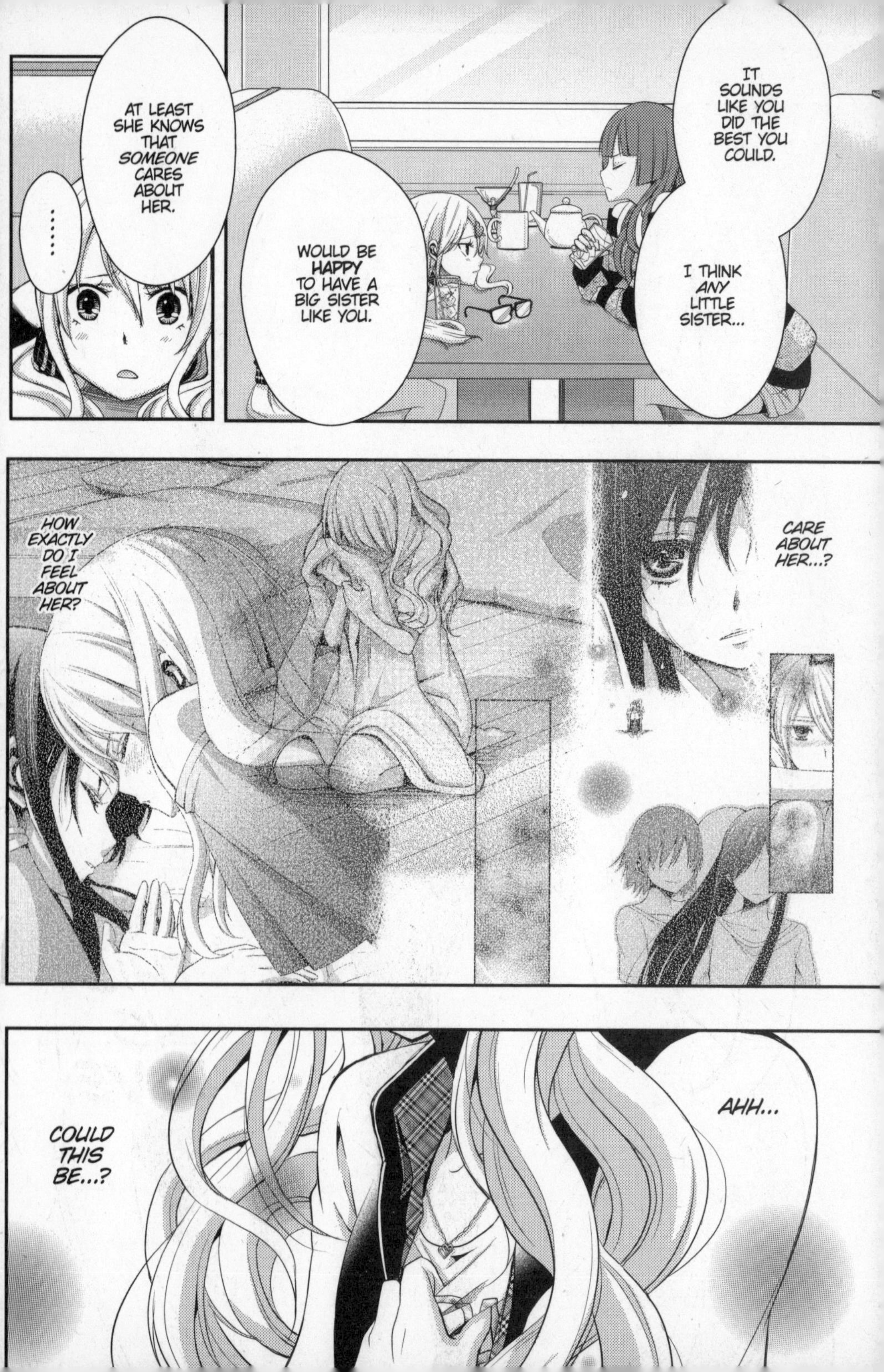
IT SOUNDS LIKE YOU DID THE BEST YOU COULD.
I THINK ANY LITTLE SISTER...
WOULD BE HAPPY TO HAVE A BIG SISTER LIKE YOU.
AT LEAST SHE KNOWS THAT SOMEONE CARES ABOUT HER.
......
CARE ABOUT HER...?
HOW EXACTLY DO I FEEL ABOUT HER?
AHH...
COULD THIS BE...?

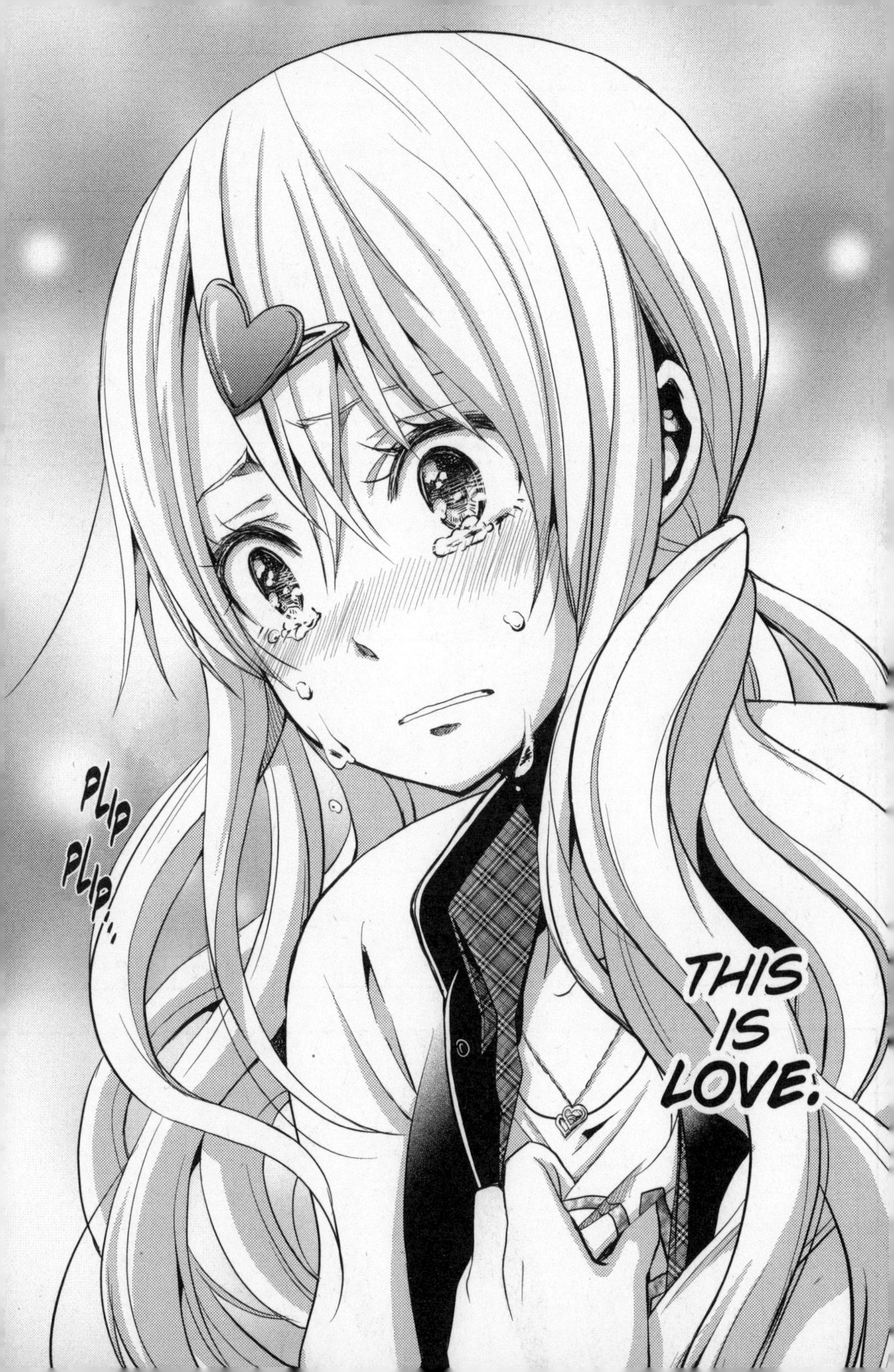

THIS IS LOVE.
PLIP PLIP...

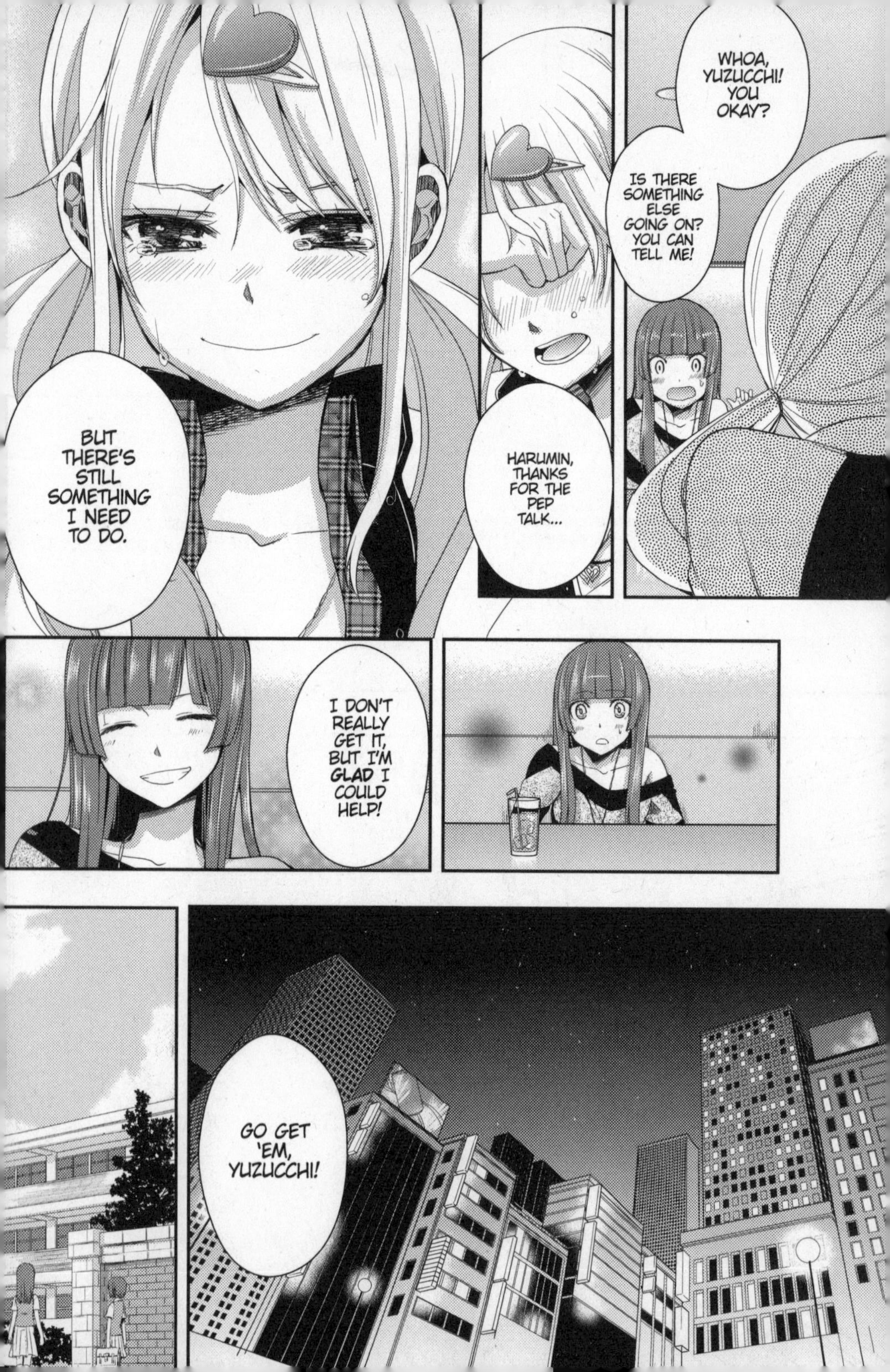
WHOA, YUZUCCHI! YOU OKAY?
IS THERE SOMETHING ELSE GOING ON? YOU CAN TELL ME!
HARUMIN, THANKS FOR THE PEP TALK...
BUT THERE'S STILL SOMETHING I NEED TO DO.
I DON'T REALLY GET IT, BUT I'M **GLAD** I COULD HELP!
GO GET 'EM, YUZUCCHI!

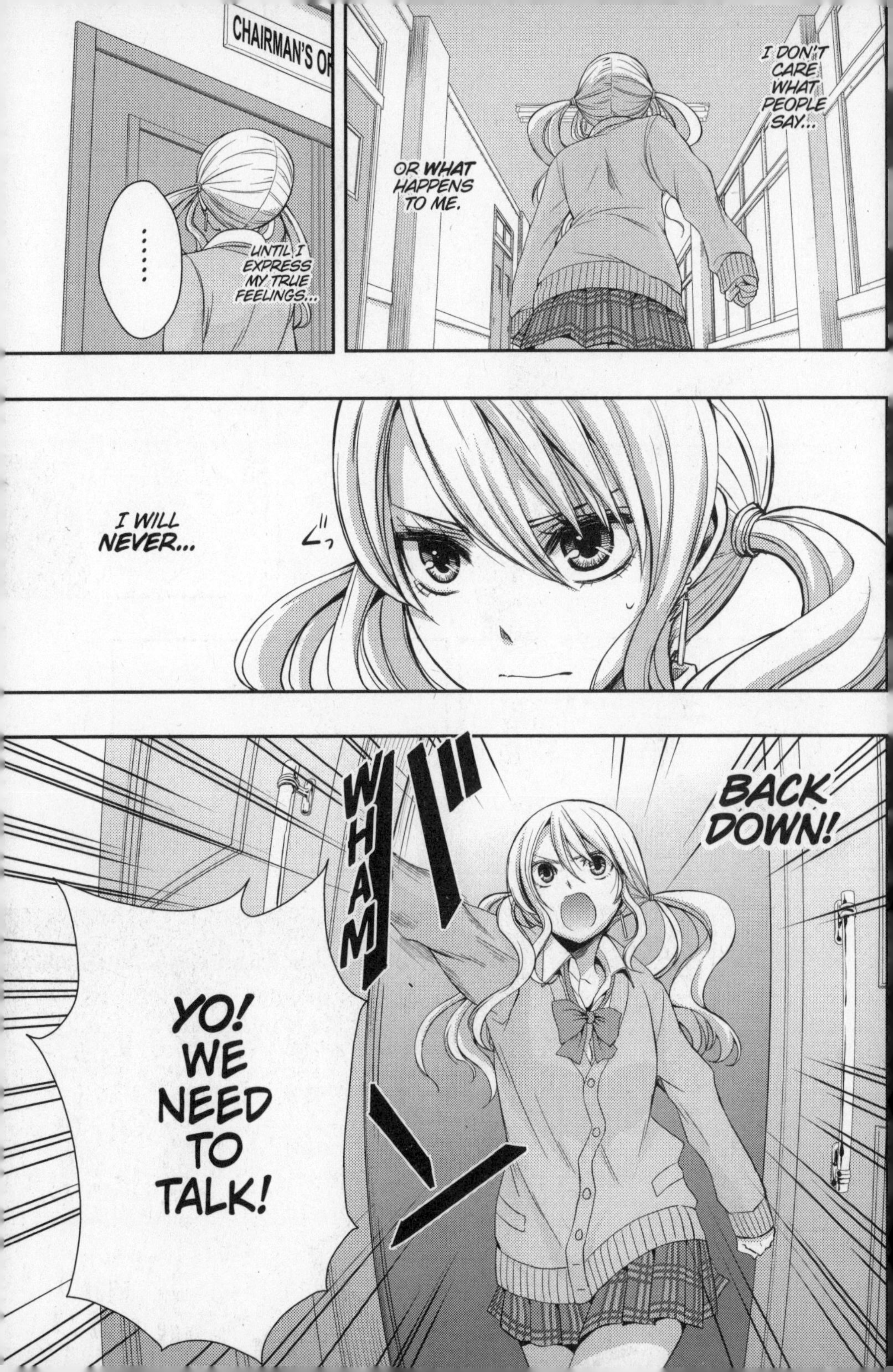
I DON'T CARE WHAT PEOPLE SAY...
OR WHAT HAPPENS TO ME.
CHAIRMAN'S OF
UNTIL I EXPRESS MY TRUE FEELINGS...
......
I WILL NEVER...
BACK DOWN!
WHAM
YO! WE NEED TO TALK!

COUGH!
COUGH!

!

Room 306

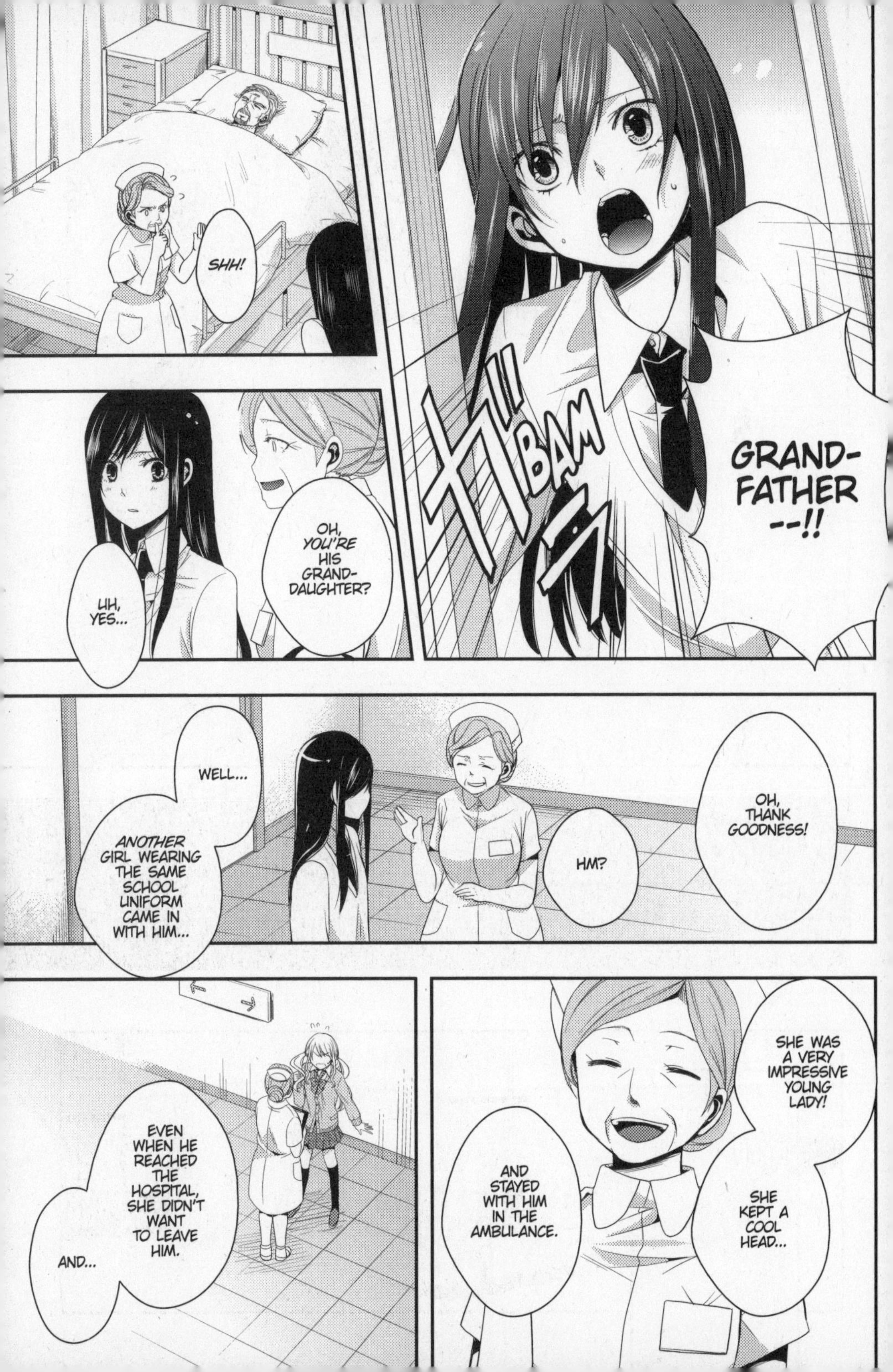
BAM
GRAND-FATHER --!!
SHH!
OH, YOU'RE HIS GRAND-DAUGHTER?
UH, YES...
OH, THANK GOODNESS!
HM?
WELL...
ANOTHER GIRL WEARING THE SAME SCHOOL UNIFORM CAME IN WITH HIM...
SHE WAS A VERY IMPRESSIVE YOUNG LADY!
SHE KEPT A COOL HEAD...
AND STAYED WITH HIM IN THE AMBULANCE.
EVEN WHEN HE REACHED THE HOSPITAL, SHE DIDN'T WANT TO LEAVE HIM.
AND...

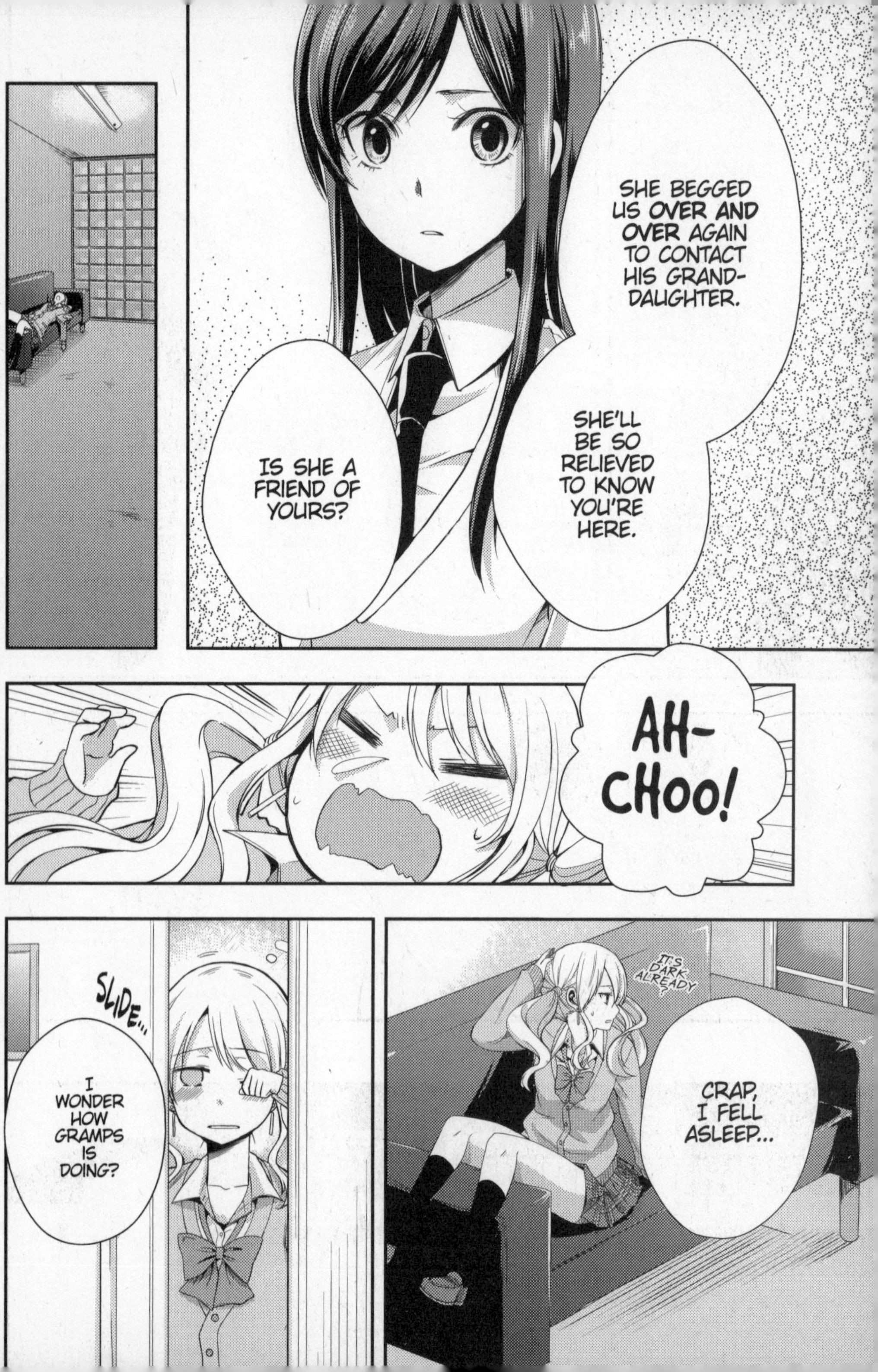
SHE BEGGED US OVER AND OVER AGAIN TO CONTACT HIS GRAND-DAUGHTER.
SHE'LL BE SO RELIEVED TO KNOW YOU'RE HERE.
IS SHE A FRIEND OF YOURS?
AH-CHOO!
IT'S DARK ALREADY?
CRAP, I FELL ASLEEP...
SLIDE...
I WONDER HOW GRAMPS IS DOING?

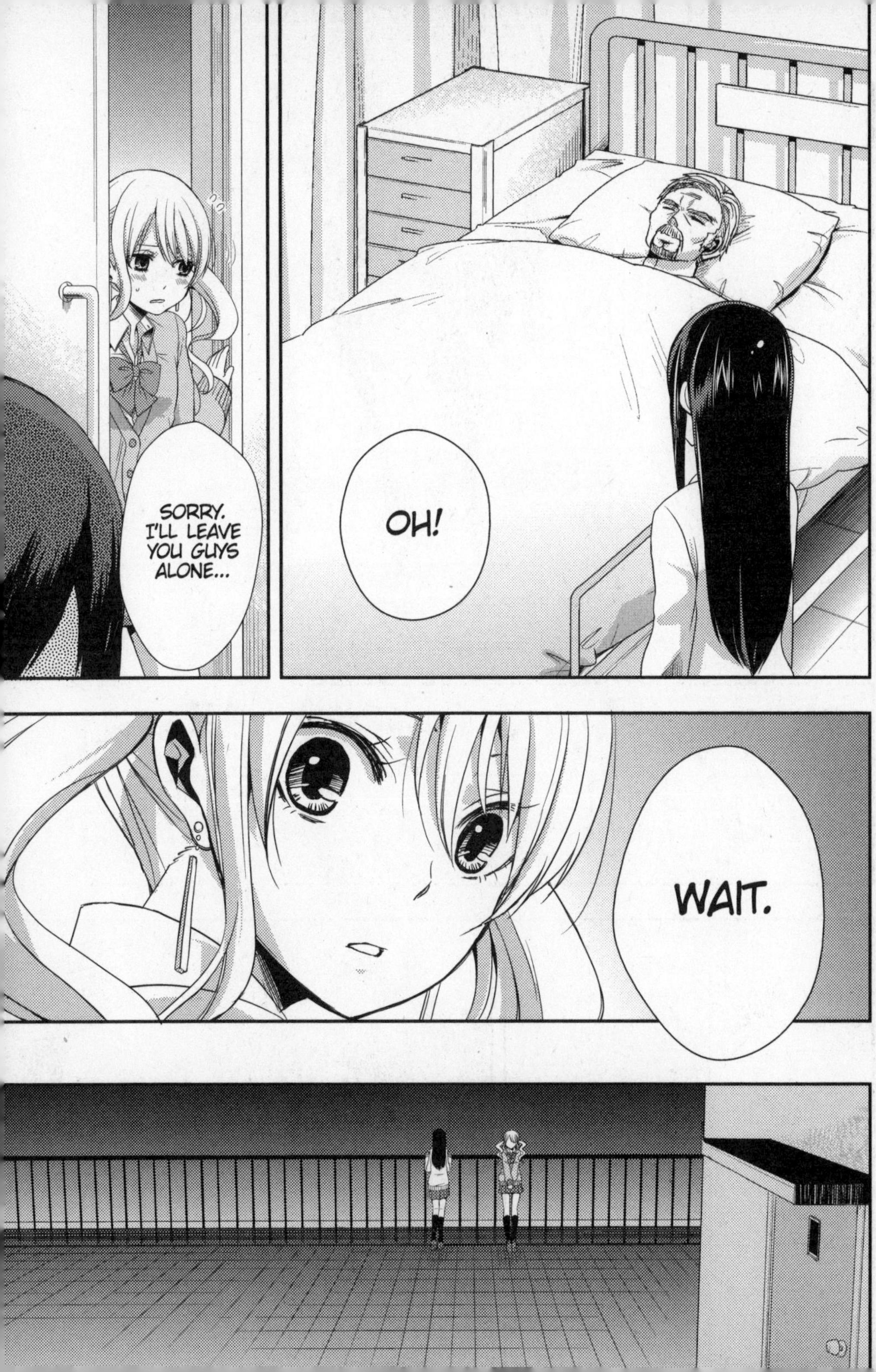
OH!
SORRY. I'LL LEAVE YOU GUYS ALONE...
WAIT.

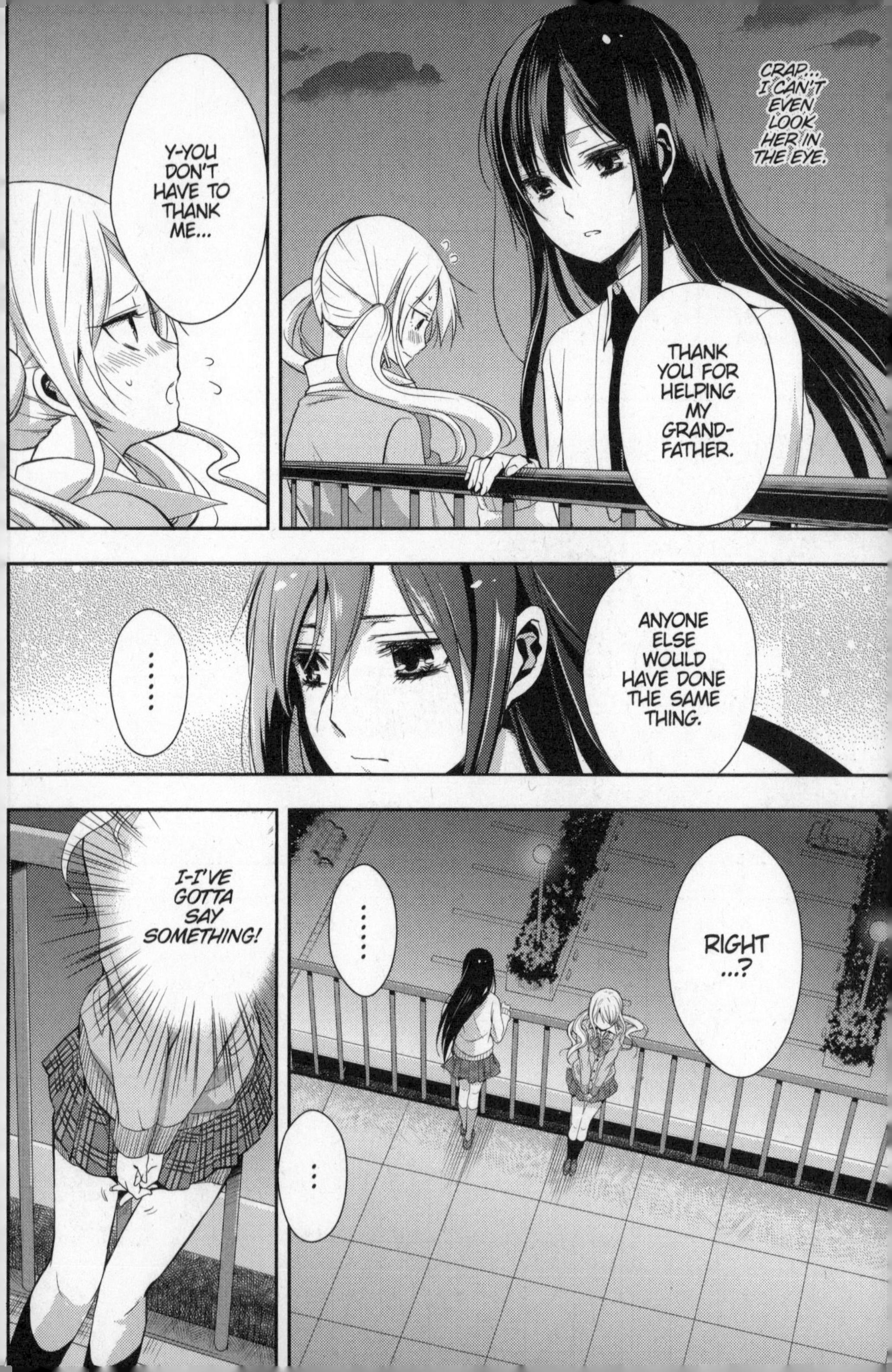
CRAP... I CAN'T EVEN LOOK HER IN THE EYE.
THANK YOU FOR HELPING MY GRAND-FATHER.
Y-YOU DON'T HAVE TO THANK ME...
ANYONE ELSE WOULD HAVE DONE THE SAME THING.
......
RIGHT ...?
......
...
I-I'VE GOTTA SAY SOMETHING!

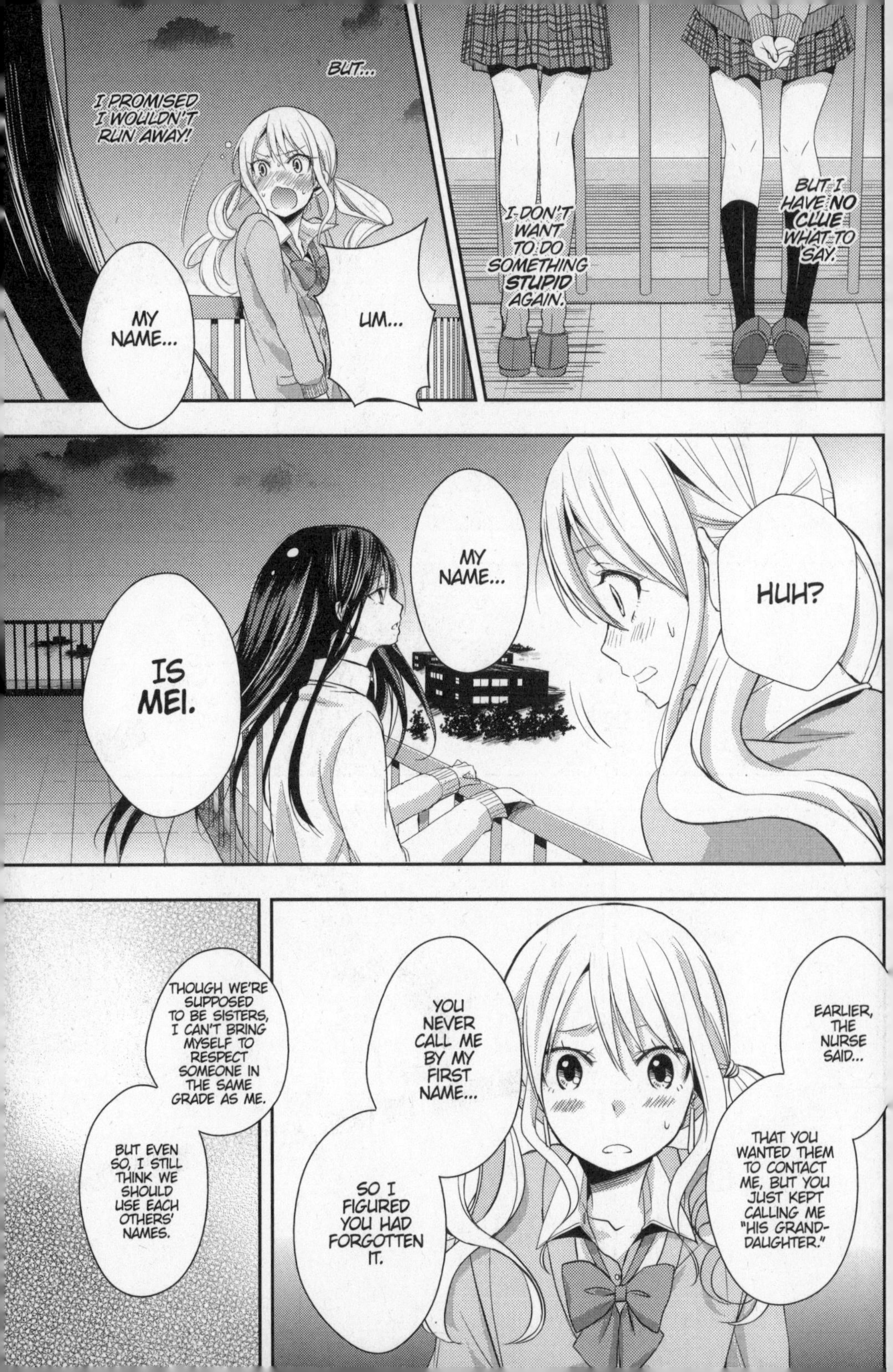
BUT I HAVE NO CLUE WHAT TO SAY.
I DON'T WANT TO DO SOMETHING STUPID AGAIN.
BUT...
I PROMISED I WOULDN'T RUN AWAY!
UM...
MY NAME...
HUH?
MY NAME...
IS MEI.
EARLIER, THE NURSE SAID...
THAT YOU WANTED THEM TO CONTACT ME, BUT YOU JUST KEPT CALLING ME "HIS GRAND-DAUGHTER."
YOU NEVER CALL ME BY MY FIRST NAME...
SO I FIGURED YOU HAD FORGOTTEN IT.
THOUGH WE'RE SUPPOSED TO BE SISTERS, I CAN'T BRING MYSELF TO RESPECT SOMEONE IN THE SAME GRADE AS ME.
BUT EVEN SO, I STILL THINK WE SHOULD USE EACH OTHERS' NAMES.

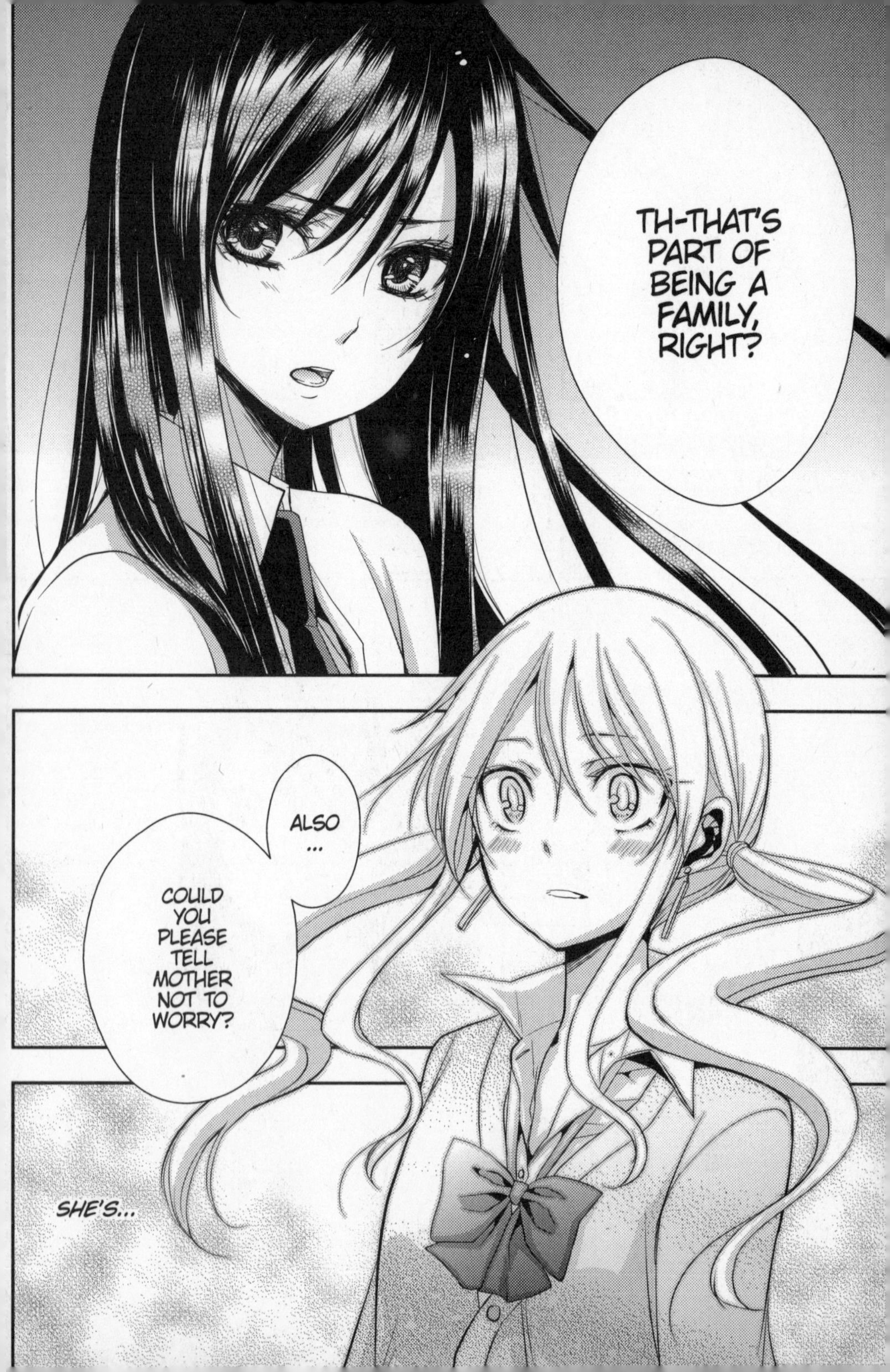
TH-THAT'S PART OF BEING A FAMILY, RIGHT?
ALSO ...
COULD YOU PLEASE TELL MOTHER NOT TO WORRY?
SHE'S...

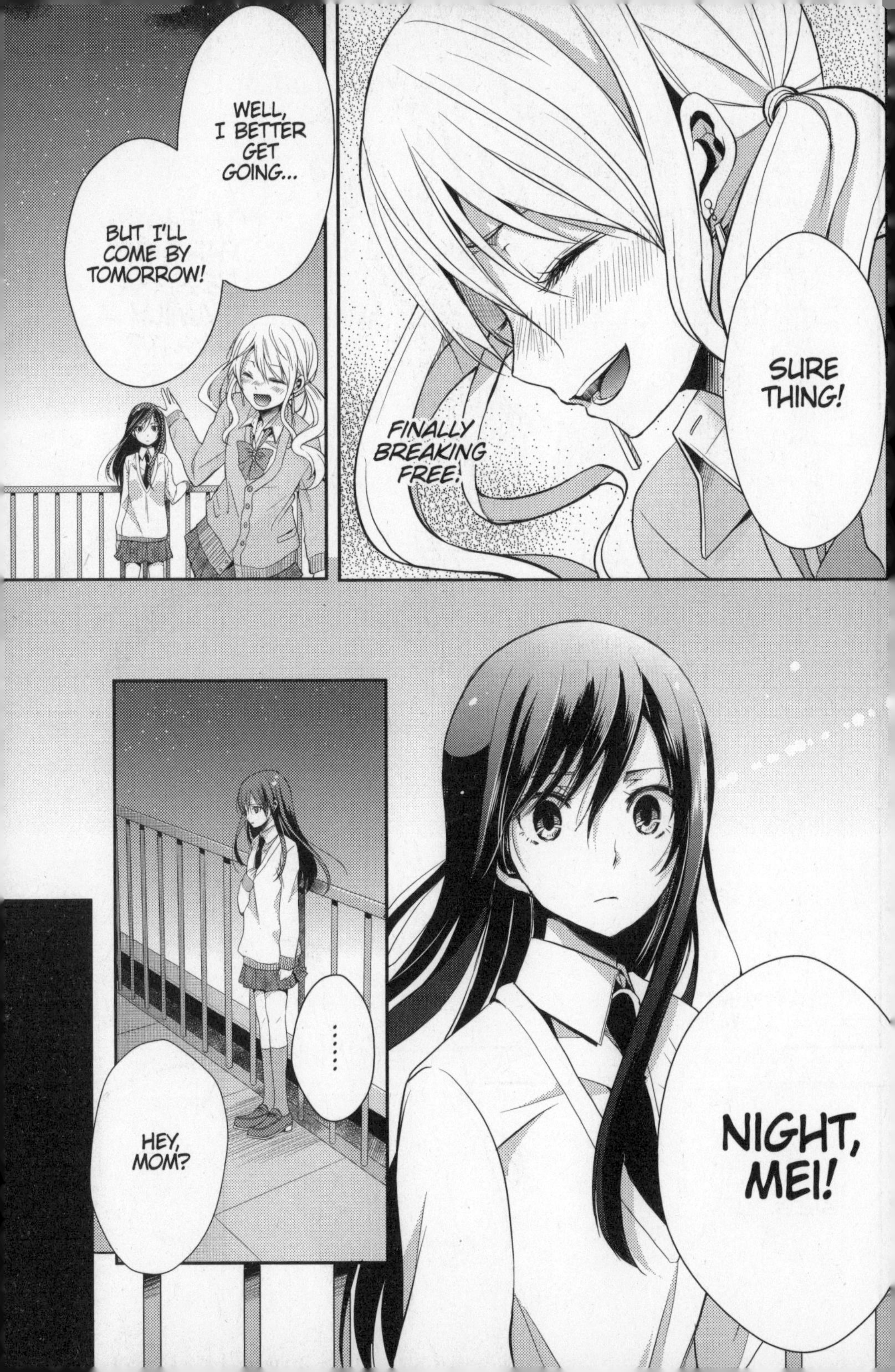
SURE THING!
FINALLY BREAKING FREE!
WELL, I BETTER GET GOING...
BUT I'LL COME BY TOMORROW!
NIGHT, MEI!
......
HEY, MOM?

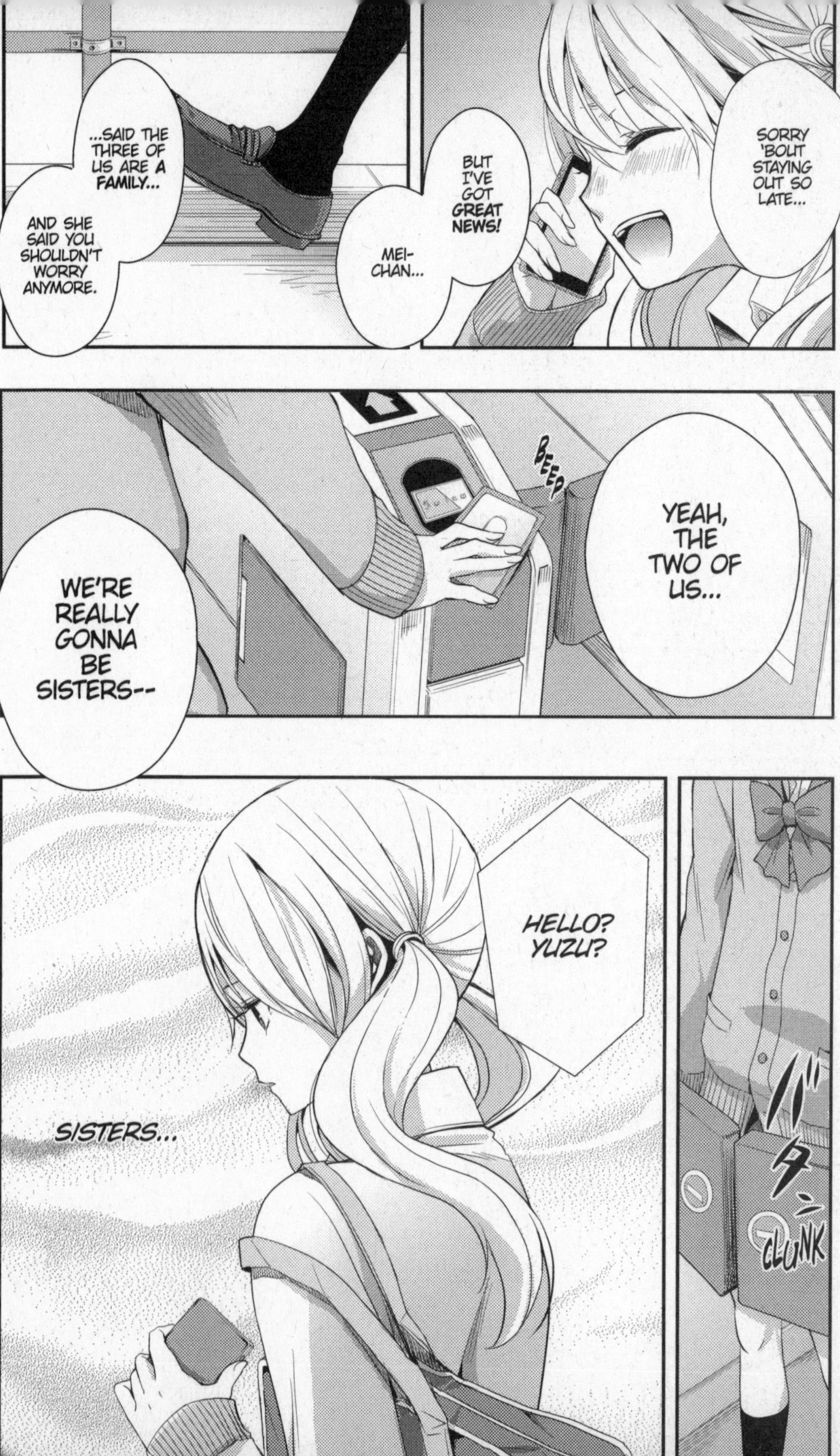
SORRY 'BOUT STAYING OUT SO LATE...
BUT I'VE GOT GREAT NEWS!
MEI-CHAN...
...SAID THE THREE OF US ARE A FAMILY...
AND SHE SAID YOU SHOULDN'T WORRY ANYMORE.
BEEP
YEAH, THE TWO OF US...
WE'RE REALLY GONNA BE SISTERS--
CLUNK
HELLO? YUZU?
SISTERS...

citrus
【シトラス】

SECRET LOVE AFFAIR WITH SISTER

citrus

SABUROUTA PRESENTS SECRET LOVE AFFAIR WITH SISTER

1

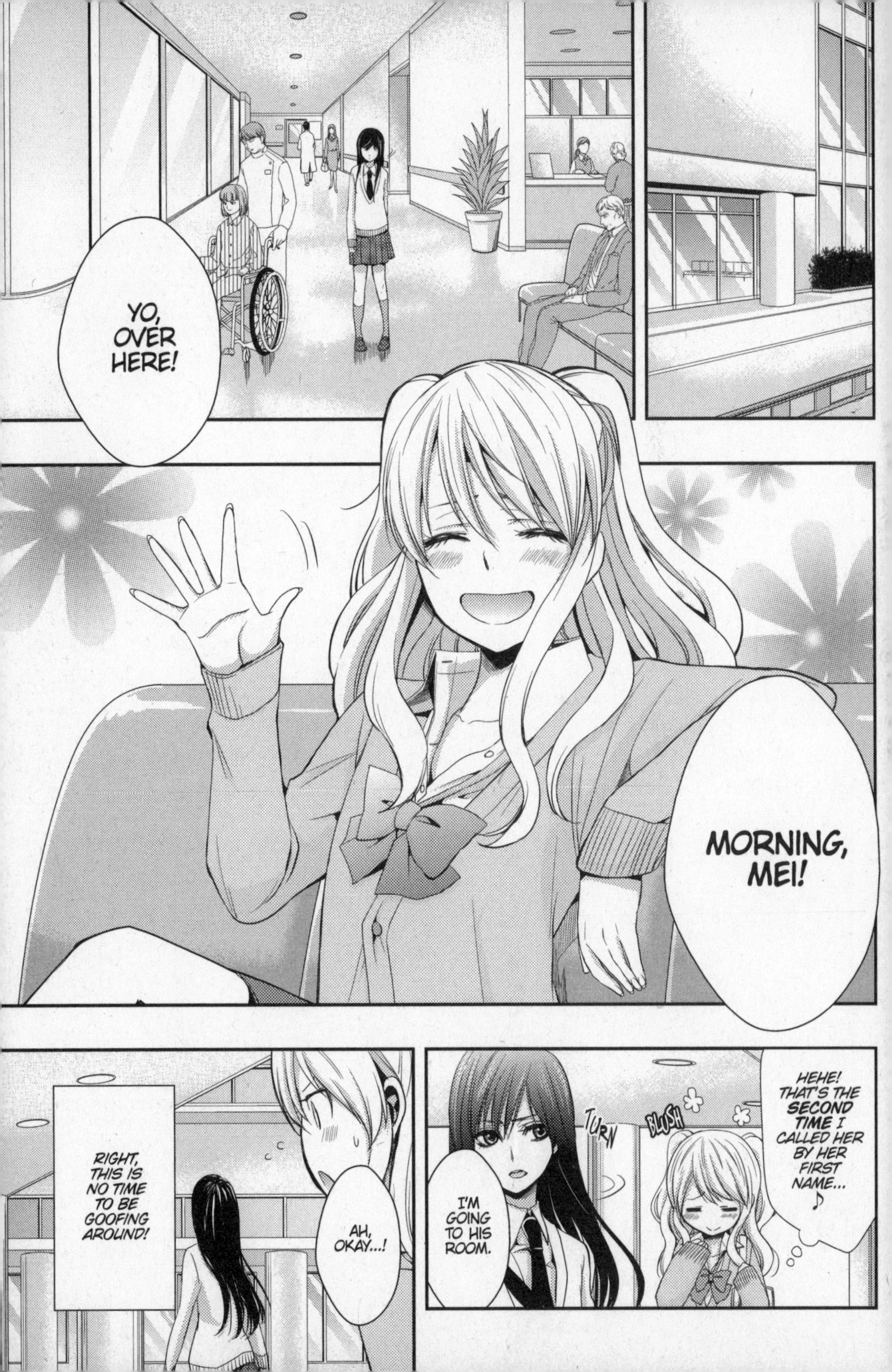
YO, OVER HERE!
MORNING, MEI!
HEHE! THAT'S THE SECOND TIME I CALLED HER BY HER FIRST NAME... ♪
BLUSH
TURN
I'M GOING TO HIS ROOM.
AH, OKAY...!
RIGHT, THIS IS NO TIME TO BE GOOFING AROUND!

4.sisterly love?

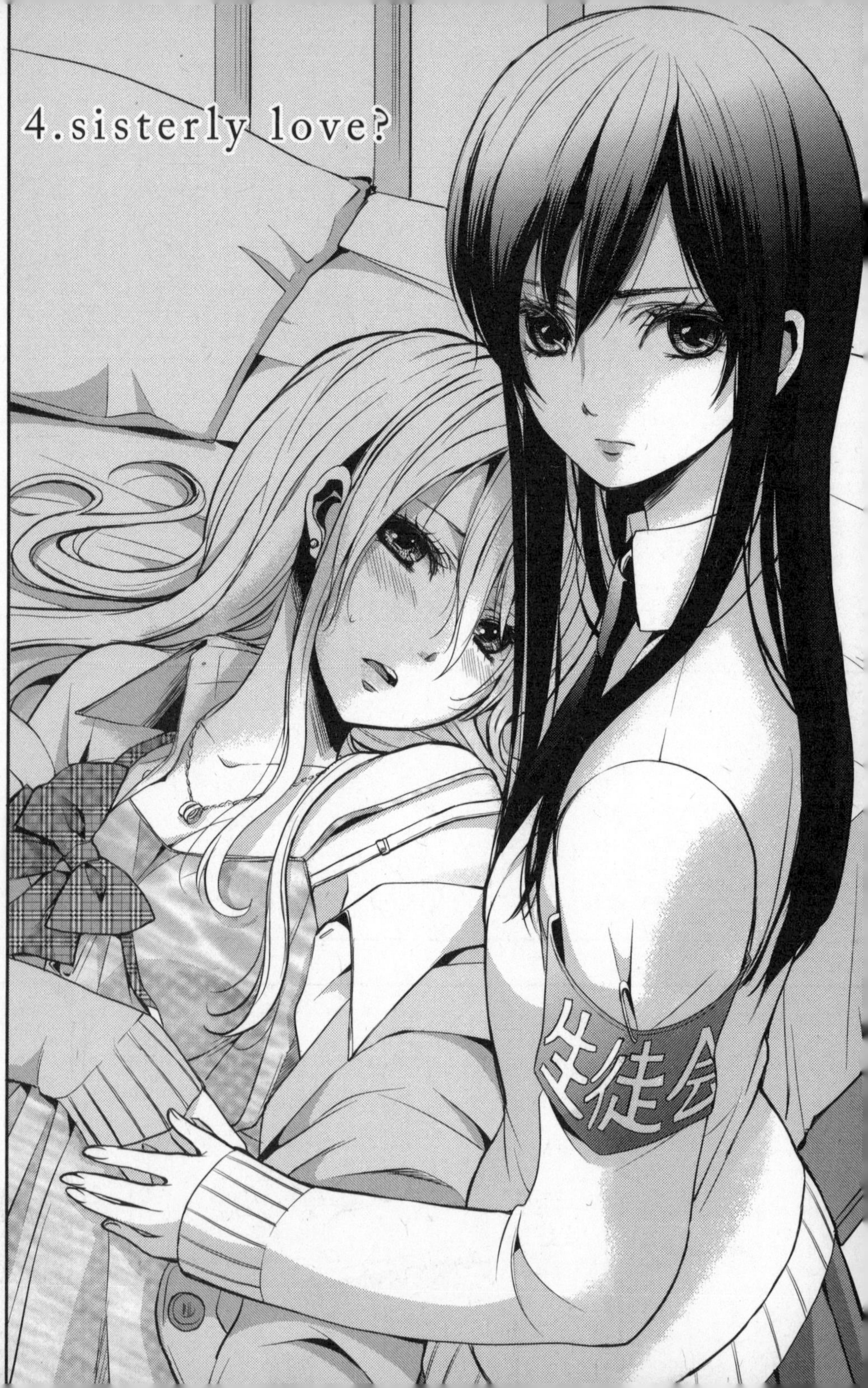
生徒会

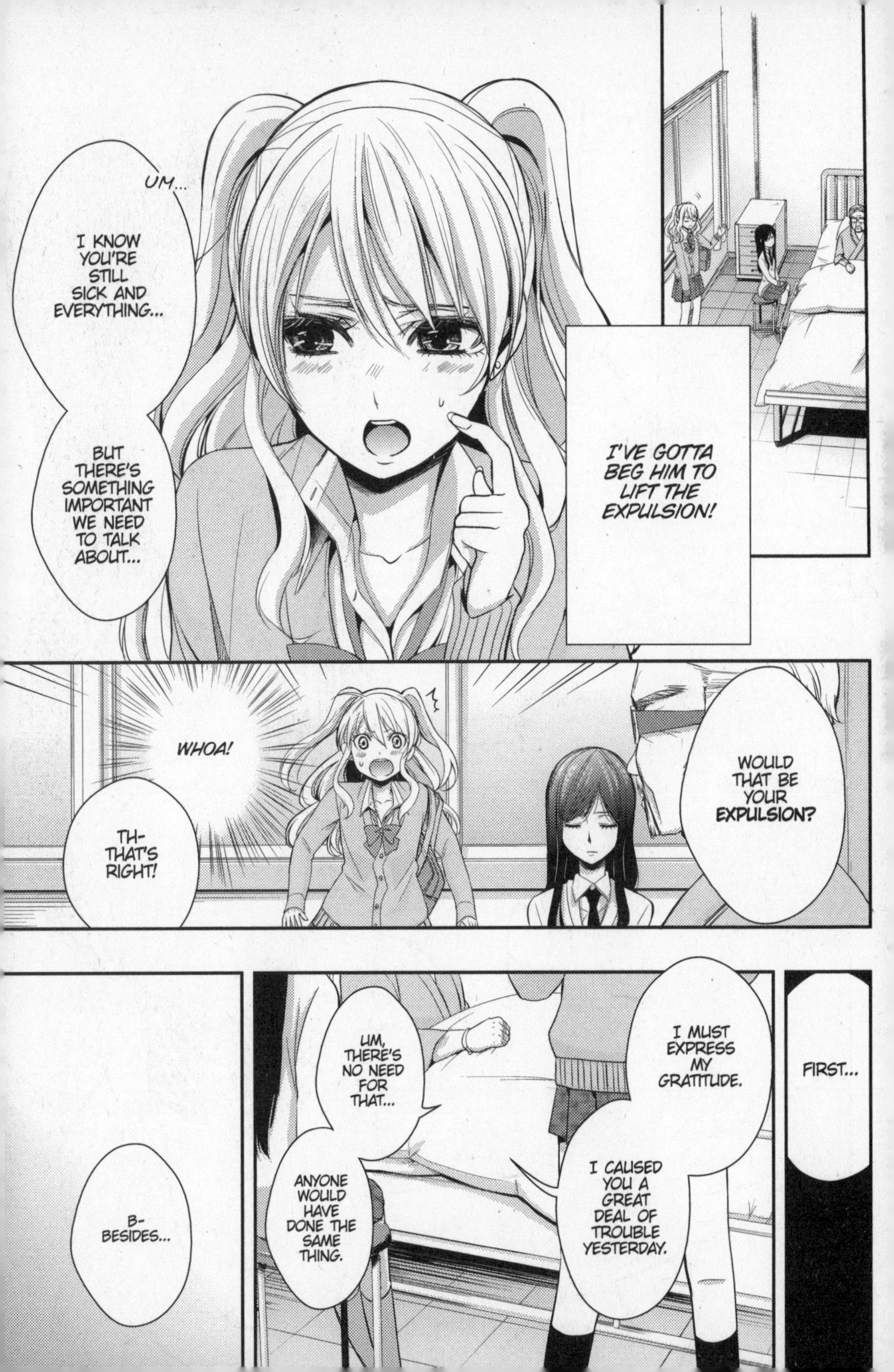
I'VE GOTTA BEG HIM TO LIFT THE EXPULSION!
UM...
I KNOW YOU'RE STILL SICK AND EVERYTHING...
BUT THERE'S SOMETHING IMPORTANT WE NEED TO TALK ABOUT...
WOULD THAT BE YOUR EXPULSION?
WHOA!
TH-THAT'S RIGHT!
FIRST...
I MUST EXPRESS MY GRATITUDE.
I CAUSED YOU A GREAT DEAL OF TROUBLE YESTERDAY.
UM, THERE'S NO NEED FOR THAT...
ANYONE WOULD HAVE DONE THE SAME THING.
B-BESIDES...

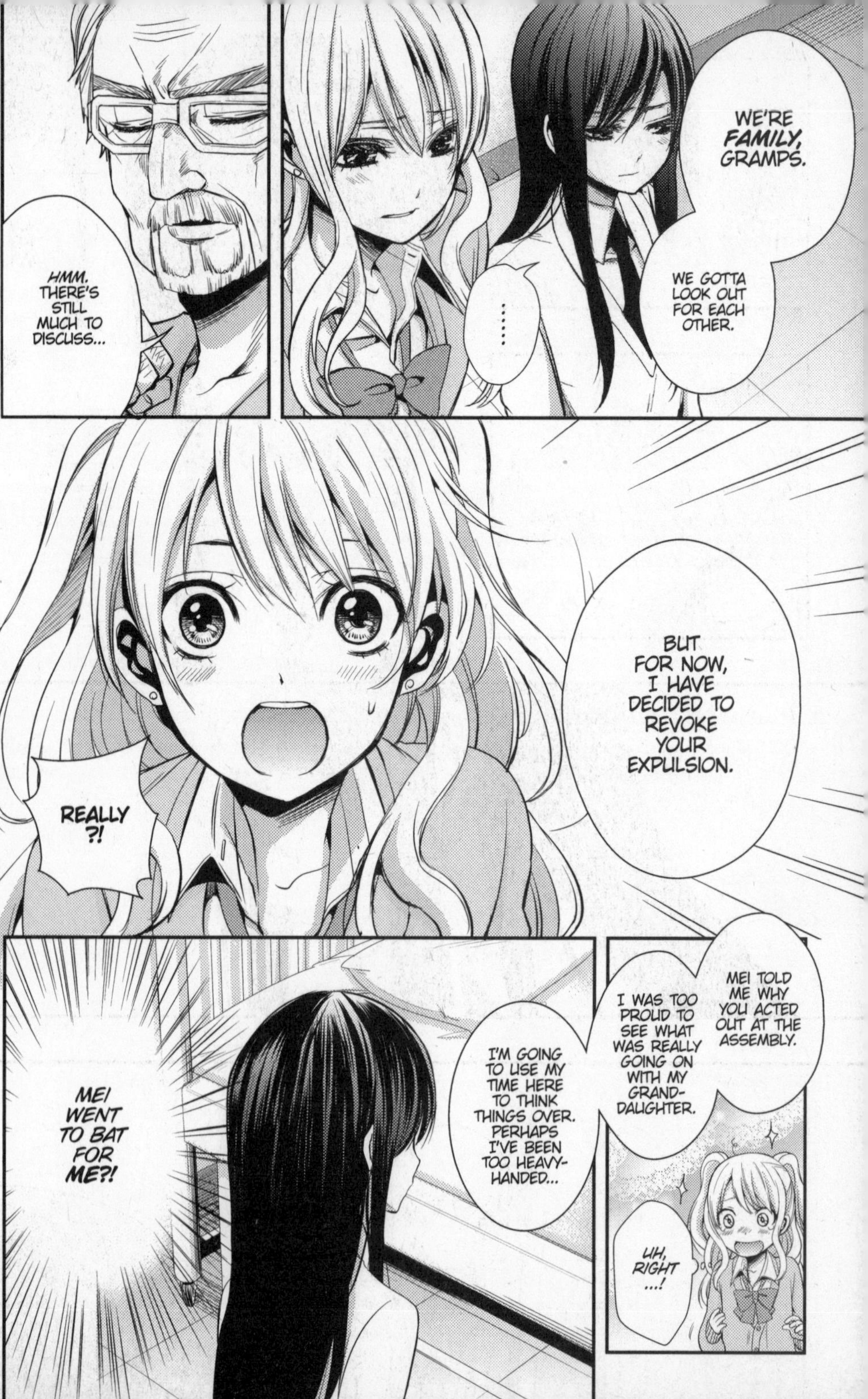
WE'RE *FAMILY,* GRAMPS.
WE GOTTA LOOK OUT FOR EACH OTHER.
……
HMM. THERE'S STILL MUCH TO DISCUSS...
BUT FOR NOW, I HAVE DECIDED TO REVOKE YOUR EXPULSION.
REALLY?!
MEI TOLD ME WHY YOU ACTED OUT AT THE ASSEMBLY.
I WAS TOO PROUD TO SEE WHAT WAS REALLY GOING ON WITH MY GRAND-DAUGHTER.
UH, RIGHT ...!
I'M GOING TO USE MY TIME HERE TO THINK THINGS OVER. PERHAPS I'VE BEEN TOO HEAVY-HANDED...
MEI WENT TO BAT FOR ME?!

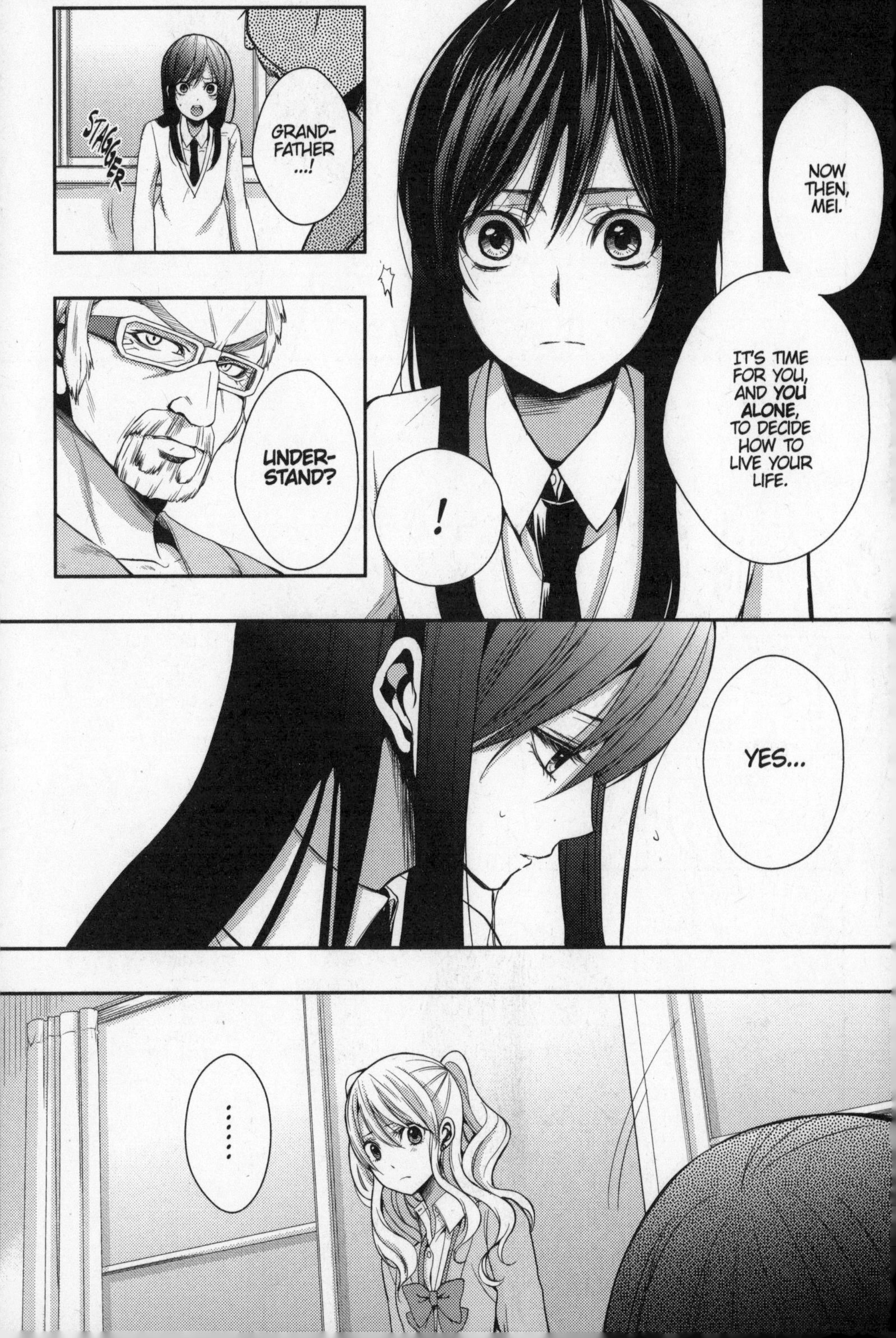
NOW THEN, MEI.
IT'S TIME FOR YOU, AND YOU ALONE, TO DECIDE HOW TO LIVE YOUR LIFE.
!
STAGGER
GRAND-FATHER ...!
UNDER-STAND?
YES...
......

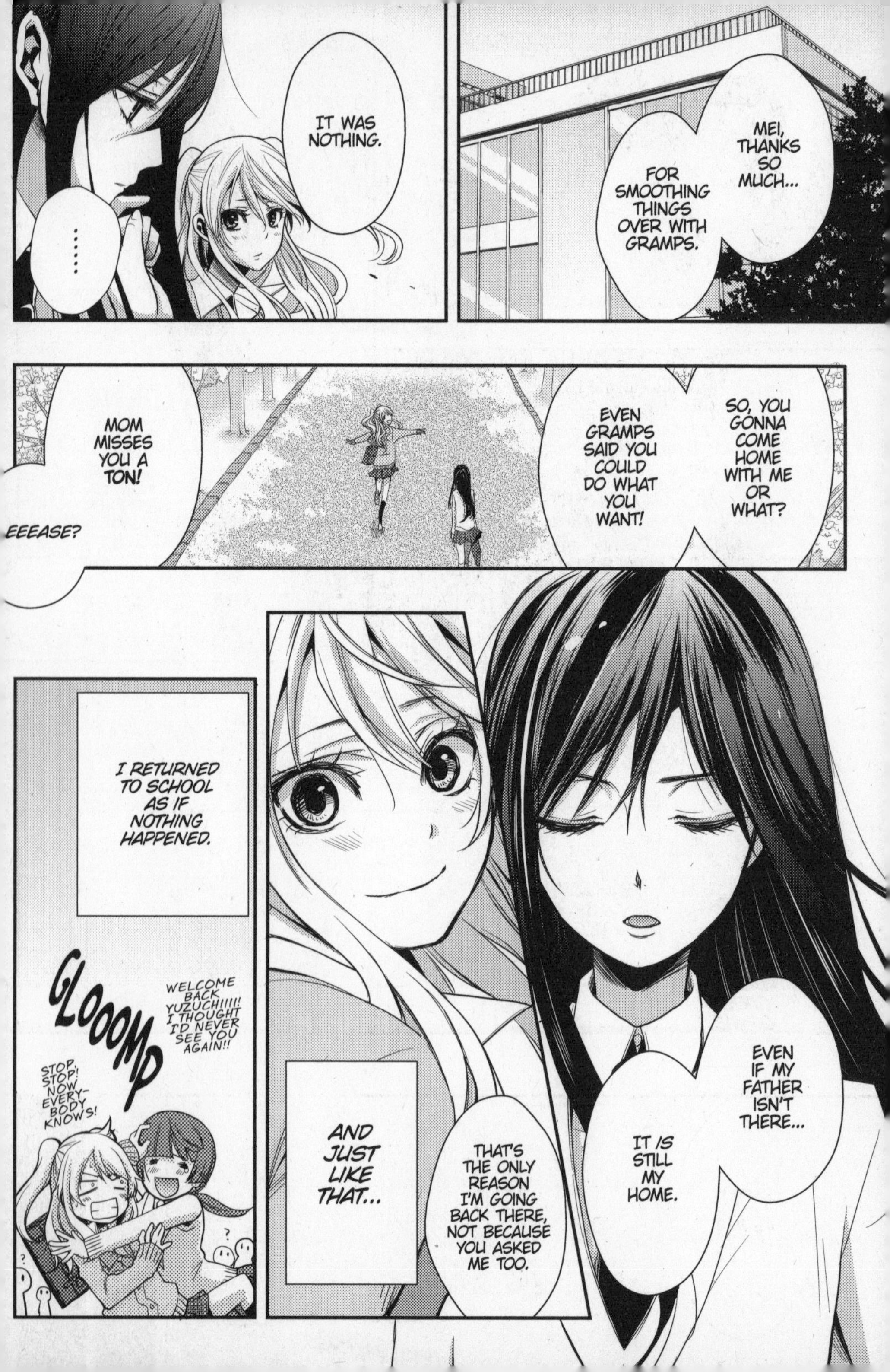

MEI, THANKS SO MUCH...
FOR SMOOTHING THINGS OVER WITH GRAMPS.
IT WAS NOTHING.
......
SO, YOU GONNA COME HOME WITH ME OR WHAT?
EVEN GRAMPS SAID YOU COULD DO WHAT YOU WANT!
MOM MISSES YOU A TON!
EEEASE?
EVEN IF MY FATHER ISN'T THERE...
IT IS STILL MY HOME.
THAT'S THE ONLY REASON I'M GOING BACK THERE, NOT BECAUSE YOU ASKED ME TOO.
AND JUST LIKE THAT...
I RETURNED TO SCHOOL AS IF NOTHING HAPPENED.
GLOOOMP
WELCOME BACK YUZUCHIIIII! I THOUGHT I'D NEVER SEE YOU AGAIN!!
STOP, STOP! NOW EVERY-BODY KNOWS!

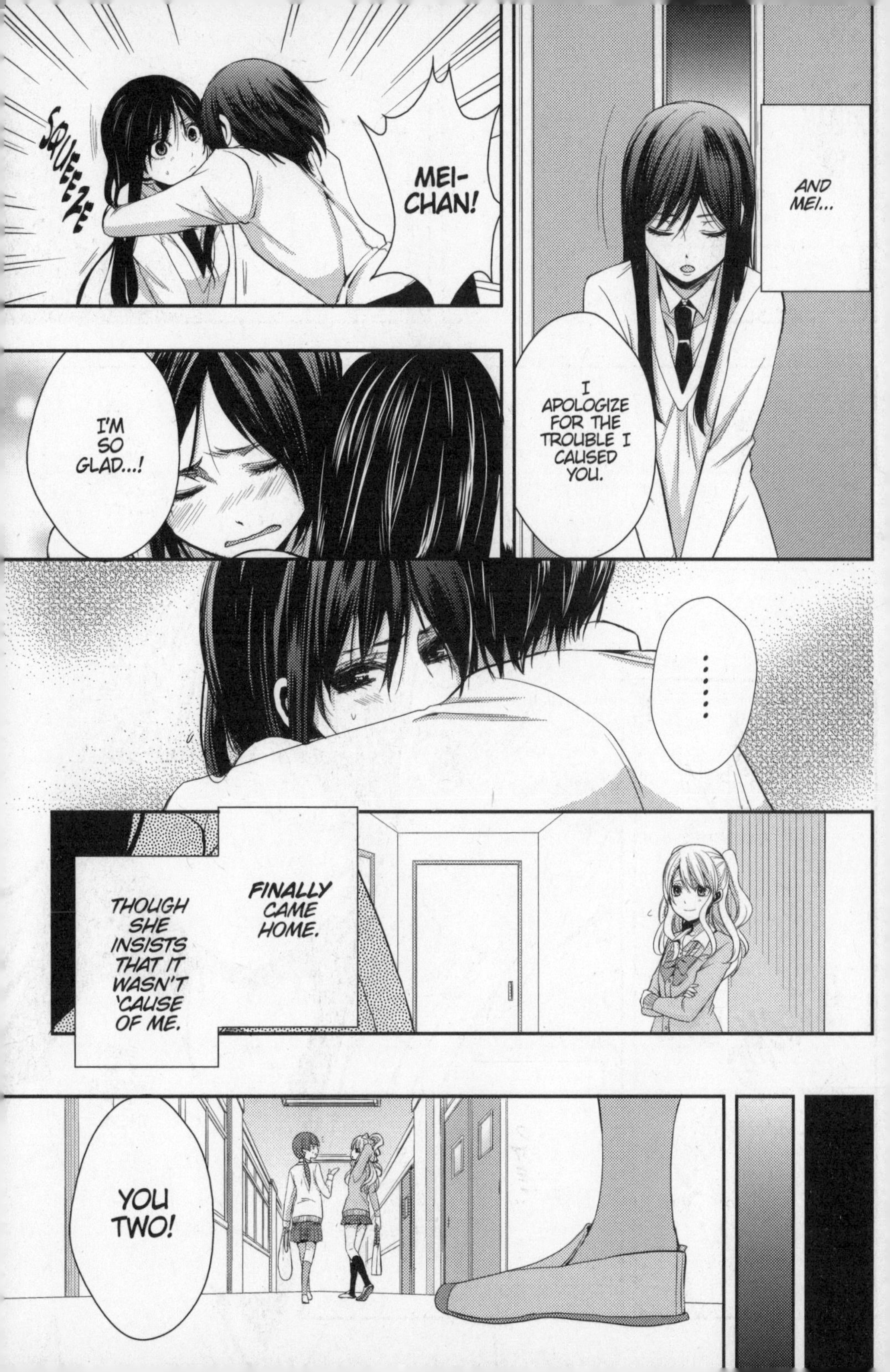
AND MEI...
I APOLOGIZE FOR THE TROUBLE I CAUSED YOU.
MEI-CHAN!
SQUEEZE
I'M SO GLAD...!
......
FINALLY CAME HOME.
THOUGH SHE INSISTS THAT IT WASN'T 'CAUSE OF ME.
YOU TWO!

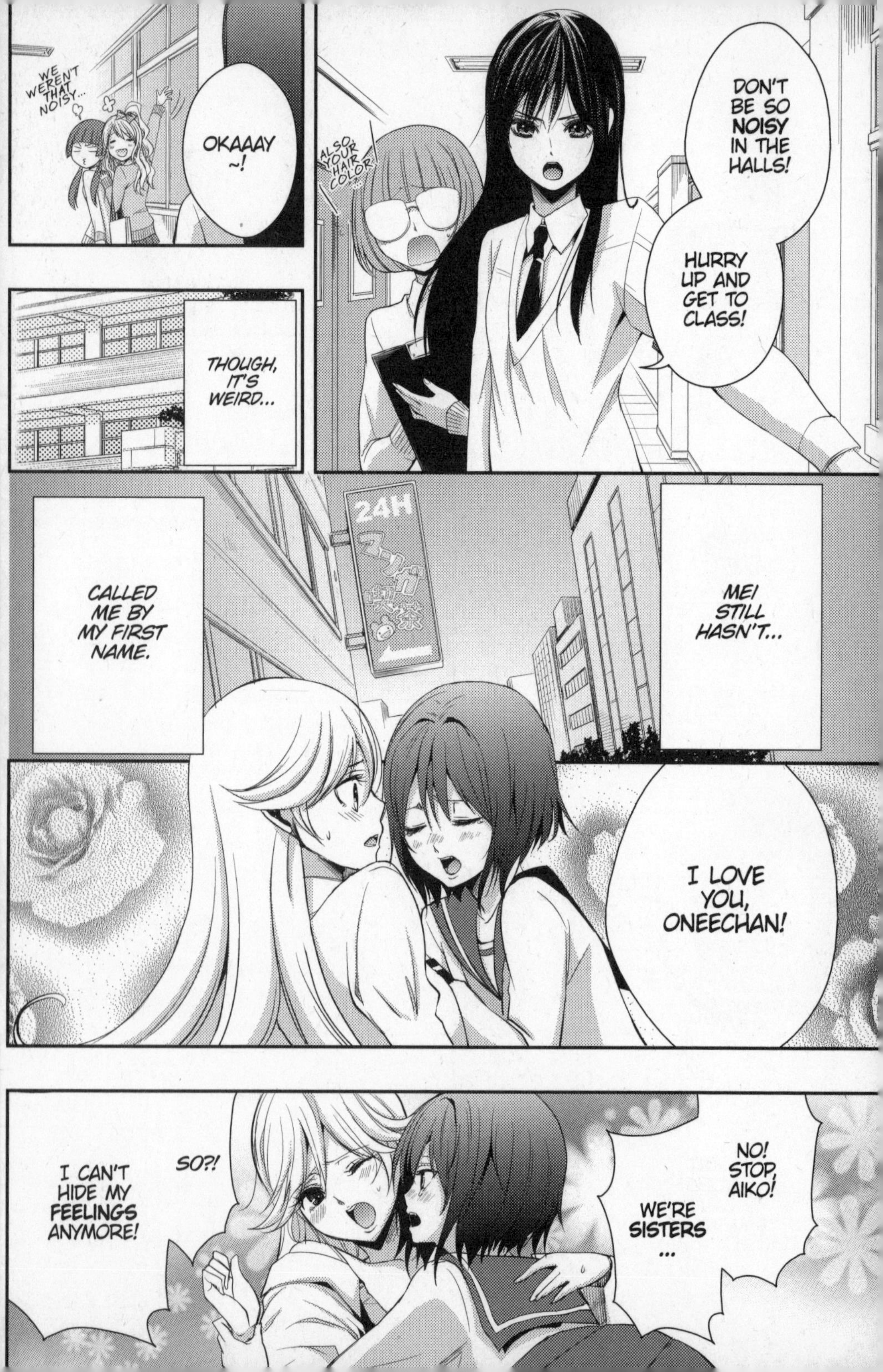
DON'T BE SO NOISY IN THE HALLS!
HURRY UP AND GET TO CLASS!
ALSO, YOUR HAIR COLOR...
OKAAAY ~!
WE WEREN'T THAT NOISY...
THOUGH, IT'S WEIRD...
MEI STILL HASN'T...
24H
CALLED ME BY MY FIRST NAME.
I LOVE YOU, ONEECHAN!
NO! STOP, AIKO!
WE'RE SISTERS ...
SO?!
I CAN'T HIDE MY FEELINGS ANYMORE!

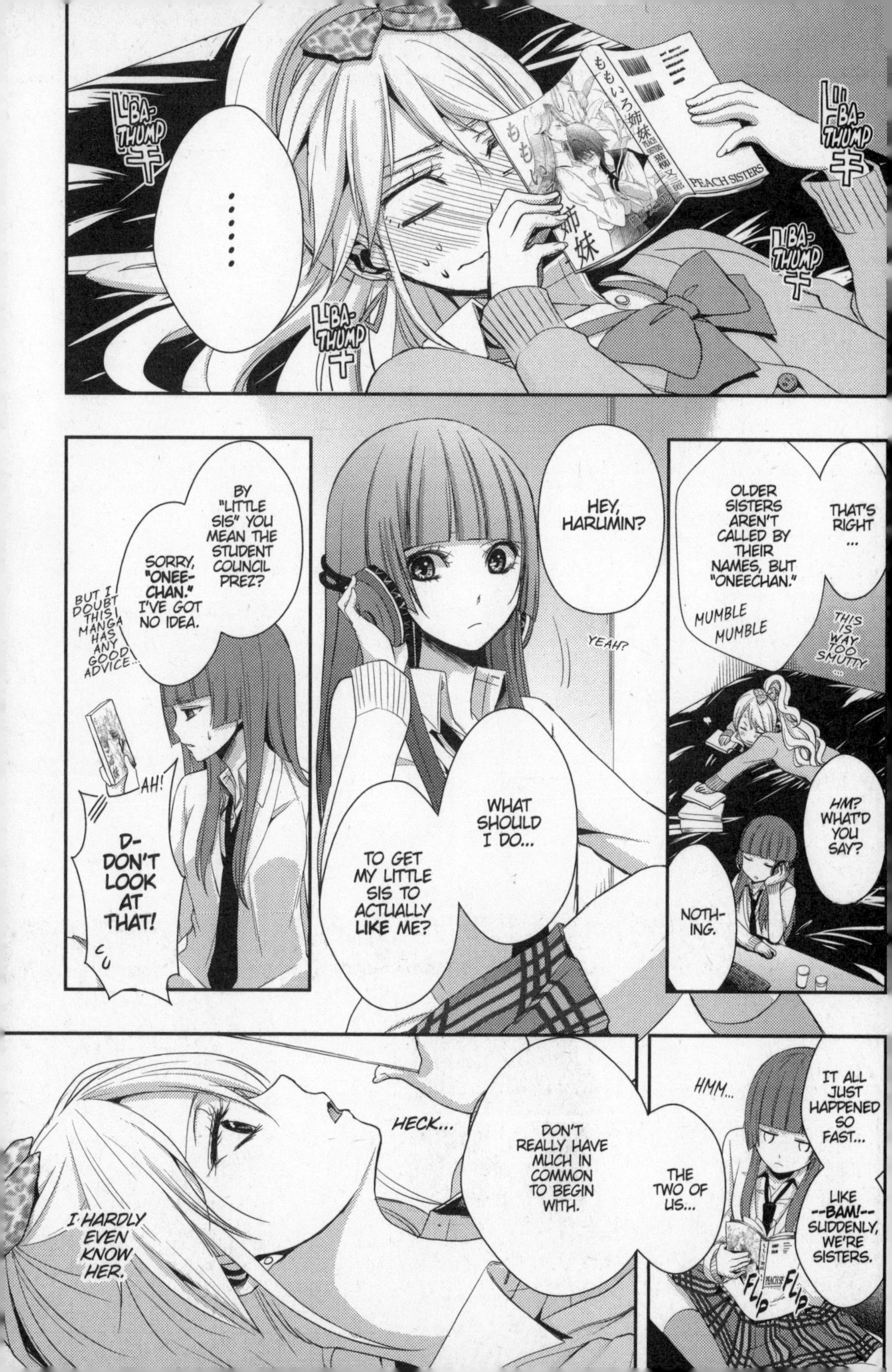
BA-THUMP
ももいろ姉妹
PEACH SISTERS
BA-THUMP
......
BA-THUMP
BA-THUMP
THAT'S RIGHT...
OLDER SISTERS AREN'T CALLED BY THEIR NAMES, BUT "ONEECHAN."
MUMBLE MUMBLE
THIS IS WAY TOO SMUTTY...
HM? WHAT'D YOU SAY?
NOTH-ING.
HEY, HARUMIN?
YEAH?
WHAT SHOULD I DO...
TO GET MY LITTLE SIS TO ACTUALLY LIKE ME?
BY "LITTLE SIS" YOU MEAN THE STUDENT COUNCIL PREZ?
SORRY, "ONEE-CHAN." I'VE GOT NO IDEA.
BUT I DOUBT THIS MANGA HAS ANY GOOD ADVICE...
AH!
D-DON'T LOOK AT THAT!
IT ALL JUST HAPPENED SO FAST...
HMM...
LIKE --BAM!-- SUDDENLY, WE'RE SISTERS.
FLIP FLIP
THE TWO OF US...
DON'T REALLY HAVE MUCH IN COMMON TO BEGIN WITH.
HECK...
I HARDLY EVEN KNOW HER.

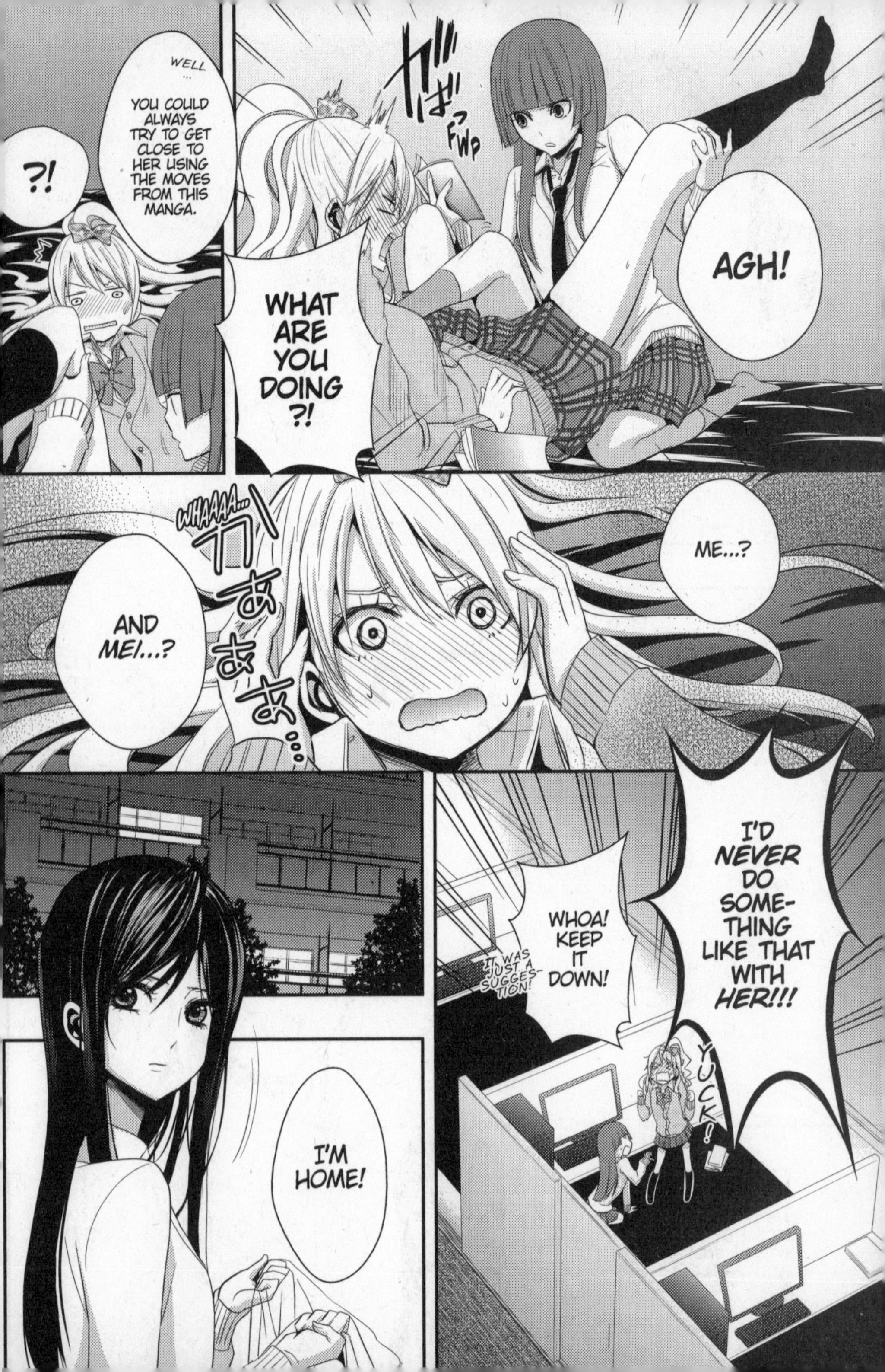
FWP
AGH!
WHAT ARE YOU DOING ?!
WELL ... YOU COULD ALWAYS TRY TO GET CLOSE TO HER USING THE MOVES FROM THIS MANGA.
?!
ME...?
WHAAAA...
AND MEI...?
I'D NEVER DO SOME-THING LIKE THAT WITH HER!!!
WHOA! KEEP IT DOWN!
IT WAS JUST A SUGGES-TION!
YUCK!
I'M HOME!

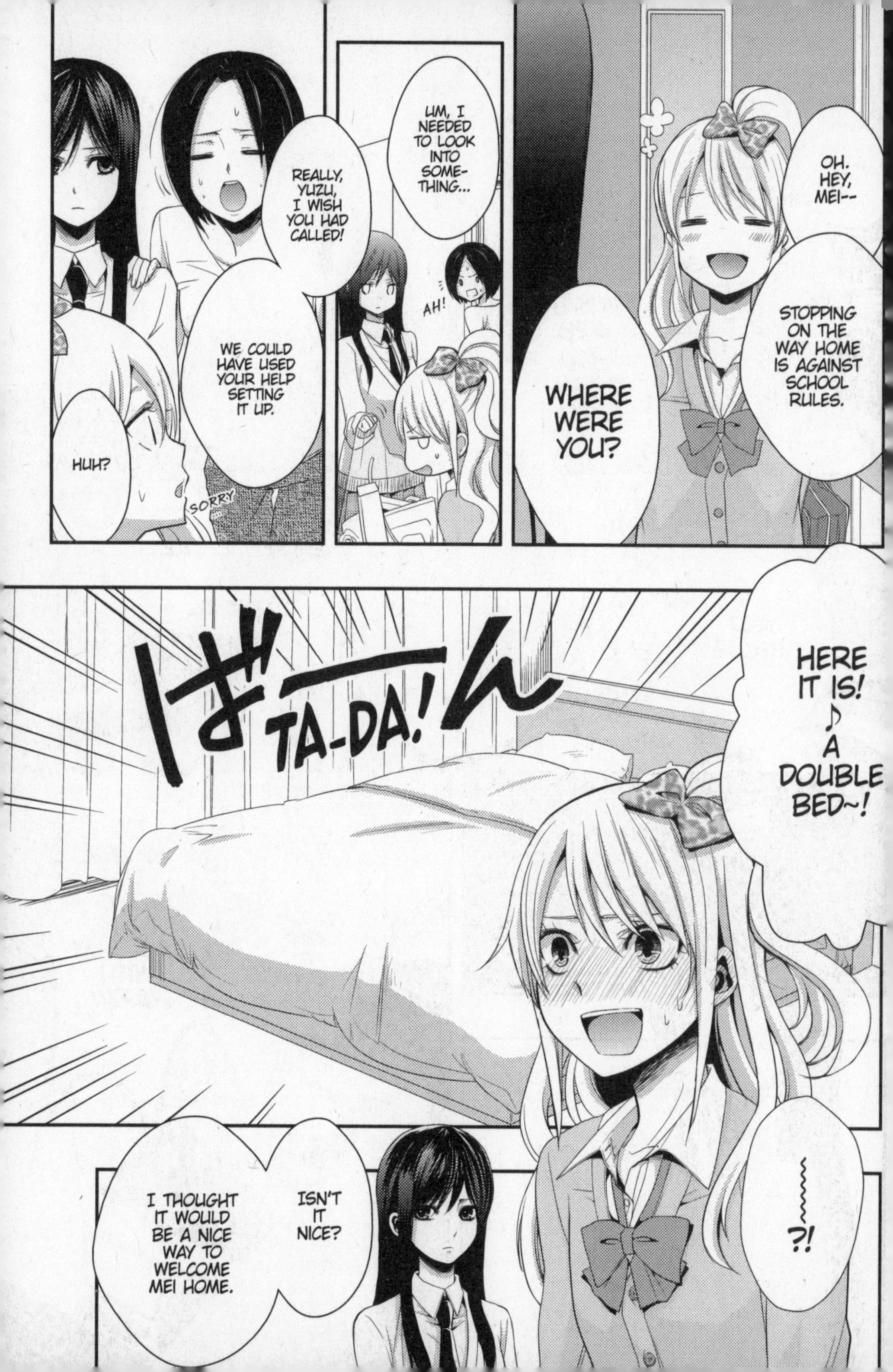
OH. HEY, MEI--
STOPPING ON THE WAY HOME IS AGAINST SCHOOL RULES.
WHERE WERE YOU?
UM, I NEEDED TO LOOK INTO SOME-THING...
AH!
REALLY, YUZU, I WISH YOU HAD CALLED!
WE COULD HAVE USED YOUR HELP SETTING IT UP.
HUH?
SORRY
HERE IT IS! ♪ A DOUBLE BED~!
ばーん
TA-DA!
~~~?!
ISN'T IT NICE?
I THOUGHT IT WOULD BE A NICE WAY TO WELCOME MEI HOME.
~~~

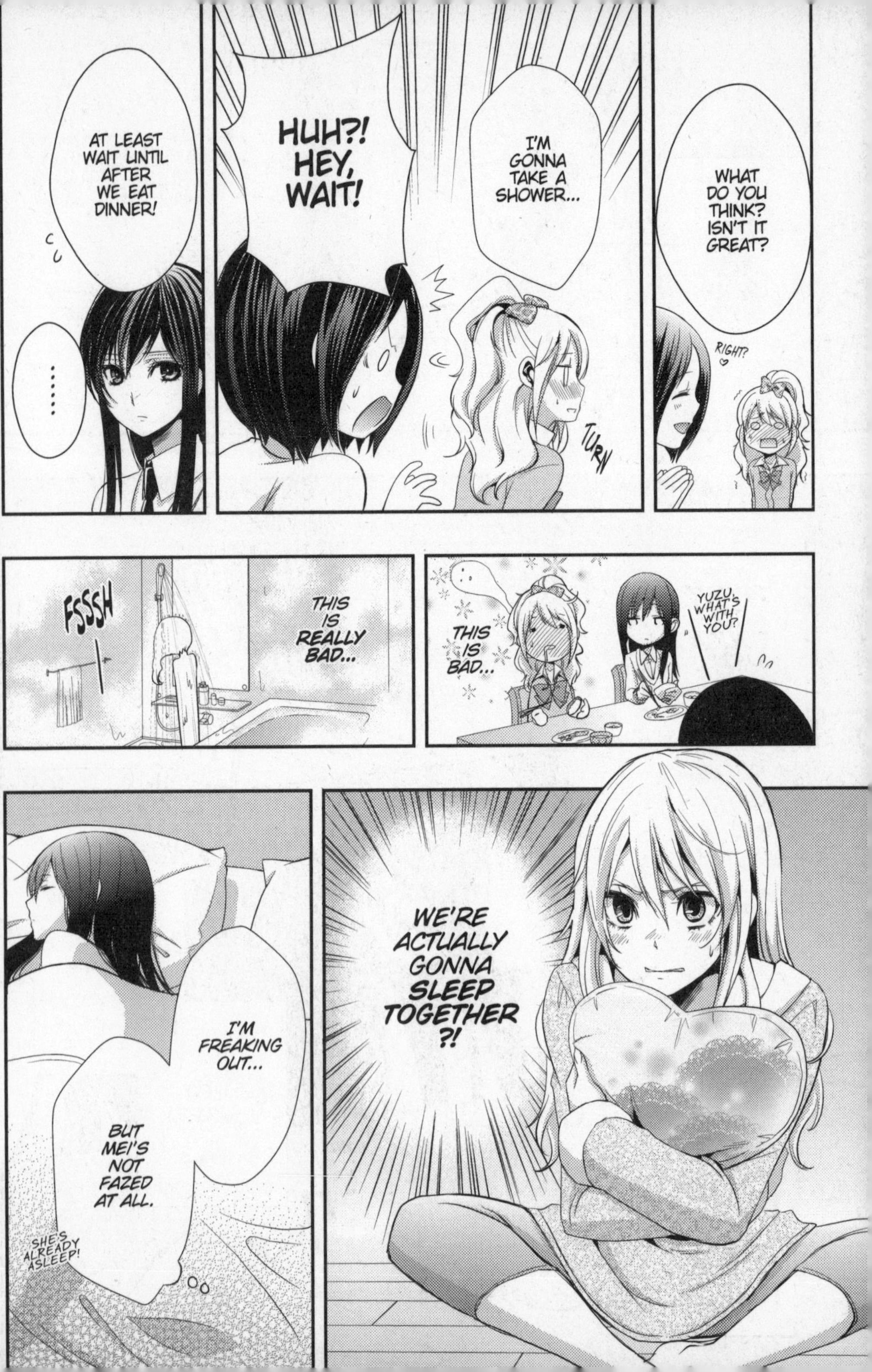

WHAT DO YOU THINK? ISN'T IT GREAT?
RIGHT? ♥
I'M GONNA TAKE A SHOWER...
TURN
HUH?! HEY, WAIT!
AT LEAST WAIT UNTIL AFTER WE EAT DINNER!
......
YUZU, WHAT'S WITH YOU?
THIS IS BAD...
THIS IS REALLY BAD...
FSSSH
WE'RE ACTUALLY GONNA SLEEP TOGETHER?!
I'M FREAKING OUT...
BUT MEI'S NOT FAZED AT ALL.
SHE'S ALREADY ASLEEP!

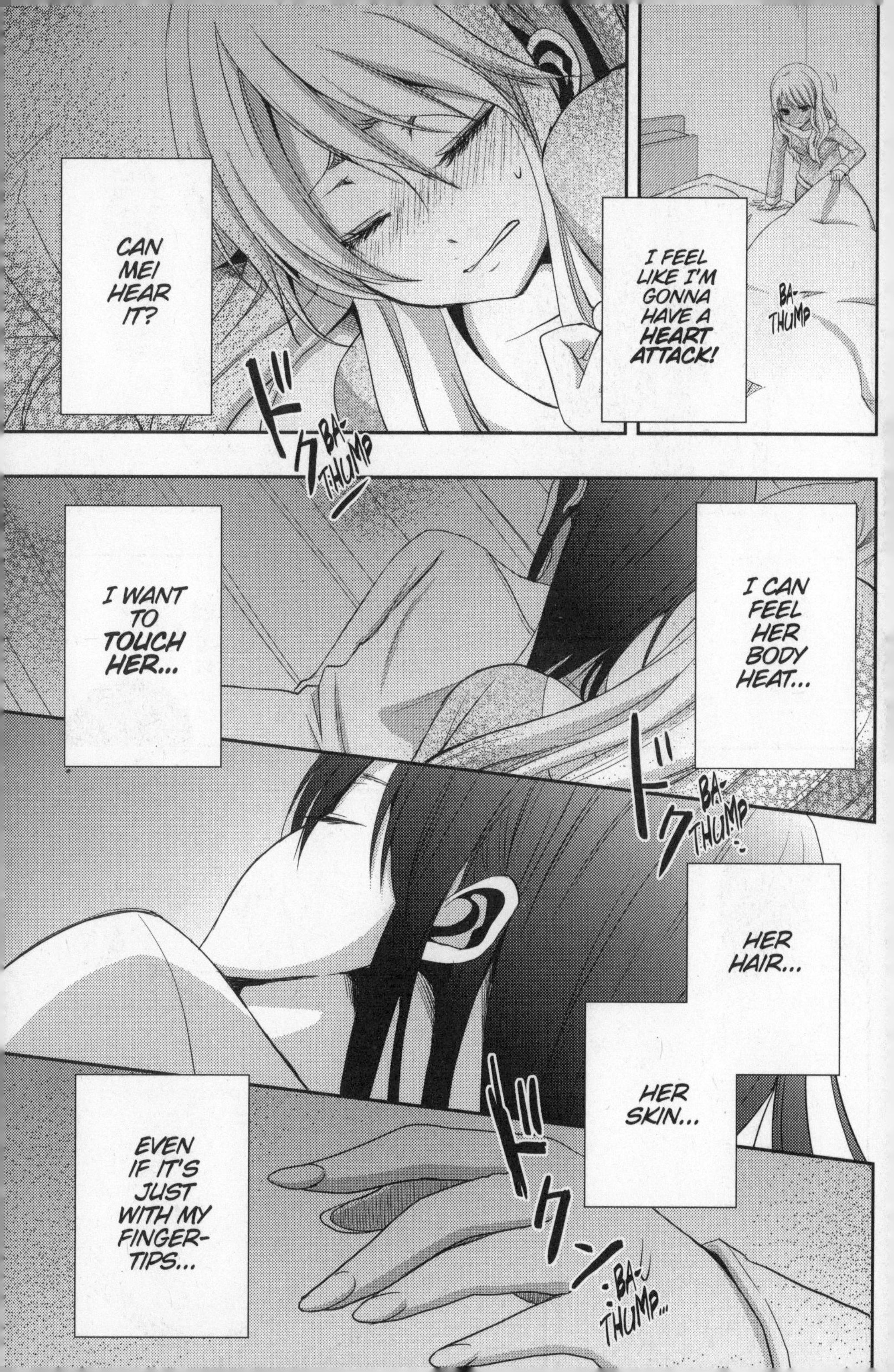

I FEEL LIKE I'M GONNA HAVE A HEART ATTACK!
BA-THUMP
CAN MEI HEAR IT?
BA-THUMP
I CAN FEEL HER BODY HEAT...
BA-THUMP...
I WANT TO TOUCH HER...
HER HAIR...
HER SKIN...
EVEN IF IT'S JUST WITH MY FINGER-TIPS...
BA-THUMP...

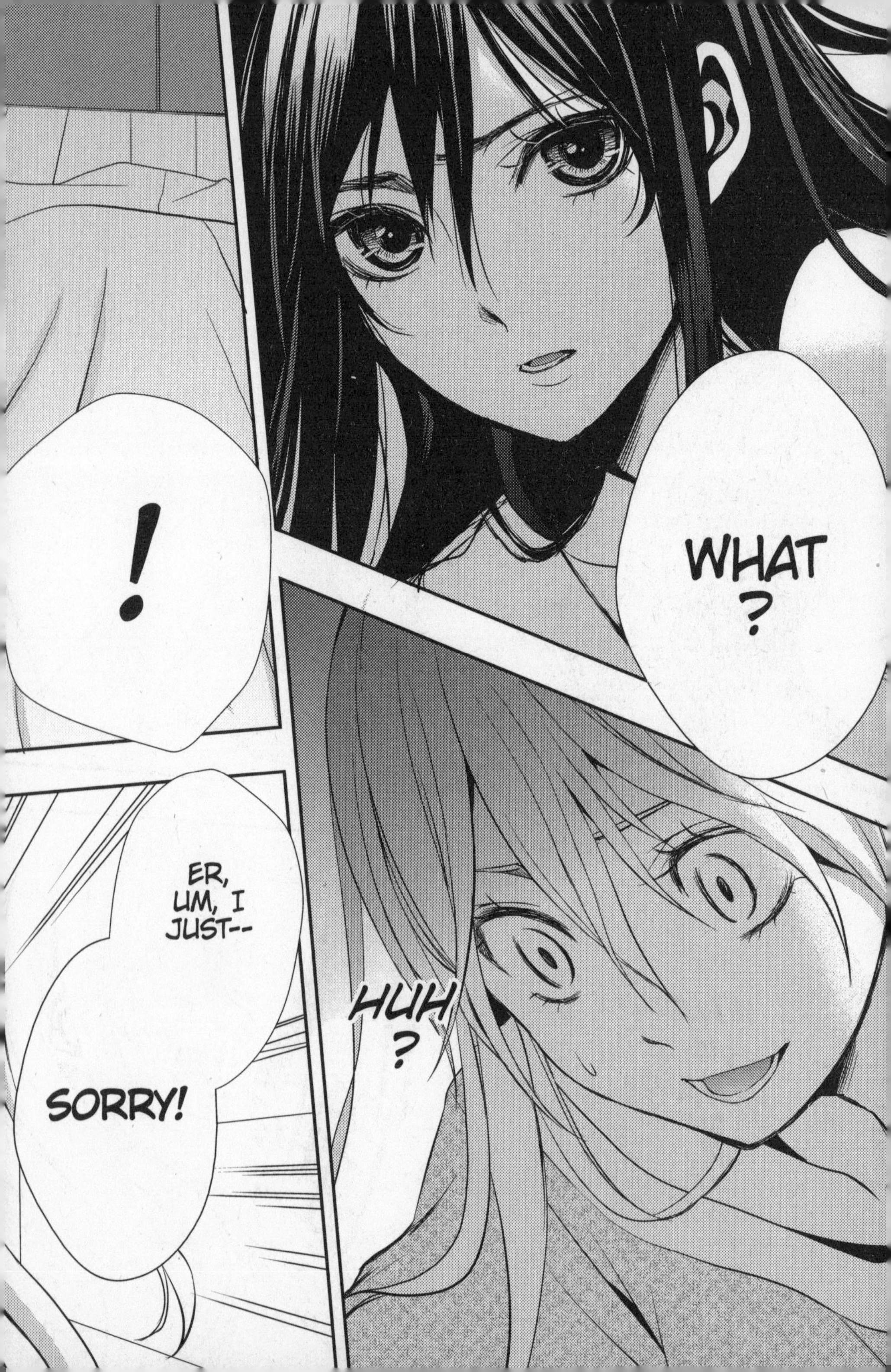
WHAT?
!
HUH?
ER, UM, I JUST--
SORRY!

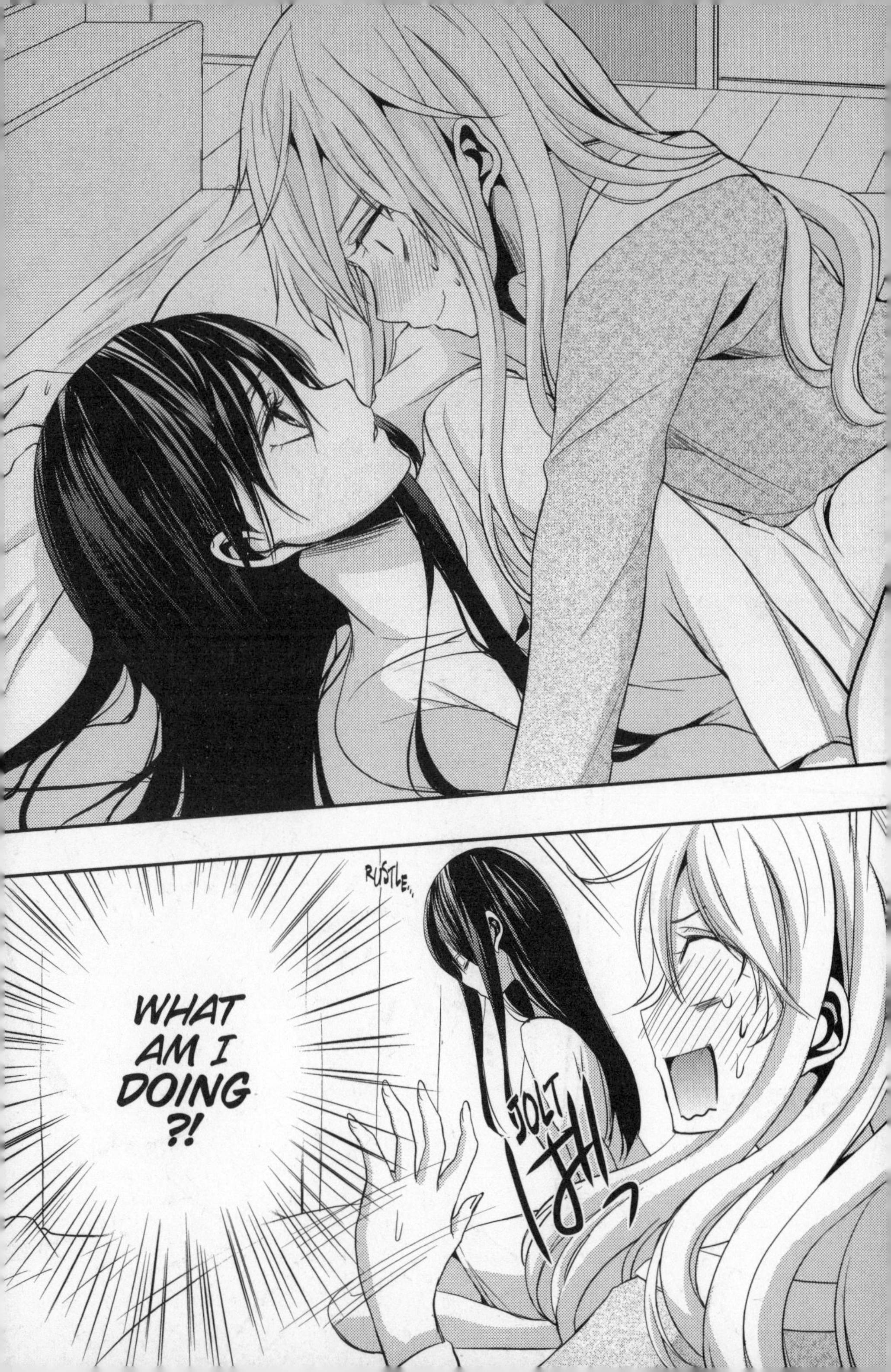
RUSTLE..
JOLT
WHAT AM I DOING?!

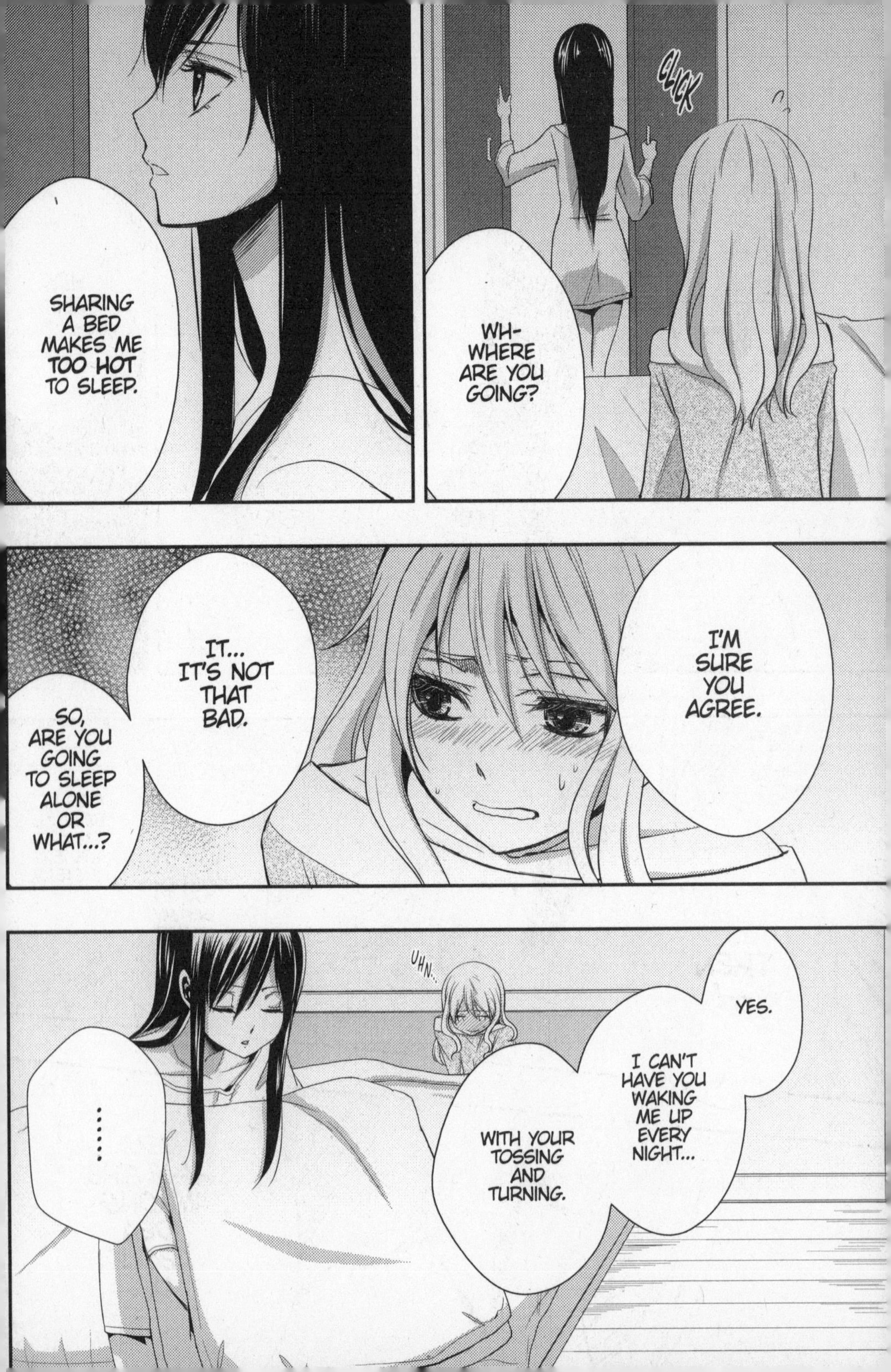
CLICK
WH- WHERE ARE YOU GOING?
SHARING A BED MAKES ME TOO HOT TO SLEEP.
I'M SURE YOU AGREE.
IT... IT'S NOT THAT BAD.
SO, ARE YOU GOING TO SLEEP ALONE OR WHAT...?
YES.
I CAN'T HAVE YOU WAKING ME UP EVERY NIGHT...
WITH YOUR TOSSING AND TURNING.
UHN...
......

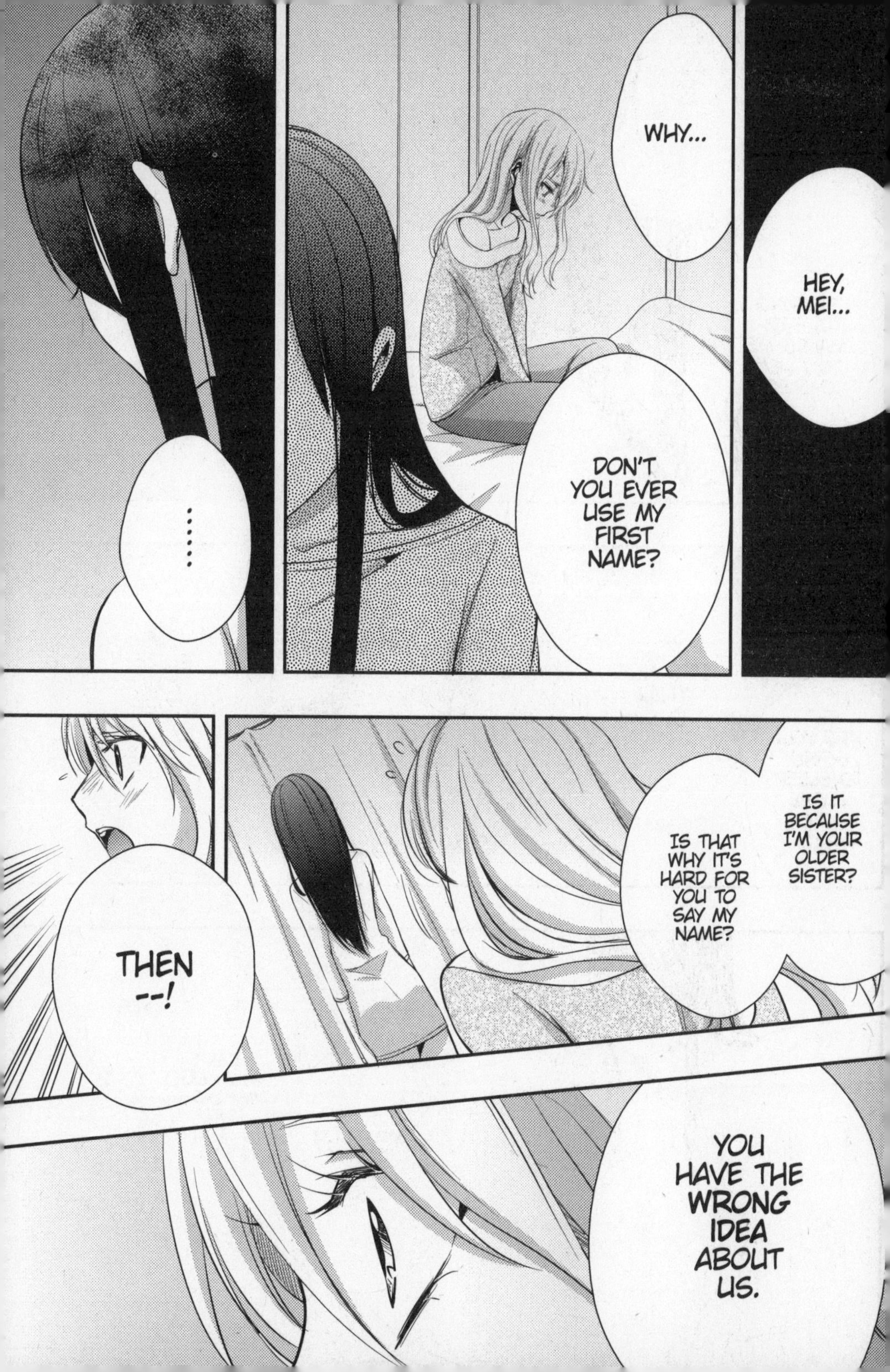
HEY, MEI...
WHY...
DON'T YOU EVER USE MY FIRST NAME?
......
IS IT BECAUSE I'M YOUR OLDER SISTER?
IS THAT WHY IT'S HARD FOR YOU TO SAY MY NAME?
THEN --!
YOU HAVE THE WRONG IDEA ABOUT US.

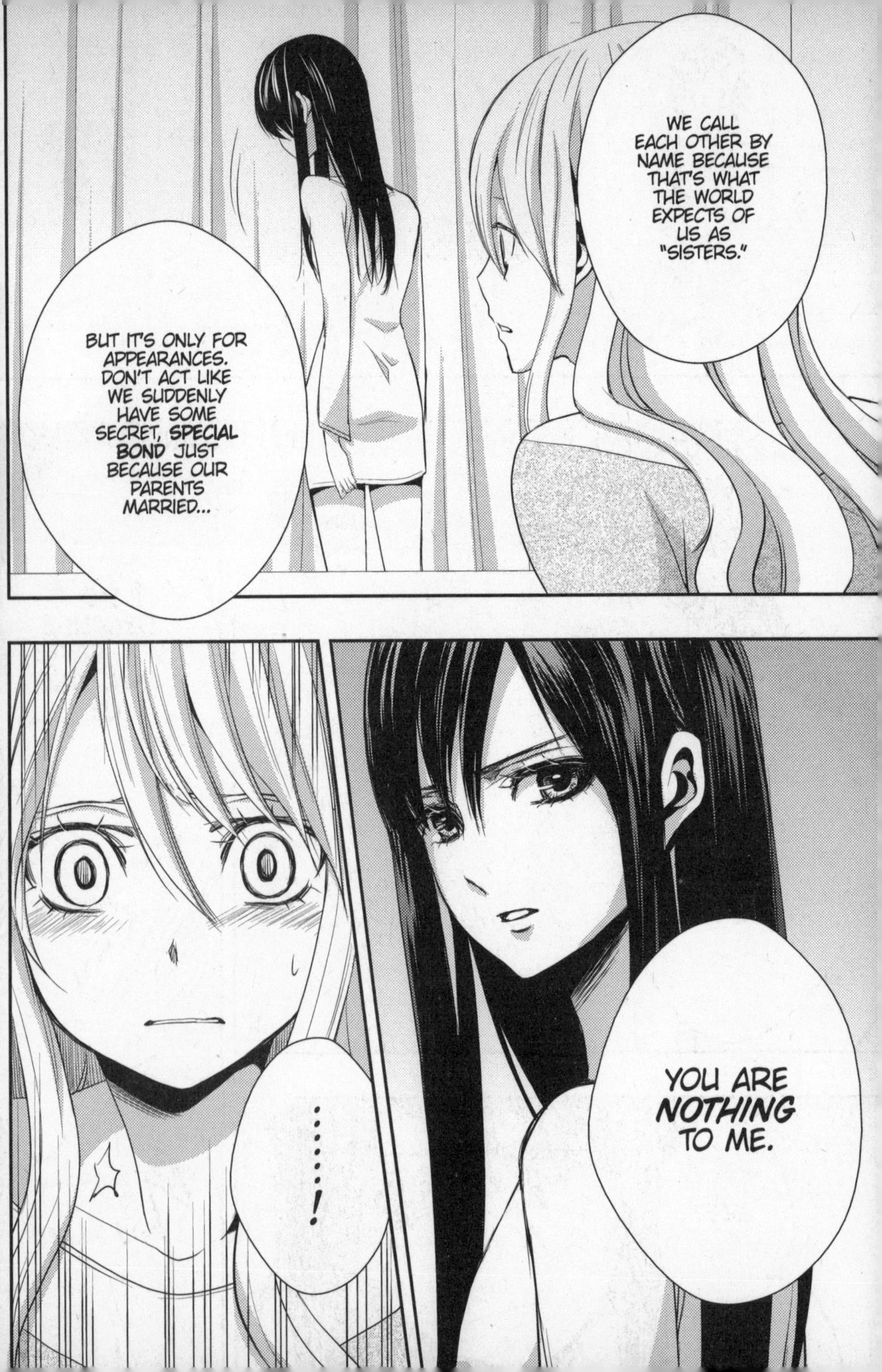
WE CALL EACH OTHER BY NAME BECAUSE THAT'S WHAT THE WORLD EXPECTS OF US AS "SISTERS."
BUT IT'S ONLY FOR APPEARANCES. DON'T ACT LIKE WE SUDDENLY HAVE SOME SECRET, **SPECIAL BOND** JUST BECAUSE OUR PARENTS MARRIED...
YOU ARE ***NOTHING*** TO ME.
......!

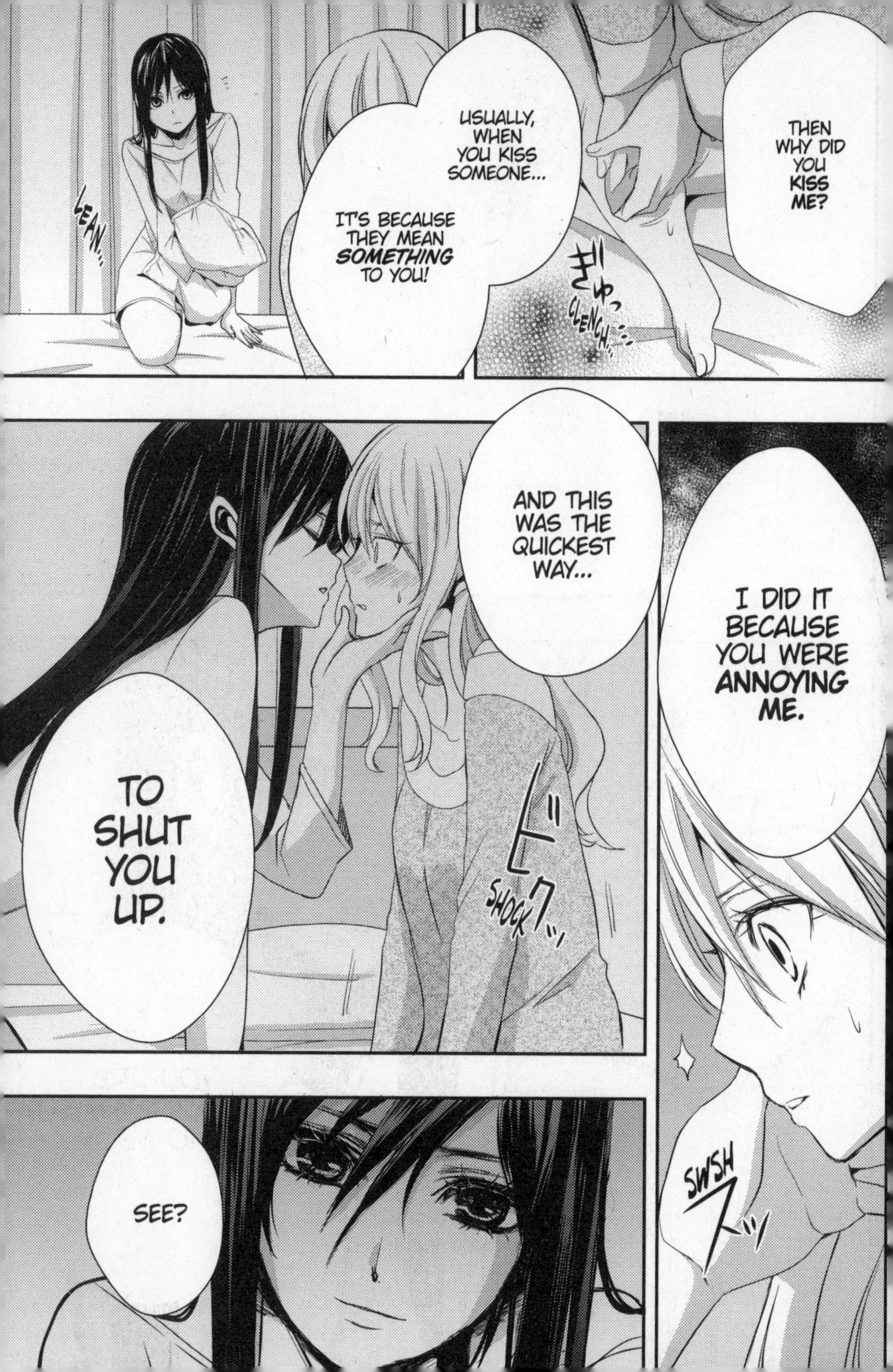
THEN WHY DID YOU KISS ME?
CLENCH...
USUALLY, WHEN YOU KISS SOMEONE...
IT'S BECAUSE THEY MEAN *SOMETHING* TO YOU!
LEAN...
I DID IT BECAUSE YOU WERE **ANNOYING** ME.
SWSH
AND THIS WAS THE QUICKEST WAY...
TO SHUT YOU UP.
SHOCK
SEE?

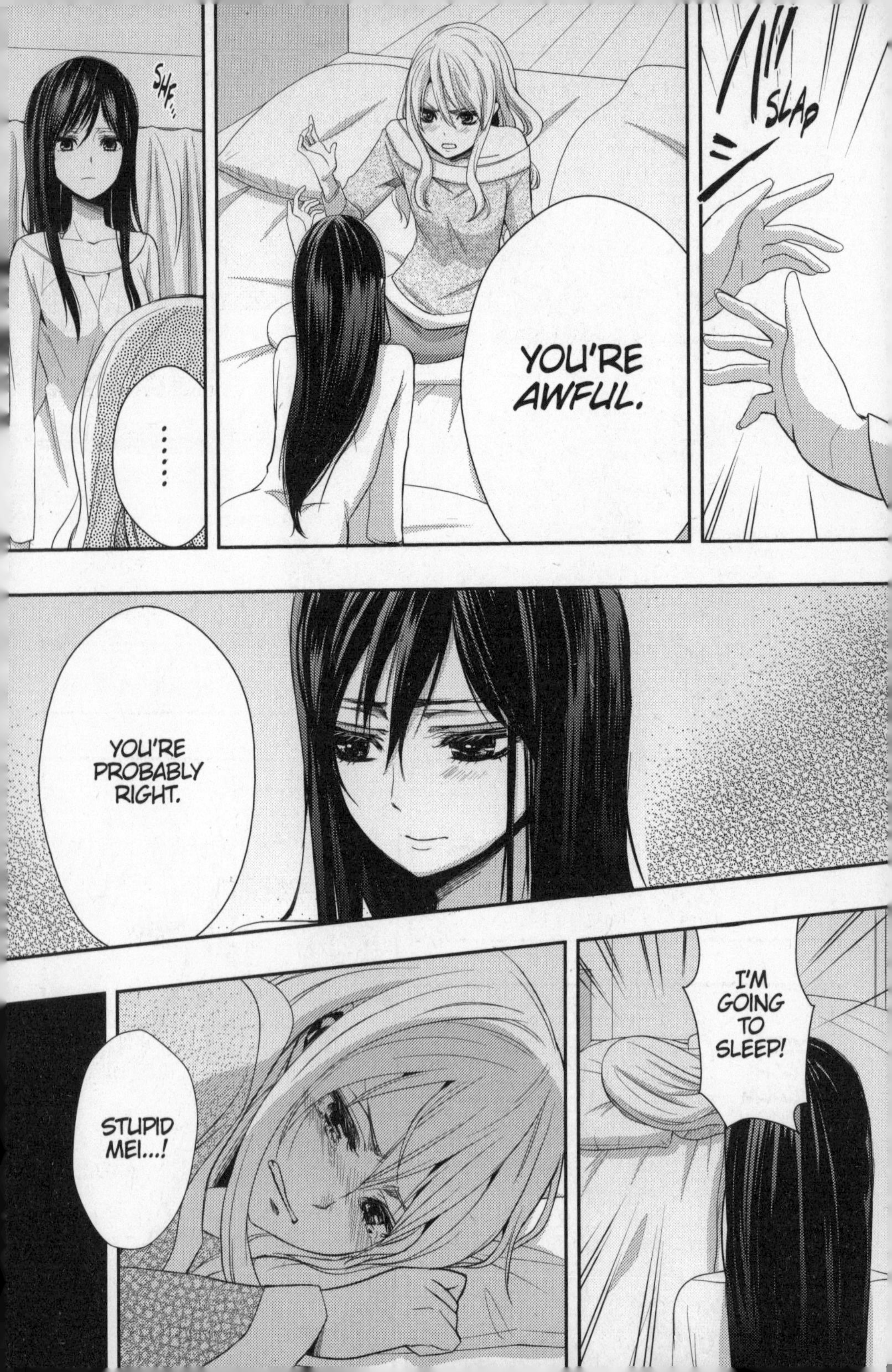
SLAP
YOU'RE AWFUL.
SHF...
......
YOU'RE PROBABLY RIGHT.
I'M GOING TO SLEEP!
STUPID MEI...!

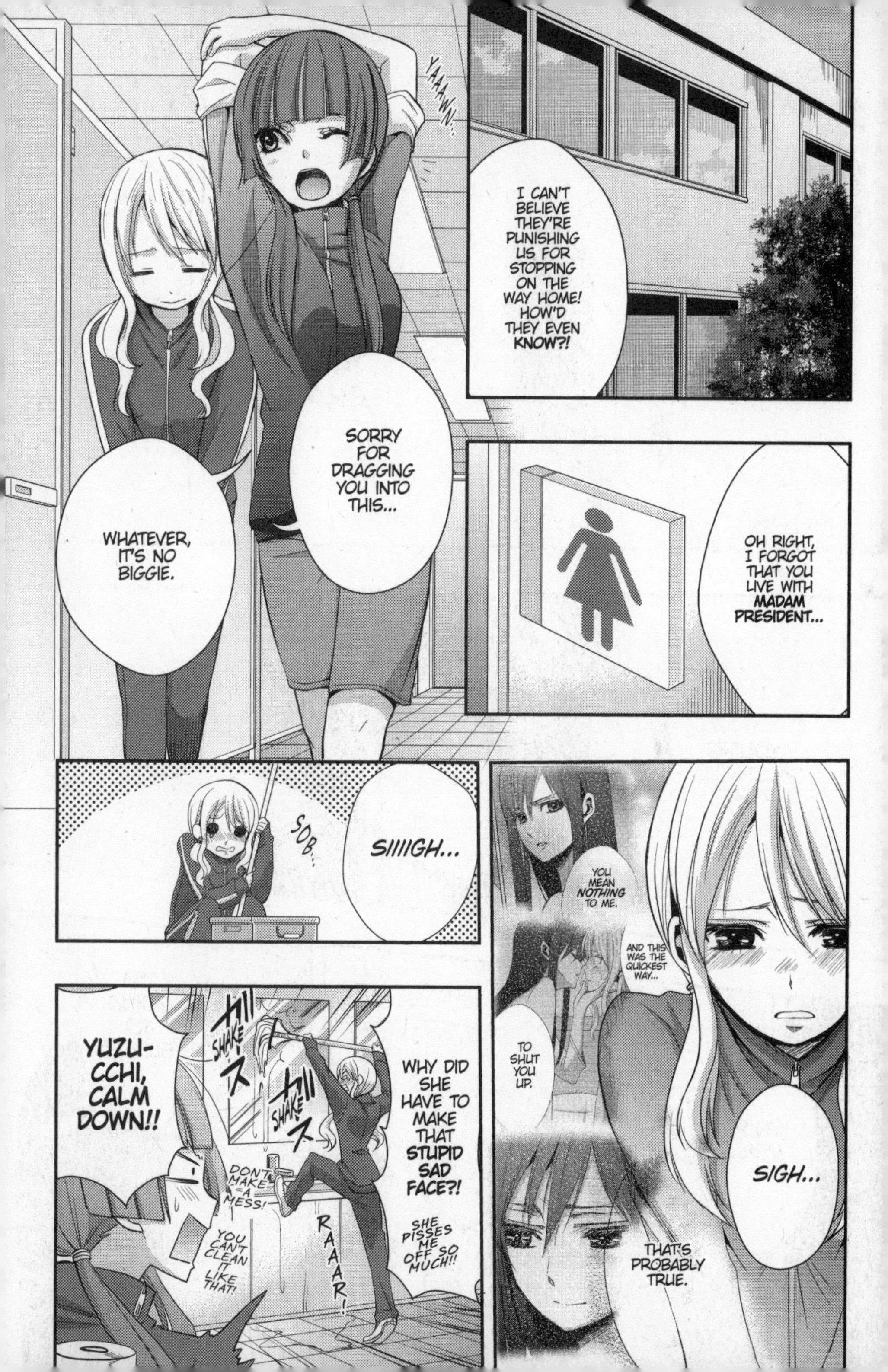
I CAN'T BELIEVE THEY'RE PUNISHING US FOR STOPPING ON THE WAY HOME! HOW'D THEY EVEN KNOW?!
OH RIGHT, I FORGOT THAT YOU LIVE WITH MADAM PRESIDENT...
YAAAAWN...
SORRY FOR DRAGGING YOU INTO THIS...
WHATEVER, IT'S NO BIGGIE.
YOU MEAN NOTHING TO ME.
AND THIS WAS THE QUICKEST WAY...
TO SHUT YOU UP.
SIGH...
THAT'S PROBABLY TRUE.
SOB...
SIIIIGH...
WHY DID SHE HAVE TO MAKE THAT STUPID SAD FACE?!
SHAKE
SHAKE
YUZU-CCHI, CALM DOWN!!
SHE PISSES ME OFF SO MUCH!!
RAAAAR!
DON'T MAKE A MESS!
YOU CAN'T CLEAN IT LIKE THAT!

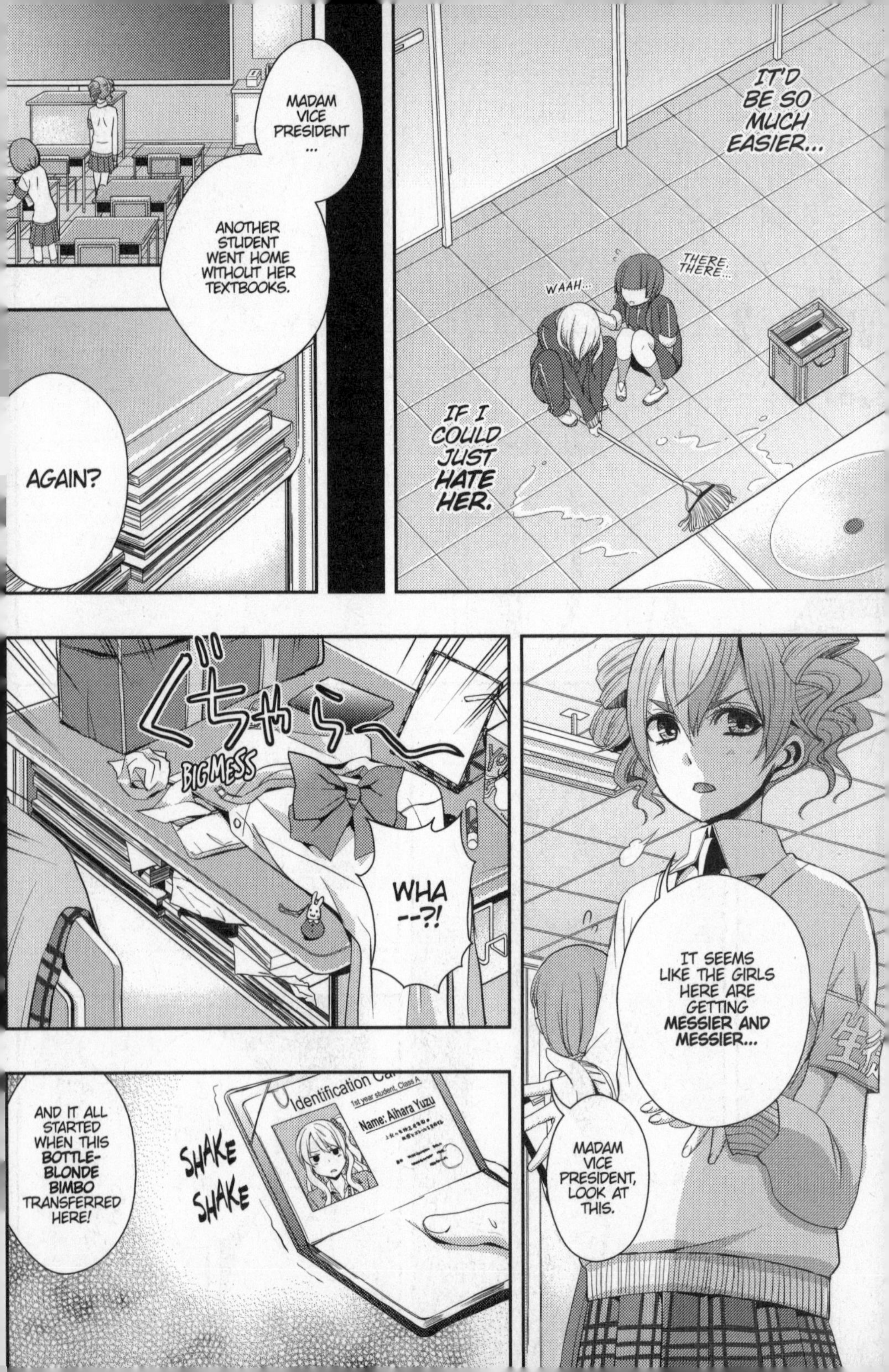
IT'D BE SO MUCH EASIER...
THERE, THERE...
WAAH...
IF I COULD JUST HATE HER.
MADAM VICE PRESIDENT ...
ANOTHER STUDENT WENT HOME WITHOUT HER TEXTBOOKS.
AGAIN?
IT SEEMS LIKE THE GIRLS HERE ARE GETTING MESSIER AND MESSIER...
MADAM VICE PRESIDENT, LOOK AT THIS.
ぐちゃら〜
BIG MESS
WHA--?!
AND IT ALL STARTED WHEN THIS BOTTLE-BLONDE BIMBO TRANSFERRED HERE!
SHAKE SHAKE
1st year student, Class A
Name: Aihara Yuzu

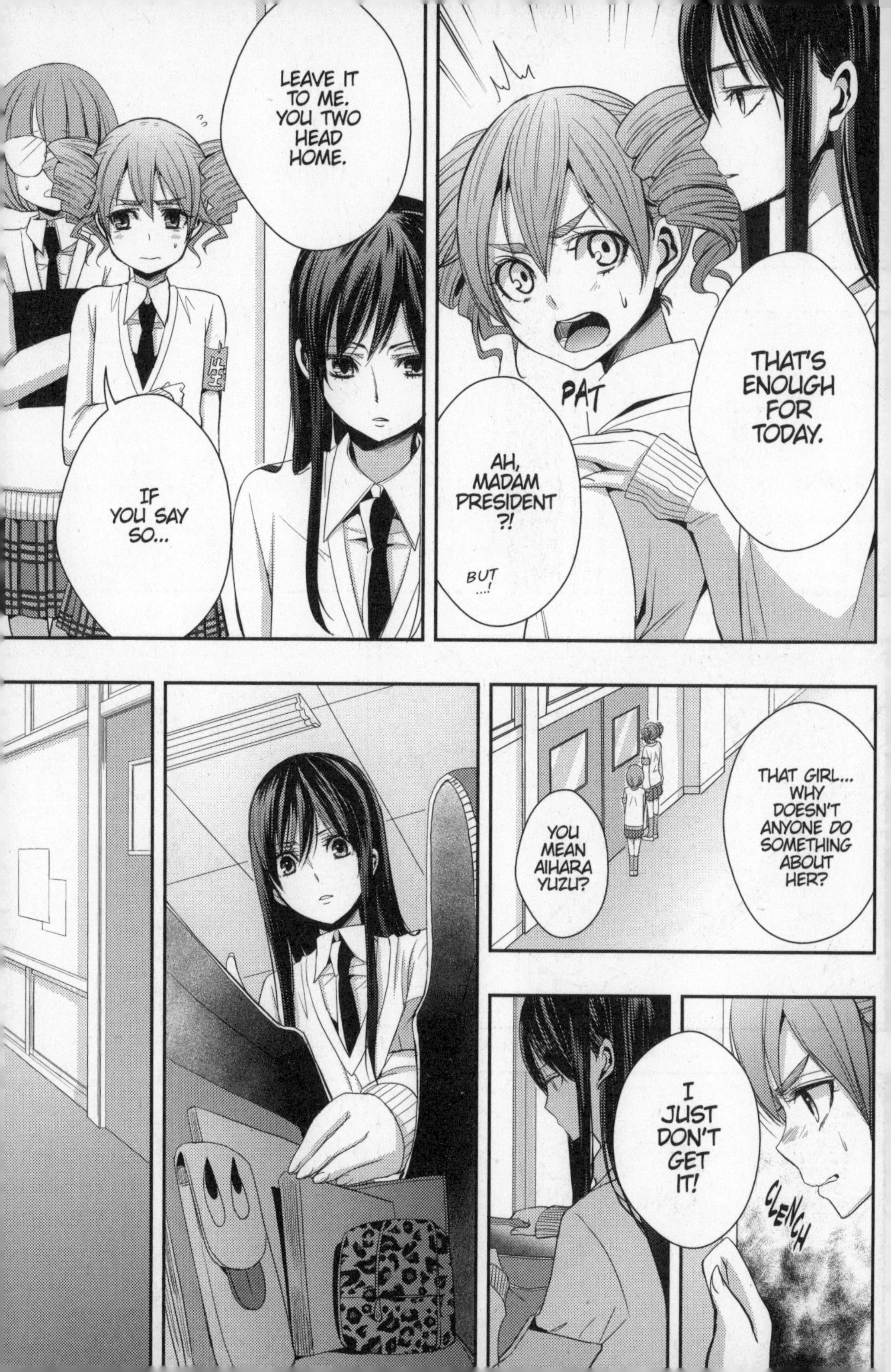
THAT'S ENOUGH FOR TODAY.
PAT
AH, MADAM PRESIDENT ?!
BUT ...!
LEAVE IT TO ME. YOU TWO HEAD HOME.
IF YOU SAY SO...
THAT GIRL... WHY DOESN'T ANYONE DO SOMETHING ABOUT HER?
YOU MEAN AIHARA YUZU?
I JUST DON'T GET IT!
CLENCH

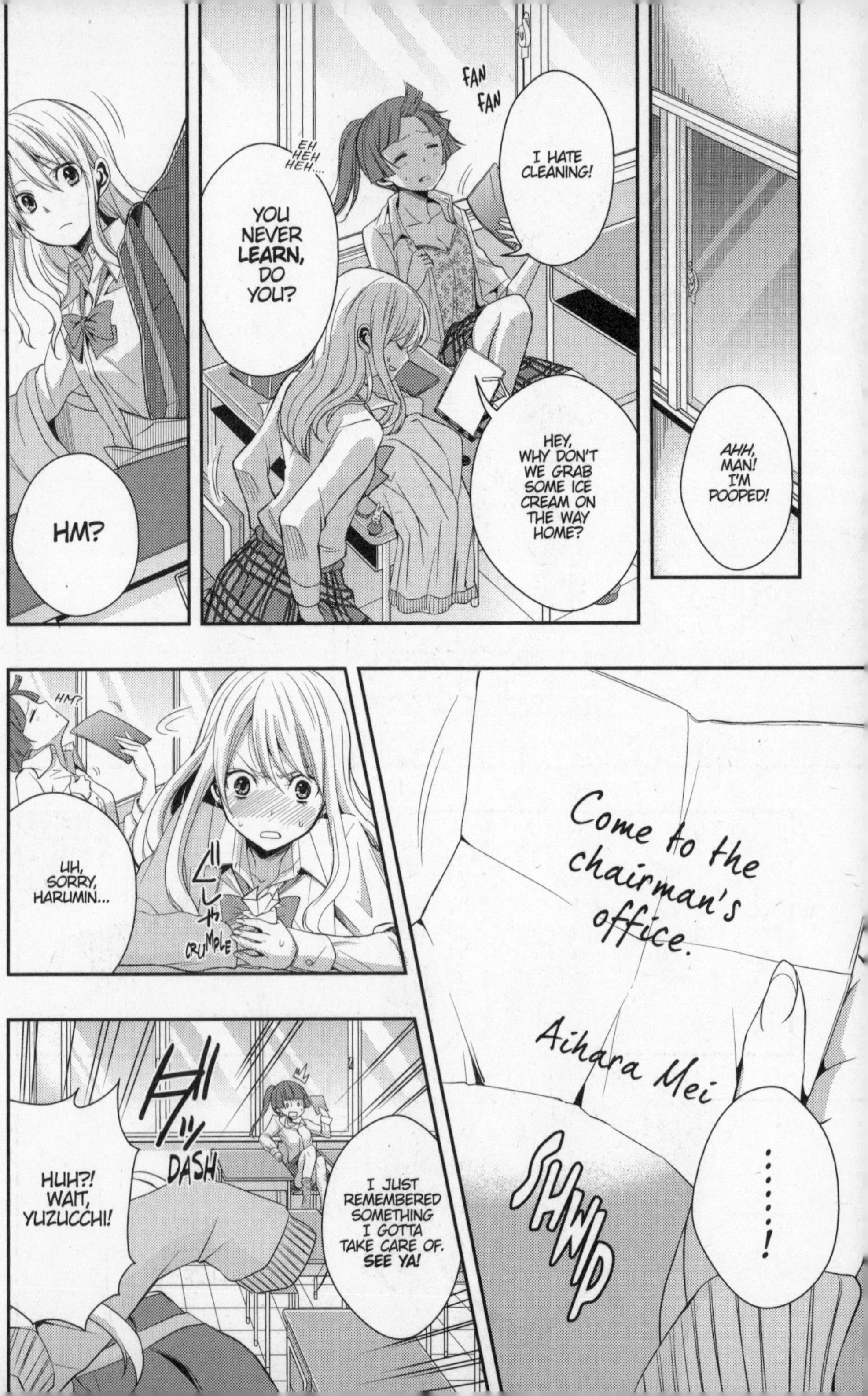
AHH, MAN! I'M POOPED!
FAN FAN
I HATE CLEANING!
HEY, WHY DON'T WE GRAB SOME ICE CREAM ON THE WAY HOME?
EH HEH HEH...
YOU NEVER LEARN, DO YOU?
HM?
Come to the chairman's office.
Aihara Mei
SHWIP
......!
HM?
UH, SORRY, HARUMIN...
CRUMPLE
I JUST REMEMBERED SOMETHING I GOTTA TAKE CARE OF. SEE YA!
DASH
HUH?! WAIT, YUZUCCHI!

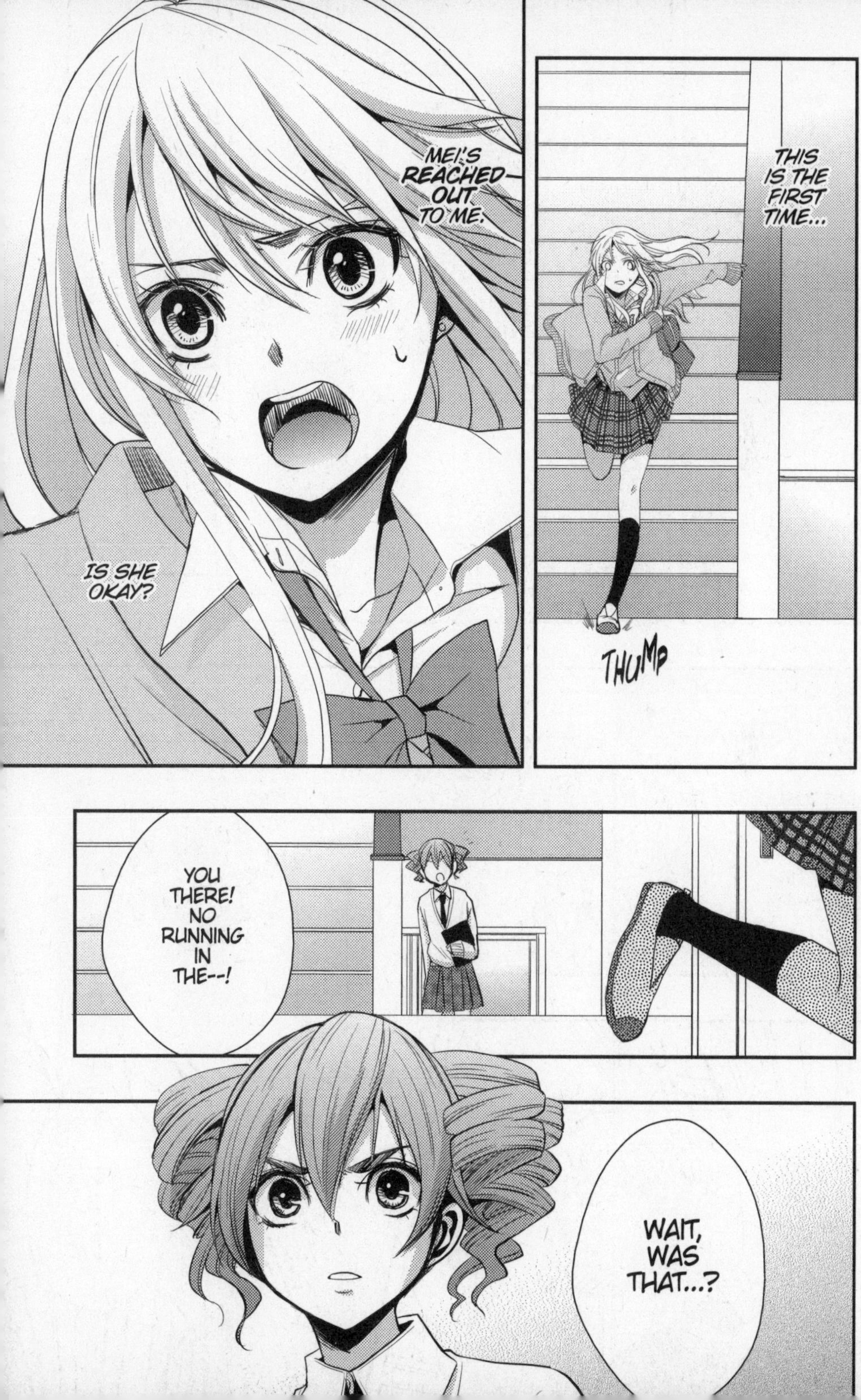
THIS IS THE FIRST TIME...
THUMP
MEI'S REACHED OUT TO ME.
IS SHE OKAY?
YOU THERE! NO RUNNING IN THE--!
WAIT, WAS THAT...?

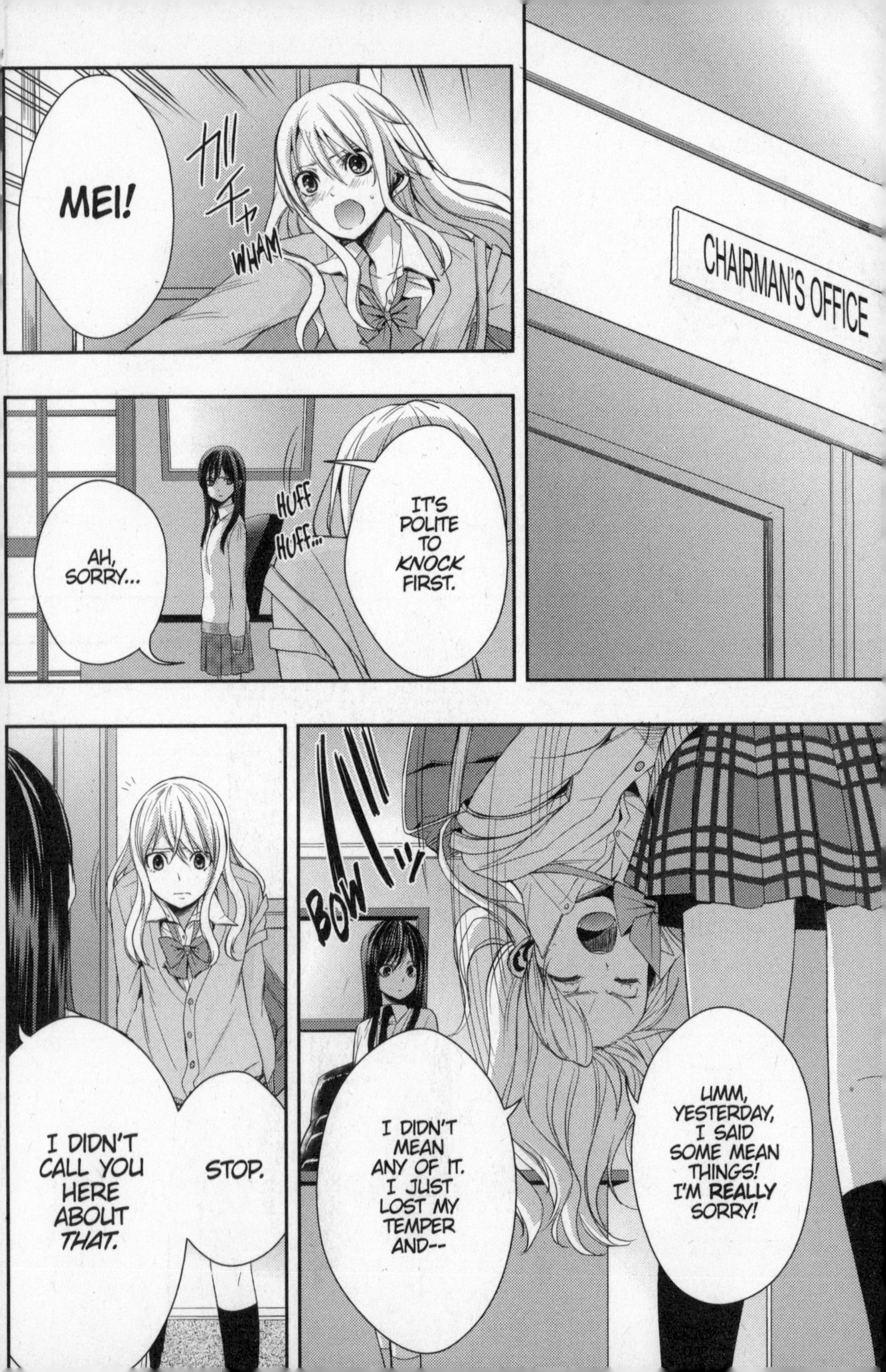
CHAIRMAN'S OFFICE
ガチャ
WHAM
MEI!
IT'S POLITE TO KNOCK FIRST.
HUFF HUFF...
AH, SORRY...
UMM, YESTERDAY, I SAID SOME MEAN THINGS! I'M REALLY SORRY!
BOW ッ
I DIDN'T MEAN ANY OF IT. I JUST LOST MY TEMPER AND--
STOP.
I DIDN'T CALL YOU HERE ABOUT THAT.

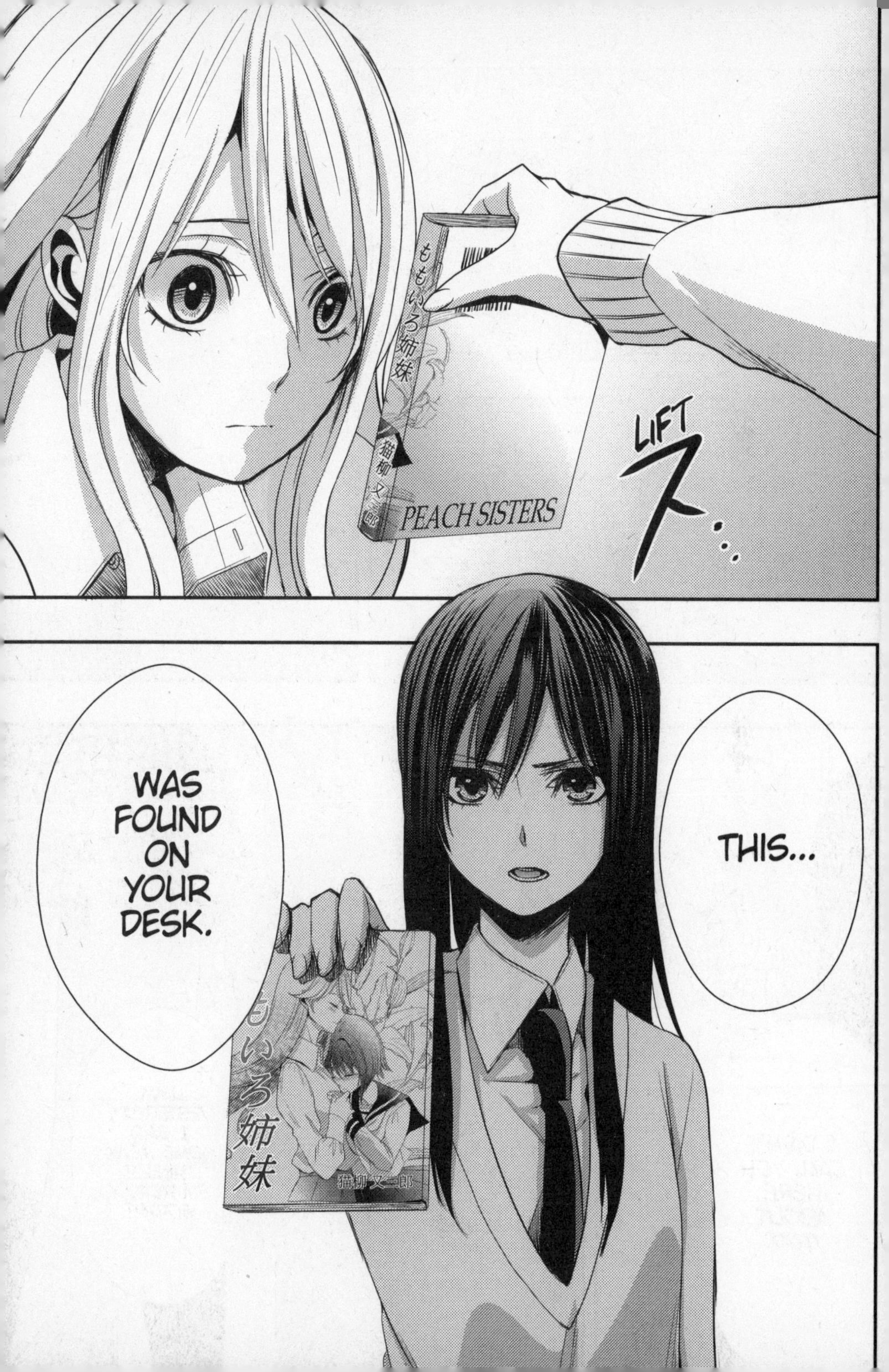
ももいろ姉妹
PEACH SISTERS
LIFT
ス...
THIS...
WAS FOUND ON YOUR DESK.
いろ姉妹
猫柳 文二郎

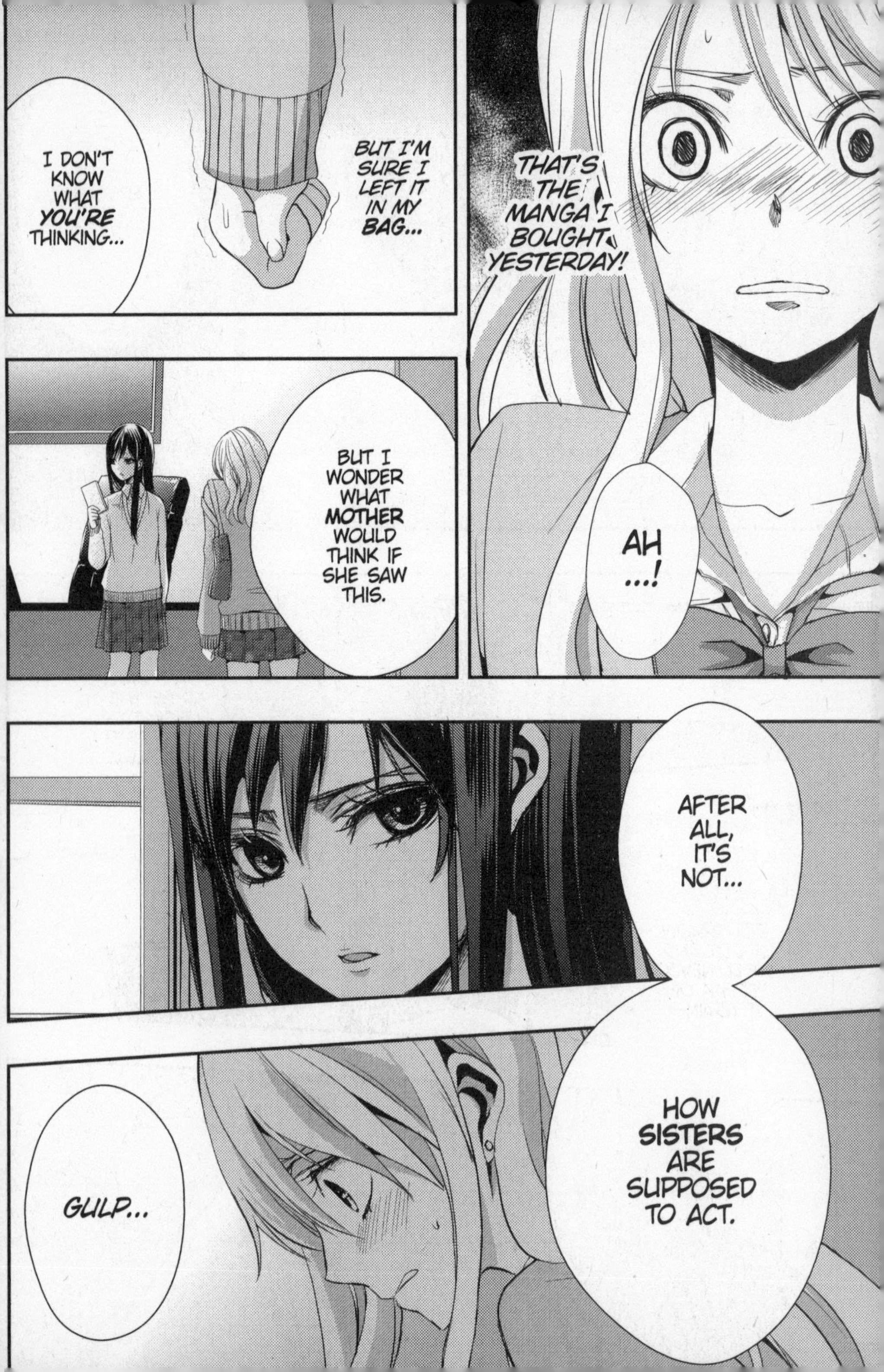
THAT'S THE MANGA I BOUGHT YESTERDAY!
AH ...!
BUT I'M SURE I LEFT IT IN MY BAG...
I DON'T KNOW WHAT YOU'RE THINKING...
BUT I WONDER WHAT MOTHER WOULD THINK IF SHE SAW THIS.
AFTER ALL, IT'S NOT...
HOW SISTERS ARE SUPPOSED TO ACT.
GULP...

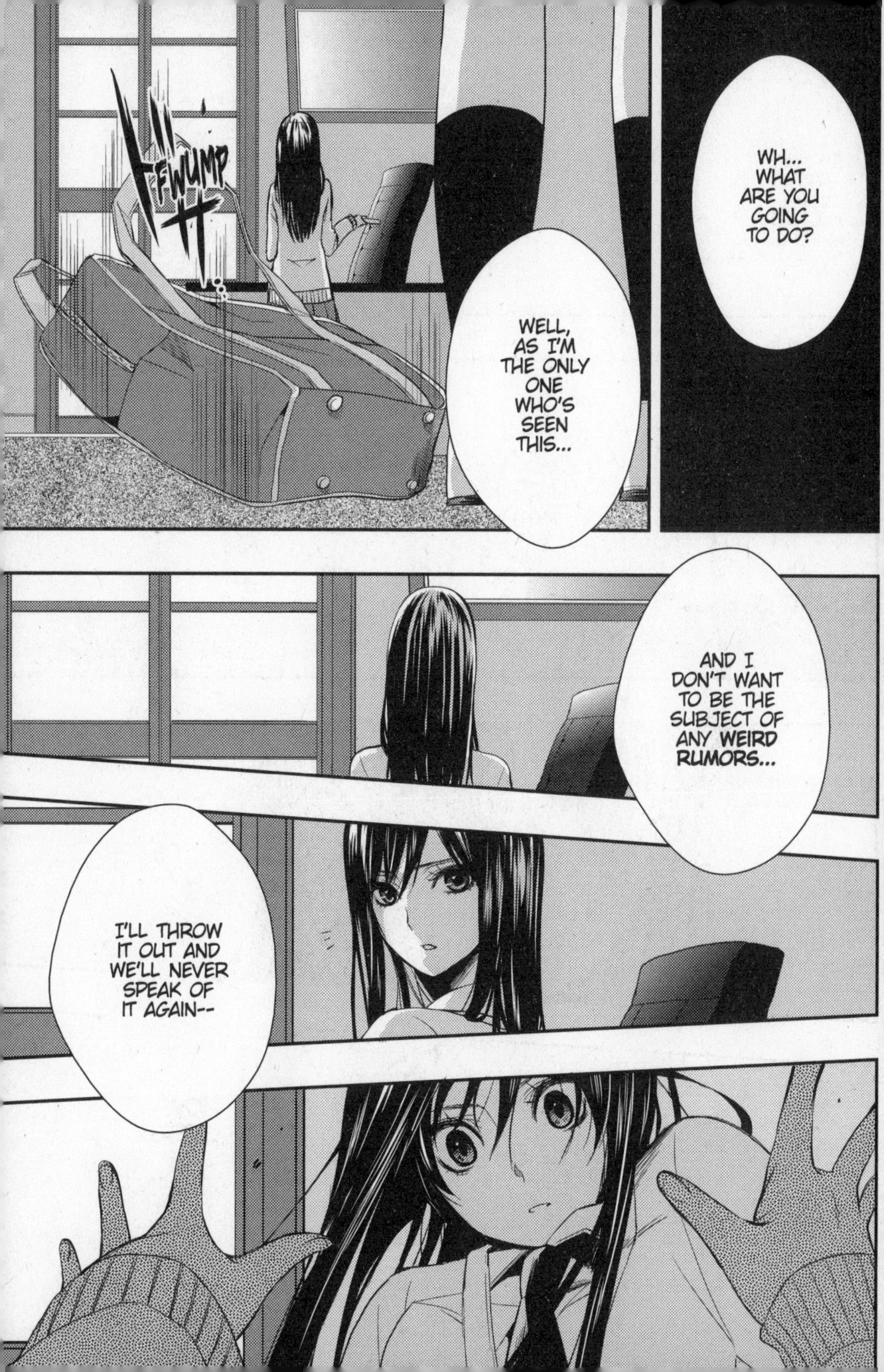
WH... WHAT ARE YOU GOING TO DO?
WELL, AS I'M THE ONLY ONE WHO'S SEEN THIS...
FWUMP
AND I DON'T WANT TO BE THE SUBJECT OF ANY WEIRD RUMORS...
I'LL THROW IT OUT AND WE'LL NEVER SPEAK OF IT AGAIN--

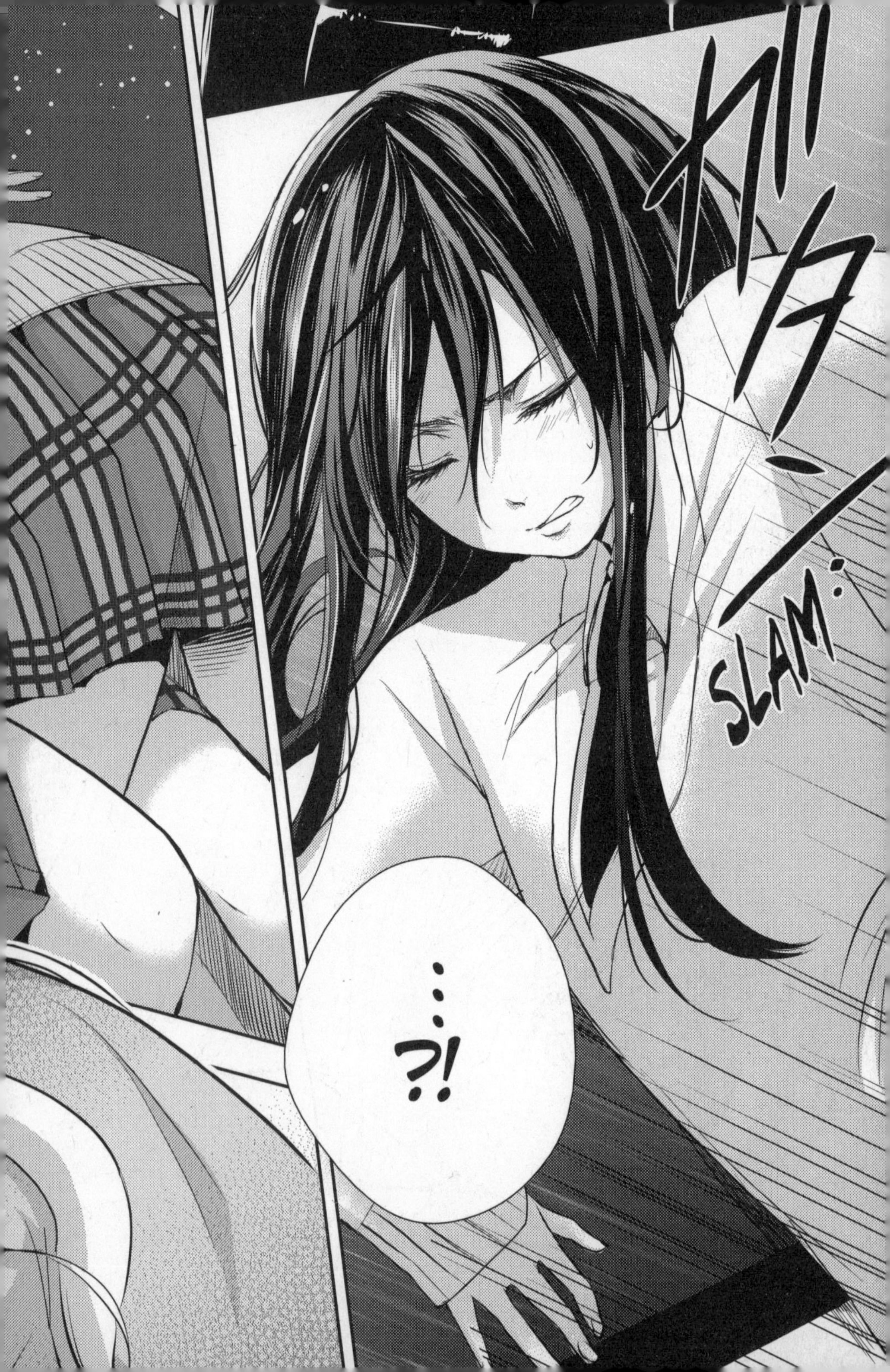
SLAM
...?!

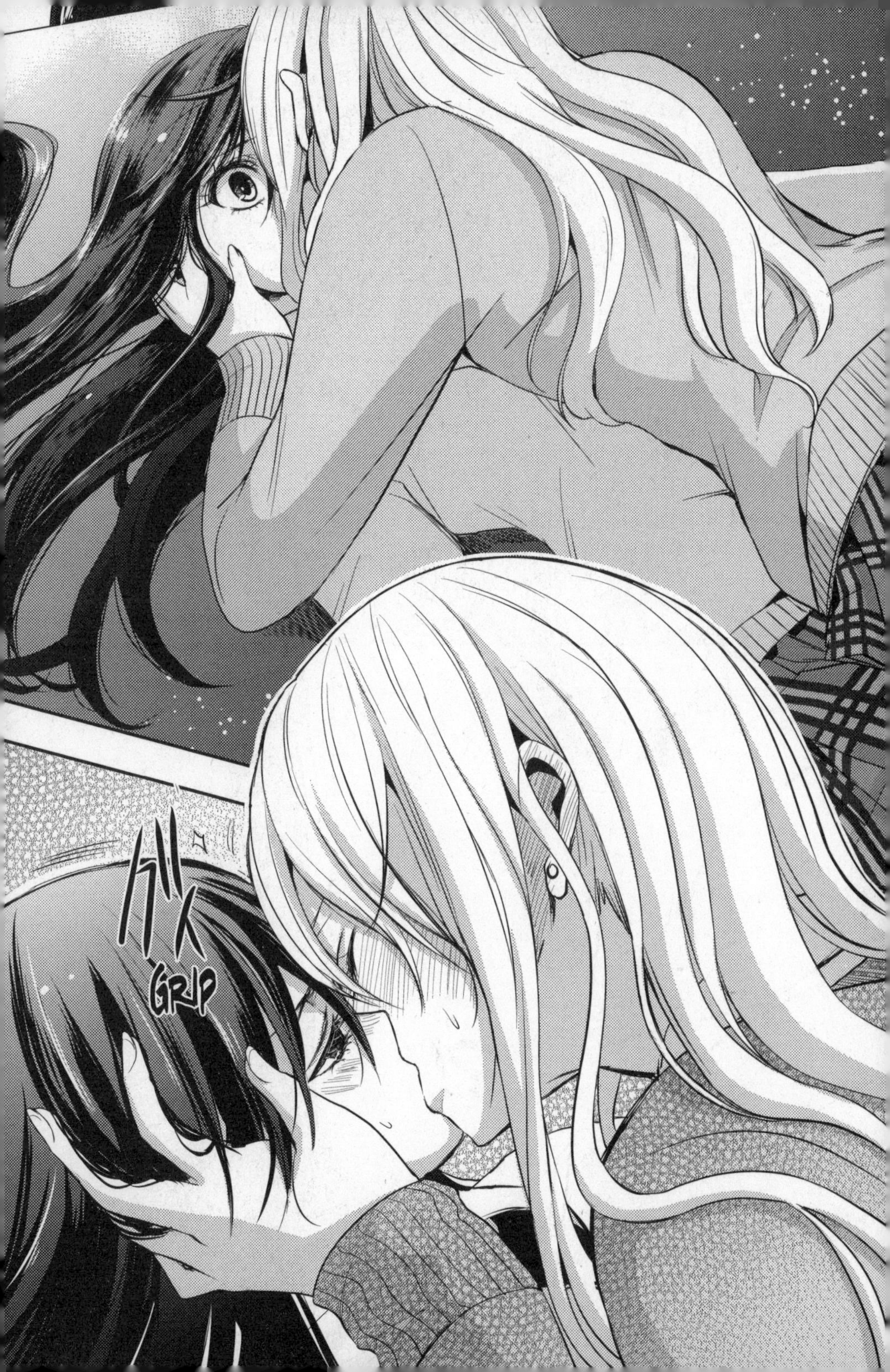
GRIP

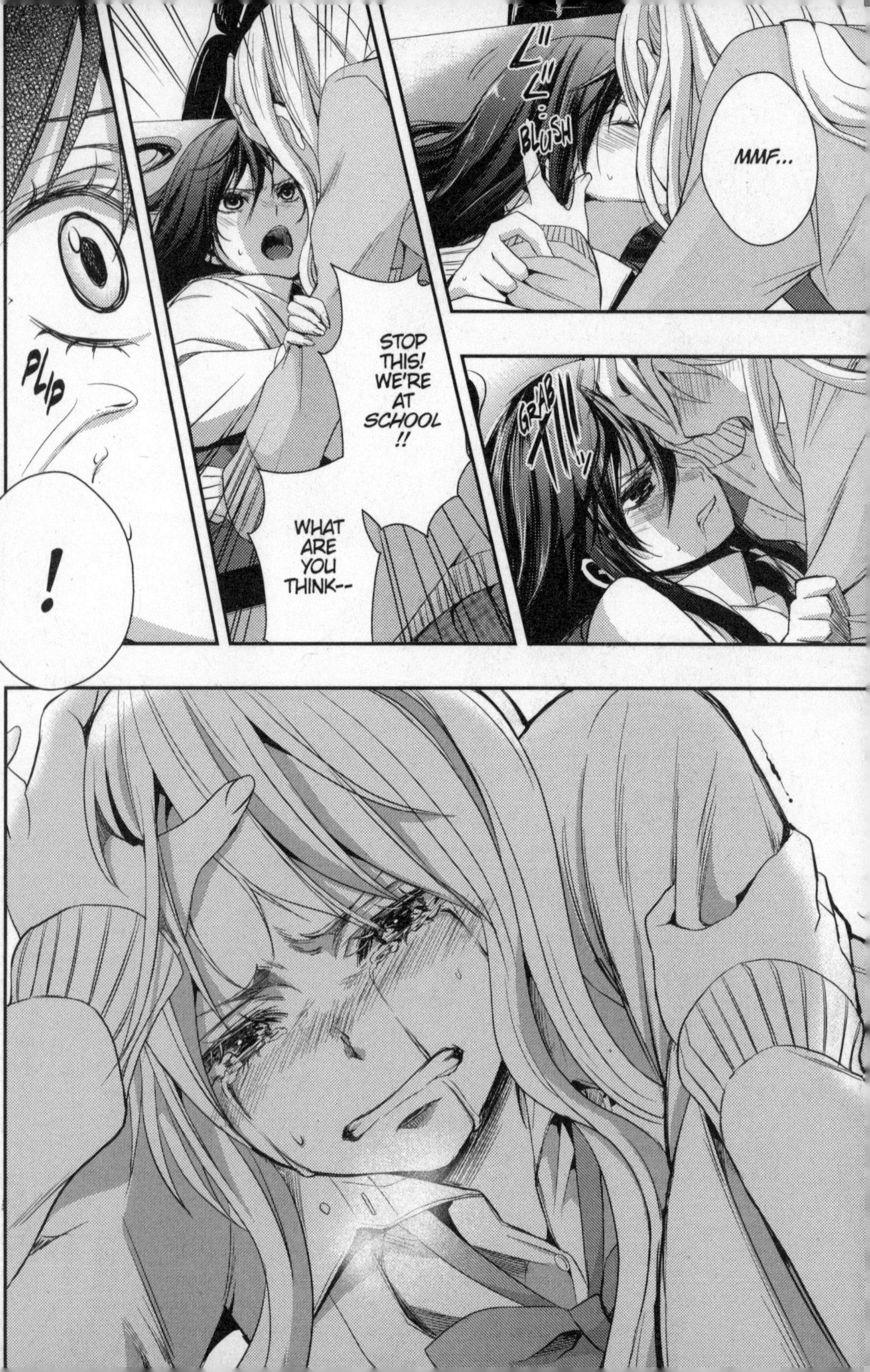

BLUSH
MMF...
GRAB
STOP THIS! WE'RE AT SCHOOL !!
WHAT ARE YOU THINK--
PLIP
!

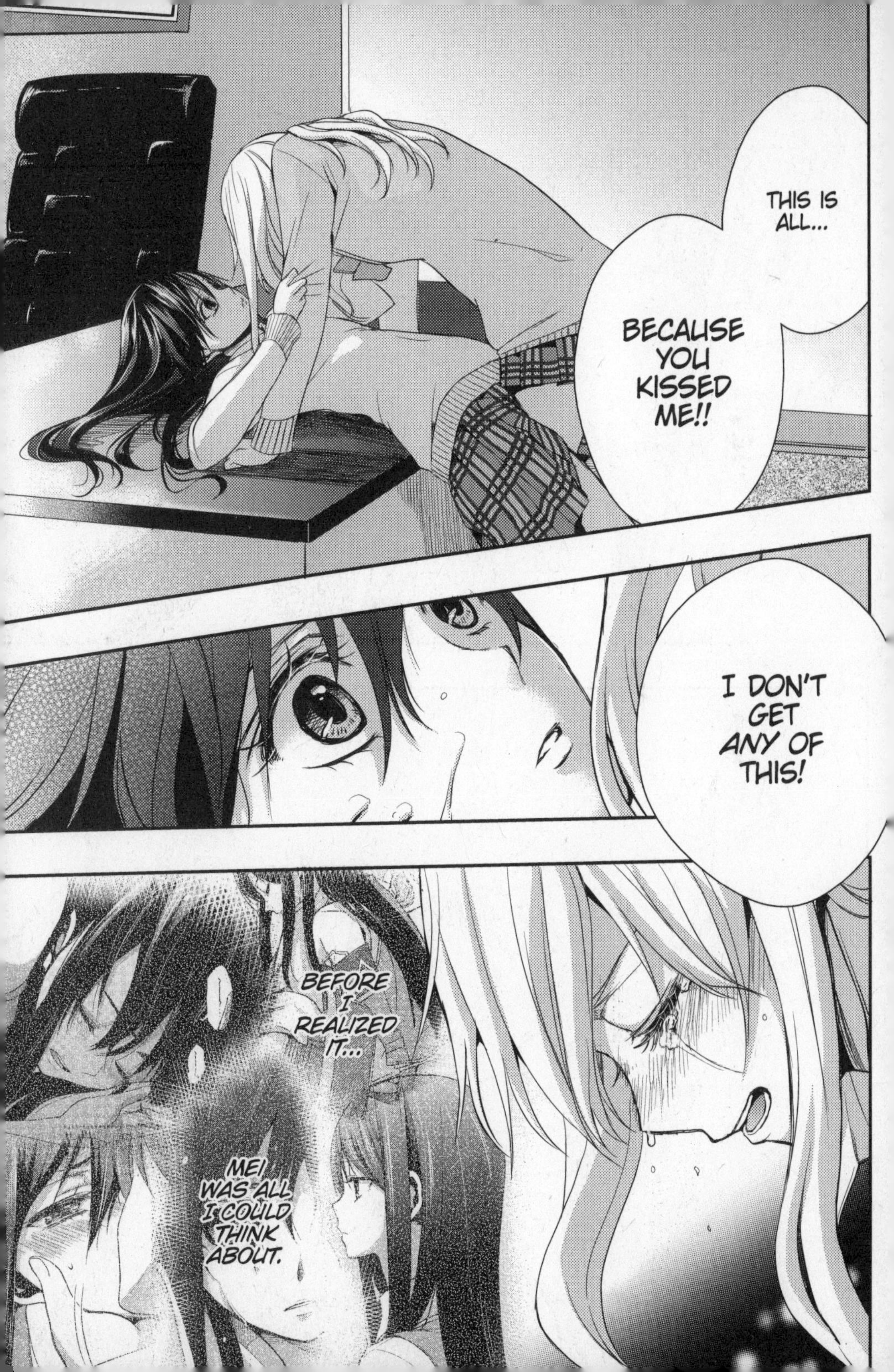
THIS IS ALL...
BECAUSE YOU KISSED ME!!
I DON'T GET ANY OF THIS!
BEFORE I REALIZED IT...
MEI WAS ALL I COULD THINK ABOUT.

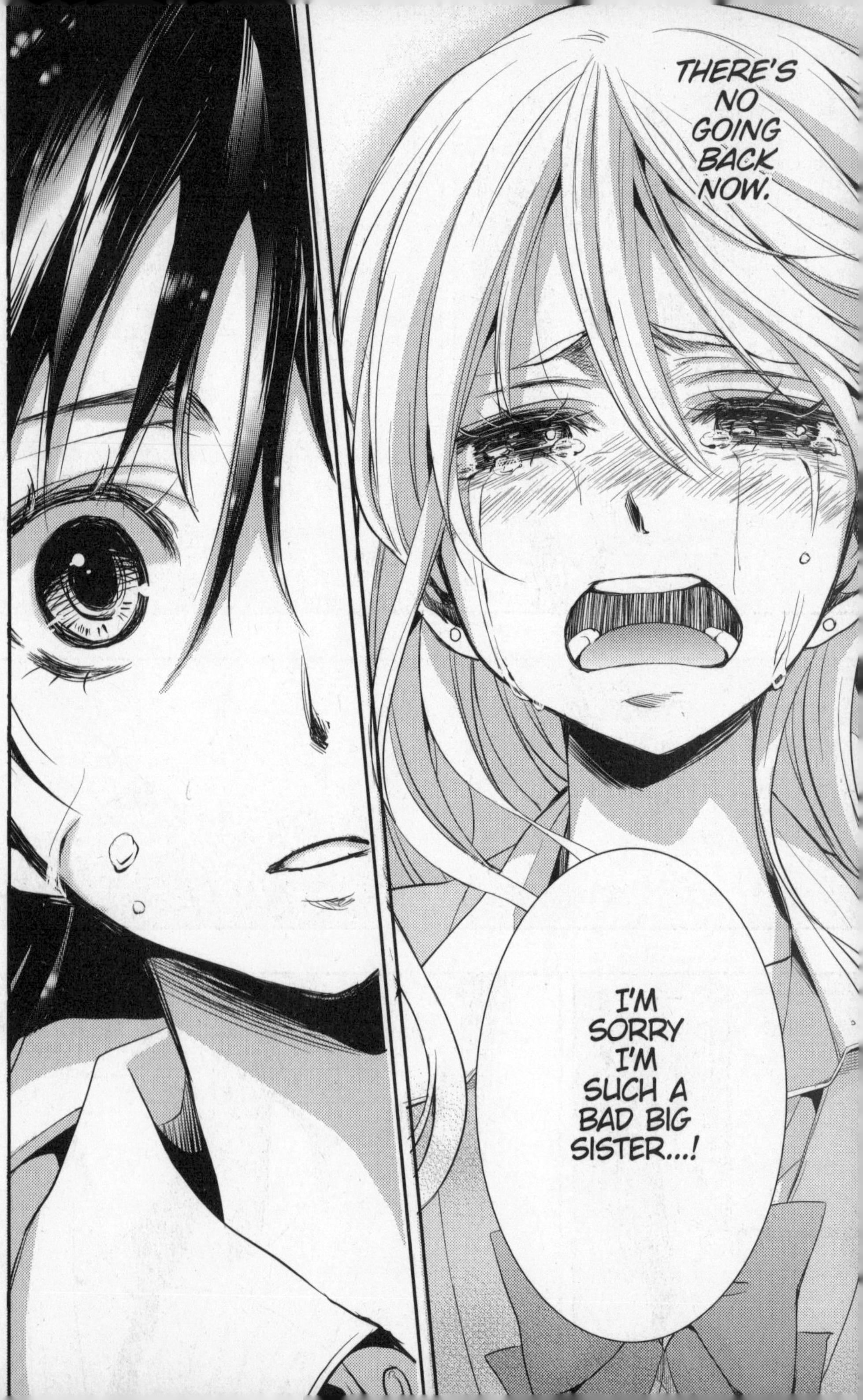
THERE'S NO GOING BACK NOW.
I'M SORRY I'M SUCH A BAD BIG SISTER...!

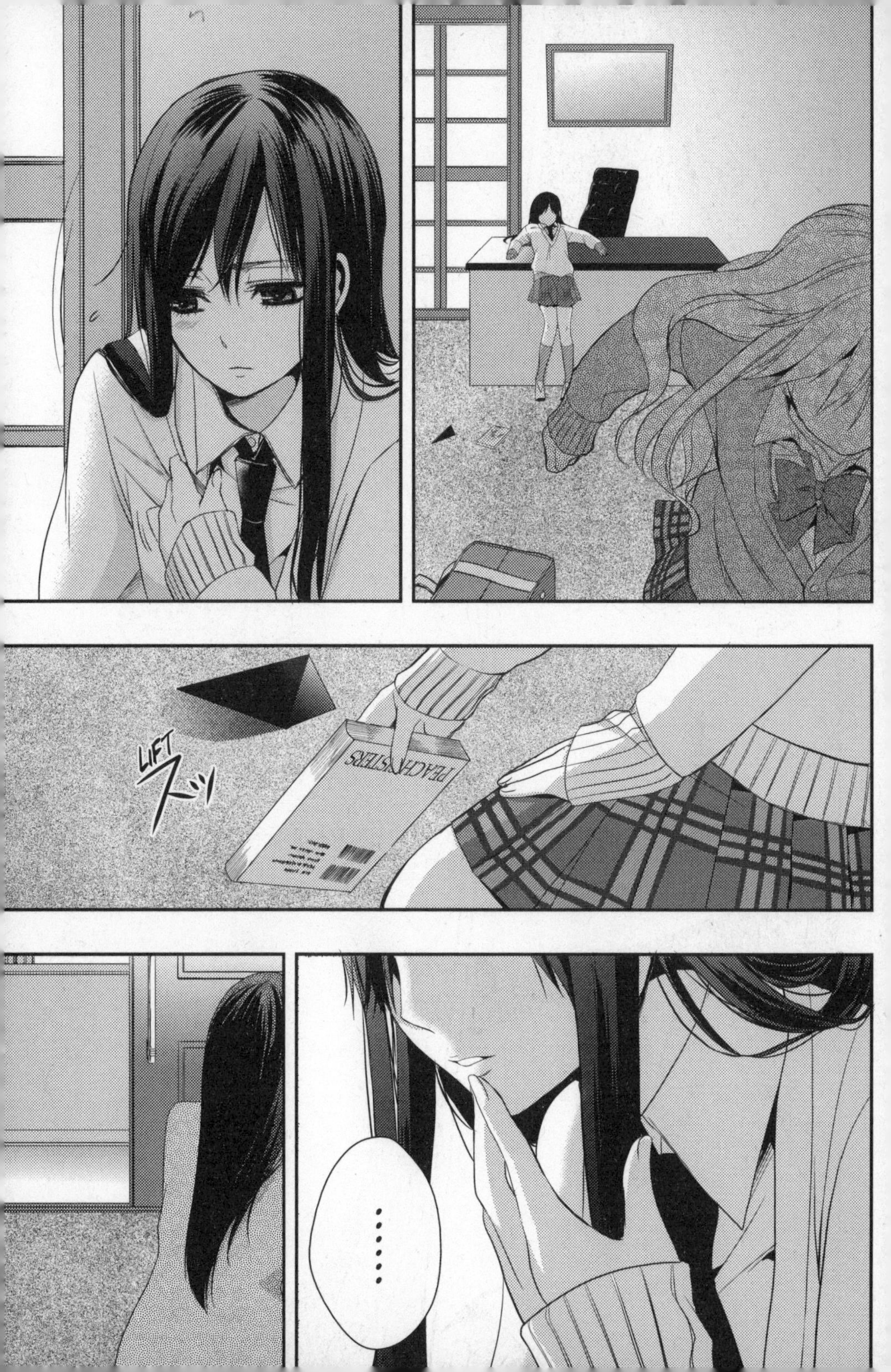
LIFT
スッ
PEACH SISTERS
……

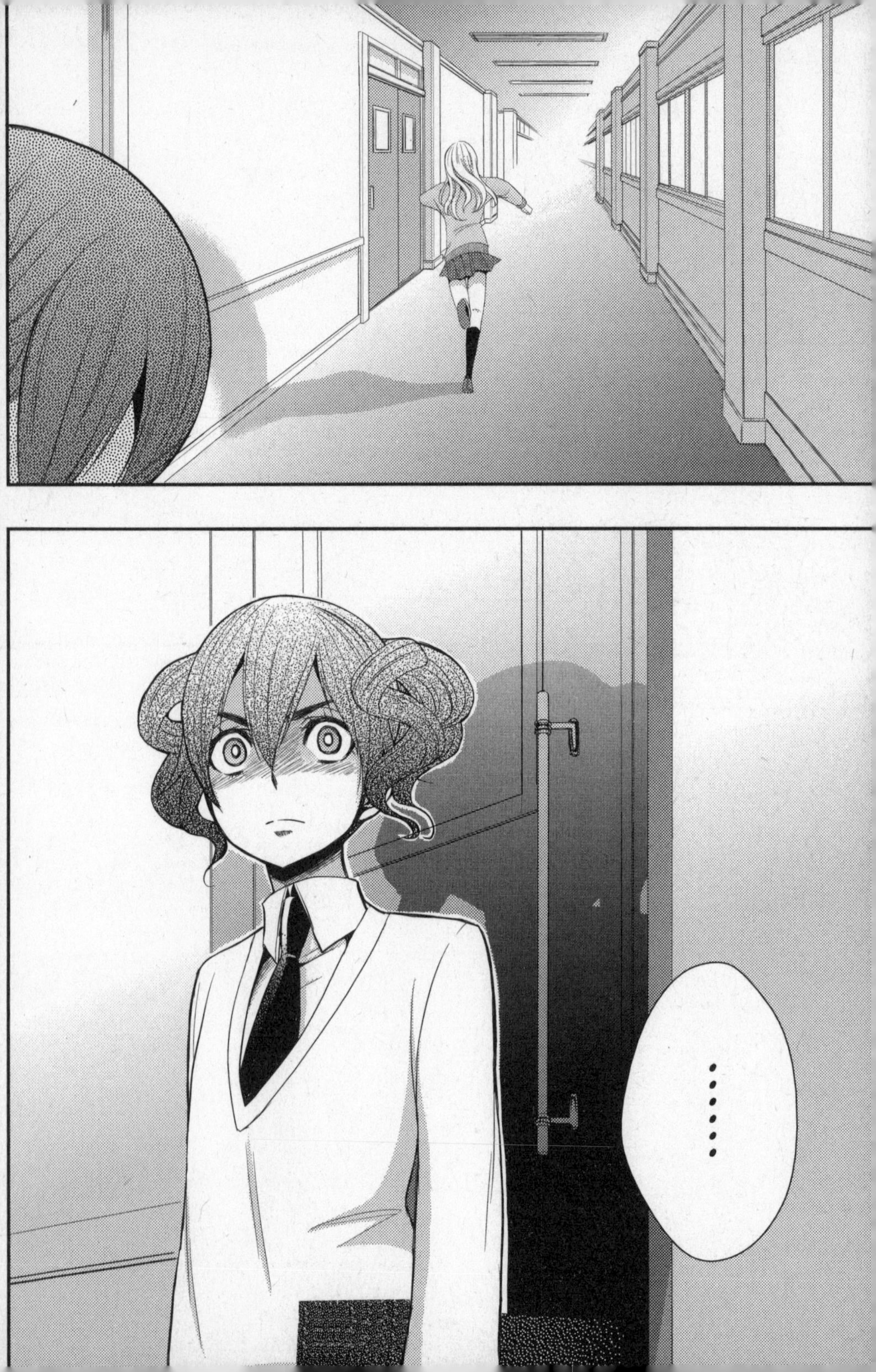
......

To be continued...

citrus

SABUROUTA PRESENTS SECRET LOVE AFFAIR WITH SISTER

1

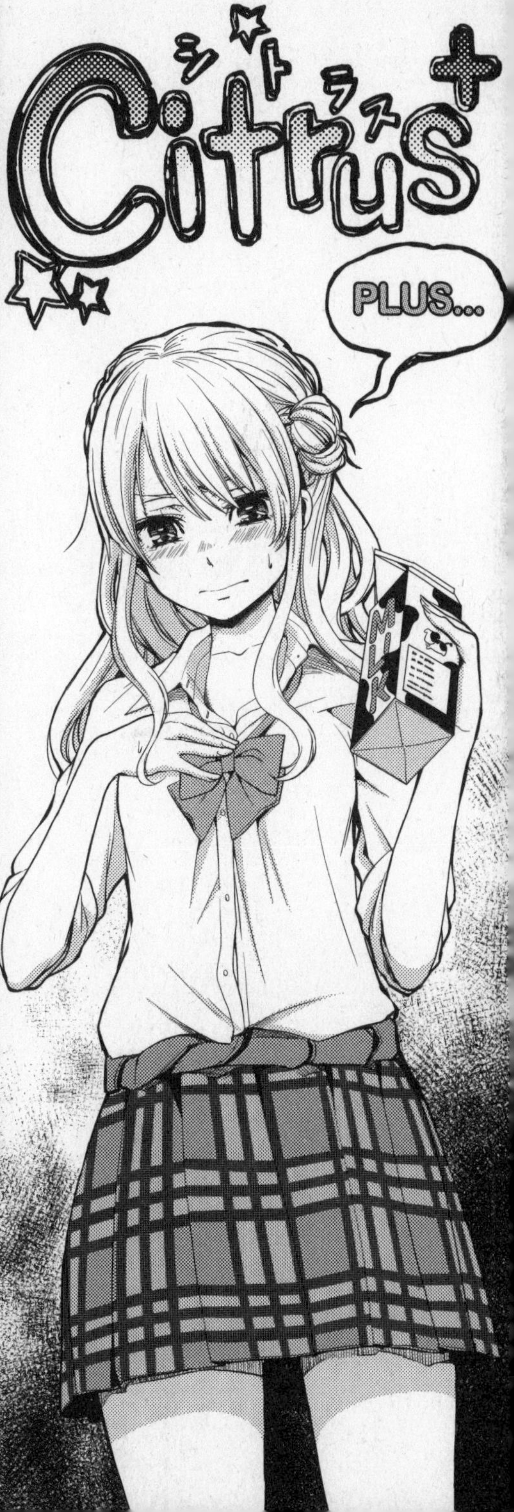
シトラス
Citrus+
PLUS...

I Couldn't Hide It

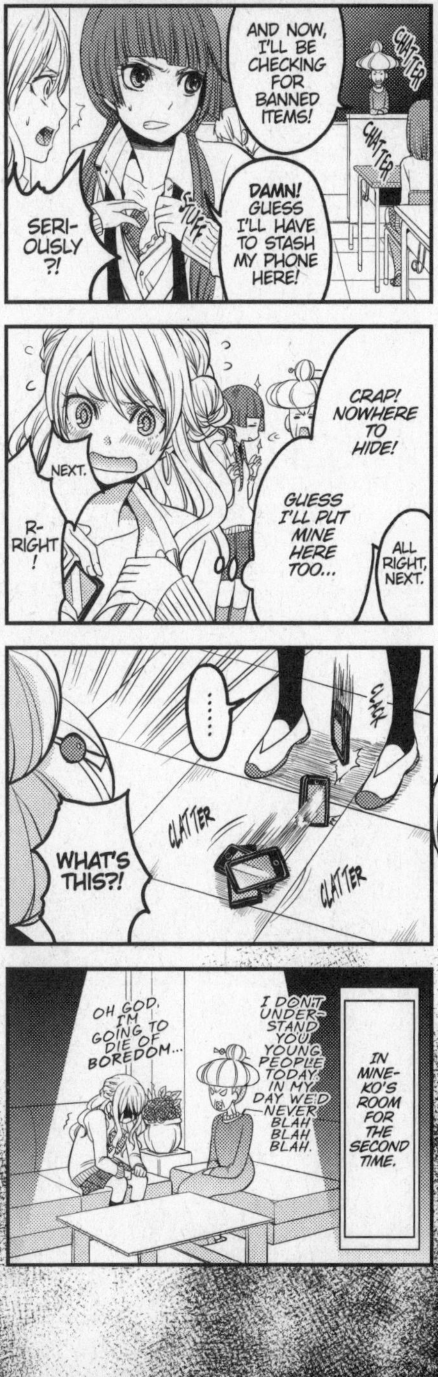
AND NOW, I'LL BE CHECKING FOR BANNED ITEMS!
CHATTER
CHATTER
DAMN! GUESS I'LL HAVE TO STASH MY PHONE HERE!
STUFF
SERIOUSLY?!
CRAP! NOWHERE TO HIDE!
GUESS I'LL PUT MINE HERE TOO...
ALL RIGHT, NEXT.
NEXT.
R-RIGHT!
CLACK
......
CLATTER
CLATTER
WHAT'S THIS?!
IN MINEKO'S ROOM FOR THE SECOND TIME.
I DON'T UNDERSTAND YOU YOUNG PEOPLE TODAY. IN MY DAY WE'D NEVER BLAH BLAH BLAH.
OH GOD, I'M GOING TO DIE OF BOREDOM...

Harumin and Megane-senpai

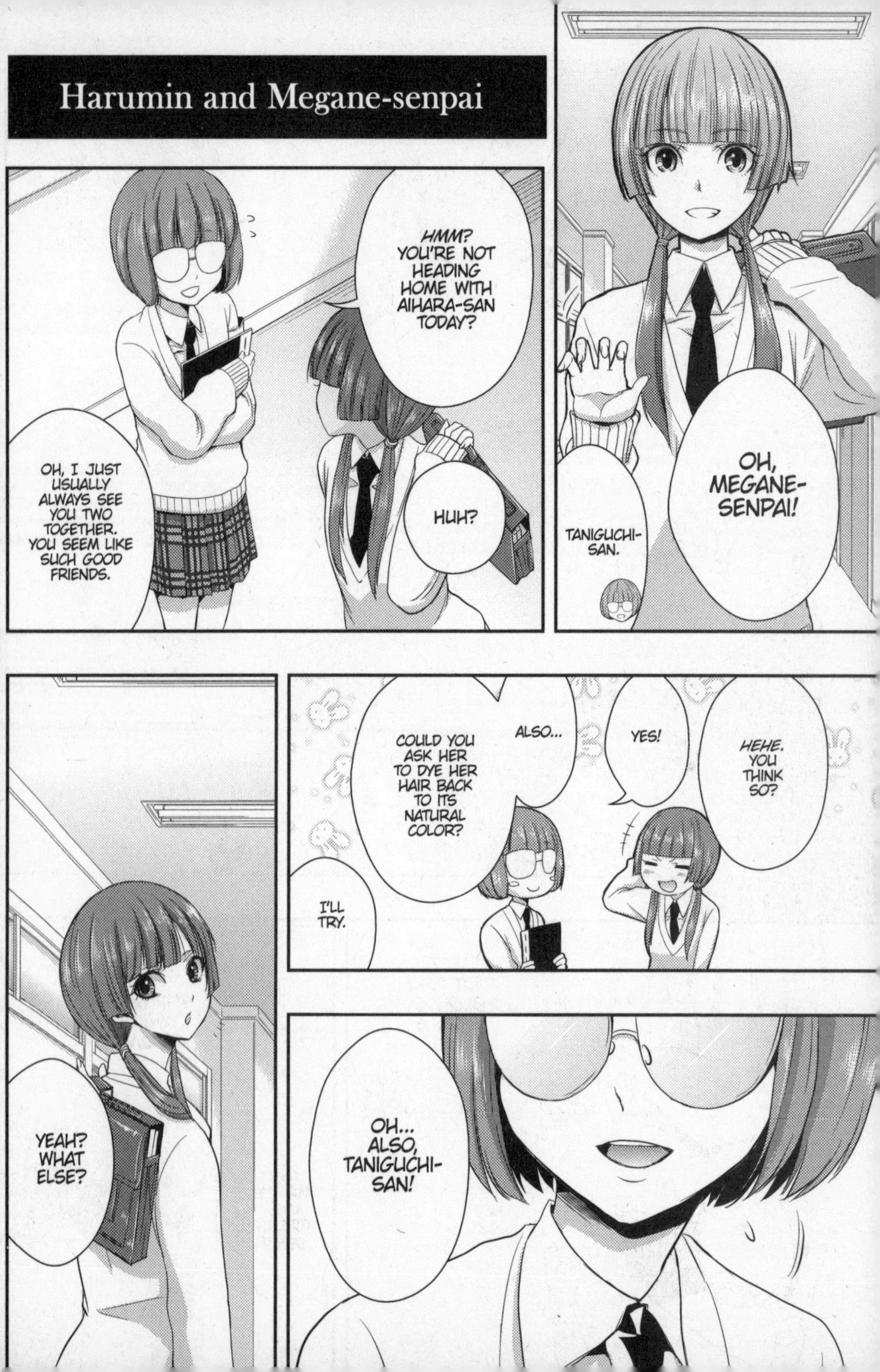
OH, MEGANE-SENPAI!
TANIGUCHI-SAN.
HMM? YOU'RE NOT HEADING HOME WITH AIHARA-SAN TODAY?
HUH?
OH, I JUST USUALLY ALWAYS SEE YOU TWO TOGETHER. YOU SEEM LIKE SUCH GOOD FRIENDS.
HEHE. YOU THINK SO?
YES!
ALSO...
COULD YOU ASK HER TO DYE HER HAIR BACK TO ITS NATURAL COLOR?
I'LL TRY.
OH... ALSO, TANIGUCHI-SAN!
YEAH? WHAT ELSE?

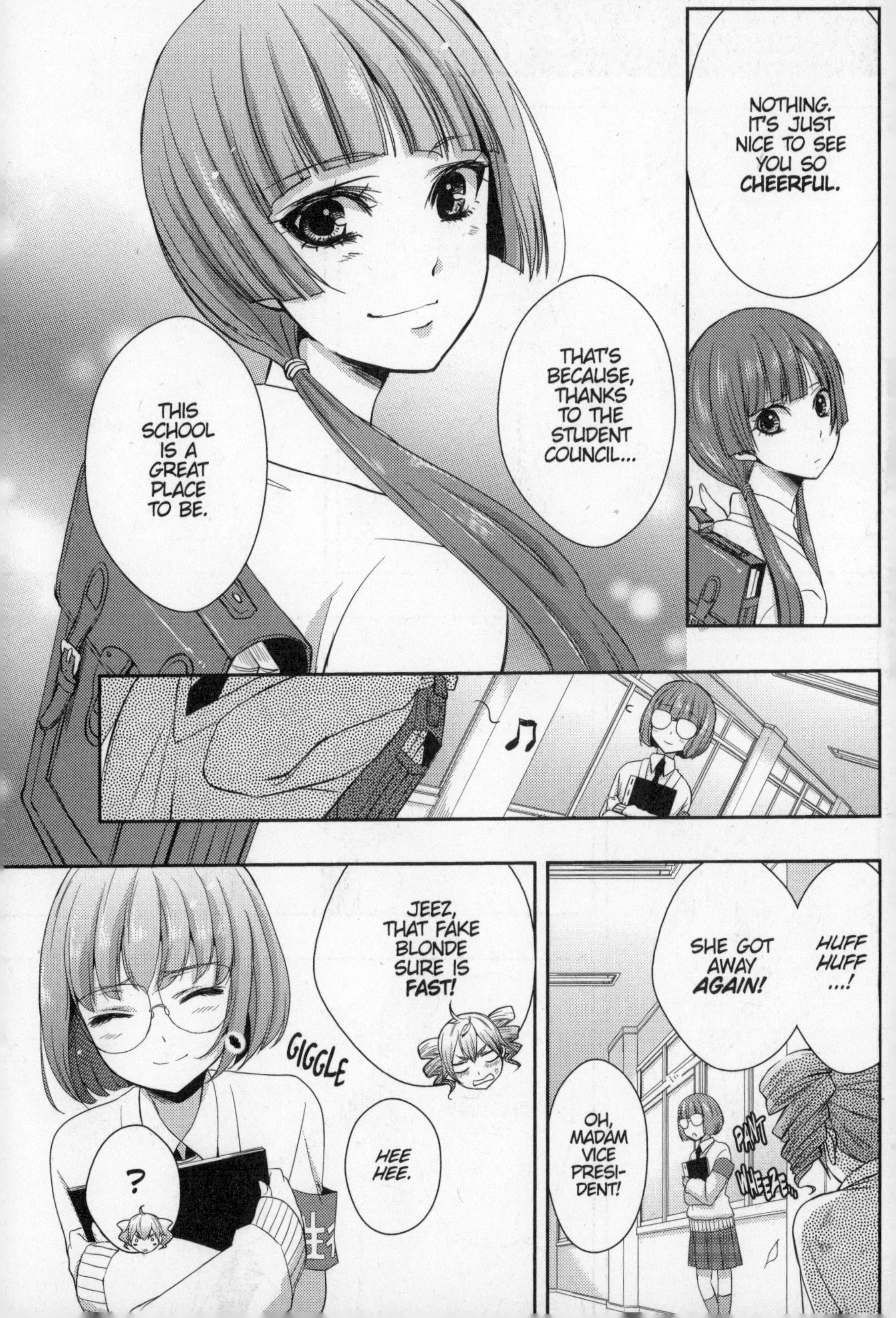

NOTHING. IT'S JUST NICE TO SEE YOU SO CHEERFUL.
THAT'S BECAUSE, THANKS TO THE STUDENT COUNCIL...
THIS SCHOOL IS A GREAT PLACE TO BE.
HUFF HUFF ...!
SHE GOT AWAY AGAIN!
OH, MADAM VICE PRESIDENT!
PANT
WHEEZE...
JEEZ, THAT FAKE BLONDE SURE IS FAST!
GIGGLE
HEE HEE.
?

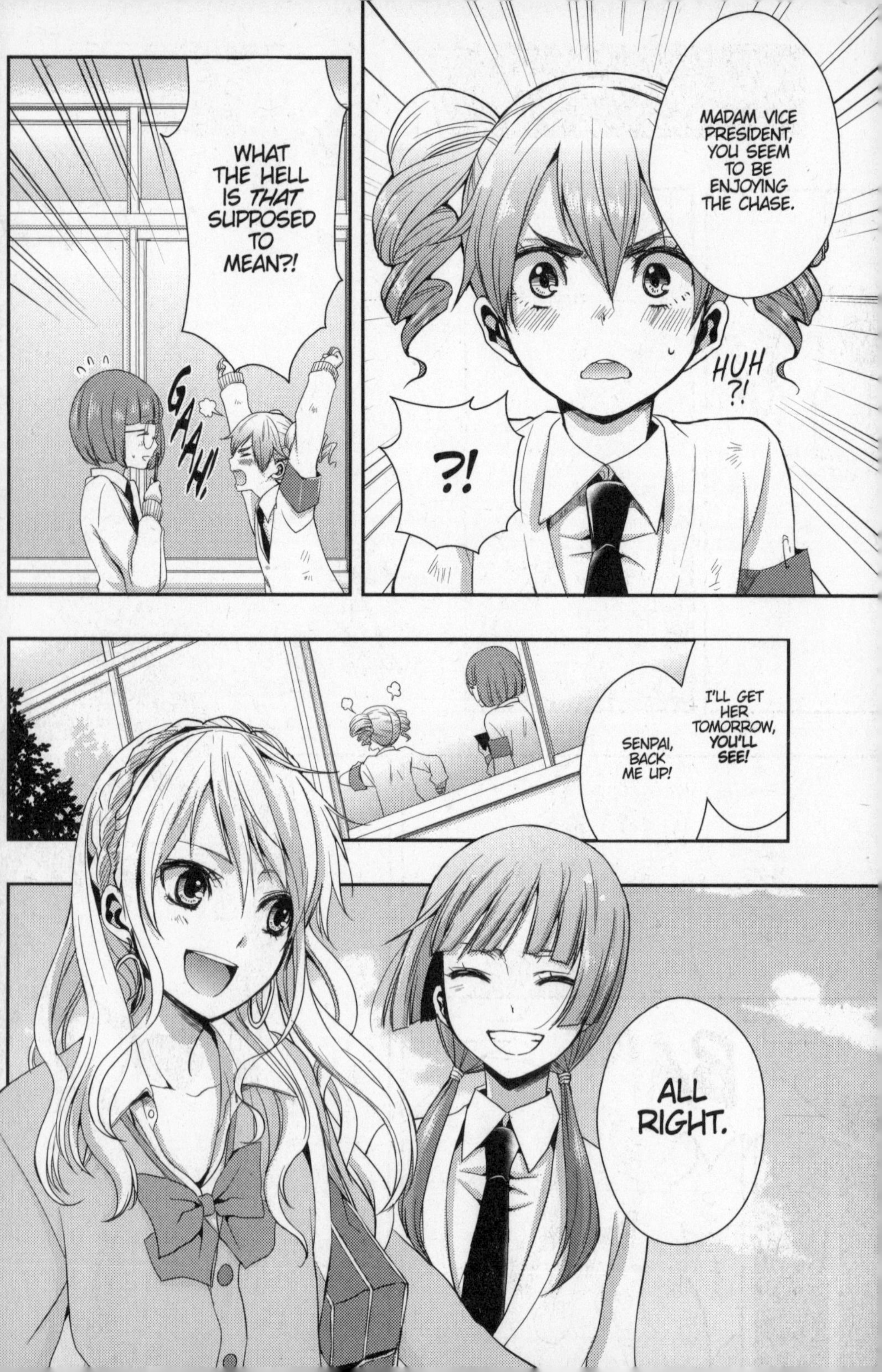
MADAM VICE PRESIDENT, YOU SEEM TO BE ENJOYING THE CHASE.
HUH ?!
?!
WHAT THE HELL IS *THAT* SUPPOSED TO MEAN?!
GAAH!
I'LL GET HER TOMORROW, YOU'LL SEE!
SENPAI, BACK ME UP!
ALL RIGHT.

Mei-chan & Mr. Bear

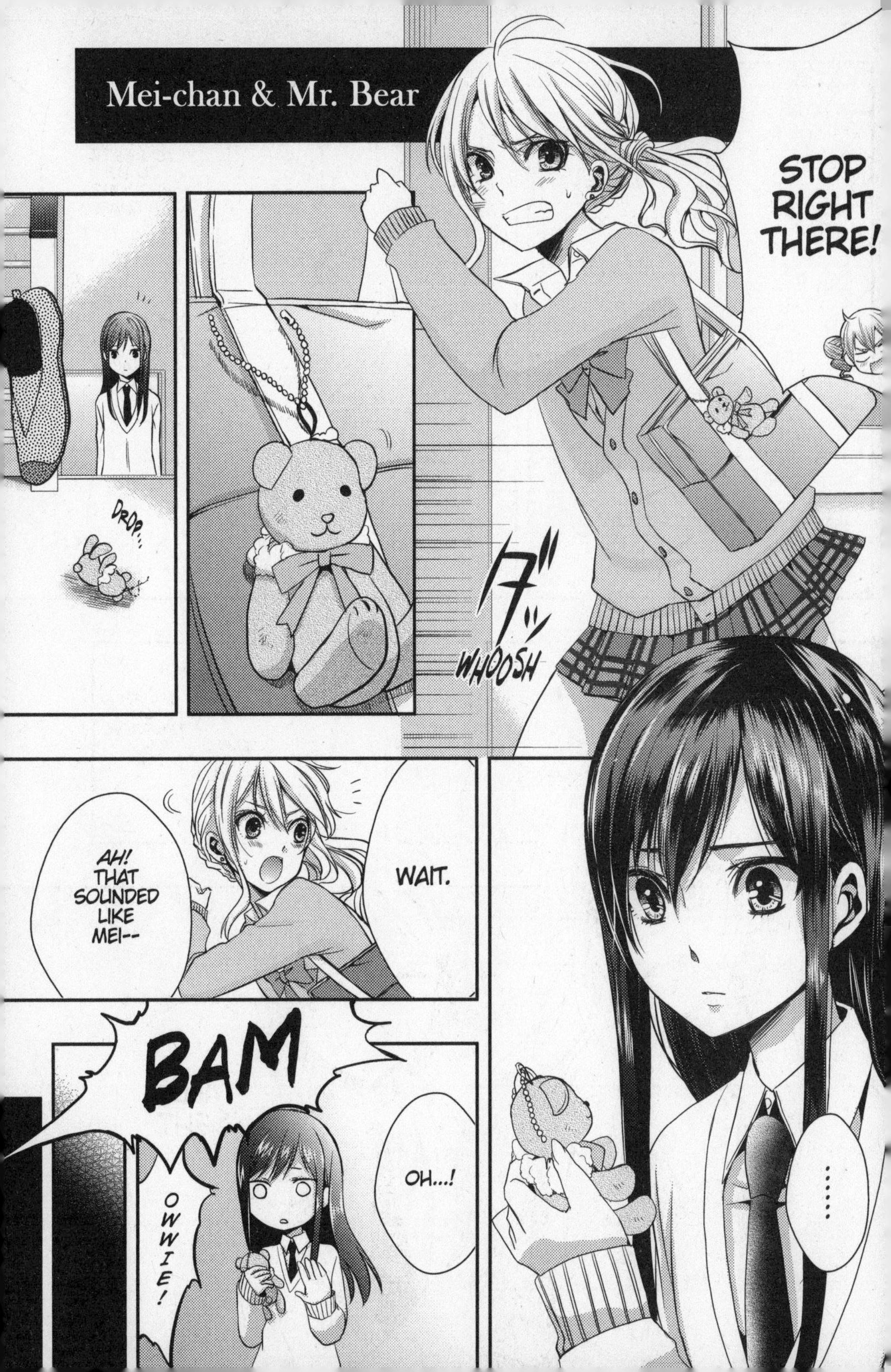
STOP RIGHT THERE!
DROP...
WHOOSH
......
WAIT.
AH! THAT SOUNDED LIKE MEI--
BAM
OH...!
OWWIE!

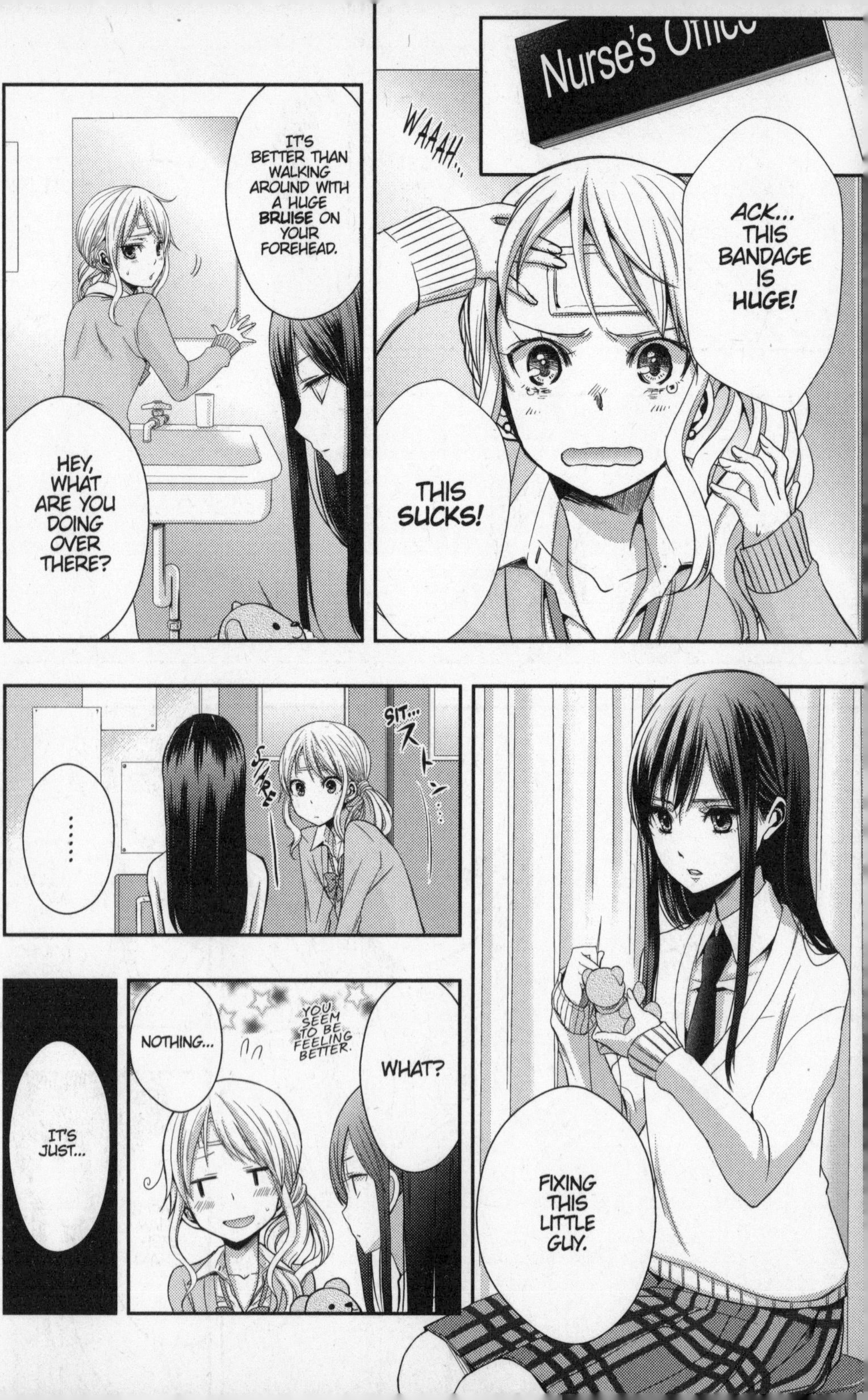
Nurse's Offic
WAAAH...
ACK... THIS BANDAGE IS HUGE!
THIS SUCKS!
IT'S BETTER THAN WALKING AROUND WITH A HUGE BRUISE ON YOUR FOREHEAD.
HEY, WHAT ARE YOU DOING OVER THERE?
FIXING THIS LITTLE GUY.
SIT...
ストン...
STARE
......
WHAT?
YOU SEEM TO BE FEELING BETTER.
NOTHING...
IT'S JUST...

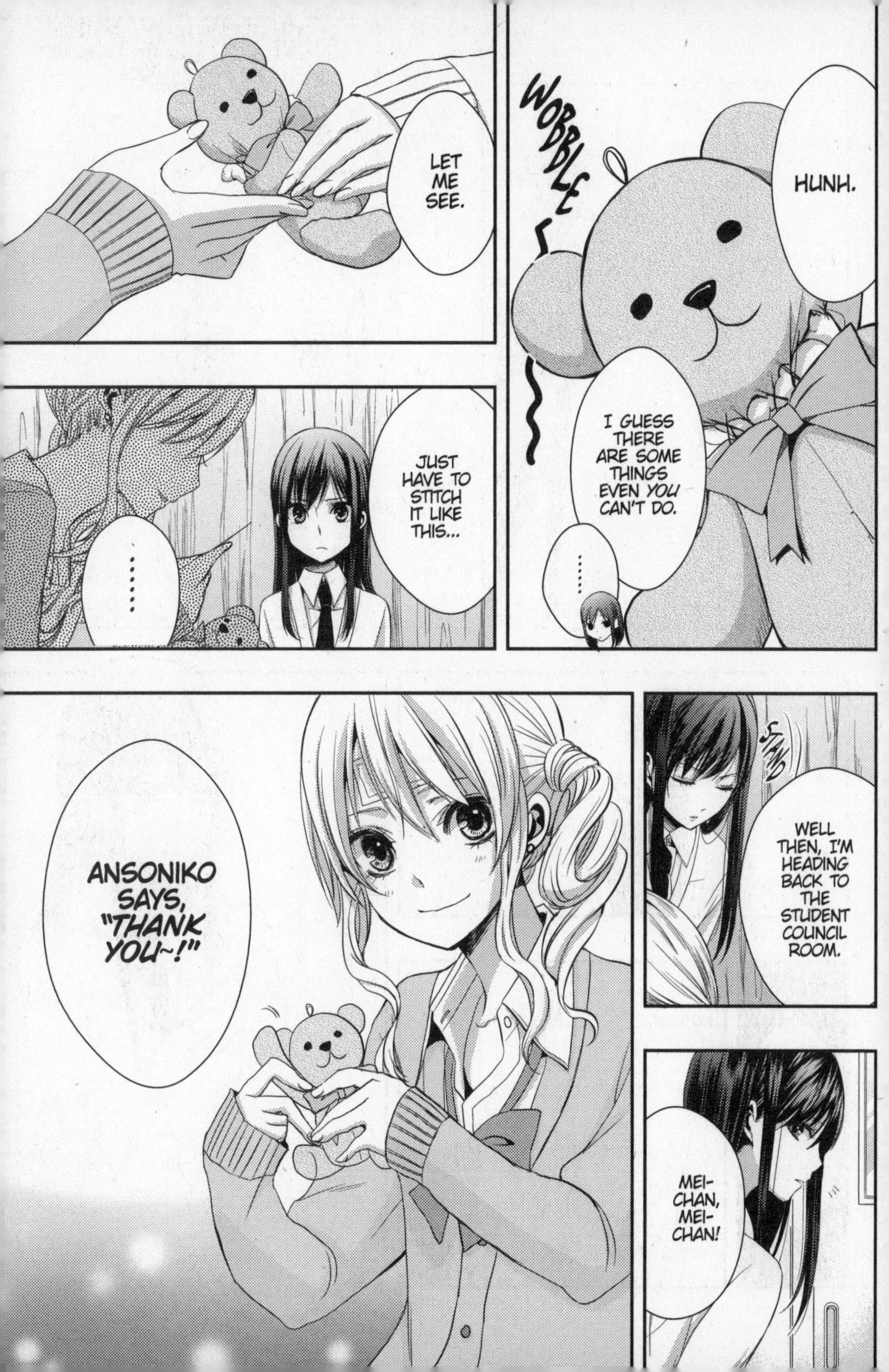
HUNH.
WOBBLE~
I GUESS THERE ARE SOME THINGS EVEN *YOU* CAN'T DO.
......
LET ME SEE.
JUST HAVE TO STITCH IT LIKE THIS...
......
STAND
WELL THEN, I'M HEADING BACK TO THE STUDENT COUNCIL ROOM.
MEI-CHAN, MEI-CHAN!
ANSONIKO SAYS, *"THANK YOU~!"*

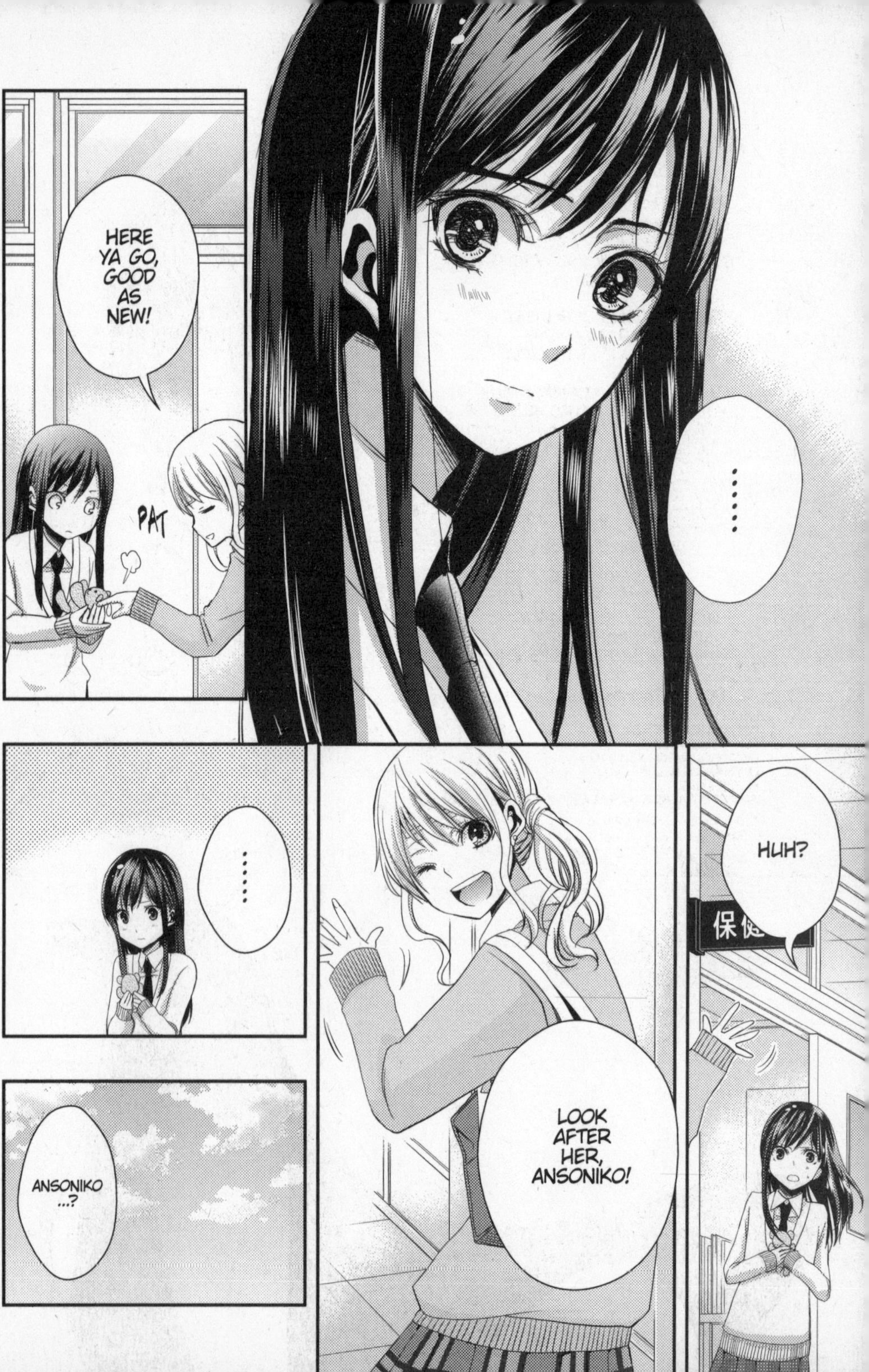
......
HERE YA GO, GOOD AS NEW!
PAT
HUH?
保健
LOOK AFTER HER, ANSONIKO!
......
ANSONIKO ...?

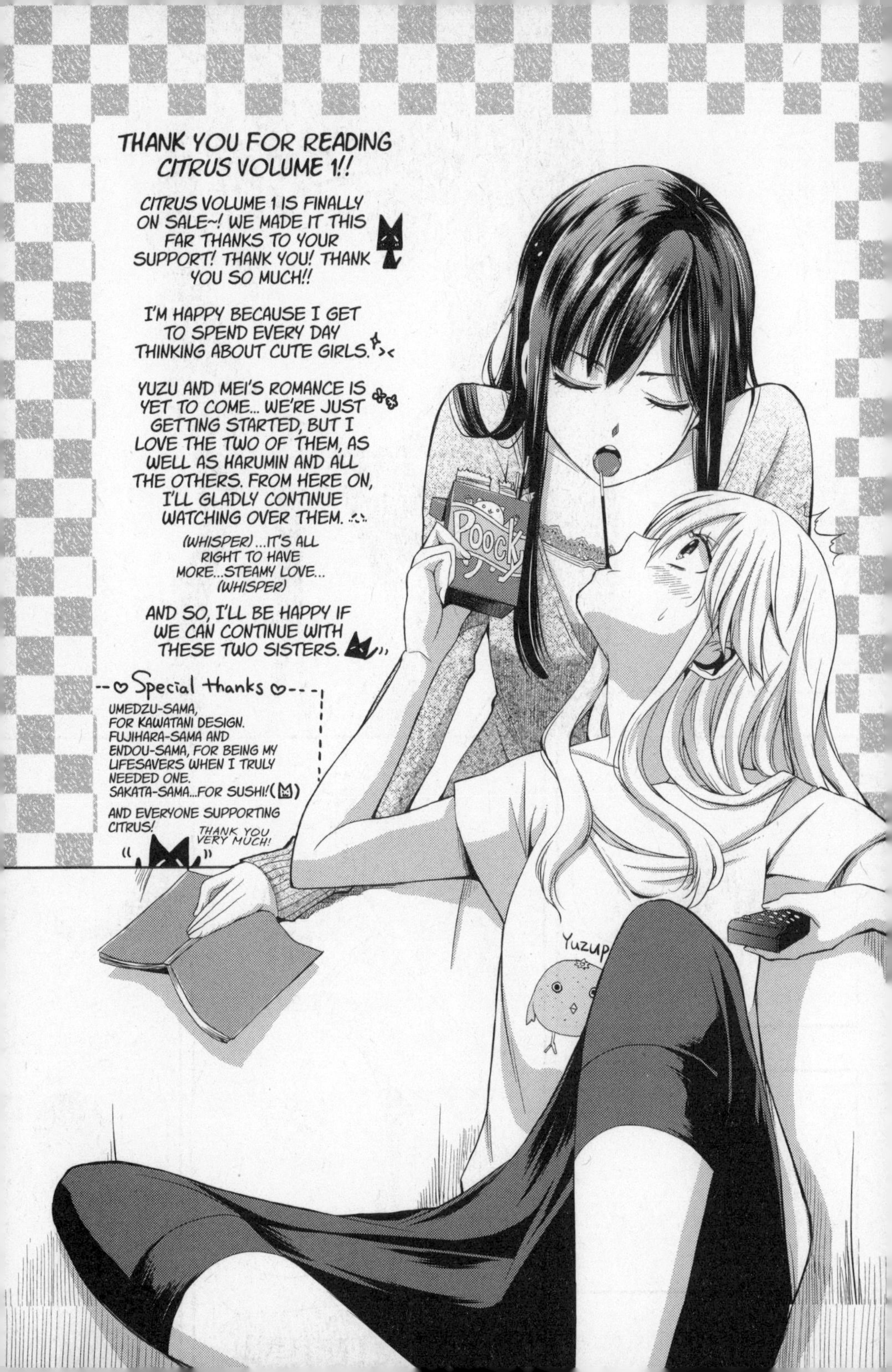
THANK YOU FOR READING CITRUS VOLUME 1!!
CITRUS VOLUME 1 IS FINALLY ON SALE~! WE MADE IT THIS FAR THANKS TO YOUR SUPPORT! THANK YOU! THANK YOU SO MUCH!!
I'M HAPPY BECAUSE I GET TO SPEND EVERY DAY THINKING ABOUT CUTE GIRLS.
YUZU AND MEI'S ROMANCE IS YET TO COME... WE'RE JUST GETTING STARTED, BUT I LOVE THE TWO OF THEM, AS WELL AS HARUMIN AND ALL THE OTHERS. FROM HERE ON, I'LL GLADLY CONTINUE WATCHING OVER THEM.
(WHISPER) ...IT'S ALL RIGHT TO HAVE MORE...STEAMY LOVE... (WHISPER)
AND SO, I'LL BE HAPPY IF WE CAN CONTINUE WITH THESE TWO SISTERS.
Special thanks
UMEDZU-SAMA, FOR KAWATANI DESIGN.
FUJIHARA-SAMA AND ENDOU-SAMA, FOR BEING MY LIFESAVERS WHEN I TRULY NEEDED ONE.
SAKATA-SAMA...FOR SUSHI!
AND EVERYONE SUPPORTING CITRUS!
THANK YOU VERY MUCH!
Poocky
Yuzup

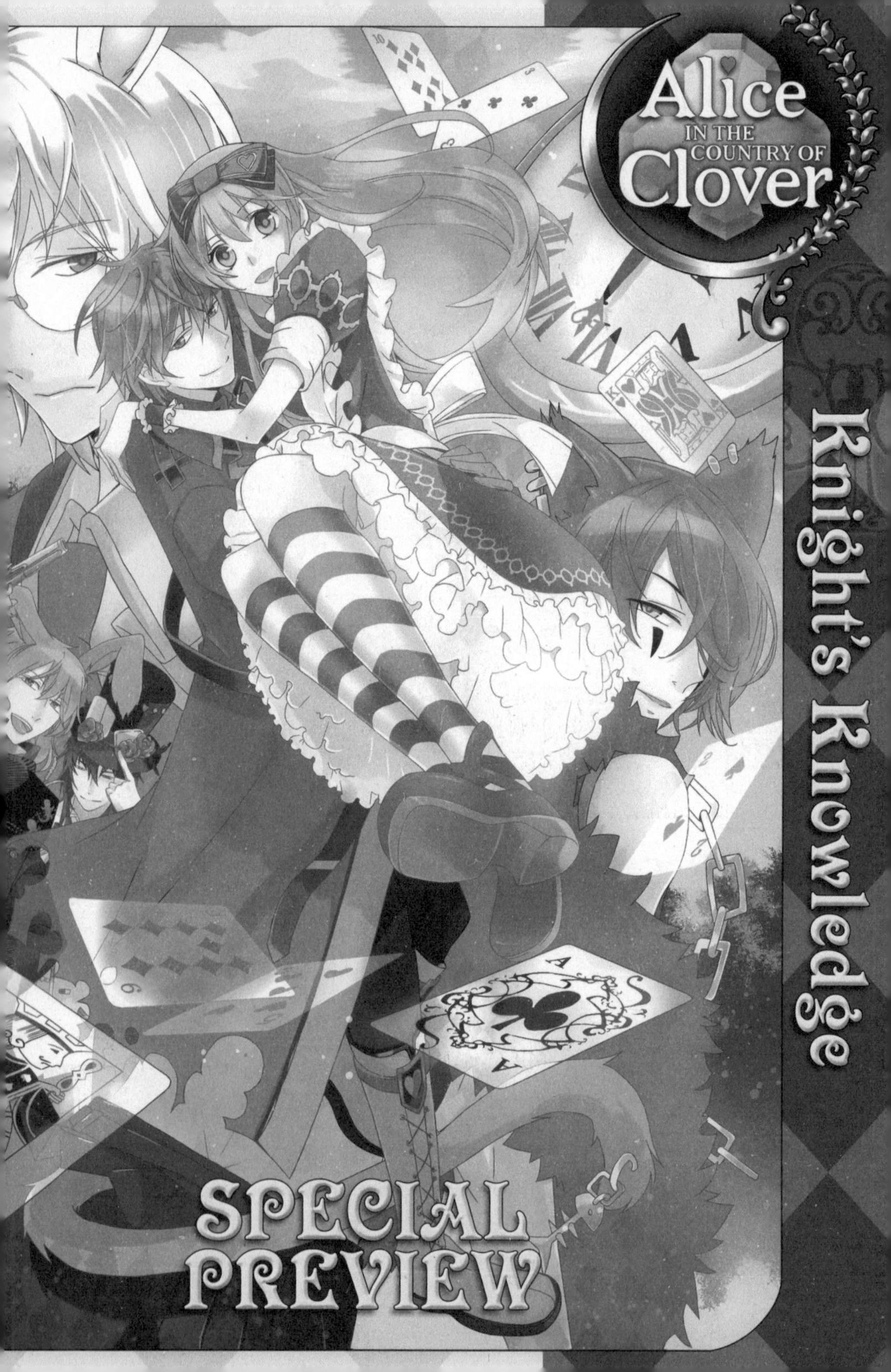
Alice
IN THE
COUNTRY OF
Clover
Knight's Knowledge
SPECIAL
PREVIEW

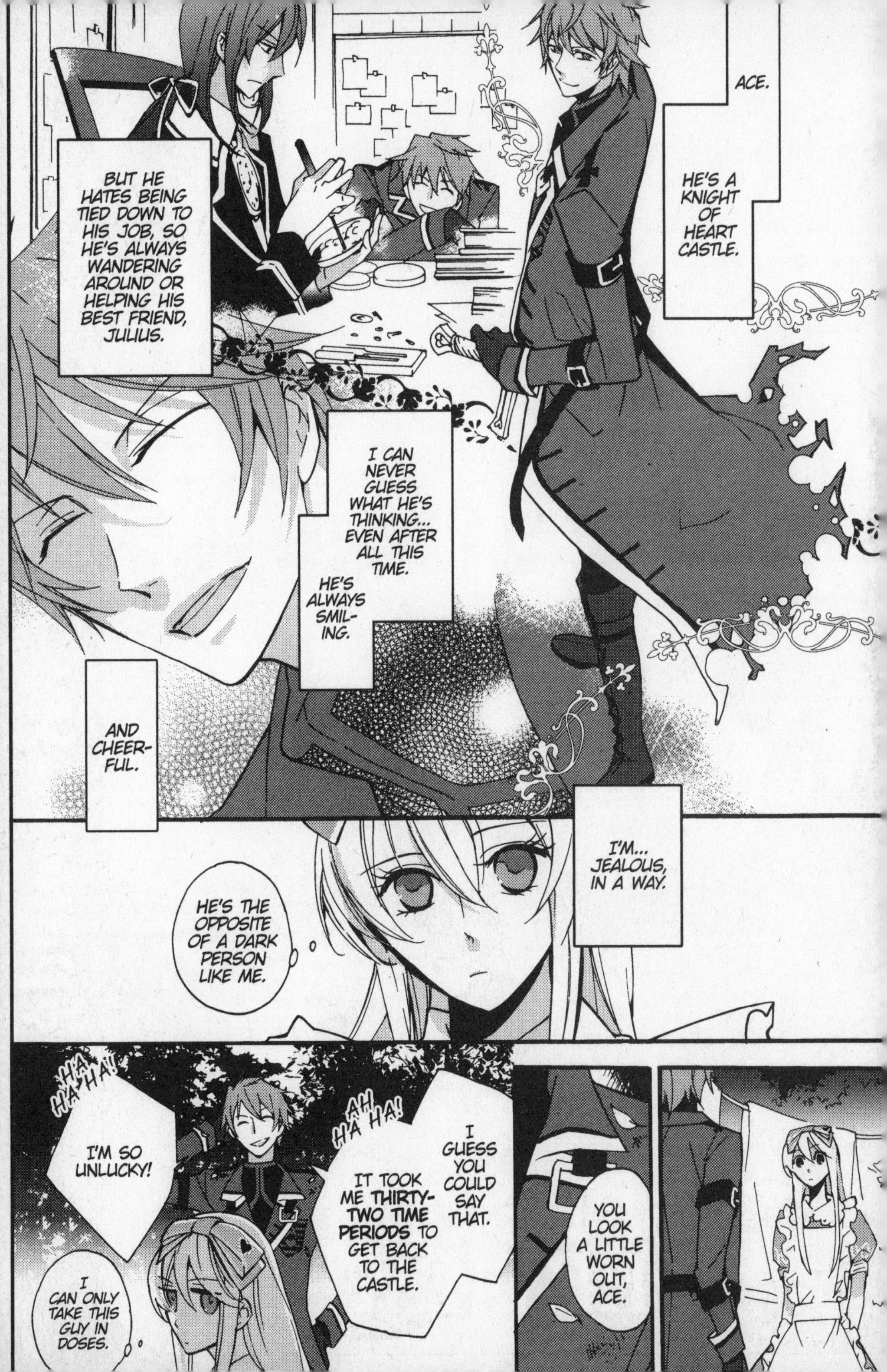
ACE.
HE'S A KNIGHT OF HEART CASTLE.
BUT HE HATES BEING TIED DOWN TO HIS JOB, SO HE'S ALWAYS WANDERING AROUND OR HELPING HIS BEST FRIEND, JULIUS.
I CAN NEVER GUESS WHAT HE'S THINKING... EVEN AFTER ALL THIS TIME.
HE'S ALWAYS SMIL-ING.
AND CHEER-FUL.
I'M... JEALOUS, IN A WAY.
HE'S THE OPPOSITE OF A DARK PERSON LIKE ME.
YOU LOOK A LITTLE WORN OUT, ACE.
AH HA HA!
I GUESS YOU COULD SAY THAT.
IT TOOK ME THIRTY-TWO TIME PERIODS TO GET BACK TO THE CASTLE.
HA HA HA!
I'M SO UNLUCKY!
I CAN ONLY TAKE THIS GUY IN DOSES.

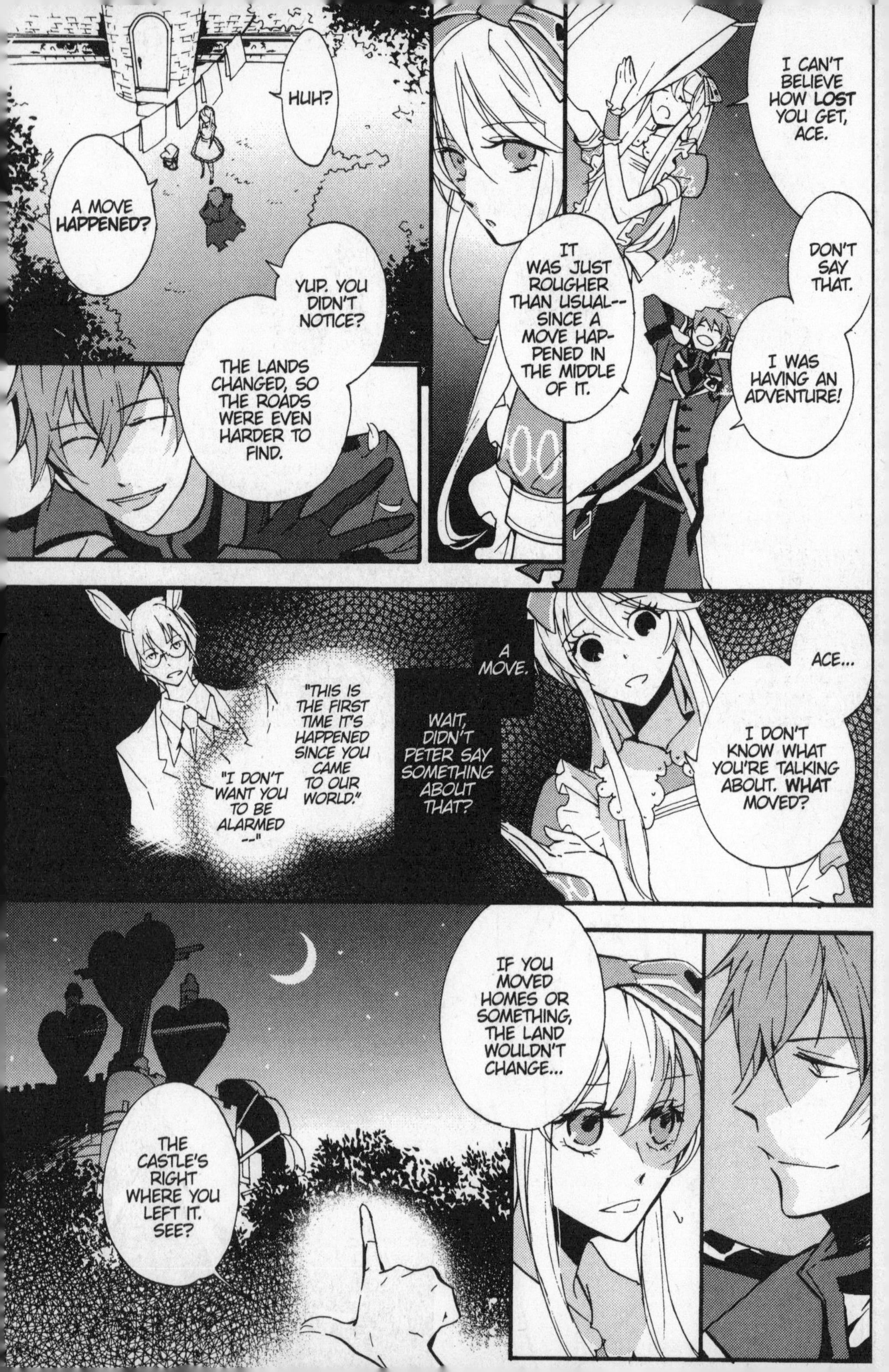
I CAN'T BELIEVE HOW LOST YOU GET, ACE.
DON'T SAY THAT.
I WAS HAVING AN ADVENTURE!
IT WAS JUST ROUGHER THAN USUAL-- SINCE A MOVE HAPPENED IN THE MIDDLE OF IT.
HUH?
A MOVE HAPPENED?
YUP. YOU DIDN'T NOTICE?
THE LANDS CHANGED, SO THE ROADS WERE EVEN HARDER TO FIND.
ACE...
I DON'T KNOW WHAT YOU'RE TALKING ABOUT. WHAT MOVED?
A MOVE.
WAIT, DIDN'T PETER SAY SOMETHING ABOUT THAT?
"THIS IS THE FIRST TIME IT'S HAPPENED SINCE YOU CAME TO OUR WORLD."
"I DON'T WANT YOU TO BE ALARMED --"
IF YOU MOVED HOMES OR SOMETHING, THE LAND WOULDN'T CHANGE...
THE CASTLE'S RIGHT WHERE YOU LEFT IT. SEE?

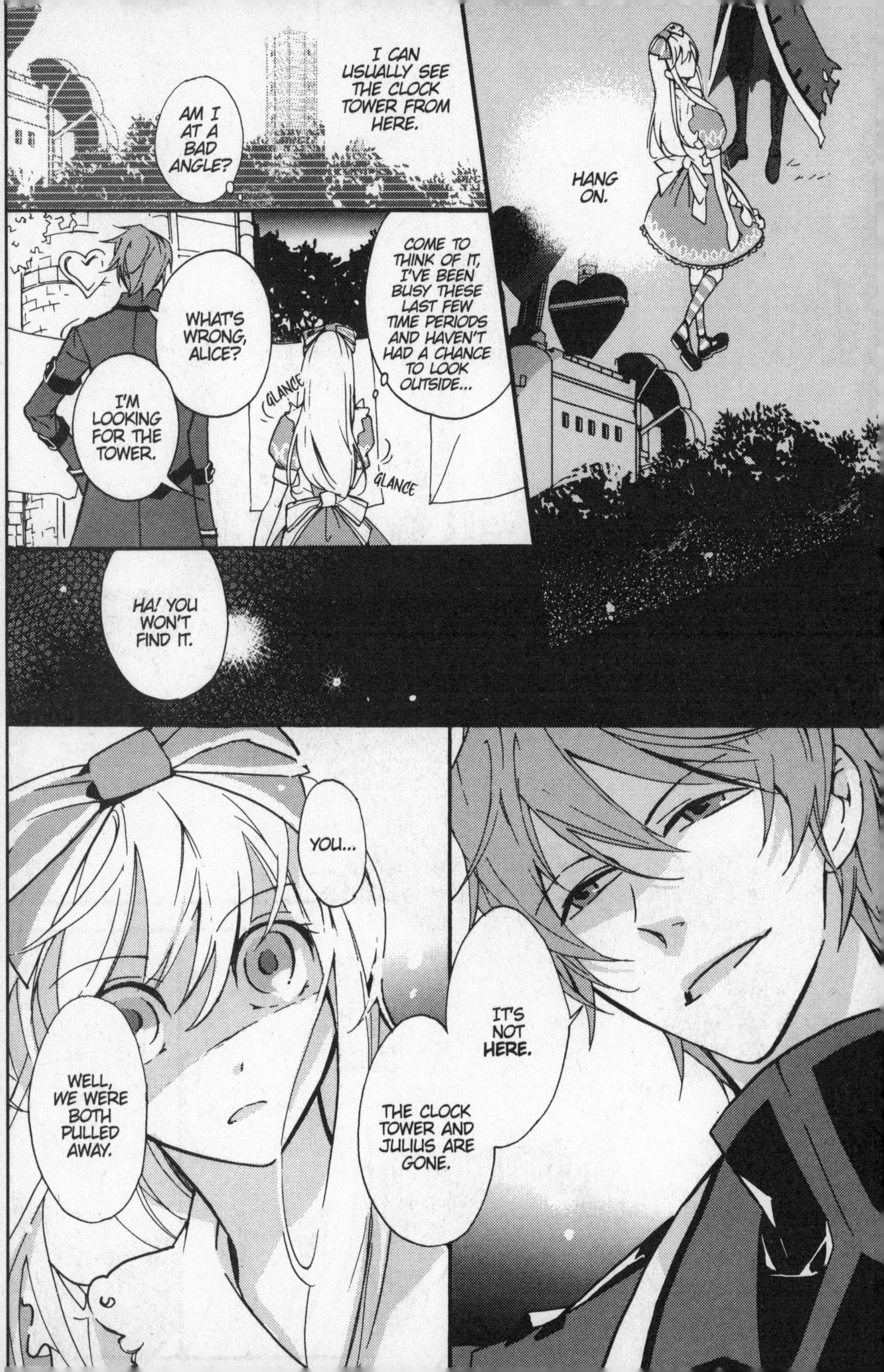
HANG ON.
I CAN USUALLY SEE THE CLOCK TOWER FROM HERE.
AM I AT A BAD ANGLE?
COME TO THINK OF IT, I'VE BEEN BUSY THESE LAST FEW TIME PERIODS AND HAVEN'T HAD A CHANCE TO LOOK OUTSIDE...
WHAT'S WRONG, ALICE?
GLANCE
GLANCE
I'M LOOKING FOR THE TOWER.
HA! YOU WON'T FIND IT.
IT'S NOT HERE.
THE CLOCK TOWER AND JULIUS ARE GONE.
YOU...
WELL, WE WERE BOTH PULLED AWAY.

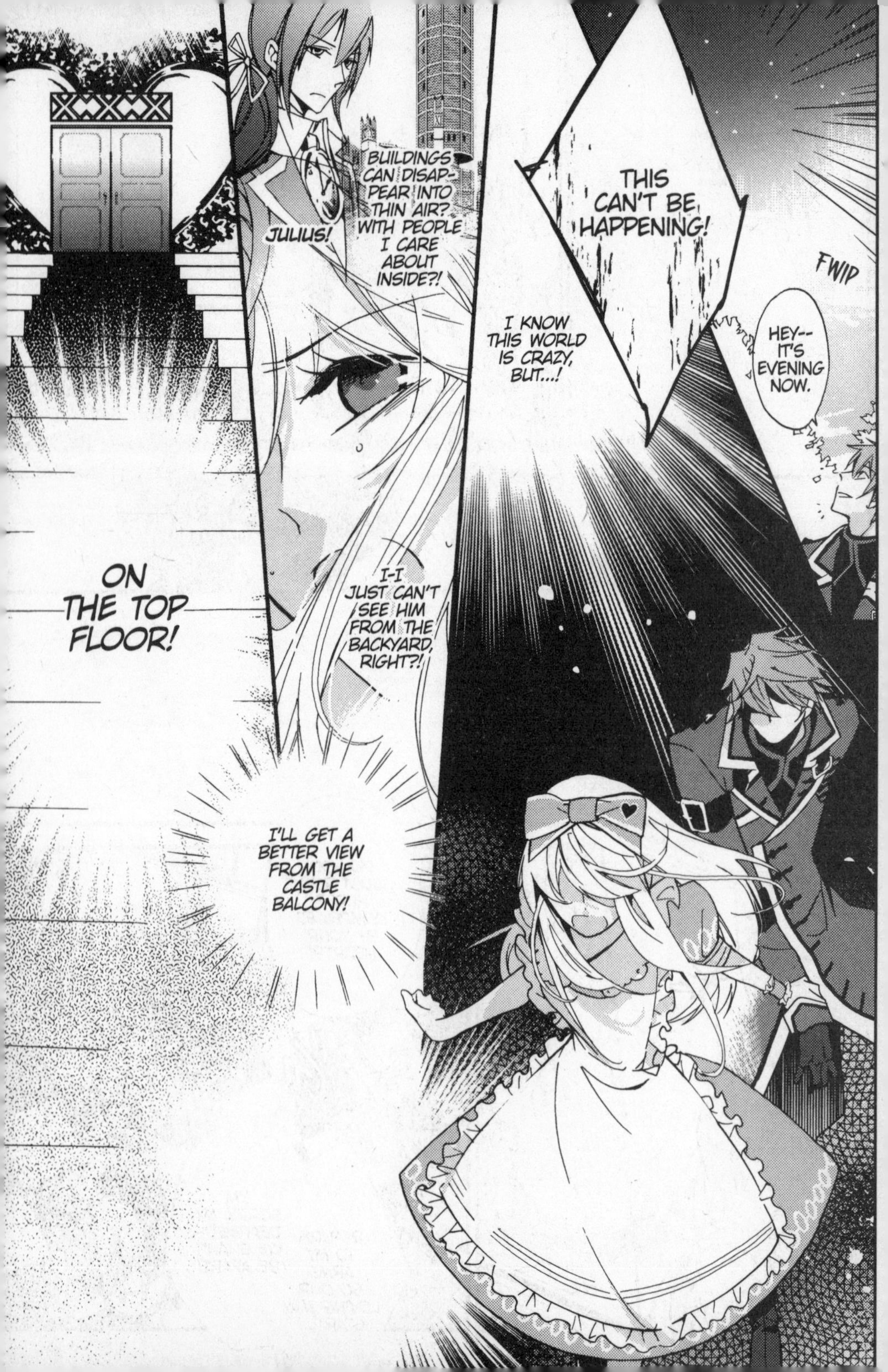
THIS CAN'T BE HAPPENING!
FWIP
HEY-- IT'S EVENING NOW.
I KNOW THIS WORLD IS CRAZY, BUT...!
BUILDINGS CAN DISAPPEAR INTO THIN AIR? WITH PEOPLE I CARE ABOUT INSIDE?!
JULIUS!
I-I JUST CAN'T SEE HIM FROM THE BACKYARD, RIGHT?!
I'LL GET A BETTER VIEW FROM THE CASTLE BALCONY!
ON THE TOP FLOOR!

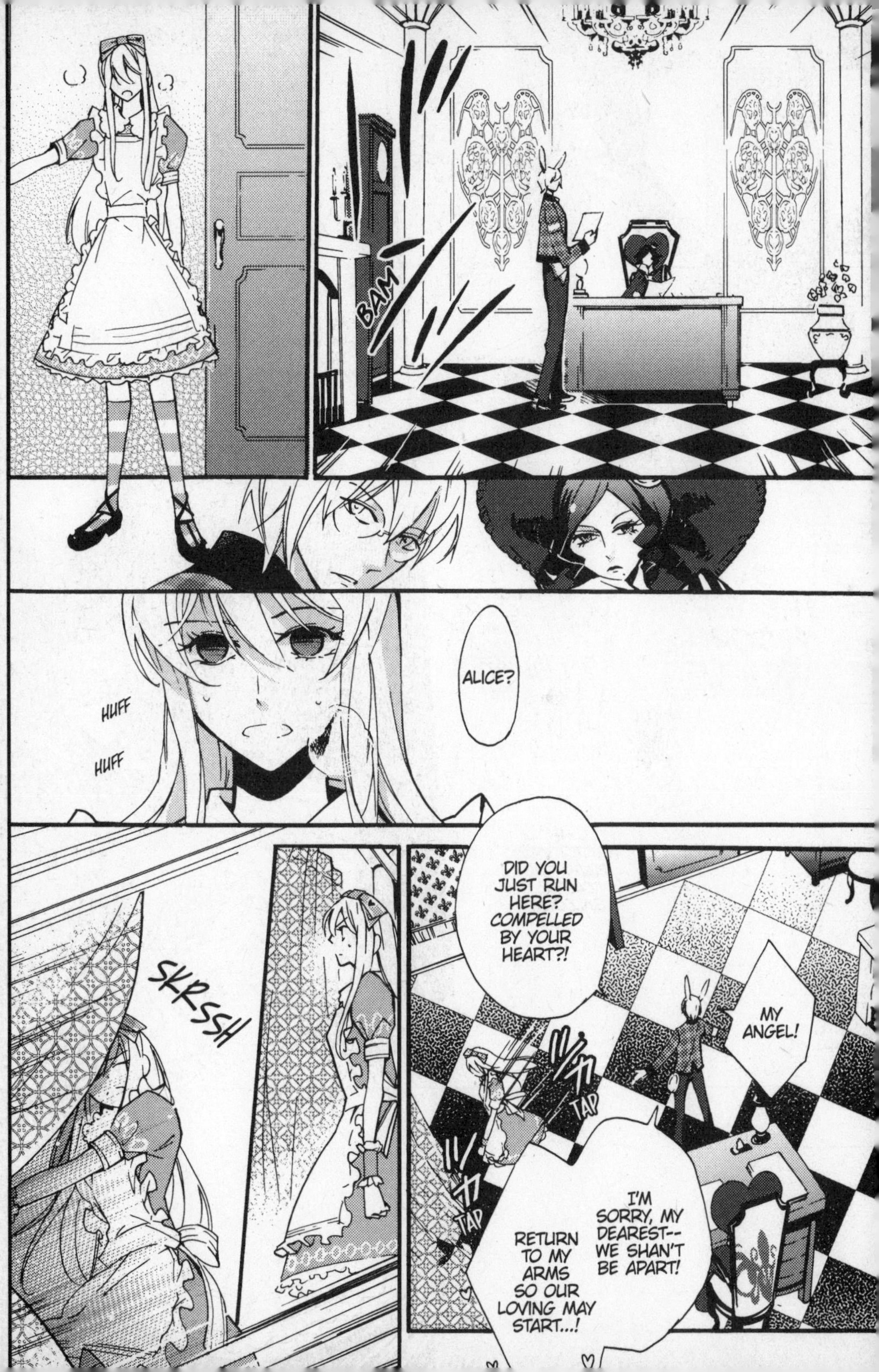
BAM
ALICE?
HUFF
HUFF
DID YOU JUST RUN HERE? COMPELLED BY YOUR HEART?!
MY ANGEL!
TAP
TAP
I'M SORRY, MY DEAREST-- WE SHAN'T BE APART!
RETURN TO MY ARMS SO OUR LOVING MAY START...!
SKRSSH

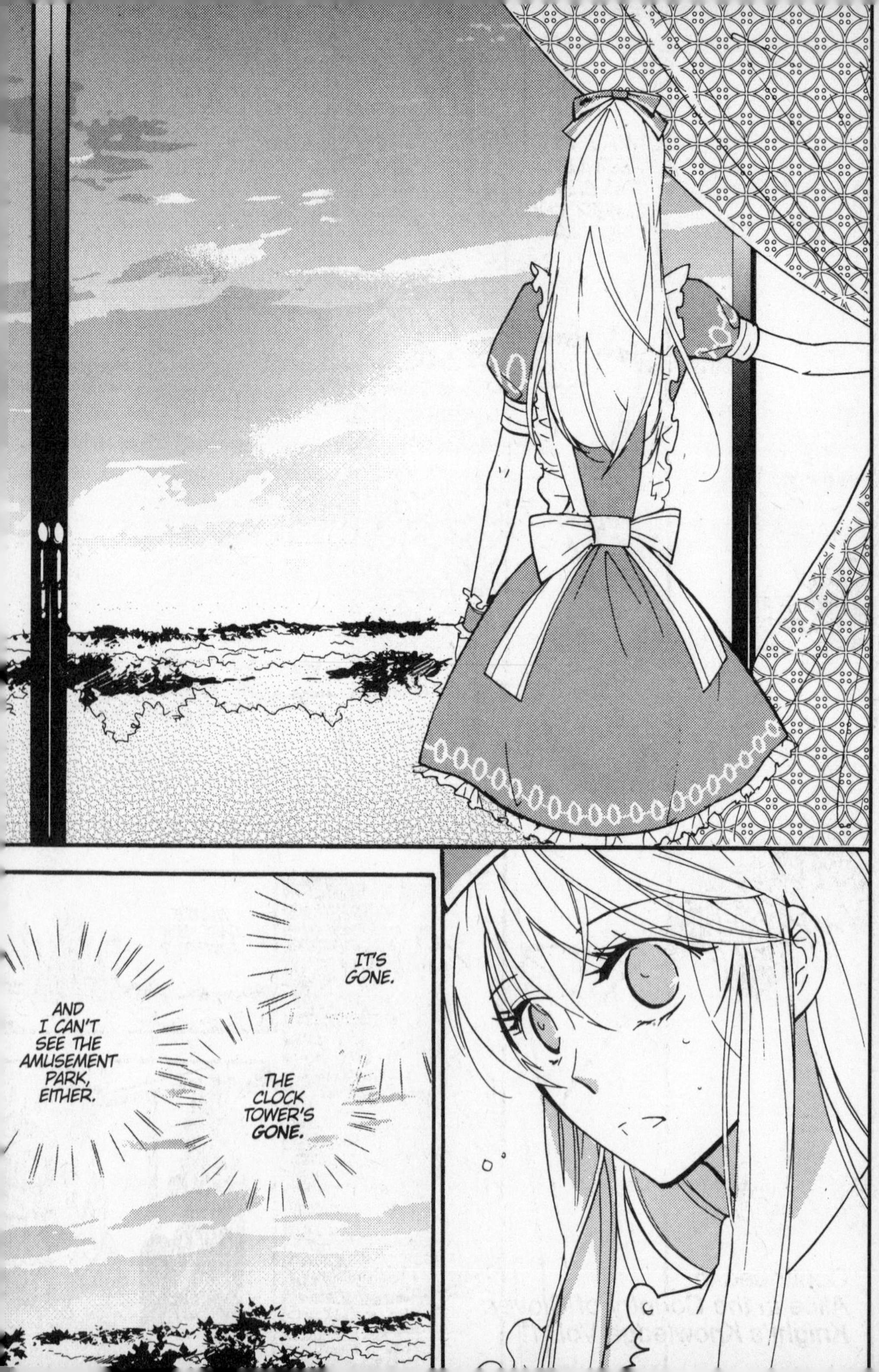
IT'S GONE.
THE CLOCK TOWER'S GONE.
AND I CAN'T SEE THE AMUSEMENT PARK, EITHER.

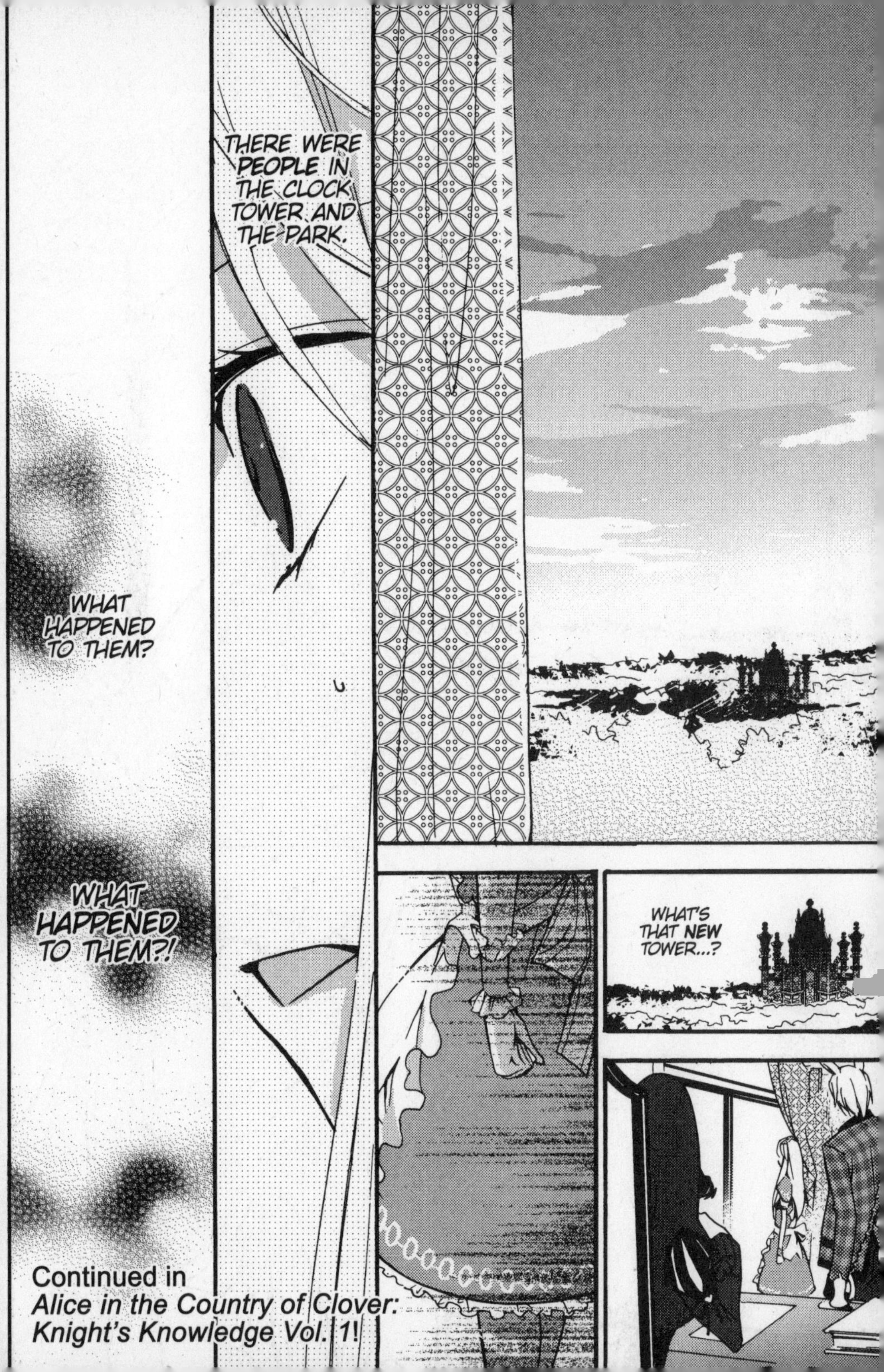
WHAT'S THAT NEW TOWER...?
THERE WERE PEOPLE IN THE CLOCK TOWER AND THE PARK.
WHAT HAPPENED TO THEM?
WHAT HAPPENED TO THEM?!

Continued in
Alice in the Country of Clover: Knight's Knowledge Vol. 1!

SEVEN SEAS ENTERTAINMENT PRESENTS

citrus

story & art by **SABUROUTA**   **VOLUME 1**

TRANSLATION
Catherine Ross

ADAPTATION
Shannon Fay

LETTERING
Roland Amago

LAYOUT
Bambi Eloriaga-Amago

COVER DESIGN
Nicky Lim

PROOFREADER
Lee Otter

MANAGING EDITOR
Adam Arnold

PUBLISHER
Jason DeAngelis

CITRUS VOLUME 1
© SABUROUTA 2013
First published in Japan in 2013 by ICHIJINSHA Inc., Tokyo.
English translation rights arranged with ICHIJINSHA Inc., Tokyo, Japan.

Seven Seas books may be purchased in bulk for educational, business, or promotional use. For information on bulk purchases, please contact Macmillan Corporate & Premium Sales Department at 1-800-221-7945 (ext 5442) or write specialmarkets@macmillan.com.

Seven Seas and the Seven Seas logo are trademarks of Seven Seas Entertainment, LLC. All rights reserved.

ISBN: 978-1-626921-40-5

Printed in Canada

First Printing: December 2014

10 9 8 7 6 5 4 3 2 1

FOLLOW US ONLINE: www.gomanga.com

READING DIRECTIONS

This book reads from *right to left*, Japanese style. If this is your first time reading manga, you start reading from the top right panel on each page and take it from there. If you get lost, just follow the numbered diagram here. It may seem backwards at first, but you□ll get the hang of it! Have fun!!

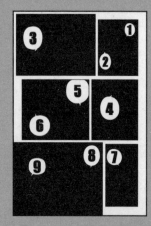